# THE VIKING PORTABLE LIBRARY

## Romantic Poets

W. H. Auden was born in England in 1907 and died in 1973. Versatile, outspoken, psychologically acute, and brilliant in literary technique, he wrote plays and libretti as well as volumes of prose and poetry—among the latter are *The Double Man, The Age of Anxiety,* and *The Shield of Achilles.*

The late Norman Holmes Pearson was chairman of American studies at Yale. His books include *American Literature, Some American Studies,* and *American Literary Fathers.*

Each volume in The Viking Portable Library either presents a representative selection from the works of a single outstanding writer or offers a comprehensive anthology on a special subject. Averaging 700 pages in length and designed for compactness and readability, these books fill a need not met by other compilations. All are edited by distinguished authorities, who have written introductory essays and included much other helpful material.

1798 – Lyrical Ballads
1832 – death of Scott

Characteristics of Romanticism

① Revolution
② Bard / Prophet → Milton
③ Secularization – the f
④ Imagination
⑤ Romantic Irony

*The Portable*

# Romantic Poets

*Edited by*

W. H. AUDEN and
NORMAN HOLMES PEARSON

PENGUIN BOOKS

PENGUIN BOOKS
Published by the Penguin Group
Penguin Books USA Inc.,
375 Hudson Street, New York, New York 10014, U.S.A.
Penguin Books Australia Ltd, Ringwood, Victoria, Australia
Penguin Books Canada Ltd, 10 Alcorn Avenue,
Toronto, Ontario, Canada M4V 3B2
Penguin Books (N.Z.) Ltd, 182–190 Wairau Road,
Auckland 10, New Zealand

Penguin Books Ltd, Registered Offices:
Harmondsworth, Middlesex, England

First published in the United States of America
by Viking Penguin Inc. 1950
First published in Great Britain
by Eyre & Spottiswoode Ltd, 1952
Viking paperbound edition published 1958
Reprinted 1960, 1961 (twice), 1962, 1963, 1965,
1966, 1967, 1968, 1969 (twice),
1972, 1973 (twice), 1974, 1975, 1976
Published in Penguin Books 1977

24   26   28   30   29   27   25   23

ISBN 0 14 015.052 8

Printed in the United States of America
Set in Linotype Caledonia

Grateful acknowledgment is made to the following for permission to re-
print selections from the books listed. J. M. Dent & Sons, Ltd., London:
"The Ploughboy" from *The Poems of John Clare*, edited by J. W. Tibble;
Harvard University Press, Cambridge, and Routledge and Kegan Paul,
Ltd., London: "I Am" and "Clock-a-clay" from *Selected Poems of John
Clare*, edited by Geoffrey Grigson; Edmund Blunden: "Autumn,"
"Badger," "Secret Love," "Invitation to Eternity," "The Frightened
Ploughman," "Gipsies," from *John Clare: Poems*, edited by Edmund
Blunden and Alan Porter; Farrar, Straus and Company, Inc., New York:
"The moon now rises to her absolute rule," "For though the caves
were rabbited," "I'm thankful that my life doth not deceive," from
*Collected Poems of Henry Thoreau*, edited by Carl Bode (copyright 1943
by Packard and Company).

# Contents

**vi** CONTENTS

# Introduction

What is man? How does he differ from the gods on the one hand and from nature on the other? What is the divine element in man? A different set of answers to such questions, or a shift of emphasis in the old answers, changes the style and subject matter of poetry and the poet's conception of his function.

For example, in the age of the heroic epic the difference between gods and men is that the former are immortal and the latter must finally all die like the beasts. In the meantime, however, some men are made godlike and separated from nature by the favor of the gods, becoming heroes who do great deeds. The poet, that is, the man inspired with the gift of tongues, celebrates the hero and his acts.

In the Middle Ages, the quality which man shares with God and which the creatures do not have is a will that can make free choices. What separates man from God is sin: that he can and does choose wrongly, love himself, act selfishly. The function of the poet is to exhibit the human soul tempted by competing loves, and to celebrate the ways in which she can be redeemed.

In the neoclassical period, the divine human quality is reason, the capacity to recognize general laws, and the function of the poet is to celebrate the Rational City and to pour scorn on its enemies.

Toward the end of the eighteenth century—Rousseau is one of the first symptoms—a new answer appears. The divine element in man is now held to be neither power nor free will nor reason, but self-consciousness. Like God and unlike the rest of nature, man can say "I": his ego stands over against his self, which to the ego is a part of nature. In this self he can see possibilities; he can imagine it and all things as being other than they are; he runs ahead of himself; he foresees his own death.

Hölderlin's poem *Der Mensch* is as complete and clear a definition as any.

> Soon he has grown up;
> The animals avoid him, for other than
>    They is man; he does not resemble
>    Thee, nor the Father, for boldly in him
>
> And alone are mingled the Father's lofty
> Spirit with thy joy, O Earth, and thy sorrow.
>    Gladly he would be like the mother
>    Of the gods, like all-embracing Nature!
>
> Oh, that is why his restless spirit drives
> Him away from thy heart, O Earth, and thy gifts
>    Are in vain, and thy gentle fetters;
>    And he seeks better things, the wild one!
>
> From the fragrant meadow of his shores, far out
> Into the flowerless water, Man must go
>    And though, like the starlit night full of
>    Golden fruit his orchard gleams, yet he digs
>
> Caves in the mountains and looks around the pit,
> Deeply hidden from his Father's cheerful light,
>    Faithless also to the sun-god who
>    Does not love the slave and scoffs at troubles.
>
> For more freely breathe the birds of the forest,
> And though Man's breast rises with greater splendour,
>    And he sees the dark future, he must
>    See death too, and he alone must fear it.
>                     —Translated by Michael Hamburger

If self-awareness and the power to conceive of possibility is the divine element in man, then the hero whom the poet must celebrate is himself, for the only con-

sciousness accessible to him is his own. When Keats
writes in his letters that the poet is the least poetical
thing in existence because he has no identity, he is say-
ing that the man of power who has this identity is less
human, more like the sun or the birds of nature, which
can only be themselves.

The romantic assertions of the supreme importance
of art—for example, Blake's statement "Art is the tree
of life. Art is Christianity," or Shelley's "Poets are the
unacknowledged legislators of the world"—are not to be
understood as vanity but as the inevitable conclusion to
be drawn from the presupposition that consciousness is
the noblest human quality.

Similarly, the romantic definitions of the poet and the
poetic imagination—for example:

. . . a disposition to be affected more than other men by
absent things as if they were present; an ability of conjuring
up in himself passions, which are indeed far from being the
same as those produced by real events, yet (especially in
those parts of the general sympathy which are pleasing and
delightful) do more nearly resemble the passions produced
by real events, than anything which, from the motions of
their own minds merely, other men are accustomed to feel
in themselves.

Wordsworth, Preface to the *Lyrical Ballads,* 1800

The primary Imagination I hold to be the living Power
and prime Agent of all human Perception, and as a repeti-
tion in the finite mind of the eternal act of creation in the
infinite I AM.

Coleridge, *Biographia Literaria,* chapter xiii

seem meaningless so long as we think of the poet as a
man with a gift for writing verse. They define, not the
writer, but the hero about whom he writes, which for
the Romantic are combined in the same person.

Thus, the subject of the greatest long poem of this period, *The Prelude,* is not a heroic action like the siege of Troy, nor a decisive choice like the Fall of Man, nor a threat to civilization like the Goddess of Dullness, but the Growth of a Poet's Mind.

### THE ROMANTIC GOD AND THE ROMANTIC DEVIL

Just as the reason which detects general laws governing the movements of natural bodies tends out of self-worship to create as an idol a purely transcendent and Unitarian god, so the idol of consciousness is a pantheistic god immanent in nature. For to my consciousness nature is a diversity of particular images present to it which have one thing in common, namely that they are *my* images: they are all flavored by the same invisible presence, myself.

Similarly, if the enemies of reason are passion and stupidity, which cause disorder, the enemies of consciousness are abstract intellectualizing and conventional codes of morality, which neglect and suppress the capacity of the consciousness to experience. Reason has to distinguish between true and false; the will, between right and wrong: consciousness can make no such distinctions; it can only ask "What is there?" For it, there is not an "either/or" but a "both-and."

### THE ROMANTIC HERO

Wordsworth is an exceptional figure in that, like Dante, in addition to and quite distinct from his poetic gift, he was granted an extraordinary vision. The peculiar experience of Nature which came to him in childhood would have made him an exception even if he had never written a line. Whether or no similar experiences have befallen other poets they have seldom informed us.

When we read Shakespeare, for instance, we are aware, not of his having enjoyed any out-of-the-way experience, but only of his unique poetic gift.

To demonstrate the identity of the romantic hero with the consciousness of the poet, therefore, it is more convincing to take works which are not professedly autobiographical, for example, Goethe's *Faust* and Byron's *Don Juan*. The Faust of Marlowe is simply an old professor who wants to be a godlike hero in the epic sense. He wants power to do great deeds and win glory, he wants to sleep with the most beautiful girls, he wants to be eternally twenty years old. Goethe's Faust has quite other aims. He doesn't want to *do anything*, he wants to *experience everything*. Hence the curious wager with Mephistopheles, for to cry to a moment of experience, "Stay: you are so beautiful," would be to renounce his quest, to exclude some possible future experience. He does not seduce Marguerite because he desires her or become a swampdrainer because he wants to do good to mankind, but because he wants to know what it feels like to be a seducer and a benefactor. The definition of Mephistopheles as the spirit who denies would be meaningless if Faust were a hero of will, for the will is as much tempted by Yes as by No; it is only the consciousness, the imagination, which is tempted solely by refusal to accept what it experiences.

Similarly, the most obvious characteristic of Byron's hero is his passivity; it is he who is always the seduced one. *Don Juan* is as much the dramatized story of the education of Byron's mind as *The Prelude* is the direct account of the education of Wordsworth's.

One more example. The occurrence which begins the Ancient Mariner's redemption is no act of penance, is not even directly concerned with his sinful act, with the albatross; it is the acceptance of the water snakes by his consciousness which previously wished to reject them.

### ROMANTIC DICTION

More fuss has been made about this than it deserves. Wordsworth's would-be polemic expression "the language really used by men," which originally ran "the language of the middle and lower classes of society," is little more than an assertion that if a poet wishes to describe his own experiences, and happens, like Wordsworth, to belong to one of those classes, his diction, however elevated, will differ from that of a poet raised among the aristocracy. Much of Byron's hostility to Wordsworth seems to have been caused by his feeling that the latter was an inverted snob who in elevating into a general principle what was a personal need was claiming that the middle and lower classes were intrinsically better, more human, than the upper classes.

### SYMBOL AND ALLEGORY

Consciousness cannot divide its *données* into the true and the false, the good and the evil; it can only measure them along a scale of intensity. Certain images present themselves charged with more affect than a rational inspection can account for. Such an image is a symbol. To the question "What does it symbolize?" only multiple and equally partial answers are possible, for, unlike an allegorical image, it has no one-to-one correspondence.

The allegorical method is to take two images, or an idea and an image, and deliberately relate them. When Gavin Douglas writes

> King Hart into his cumlie castell strang

we know without possibility of contradiction that King Hart is the soul and his castle is the body. But there can be no method of symbolism. An image is presented to the poet's consciousness either charged with symbolic affect or not; all that the poet can do is to pick out one or several which are and arrange them. We may say, if we like, that the sun and the moon in *The Ancient Mariner* symbolize respectively the punishing justice-demanding Father and the forgiving merciful Mother; we are not wrong but we are very little nearer understanding the poem, for a hundred equally valid allegorical identifications can be made.

Allegory is a form of rhetoric, a device for making the abstract concrete; in nearly all successful allegory the images used do in fact have a symbolic value over and above their allegorical use, but that is secondary to the poet's purpose. In poetry of which the subject, the hero, is consciousness, the symbols are the primary material.

## ORGANIZATION

A poem that attempts to follow the motions of consciousness will have to organize itself into a whole in ways which consciousness itself suggests, not as logic dictates.

The real novelty in Romantic poetry is not its diction but its structure. If the Romantic poets, after rejecting Pope and Dryden, did not rediscover Donne and the metaphysical poets, this was because the latter, no less than the former, organized their poems logically. For example, Marvell's poem "To His Coy Mistress" is constructed syllogistically upon three conjunctions: if—but—therefore. In contrast to this, take the structure of Keats's "Ode to a Nightingale." The poem opens with a description of a state of feeling, a desire for death; it shifts to the nightingale singing of summer; it shifts back to the "I" of the poem wishing for wine and the Golden Age; it returns to the bird in the forest and what it does not know but the "I" describes: mortality, sorrow, unrequited love; the "I" again is listening to the bird and desires again to die; now the "I" disappears completely for a stanza and the bird is heard singing to various others in the far past and faery lands forlorn. The word forlorn by its suggestion brings back the "I" to himself listening to the bird song fading away. The roles of the nightingale and of the poet have kept varying throughout the poem. Sometimes the bird has been seen in contrast to the poet, as the unconscious creature contrasted with the conscious man; sometimes his bird's song has been considered not as distinct from the poet but as a part of his experience, and a symbol of himself as poet; sometimes again it is the poet who is singing of the bird and thereby doing what a bird cannot do, immortalizing the immediate moment.

### ROMANTICISM AND SOCIETY

A new aesthetic is always accompanied by and related to religious and political changes, though none can be explained away in terms of another.

While the Pope couplet and the neoclassical aesthetic were still the poetic gospel, the Wesleyan religious revival cast doubts. Ignoring rational arguments, from design, for the existence of God, scorning utilitarian arguments for morality, it insisted upon a catastrophic personal experience of sin and divine redemption. To describe such experiences neither the form nor the diction of Pope would do, and the evangelical hymn writers like Charles Wesley were, in technique as well as in spirit, the forerunners of the English Romantic poets. This was, however, a local influence. The dominating event which affected all the Romantics is, of course, the French Revolution.

The uniqueness of this revolution is that it was the

work of talented intellectuals, of orators and men of
letters.[1] Its achievement was not the liberation of any
social or economic class but freedom for the talented in-
dividual to profit from and earn full credit for his talents.
Its hero is Figaro, the gifted barber of Beaumarchais'
comedy, its enemy the count who claims privileges as a
member of a social class to which his gifts as a natural
individual do not entitle him. The French Revolution did
not believe that all men were equal or should be equally
rewarded by society, but that the inequalities should be
natural, not artificial. In France the interest was con-
centrated upon politics and culture; in England the
same principles were applied to economics: the mill
owners of the North of England were the brothers of the
Jacobins. Fouché's comment upon Napoleon at his fall,
"C'est un acteur usé," was cruel but true. He had been
not an emperor but an employee of the French Muse.
His political achievement was nil, his cultural very great,
for he created Europe, which is neither a political nor a
geographical entity. Europe—and this is why England
has never thought of herself as a part of Europe—is sim-
ply the area dominated by the ideals of French litera-
ture.

A revolution to emancipate the individual must neces-
sarily regard tradition, the control of the present by the
past, as its enemy; if the human individual is to be really
free, then time must also be individualized into a succes-
sion of immediate moments. The kind of society, there-
fore, which it tends to create, is an atomized society of
individuals, with neither a common myth nor a common

[1] The Russian Revolution was the work of martyrs. Some
of its leaders were intellectuals but it was not their intellects
which gave them their authority, but the fact that they had
suffered imprisonment and exile.

cult, but united moment by moment by what they are reading.

In France the danger of this was postponed by the importance to her economy of the peasant proprietor. In England, where the Industrial Revolution developed more rapidly, it was much sooner apparent. For the industrial system, by destroying the family as an economic unit, and converting the working individual into an impersonal labor force to be used like water or electricity for so many hours a day, destroys the one social bond which is natural—that is, independent of myth or cult and capable of surviving a change in or the disappearance of both. When it too is lost, then society degenerates into the city crowds described by Wordsworth:

> The slaves unrespited of low pursuits
> Living amid the same perpetual flow
> Of trivial objects, melted and reduced
> To one identity, by differences
> That have no law, no meaning, and no end.
> *The Prelude*

## AMERICA

If we apply the term revolution to what happened in North America between 1776 and 1829, it has a special meaning.

Normally the word describes the process by which man transforms himself from one kind of man, living in one kind of society, with one way of looking at the world, into another kind of man, another society, another conception of life. So it is with the papal, the Lutheran, the English, and the French revolutions. The American case is different; it is not a question of the Old Man transforming himself into the New, but of the New Man becoming alive to the fact that he is new, that he has been transformed already without his having realized it.

The War of Independence was the first step, the leaving of the paternal roof in order to find out who one is; the second and more important step, the actual discovery, came with Jackson. It was then that it first became clear that, despite similarities of form, representative government in America was not to be an imitation of the English parliamentary system, and that, though the vocabulary of the Constitution may be that of the French Enlightenment, its American meaning is quite distinct.

The American had not intended to become what he was; he had been made so by emigration and the nature of the American continent. An emigrant never knows what he wants, only what he does not want. A man who comes from a land settled for centuries to a virgin wilderness where he faces problems with which none of his traditions and habits was intended to deal cannot foresee the future but must improvise himself from day to day. It is not surprising, therefore, that the first clear realization of the novelty and importance of the United States should have come not from an American but from outsiders, like Crèvecoeur and de Tocqueville.

In a society whose dominant task is still that of the pioneer—the physical struggle with nature, and a nature, moreover, particularly recalcitrant and violent—the intellectual is not a figure of much importance. Those with intellectual and artistic tastes, finding themselves a despised or at best an ignored minority, are apt in return to despise the society in which they live as vulgar and think nostalgically of more leisured and refined cultures. The situation of the first important American poets—Emerson, Thoreau, Poe—was therefore doubly difficult. As writers, and therefore intellectuals, they were without status with the majority; and, on the other hand, the cultured minority of which they were members looked to England for its literary standards and did not want to think or read about America.

This dependence on English literature was a hindrance to their development in a way which it would not have been had they lived elsewhere. A poet living in England, for instance, might read nothing but French poetry, or he might move to Italy and know only English, without raising any serious barrier between himself and his experiences. Indeed, in Europe whenever some journalist raises the patriotic demand for an English or French or Dutch literature free from foreign influences, we know him at once to be a base fellow. The wish for an American literature, on the other hand, has nothing to do, really, with politics or national conceit; it is a demand for honesty. All European literature presupposes two things: a nature which is humanized, mythologized, usually friendly, and a human society in which most men stay where they were born and do not move about much. Neither of these presuppositions was valid for America, where nature was virgin, devoid of history, usually hostile; and society was fluid, its groupings always changing as men moved on somewhere else.

The European Romantics may praise the charms of wild desert landscape, but they know that for them it is never more than a few hours' walk from a comfortable inn: they may celebrate the joys of solitude but they know that any time they choose they can go back to the family roof or to town and that there their cousins and nephews and nieces and aunts, the club and the salons, will still be going on exactly as they left them. Of real desert, of a loneliness which knows of no enduring relationships to cherish or reject, they have no conception.

The achievement of Emerson and Thoreau was twofold: they wrote of the American kind of nature, and they perceived what qualities were most needed by members of the American kind of society, which was threatened not by the petrified injustice of any tradition but by the fluid irresponsibility of crowd opinion. Their work has both the virtues and the vices of the isolated and the protestant: on the one hand it is always genuine and original, it is never superficial; on the other it is a little too cranky, too earnest, too scornful of elegance. Just as in their political thinking Americans are apt to identify the undemocratic with monarchy, so in their aesthetics they are apt to identify the falsely conventional with rhyme and meter. The prose of Emerson and Thoreau is superior to their verse, because verse in its formal nature protests against protesting; it demands that to some degree we accept things as they are, not for any rational or moral reason, but simply because they happen to be that way; it implies an element of frivolity in the creation.

Poe, on the other hand, has nothing to say directly about nature or society. He is the first poet to create an entirely imaginary landscape, a subjective *paysage moralisé,* the implication of which is that, where nature is not humanized, where there is no common mythology, each poet has to invent one for himself—nature by herself is meaningless. His love stories, without any conscious intention on his part, are terrible warnings of what can happen in a society where human relations are few in number and character, and where in consequence the whole range of human emotions may attach themselves to a single relation. One has often to decipher his work in order to see that, for all its cheapness and flashiness of execution, it is intensely serious. He may strike dramatic attitudes, but behind them there is a man who is really in great pain.

As the nineteenth century progressed, the destruction

of the popular mythographic imagination by popular science and the spread of universal suffrage and the influence of the press made conditions in Europe to approximate more and more closely to the American case, and European writers came to see in Poe the heroic forerunner who had suffered and understood, who had really been what Byron, for instance, never was, the *poète maudit,* the alienated dandy.

# General Principles

## SELECTIONS

The central cluster of poets represented in this volume marks the Romantic Movement at the period of its greatest vigor, though as always there are strains other than the dominant one which had persisted or were being initiated. American verse, in this volume, begins to assume dimensions of some significance, and the intermingling of American with British poems from the same age should be variously suggestive. Certain cultural lags as well as certain distinctions in diction are apparent. Ordinarily one is accustomed, in anthologies, to find the two poetries completely separated, as though they were distinct and self-sufficient, but it is time for us to recognize how the poetical consciousness and training in craft depends upon a common or at least a joint tradition. The separation of British and American strains provides some useful insights, but we need to be reminded that poets did not work that way as poets.

# A Calendar of British and American Poetry

| GENERAL BACKGROUND | DATE | DIRECT HISTORY |
|---|---|---|
| J. S. Bach, *Die Kunst der Fuge:* end of polyphonic period | 1750 | |
| Rousseau, *Discours sur les arts et les sciences* | | |
| Johnson, *The Rambler:* a bi-weekly | 1750–52 | |
| French *Encyclopédie*, Vols. I–II | 1751 | Gray, *Elegy Written in a Country Church Yard* |
| Hume, *An Enquiry concerning the Principles of Morals* | | |
| Franklin, *Experiments and Observations on Electricity* | 1751–54 | |
| Gregorian Calendar adopted for England and her colonies | 1752 | Smart, *Poems on Several Occasions* |
| British Museum founded | 1753 | |
| Mrs. Charlotte Lennox, *Shakespear Illustrated:* first collection of Shakespearean sources | | |
| Jonathan Edwards, *Freedom of the Will* | 1754 | |
| Hume, *History of Great Britain*, Vol. I | | |
| Johnson, *A Dictionary of the English Language* | 1755 | |
| Burke, *On the Sublime and Beautiful* | 1756 | |
| Walpole establishes Strawberry Hill Press | 1757 | *The Beauties of Poetry Display'd:* "common-place book" |
| | | Collins, *Oriental Eclogues* |
| | | Dyer, *The Fleece* |
| | | Gray, *Odes:* "Progress of Poesy," "The Bard" |
| Franklin, "Way to Wealth" (in *Poor Richard's Almanac*) | 1758 | |
| Helvétius, *De l'Esprit* | | |
| Johnson, *The Idler:* weekly gazette | 1758–60 | |
| Johnson, *The History of Rasselas* | 1759 | |

# A CALENDAR

| GENERAL BACKGROUND | DATE | DIRECT HISTORY |
|---|---|---|
| Lessing, *Briefe, die neuste Litteratur betreffend* | 1759 | |
| Robertson, *History of Scotland during the Reign of Queen Mary* | | |
| Voltaire, *Candide* | | |
| Rousseau, *La Nouvelle Héloïse* | 1760 | |
| Sterne, *Tristram Shandy* | 1760–67 | |
| Piranesi, *Della magnificenza ed architettura de' Romani* | 1761 | Churchill, *The Rosciad* |
| | | Derrick, *A Poetical Dictionary:* dictionary of familiar quotations |
| Goldsmith, *The Citizen of the World* | 1762 | Macpherson, *Fingal, An Ancient Epic Poem* |
| Gluck, *Orfeo ed Euridice,* Vienna | | |
| Kames, *Elements of Criticism* | | |
| Rousseau, *Le contrat social* | | |
| Stuart and Revett, *Antiquities of Athens* | | |
| | 1763 | Smart, *A Song to David* |
| Rousseau, *Emile* | 1764 | Churchill, *Gotham* |
| Voltaire, *Dictionnaire philosophique* | | |
| Winckelmann, *Geschichte der Kunst des Altertums* | | |
| Goldsmith, *Essays* collected | 1765 | Percy, *Reliques of Ancient English Poetry* |
| The Stamp Act | | |
| Walpole, *The Castle of Otranto* | | |
| Blackstone, *Commentaries on the Laws of England* | 1765–68 | |
| Goldsmith, *The Vicar of Wakefield* | 1766 | |
| Lessing, *Láokoön* | | |
| Herder, *Uber die neuere deutsche Litteratur:* program for Sturm und Drang | 1767 | |
| Dickinson, *Letters from a Farmer in Pennsylvania to the Inhabitants of the British Colonies* | 1768 | Gray, *Poems* |
| Royal Academy of Arts founded; Reynolds president | | |
| Sterne, *A Sentimental Journey through France and Italy* | | |
| Watt's steam engine patented | 1769 | |
| Reynolds, *Discourses* | 1769–91 | |
| Hargreaves's spinning jenny patented | 1770 | Goldsmith, *The Deserted Village* |
| Holbach, *La Système de la nature* | | |

# A CALENDAR

| GENERAL BACKGROUND | DATE | DIRECT HISTORY |
|---|---|---|
| | 1771–74 | Beattie, *The Minstrel* |
| | 1772 | John Trumbull, *The Progress of Dullness* |
| Goldsmith, *She Stoops to Conquer* | 1773 | John Byrom, *Miscellaneous Poems* |
| First American museum organized at Charleston, S. C. | | Phillis Wheatley, *Poems on Various Subjects*: first book of poems by a Negro in America |
| Chesterfield, *Letters Written by the Earl of Chesterfield to His Son, Philip Stanhope* | 1774 | Goldsmith, *Retaliation* |
| Gluck, *Iphigénie en Aulide*, first performance, Paris | | |
| Goethe, *Die Leiden des jungen Werthers* | | |
| | 1774–81 | Thomas Warton, *The History of English Poetry* |
| Beaumarchais, *Le Barbier de Séville*, first performance | 1775 | Walker, *A Dictionary of the English Language, answering at once the Purposes of Rhyming, Spelling and Pronouncing* |
| Burke, *Speech . . . on Moving his Resolution for Conciliation with the Colonies* | | |
| Sheridan, *The Rivals* | | |
| Declaration of American Independence | 1776 | |
| Paine, *Common Sense* | | |
| Adam Smith, *Wealth of Nations* | | |
| Gibbon, *Decline and Fall of the Roman Empire* | 1776–88 | |
| | 1777 | Chatterton, *Poems* (presented as though written by Thomas Rowley in the 15th century) |
| | | Thomas Warton, *Poems* |
| Frances Burney, *Evelina* | 1778 | |
| Hume, *Dialogues concerning Natural Religion* | 1779 | Cowper, *Olney Hymns* |
| Mesmer, *Mémoire sur la découverte du magnétisme animal*: theory of hypnotism | | |
| | 1779–81 | Johnson, *Prefaces, Biographical and Critical, to the English Poets* |
| Wieland, *Oberon* | 1780 | |
| Kant, *Kritik der reinen Vernunft* (Critique of Pure Reason) | 1781 | |
| Schiller, *Die Räuber* | | |
| Rousseau, *Confessions* | 1781–88 | |
| Crèvecœur, *Letters from an American Farmer* | 1782 | Cowper, "John Gilpin": first appearance |

# A CALENDAR

| GENERAL BACKGROUND | DATE | DIRECT HISTORY |
|---|---|---|
| Trimmer, *An Easy Introduction to the Knowledge of Nature* | 1782 | Trumbull, *M'Fingal* |
| Noah Webster, *Spelling Book* | 1782–83 | |
| Blair, *Lectures on Rhetoric and Belles Lettres* | 1783 | Blake, *Poetical Sketches* |
| William Herschel, *On the Proper Motion of the Sun and Solar Systems* | | Crabbe, *The Village*<br>Trusler, *Poetic Endings, or, A Dictionary of Rhymes* |
| Sheridan, *The School for Scandal* | | |
| Jefferson, *Notes on the State of Virginia,* published at Paris | 1784 | |
| Kant, *Ideen zu einer allgemeiner Geschichte in weltbürgerliche Absicht* | | |
| Herder, *Ideen zur Philosophie der Geschichte der Menschheit* | 1784–91 | |
| Kant, *Grundlegung zur Metaphysik der Sitten:* metaphysics of morals | 1785 | Cowper, *The Task*<br>Dwight, *The Conquest of Canaan* |
| Charles Wilkins's translation of the *Bhagavadgita:* first in English | | |
| Beckford, *Vathek* | 1786 | Burns, *Poems chiefly in the Scottish Dialect* |
| | | Freneau, *Poems* |
| | | Rogers, *An Ode to Superstition* |
| | | Wolcot, *Bozzy and Piozzi* |
| Goethe, *Iphigenie auf Tauris* | 1787 | Barlow, *The Vision of Columbus (The Columbiad)* |
| Mozart, *Don Giovanni* | | |
| *The Federalist* | 1787–88 | |
| Goethe, *Egmont* | 1788 | Collins, *An Ode on Popular Superstitions of the Highlands of Scotland* |
| Kant, *Kritik der practischen Vernunft* (Critique of Practical Reason) | | Whitehead, *Poems* |
| United States Constitution ratified | | |
| Bentham, *An Introduction to the Principles of Morals and Legislation:* utilitarianism | 1789 | Blake, *The Book of Thel; Songs of Innocence* |
| Erasmus Darwin, *The Loves of the Plants* | | |
| Fall of the Bastille | | |
| White, *Natural History and Antiquities of Selborne* | | |
| Bewick, *A General History of Quadrupeds* | 1790 | Blake, *The Marriage of Heaven and Hell* |
| Malone's edition of Shakespeare | | |

# A CALENDAR

| GENERAL BACKGROUND | DATE | DIRECT HISTORY |
|---|---|---|
| William Bartram, *Travels through North and South Carolina, Georgia, East and West Florida . . .*<br>Boswell, *The Life of Samuel Johnson*<br>De Sade, *Justine* | 1791 | Burns, "Tam o' Shanter": first appearance |
| Brackenridge, *Modern Chivalry*, Parts I–II: a novel<br>Wollstonecraft, *A Vindication of the Rights of Woman* | 1792 | Ritson, *Ancient Songs from the Time of King Henry III to the Revolution*<br>Rogers, *The Pleasures of Memory* |
| Carnot's *levée en masse*: beginning of universal military conscription; cult of the Goddess of Reason; decimal system adopted by the National Assembly; execution of Louis XVI and Reign of Terror<br>Dalton, *Meteorological Observations and Essays*: ultimately leading to atomic theory<br>Godwin, *Political Justice*<br>Louvre established | 1793 | Blake, *America, A Prophecy*<br>Wordsworth, *An Evening Walk* |
| Paley, *A View of the Evidences of Christianity*<br>Radcliffe, *Mysteries of Udolpho*<br>Slavery in French colonies abolished by the National Assembly<br>Whitney patents his cotton gin | 1794 | Blake, *Songs of Innocence and Experience*<br>Dwight, *Greenfield Hill* |
| Murray, *English Grammar*: widely used in American schools | 1795 | *The Poems of Walter Savage Landor*, suppressed by Landor |
| Goethe, *Wilhelm Meisters Lehrjahre* | 1795–96 | |
| Lewis, *The Monk*<br>Jean Paul Richter, *Quintus Fixlein*<br>Washington, "Farewell Address" | 1796 | Barlow, *The Hasty Pudding*<br>Coleridge, *Poems on Various Subjects* |
| Goethe, *Hermann und Dorothea* | 1797 | |
| C. B. Brown, *Wieland*<br>Malthus, *Principle of Population as it affects the Future of Society* | 1798 | Wordsworth and Coleridge, *Lyrical Ballads* |
| Napoleon's *coup* of the 18th Brumaire<br>Mme de Staël, *De la Littérature considerée dans ses* | 1799 | Moore, *Odes of Anacreon, translated into English Verse*<br>Scott, *The Eve of St. John* |

# A CALENDAR

| GENERAL BACKGROUND | DATE | DIRECT HISTORY |
|---|---|---|
| *rapports avec les institutions sociales:* the advent of democracy requires a pure language | 1799 | Wordsworth and Coleridge, *Lyrical Ballads,* Vol. II |
| Gauss, *Disquisitiones Arithmeticae:* higher mathematics developed as an independent science | 1801 | |
| Pestalozzi, *Wie Gertrud ihre Kinder lehrt:* doctrine of direct experiences for the child in education | | |
| | 1802–03 | Scott, ed., *Minstrelsy of the Scottish Border* |
| Louisiana Purchase | 1803 | |
| *Code Napoléon* | 1804 | Blake, *Milton;* "Jerusalem" |
| Lewis and Clark Expedition | 1804–06 | |
| Beethoven, *Fidelio,* first performance, rewritten in present form and presented 1814 | 1805 | Scott, *The Lay of the Last Minstrel*<br>Southey, *Madoc* |
| | 1805–06 | Wordsworth, *The Prelude,* written; this version first published 1926 |
| | 1806 | Byron, *Fugitive Pieces*<br>Scott, *Ballads and Lyrical Pieces* |
| Hegel, *Phänomenologie des Geistes* | 1807 | Moore, *A Selection of Irish Melodies* |
| Charles and Mary Lamb, *Tales from Shakespeare*<br>Mme de Staël, *Corinne* | | Wordsworth, *Poems in Two Volumes:* including "Intimations of Immortality" |
| Fichte, *Reden an die deutsche Nation* | 1807–08 | |
| Goethe, *Faust,* Part I | 1808 | Bryant, *The Embargo*<br>Scott, *Marmion* |
| Lamarck, *Philosophie zoölogique* | 1809 | Byron, *English Bards and Scotch Reviewers*<br>Campbell, *Gertrude of Wyoming, A Pennsylvanian Tale* |
| Schlegel, *Vorlesungen über dramatische Kunst und Litteratur:* a key book of European romanticism | 1809–11 | |
| Porter, *The Scottish Chiefs*<br>Mme de Stael, *De l'Allemagne* | 1810 | Crabbe, *The Borough*<br>Scott, *The Lady of the Lake* |
| Goya, *Los Desastres de la guerra* | 1810–13 | |
| Austen, *Sense and Sensibility* | 1811 | |
| Goethe, *Aus meinem Leben: Dichtung und Wahrheit* | 1811–33 | |
| Grimm, *Kinder- und Hausmärchen* | 1812–15 | |
| Hegel, *Wissensohaft der Logik* | 1812–16 | |

# A CALENDAR

# A CALENDAR

| GENERAL BACKGROUND | DATE | DIRECT HISTORY |
|---|---|---|
| Lamb, *Essays of Elia*, periodical appearance | 1820–23 | |
| Cooper, *The Spy* | 1821 | Beddoes, *The Improvisatore* |
| James Mill, *Elements of Political Economy*: first English textbook on economics | | Bryant, *Poems*, expanded 1832 |
| | | Clare, *The Village Minstrel* |
| Saint-Simon, *Le Système industriel* | | James Gates Percival, *Poems* |
| Scott, *Kenilworth* | | Shelley, *Adonais; Epipsychidion* |
| | | Southey, *A Vision of Judgement* |
| Hazlitt, *Table Talk* | 1821–22 | |
| De Quincey, *Confessions of an English Opium Eater* | 1822 | Byron, *The Vision of Judgement* |
| Scott, *Peveril of the Peak* | | Beddoes, *The Bride's Tragedy* |
| | | Darley, *The Errors of Ecstasie* |
| | | Rogers, *Italy*, Part I |
| Samuel Brown's gas engine: internal combustion | 1823 | |
| Cooper, *The Pioneers; The Pilot* | | |
| The Monroe Doctrine | | |
| Carlyle, *William Meister's Apprenticeship*: a translation from Goethe | 1824 | |
| Scott, *Redgauntlet* | | |
| Landor, *Imaginary Conversations of Literary Men and Statesmen* | 1824–28 | |
| Mitford, *Our Village* | 1824–32 | |
| Coleridge, *Aids to Reflection* | 1825 | E. C. Pinkney, *Poems* |
| Hazlitt, *The Spirit of the Age* | | |
| Manzoni, *I Promessi sposi* | 1825–27 | |
| Grimm, *Irische Elfenmärchen* | 1826 | Hood, *Whims and Oddities*, first series |
| Graham's *Magazine*, published in Philadelphia | 1826–64 | |
| Cooper, *The Prairie* | 1827 | Clare, *The Shepherd's Calendar* |
| Heine, *Buch der Lieder* | | Keble, *The Christian Year* |
| Niepce's first camera image | | Poe, *Tamerlane and other Poems* |
| | | Mrs. Sigourney, *Poems* |
| | | Simms, *Lyrical and Other Poems* |
| | | Alfred and Charles Tennyson, *Poems by Two Brothers* |
| Webster, *An American Dictionary of the English Language* | 1828 | |
| Catholic Emancipation Act in Great Britain | 1829 | Addington, *Poetical Quotations* |

# A CALENDAR

| GENERAL BACKGROUND | DATE | DIRECT HISTORY |
|---|---|---|
| James Mill, *Analysis of the Phenomena of the Human Mind:* beginning of associationist psychology | 1829 | Poe, *Al Aaraaf, Tamerlane and Minor Poems* |
| Hugo, *Hernani* | 1830 | Tennyson, *Poems, Chiefly Lyrical* |
| Lyell, *The Principles of Geology* | 1830–33 | |
| Hood's *Comic Annual* | 1830–42 | |
| Comte, *Cours de philosophie positive* | 1830–42 | |
| Godey's *Lady's Book* | 1830–98 | |
| Faraday's dynamo, discovery of magneto-electricity | 1831 | Elliott, *Corn-Law Rhymes* |
| Stendhal, *Le Rouge et le noir* | | Whittier, *Legends of New England* |
| H.M.S. *Beagle* starts its voyage, with young Darwin aboard | | |
| Irving, *The Alhambra* | 1832 | Hunt, *Poetical Works* |
| Reform Bill: disfranchisement of pocket and rotten boroughs, extension of the franchise to the middle class | | Tennyson, *Poems* |
| Frances Trollope, *Domestic Manners of the Americans* | | |
| Abolition of slavery in British colonies | 1833 | Robert Browning, *Pauline* |
| Balzac, *Eugénie Grandet* | | Hartley Coleridge, *Poems* |
| Factory Act: government regulation of working conditions | | |
| Keble's sermon on Irish Church Bill initiates the Oxford Movement | | |
| Balzac, *Le Père Goriot* | 1834 | |
| Bancroft, *A History of the United States* | 1834–74 | |
| Andersen, *Fairy Tales,* first series | 1835 | Browning, *Paracelsus* |
| Longstreet, *Georgia Scenes* | | Clare, *The Rural Muse* |
| Lytton, *Rienzi* | | Darley, *Nepenthe* |
| D. F. Strauss, *Das Leben Jesu* | 1835–36 | Drake, *The Culprit Fay* |
| Tocqueville, *De la Démocratie en Amérique* | 1835–40 | |
| Emerson, *Nature* | 1836 | O. W. Holmes, *Poems* |
| Landor, *Pericles and Aspasia* | | |
| Hegel, *Vorlesungen über die Aesthetik* | 1836–38 | |
| Carlyle, *French Revolution* | 1837 | |
| Dickens, *Pickwick Papers* | | |
| Emerson, *The American Scholar* | | |
| Hawthorne, *Twice-Told Tales* | | |

# A CALENDAR

| GENERAL BACKGROUND | DATE | DIRECT HISTORY |
|---|---|---|
| Carlyle, *Sartor Resartus*<br>Hugo, *Ruy Blas* | 1838 | Tupper, *Proverbial Philosophy* |
| Stendhal, *La Chartreuse de Parme* | 1839 | Bailey, *Festus*<br>Longfellow, *Voices of the Night*<br>Very, *Essays and Poems* |
| Faraday, *Experimental Researches in Electricity* | 1839–55 | |
| Carlyle, *Chartism*<br>Dana, *Two Years before the Mast*<br>Poe, *Tales of the Grotesque and Arabesque* | 1840 | Browning, *Sordello* |
| | 1840–47 | Barham, *The Ingoldsby Legends* |
| Carlyle, *On Heroes, Hero-Worship, and the Heroic in History*<br>Emerson, *Essays*, first series<br>Newman, *Tracts for the Times, No. 90; Remarks on Certain Passages in the Thirty-Nine Articles* | 1841 | |
| | 1842 | Browning, *Dramatic Lyrics*<br>Macaulay, *Lays of Ancient Rome*<br>Tennyson, *Poems* |
| Borrow, *The Bible in Spain*<br>O. W. Holmes, *The Contagiousness of Puerperal Fever*<br>Kierkegaard, *Either/Or*<br>John Stuart Mill, *A System of Logic*<br>Poe, *The Murders in the Rue Morgue*<br>Surtees, *Handley Cross* | 1843 | W. E. Channing, *Poems*<br>Hood, "Song of the Shirt"<br>Longfellow, *The Spanish Student* |
| Ruskin, *Modern Painters* | 1843–60 | |
| Disraeli, *Coningsby*<br>Musée de Cluny opened: medieval arts and crafts | 1844 | Barnes, *Poems of Rural Life in the Dorset Dialect*<br>E. B. Browning, *Poems*<br>Cranch, *Poems*<br>Emerson, "The Poet," in *Essays: Second Series*<br>Lowell, *Poems*<br>Patmore, *Poems* |
| Engels, *Die Lage der arbeitenden Klasse in England*<br>Margaret Fuller, *Woman in the Nineteenth Century* | 1845 | Longfellow, ed., *The Poets and Poetry of Europe*: historical anthology of translations by Longfellow and others |

# A CALENDAR

| GENERAL BACKGROUND | DATE | DIRECT HISTORY |
|---|---|---|
| Newman received into the Roman Church | 1845 | Poe, *The Raven and Other Poems* |
| Wagner, *Tannhäuser* | | |
| Hawthorne, *Mosses from an Old Manse* | 1846 | Charlotte, Emily, and Anne Brontë, *Poems* |
| Melville, *Typee* | | Lear, *A Book of Nonsense* |
| Smithsonian Institution established | | Poe, "The Philosophy of Composition," in *Graham's Magazine* |
| | | Whittier, *Voices of Freedom* |
| War between United States and Mexico | 1846–47 | |
| Charlotte Brontë, *Jane Eyre* | 1847 | Emerson, *Poems* |
| Emily Brontë, *Wuthering Heights* | | Landor, *The Hellenics* |
| | | Longfellow, *Evangeline* |
| | | Tennyson, *The Princess* |
| Bartlett, *Dictionary of Americanisms* | 1848 | Foster, *Songs of the Sable Harmonists*: including "Oh! Susannah," etc.; later songs published in *Ethiopian Melodies*, etc. |
| Grimm, *Die Geschichte der Deutschen Sprache:* laws of sound changes and idea of particular national spirit in words | | Lowell, *Biglow Papers*, first series; *A Fable for Critics* |
| Anna Jameson, *Sacred and Legendary Art* | | |
| Marx and Engels, *Manifest der kommunistischen Partei* | | |
| John Stuart Mill, *Principles of Political Economy* | | |
| Thackeray, *Vanity Fair* | | |
| California Gold Rush | 1849 | |
| Coleridge, *Notes and Lectures upon Shakespeare and Some of the Old Poets and Dramatists* | | |
| Parkman, *The Oregon Trail* | | |
| Ruskin, *The Seven Lamps of Architecture* | | |
| Thoreau, *Civil Disobedience; A Week on the Concord and Merrimack Rivers* | | |
| Macaulay, *The History of England from the Accession of James II* | 1849–61 | |

# William Blake

(1757–1827)

## Song

Memory, hither come,
And tune your merry notes:
And, while upon the wind
Your music floats,
I'll pore upon the stream
Where sighing lovers dream,
And fish for fancies as they pass
Within the watery glass.

I'll drink of the clear stream,
And hear the linnet's song;
And there I'll lie and dream
The day along:
And, when night comes, I'll go
To places fit for woe,
Walking along the darken'd valley
With silent Melancholy.

## Mad Song

The wild winds weep,
And the night is a-cold;
Come hither, Sleep,
And my griefs unfold:

But lo! the mornmg peeps
Over the eastern steeps,
And the rustling birds of dawn
The earth do scorn.

Lo! to the vault
Of pavèd heaven,
With sorrow fraught
My notes are driven:
They strike the ear of night,
Make weep the eyes of day;
They make mad the roaring winds,
And with tempests play.

Like a fiend in a cloud,
With howling woe
After night I do croud,
And with night will go;
I turn my back to the east
From whence comforts have increas'd;
For light doth seize my brain
With frantic pain.

## Song

How sweet I roam'd from field to field
And tasted all the summer's pride,
'Til I the prince of love beheld
Who in the sunny beams did glide!

He shew'd me lilies for my hair,
And blushing roses for my brow;
He led me through his gardens fair,
Where all his golden pleasures grow.

With sweet May dews my wings were wet,
And Phœbus fir'd my vocal rage;
He caught me in his silken net,
And shut me in his golden cage.

He loves to sit and hear me sing,
Then, laughing, sports and plays with me;
Then stretches out my golden wing,
And mocks my loss of liberty.

## To Spring

O thou with dewy locks, who lookest down
Thro' the clear windows of the morning, turn
Thine angel eyes upon our western isle,
Which in full choir hails thy approach, O Spring!

The hills tell each other, and the list'ning
Vallies hear; all our longing eyes are turned
Up to thy bright pavillions: issue forth,
And let thy holy feet visit our clime.

Come o'er the eastern hills, and let our winds
Kiss thy perfumèd garments; let us taste
Thy morn and evening breath; scatter thy pearls
Upon our love-sick land that mourns for thee.

O deck her forth with thy fair fingers; pour
Thy soft kisses on her bosom; and put
Thy golden crown upon her languish'd head,
Whose modest tresses were bound up for thee!

## FROM *Songs of Innocence*

### INTRODUCTION

Piping down the valleys wild,
Piping songs of pleasant glee,
On a cloud I saw a child,
And he laughing said to me:

"Pipe a song about a Lamb!"
So I piped with a merry chear.
"Piper, pipe that song again";
So I piped: he wept to hear.

"Drop thy pipe, thy happy pipe;
Sing thy songs of happy chear":
So I sung the same again,
While he wept with joy to hear.

"Piper, sit thee down and write
In a book, that all may read."
So he vanish'd from my sight,
And I pluck'd a hollow reed,

And I made a rural pen,
And I stain'd the water clear,
And I wrote my happy songs
Every child may joy to hear.

### THE LITTLE BLACK BOY

My mother bore me in the southern wild,
And I am black, but O my soul is white;
White as an angel is the English child,
But I am black, as if bereav'd of light.

My mother taught me underneath a tree,
And sitting down before the heat of day,
She took me on her lap and kissèd me,
And, pointing to the east, began to say:

"Look on the rising sun—there God does live,
And gives his light, and gives his heat away;
And flowers and trees and beasts and men receive
Comfort in morning, joy in the noon day.

"And we are put on earth a little space,
That we may learn to bear the beams of love;
And these black bodies and this sun-burnt face
Is but a cloud, and like a shady grove.

"For when our souls have learn'd the heat to bear,
The cloud will vanish; we shall hear his voice,
Saying: 'come out from the grove, my love and care,
And round my golden tent like lambs rejoice.'"

Thus did my mother say, and kissèd me;
And thus I say to little English boy:
When I from black, and he from white cloud free,
And round the tent of God like lambs we joy,

I'll shade him from the heat, till he can bear
To lean in joy upon our father's knee;
And then I'll stand and stroke his silver hair,
And be like him, and he will then love me.

## THE DIVINE IMAGE

To Mercy, Pity, Peace, and Love
All pray in their distress;
And to these virtues of delight
Return their thankfulness.

For Mercy, Pity, Peace, and Love
Is God, our father dear,
And Mercy, Pity, Peace, and Love
Is Man, his child and care.

For Mercy has a human heart,
Pity a human face,
And Love, the human form divine,
And Peace, the human dress.

Then every man, of every clime,
That prays in his distress,
Prays to the human form divine,
Love, Mercy, Pity, Peace.

And all must love the human form,
In heathen, Turk, or jew;
Where Mercy, Love, and Pity dwell
There God is dwelling too.

## ON ANOTHER'S SORROW

Can I see another's woe,
And not be in sorrow too?
Can I see another's grief,
And not seek for kind relief?

Can I see a falling tear,
And not feel my sorrow's share?
Can a father see his child
Weep, nor be with sorrow fill'd?

Can a mother sit and hear
An infant groan an infant fear?
No, no! never can it be!
Never, never can it be!

And can he who smiles on all
Hear the wren with sorrows small,
Hear the small bird's grief and care,
Hear the woes that infants bear,

And not sit beside the nest,
Pouring pity in their breast;
And not sit the cradle near,
Weeping tear on infant's tear;

And not sit both night and day,
Wiping all our tears away?
O, no! never can it be!
Never, never can it be!

He doth give his joy to all;
He becomes an infant small;
He becomes a man of woe;
He doth feel the sorrow too.

Think not thou canst sigh a sigh
And thy maker is not by;
Think not thou canst weep a tear
And thy maker is not near.

O! he gives to us his joy
That our grief he may destroy;
Till our grief is fled and gone
He doth sit by us and moan.

## FROM *Songs of Experience*

### INTRODUCTION

Hear the voice of the Bard!
Who Present, Past, and Future, sees;
Whose ears have heard

The Holy Word
That walk'd among the ancient trees,

Calling the lapsèd Soul,
And weeping in the evening dew;
That might controll
The starry pole,
And fallen, fallen light renew!

"O Earth, O Earth, return!
Arise from out the dewy grass;
Night is worn,
And the morn
Rises from the slumberous mass.

"Turn away no more;
Why wilt thou turn away?
The starry floor,
The wat'ry shore,
Is giv'n thee till the break of day."

## THE TYGER

Tyger! Tyger! burning bright
In the forests of the night,
What immortal hand or eye
Could frame thy fearful symmetry?

In what distant deeps or skies
Burnt the fire of thine eyes?
On what wings dare he aspire?
What the hand dare sieze the fire?

And what shoulder, and what art,
Could twist the sinews of thy heart?
And when thy heart began to beat,
What dread hand? and what dread feet?

What the hammer? what the chain?
In what furnace was thy brain?
What the anvil? what dread grasp
Dare its deadly terrors clasp?

When the stars threw down their spears,
And water'd heaven with their tears,
Did he smile his work to see?
Did he who made the Lamb make thee?

Tyger! Tyger! burning bright
In the forests of the night,
What immortal hand or eye,
Dare frame thy fearful symmetry?

## A POISON TREE

I was angry with my friend:
I told my wrath, my wrath did end.
I was angry with my foe:
I told it not, my wrath did grow.

And I water'd it in fears,
Night and morning with my tears;
And I sunnèd it with smiles,
And with soft deceitful wiles.

And it grew both day and night,
Till it bore an apple bright;
And my foe beheld it shine,
And he knew that it was mine,

And into my garden stole
When the night had veil'd the pole:
In the morning glad I see
My foe outstretch'd beneath the tree.

## THE SICK ROSE

O Rose, thou art sick!
The invisible worm,
That flies in the night,
In the howling storm,

Has found out thy bed
Of crimson joy;
And his dark secret love
Does thy life destroy.

## AH! SUN-FLOWER

Ah, Sun-flower! weary of time,
Who countest the steps of the Sun;
Seeking after that sweet golden clime,
Where the traveller's journey is done;

Where the Youth pined away with desire,
And the pale Virgin shrouded in snow,
Arise from their graves, and aspire
Where my Sun-flower wishes to go.

## LONDON

I wander thro' each charter'd street,
Near where the charter'd Thames does flow,
And mark in every face I meet
Marks of weakness, marks of woe.

In every cry of every Man,
In every Infant's cry of fear,
In every voice, in every ban,
The mind-forg'd manacles I hear.

How the Chimney-sweeper's cry
Every black'ning Church appalls;
And the hapless Soldier's sigh
Runs in blood down Palace walls.

But most thro' midnight streets I hear
How the youthful Harlot's curse
Blasts the new born Infant's tear,
And blights with plagues the Marriage hearse.

## INFANT SORROW

My mother groan'd, my father wept,
Into the dangerous world I leapt;
Helpless, naked, piping loud,
Like a fiend hid in a cloud.

Struggling in my father's hands,
Striving against my swadling bands,
Bound and weary, I thought best
To sulk upon my mother's breast.

## THE HUMAN ABSTRACT

Pity would be no more
If we did not make somebody Poor;
And Mercy no more could be
If all were as happy as we.

And mutual fear brings peace,
Till the selfish loves increase;
Then Cruelty knits a snare,
And spreads his baits with care.

He sits down with holy fears,
And waters the ground with tears;

Then Humility takes its root
Underneath his foot.

Soon spreads the dismal shade
Of Mystery over his head;
And the Catterpiller and Fly
Feed on the Mystery.

And it bears the fruit of Deceit,
Ruddy and sweet to eat;
And the Raven his nest has made
In its thickest shade.

The Gods of the earth and sea
Sought thro' Nature to find this Tree;
But their search was all in vain:
There grows one in the Human Brain.

## Never seek to tell thy love

Never seek to tell thy love
Love that never told can be;
For the gentle wind does move
Silently, invisibly.

I told my love, I told my love,
I told her all my heart,
Trembling, cold, in ghastly fears—
Ah, she doth depart.

Soon as she was gone from me
A traveller came by
Silently, invisibly—
O, was no deny.

# Mock on, Mock on, Voltaire, Rousseau

Mock on, Mock on, Voltaire, Rousseau;
Mock on, Mock on; 'tis all in vain!
You throw the sand against the wind,
And the wind blows it back again.

And every sand becomes a Gem
Reflected in the beams divine;
Blown back they blind the mocking eye,
But still in Israel's paths they shine.

The Atoms of Democritus
And Newton's Particles of light
Are sands upon the Red sea shore,
Where Israel's tents do shine so bright.

# The Mental Traveller

I travel'd thro' a Land of Men,
A Land of Men and Women too,
And heard and saw such dreadful things
As cold Earth-wanderers never knew.

For there the Babe is born in joy
That was begotten in dire woe;
Just as we reap in joy the fruit
Which we in bitter tears did sow.

And if the Babe is born a Boy
He's given to a Woman Old,

Who nails him down upon a rock,
Catches his Shrieks in Cups of gold.

She binds iron thorns around his head,
She pierces both his hands and feet,
She cuts his heart out at his side
To make it feel both cold and heat.

Her fingers number every Nerve,
Just as a Miser counts his gold;
She lives upon his shrieks and cries,
And she grows young as he grows old.

Till he becomes a bleeding youth,
And she becomes a Virgin bright;
Then he rends up his Manacles
And binds her down for his delight.

He plants himself in all her Nerves,
Just as a Husbandman his mould;
And she becomes his dwelling-place
And Garden fruitful seventy-fold.

An Agèd Shadow, soon he fades,
Wand'ring round an Earthly Cot,
Full-fillèd all with gems and gold
Which he by industry had got.

And these are the gems of the Human Soul,
The rubies and pearls of a love-sick eye,
The countless gold of the akeing heart,
The martyr's groan and the lover's sigh.

They are his meat, they are his drink;
He feeds the Beggar and the Poor
And the wayfaring Traveller:
For ever open is his door.

His grief is their eternal joy;
They make the roofs and walls to ring.
Till from the fire on the hearth
A little Female Babe does spring;

And she is all of solid fire
And gems and gold, that none his hand
Dares stretch to touch her Baby form,
Or wrap her in his swaddling band.

But She comes to the Man she loves,
If young or old, or rich or poor;
They soon drive out the agèd Host,
A Beggar at another's door.

He wanders weeping far away,
Until some other take him in;
Oft blind and age-bent, sore distrest,
Until he can a Maiden win.

And to allay his freezing Age,
The Poor Man takes her in his arms;
The Cottage fades before his sight,
The Garden and its lovely Charms.

The Guests are scatter'd thro' the land,
For the Eye altering alters all;
The Senses roll themselves in fear,
And the flat Earth becomes a Ball;

The Stars, Sun, Moon, all shrink away,
A desart vast without a bound,
And nothing left to eat or drink,
And a dark desart all around.

The honey of her Infant lips,
The bread and wine of her sweet smile,

The wild game of her roving Eye,
Does him to Infancy beguile;

For as he eats and drinks he grows
Younger and younger every day;
And on the desart wild they both
Wander in terror and dismay.

Like the wild Stag she flees away,
Her fear plants many a thicket wild;
While he pursues her night and day,
By various arts of love beguil'd,

By various arts of Love and Hate,
Till the wide desart planted o'er
With Labyrinths of wayward Love,
Where roam the Lion, Wolf, and Boar,

Till he becomes a wayward Babe,
And she a weeping Woman Old.
Then many a Lover wanders here;
The Sun and Stars are nearer roll'd;

The trees bring forth sweet extacy
To all who in the desart roam;
Till many a City there is Built,
And many a pleasant Shepherd's home.

But when they find the frowning Babe,
Terror strikes thro' the region wide:
They cry "The Babe! the Babe is Born!"
And flee away on Every side.

For who dare touch the frowning form,
His arm is wither'd to its root;
Lions, Boars, Wolves, all howling flee,
And every Tree does shed its fruit.

And none can touch that frowning form,
Except it be a Woman Old;
She nails him down upon the Rock,
And all is done as I have told.


## The Crystal Cabinet

The Maiden caught me in the Wild,
Where I was dancing merrily;
She put me into her Cabinet,
And Lock'd me up with a golden Key.

This Cabinet is form'd of Gold
And Pearl and Crystal shining bright,
And within it opens into a World
And a little lovely Moony Night.

Another England there I saw,
Another London with its Tower,
Another Thames and other Hills,
And another pleasant Surrey Bower,

Another Maiden like herself,
Translucent, lovely, shining clear,
Threefold each in the other clos'd,—
O what a pleasant trembling fear!

O what a smile! a threefold smile
Fill'd me that like a flame I burn'd;
I bent to kiss the lovely Maid,
And found a Threefold Kiss return'd.

I strove to sieze the inmost Form
With ardor fierce and hands of flame,
But burst the Crystal Cabinet,
And like a Weeping Babe became—

A weeping Babe upon the wild,
And Weeping Woman pale reclin'd,
And in the outward air again
I fill'd with woes the passing Wind.

## Auguries of Innocence

To see a World in a Grain of Sand,
And a Heaven in a Wild Flower,
Hold Infinity in the palm of your hand,
And Eternity in an hour.
A Robin Redbreast in a Cage
Puts all Heaven in a Rage.
A dove-house fill'd with Doves and Pigeons
Shudders Hell thro' all its regions.
A dog starv'd at his Master's Gate
Predicts the ruin of the State.
A Horse misus'd upon the Road
Calls to Heaven for Human blood.
Each outcry of the hunted Hare
A fibre from the Brain does tear.
A Skylark wounded in the wing,
A Cherubim does cease to sing.
The Game Cock clip'd and arm'd for fight
Does the Rising Sun affright.
Every Wolf's and Lion's howl
Raises from Hell a Human Soul.
The wild Deer, wand'ring here and there,
Keeps the Human Soul from Care.
The Lamb misus'd breeds Public Strife
And yet forgives the Butcher's knife.
The Bat that flits at close of Eve
Has left the Brain that won't Believe.

The Owl that calls upon the Night
Speaks the Unbeliever's fright.
He who shall hurt the little Wren
Shall never be belov'd by Men.
He who the Ox to wrath has mov'd
Shall never be by Woman lov'd.
The wanton Boy that kills the Fly
Shall feel the Spider's enmity.
He who torments the Chafer's Sprite
Weaves a Bower in endless Night.
The Catterpiller on the Leaf
Repeats to thee thy Mother's grief.
Kill not the Moth nor Butterfly,
For the Last Judgment draweth nigh.
He who shall train the Horse to war
Shall never pass the Polar Bar.
The Beggar's Dog and Widow's Cat,
Feed them and thou wilt grow fat.
The Gnat that sings his Summer's Song
Poison gets from Slander's tongue.
The poison of the Snake and Newt
Is the sweat of Envy's Foot.
The poison of the Honey Bee
Is the Artist's Jealousy.
The Prince's Robes and Beggar's Rags
Are Toadstools on the Miser's Bags.
A Truth that's told with bad intent
Beats all the Lies you can invent.
It is right it should be so;
Man was made for Joy and Woe;
And when this we rightly know,
Thro' the World we safely go,
Joy and Woe are woven fine,
A Clothing for the soul divine.
Under every grief and pine

Runs a joy with silken twine.
The Babe is more than Swadling Bands;
Throughout all these Human Lands
Tools were made, and Born were hands,
Every Farmer Understands.
Every Tear from Every Eye
Becomes a Babe in Eternity;
This is caught by Females bright
And return'd to its own delight.
The Bleat, the Bark, Bellow and Roar,
Are Waves that Beat on Heaven's Shore.
The Babe that weeps the Rod beneath
Writes Revenge in realms of Death.
The Beggar's Rags, fluttering in Air,
Does to Rags the Heavens tear.
The Soldier, arm'd with Sword and Gun,
Palsied strikes the Summer's Sun.
The poor Man's Farthing is worth more
Than all the Gold on Afric's Shore.
One Mite wrung from the Lab'rer's hands
Shall buy and sell the Miser's Lands;
Or, if protected from on high,
Does that whole Nation sell and buy.
He who mocks the Infant's Faith
Shall be mock'd in Age and Death.
He who shall teach the Child to Doubt
The rotting Grave shall ne'er get out.
He who respects the Infant's faith
Triumphs over Hell and Death.
The Child's Toys and the Old Man's Reasons
Are the Fruits of the Two seasons.
The Questioner, who sits so sly,
Shall never know how to Reply.
He who replies to words of Doubt

Doth put the Light of Knowledge out.
The Strongest Poison ever known
Came from Caesar's Laurel Crown.
Nought can Deform the Human Race
Like to the Armour's iron brace.
When Gold and Gems adorn the Plow
To Peaceful Arts shall Envy Bow.
A Riddle, or the Cricket's Cry,
Is to Doubt a fit Reply.
The Emmet's Inch and Eagle's Mile
Make Lame Philosophy to smile.
He who Doubts from what he sees
Will ne'er Believe, do what you Please.
If the Sun and Moon should Doubt,
They'd immediately Go Out.
To be in a Passion you Good may do,
But no Good if a Passion is in you.
The Whore and Gambler, by the State
Licensed, build that Nation's Fate.
The Harlot's cry from Street to Street
Shall weave Old England's winding Sheet.
The Winner's Shout, the Loser's Curse,
Dance before dead England's Hearse.
Every Night and every Morn
Some to Misery are Born.
Every Morn and every Night
Some are Born to Sweet Delight.
Some are Born to Sweet Delight,
Some are Born to Endless Night.
We are led to Believe a Lie
When we see not Thro' the Eye,
Which was Born in a Night to perish in a Night,
When the Soul Slept in Beams of Light.
God Appears, and God is Light,

To those poor souls who dwell in Night;
But does a Human Form Display
To those who Dwell in Realms of Day.

# For the Sexes:
## The Gates of Paradise

### PROLOGUE

Mutual Forgiveness of each Vice,
Such are the Gates of Paradise,
Against the Accuser's chief desire,
Who walk'd among the Stones of Fire.
Jehovah's Finger Wrote the Law;
Then Wept; then rose in Zeal and Awe,
And the Dead Corpse, from Sinai's heat,
Buried beneath his Mercy Seat.
O Christians! Christians! tell me Why
You rear it on your Altars high?

### THE KEYS

The Catterpiller on the Leaf
Reminds thee of thy Mother's Grief.

### OF THE GATES

My Eternal Man set in Repose,
The Female from his darkness rose;
And She found me beneath a Tree,
A Mandrake, and in her Veil hid me.
Serpent Reasonings us entice
Of Good and Evil, Virtue and Vice,

Doubt Self Jealous, Watry folly,
Struggling thro' Earth's Melancholy,
Naked in Air, in Shame and Fear,
Blind in Fire, with shield and spear,
Two Horn'd Reasoning, Cloven Fiction,
In Doubt, which is Self contradiction,
A dark Hermaphrodite We stood,—
Rational Truth, Root of Evil and Good.
Round me flew the Flaming Sword;
Round her snowy Whirlwinds roar'd,
Freezing her Veil, the Mundane Shell.
I rent the Veil where the Dead dwell:
When weary Man enters his Cave,
He meets his Saviour in the Grave.
Some find a Female Garment there,
And some a Male, woven with care,
Lest the Sexual Garments sweet
Should grow a devouring Winding sheet.
One Dies! Alas! the Living and Dead!
One is slain! and One is fled!
In Vain-glory hatcht and nurst,
By double Spectres, Self Accurst,
My Son! my Son! thou treatest me
But as I have instructed thee.
On the shadows of the Moon
Climbing thro' Night's highest noon:
In Time's Ocean falling drown'd:
In Aged Ignorance profound,
Holy and cold, I clip'd the Wings
Of all Sublunary Things,
And in depths of my Dungeons
Closed the Father and the Sons.
But when once I did descry
The Immortal Man that cannot Die,
Thro' evening shades I haste away

To close the Labours of my Day.
The Door of Death I open found,
And the Worm Weaving in the Ground:
Thou'rt my Mother from the Womb,
Wife, Sister, Daughter, to the Tomb:
Weaving to Dreams the Sexual strife,
And weeping over the Web of Life.

## EPILOGUE

### (TO THE ACCUSER WHO IS THE GOD OF THIS WORLD)

Truly, My Satan, thou art but a Dunce,
And dost not know the Garment from the Man;
Every Harlot was a Virgin once,
Nor can'st thou ever change Kate into Nan.

Tho' thou art Worshippèd by the Names Divine
Of Jesus and Jehovah, thou art still
The Son of Morn in weary Night's decline,
The lost Traveller's Dream under the Hill.

## FROM *Milton*

And did those feet in ancient time
Walk upon England's mountains green?
And was the holy Lamb of God
On England's pleasant pastures seen?

And did the Countenance Divine
Shine forth upon our clouded hills?
And was Jerusalem builded here
Among these dark Satanic Mills?

Bring me my Bow of burning gold!
Bring me my Arrows of desire!
Bring me my Spear! O clouds unfold!
Bring me my Chariot of fire!

I will not cease from Mental Fight,
Nor shall my Sword sleep in my hand,
Till we have built Jerusalem
In England's green and pleasant Land.


# The Book of Thel

### THEL'S MOTTO

Does the Eagle know what is in the pit,
Or wilt thou go ask the Mole?
Can Wisdom be put in a silver rod?
Or Love in a golden bowl?

### I

The daughters of the Seraphim led round their sunny
    flocks,
All but the youngest: she in paleness sought the secret
    air,
To fade away like morning beauty from her mortal day.
Down by the river of Adona her soft voice is heard,
And thus her gentle lamentation falls like morning dew:

"O life of this our spring! why fades the lotus of the
    water?
Why fade these children of the spring, born but to smile
    and fall?
Ah! Thel is like a wat'ry bow, and like a parting cloud;
Like a reflection in a glass; like shadows in the water,

Like dreams of infants, like a smile upon an infant's
    face,
Like the dove's voice, like transient day, like music in
    the air.
Ah! gentle may I lay me down, and gentle rest my head,
And gentle sleep the sleep of death, and gentle hear the
    voice
Of him that walketh in the garden in the evening time."

The Lilly of the valley, breathing in the humble grass
Answer'd the lovely maid and said: "I am a wat'ry
    weed,
And I am very small and love to dwell in lowly vales;
So weak, the gilded butterfly scarce perches on my
    head.
Yet I am visited from heaven, and he that smiles on all
Walks in the valley, and each morn over me spreads his
    hand,
Saying, 'Rejoice, thou humble grass, thou new-born lilly
    flower,
Thou gentle maid of silent valleys and of modest brooks;
For thou shalt be clothed in light, and fed with morn-
    ing manna,
Till summer's heat melts thee beside the fountains and
    the springs
To flourish in eternal vales': then why should Thel com-
    plain?
Why should the mistress of the vales of Har utter a
    sigh?"

She ceas'd and smil'd in tears, then sat down in her
    silver shrine.

Thel answer'd: "O thou little virgin of the peaceful
    valley,
Giving to those that cannot crave, the voiceless, the
    o'ertired.

Thy breath doth nourish the innocent lamb; he smells
    thy milky garments;
He crops thy flowers while thou sittest smiling in his
    face,
Wiping his mild and meekin mouth from all contagious
    taints.
Thy wine doth purify the golden honey; thy perfume,
Which thou dost scatter on every little blade of grass
    that springs,
Revives the milked cow and tames the fire-breathing
    steed.
But Thel is like a faint cloud kindled at the rising sun:
I vanish from my pearly throne, and who shall find my
    place?"

"Queen of the vales," the Lilly answer'd, "ask the tender
    cloud,
And it shall tell thee why it glitters in the morning sky,
And why it scatters its bright beauty thro' the humid air.
Descend, O little Cloud, and hover before the eyes of
    Thel."

The Cloud descended, and the Lilly bow'd her modest
    head,
And went to mind her numerous charge among the
    verdant grass.

## II

"O little Cloud," the virgin said, "I charge thee tell to
    me
Why thou complainest not when in one hour thou fade
    away.
Then we shall seek thee, but not find. Ah, Thel is like to
    thee.
I pass away; yet I complain, and no one hears my
    voice."

The Cloud then shew'd his golden head and his bright
    form emerg'd,
Hovering and glittering on the air before the face of
    Thel.

"O virgin, know'st thou not our steeds drink of the
    golden springs
Where Luvah doth renew his horses? Look'st thou on
    my youth,
And fearest thou, because I vanish and am seen no
    more?
Nothing remains? O maid, I tell thee, when I pass away,
It is to tenfold life, to love, to peace and raptures holy.
Unseen descending, weigh my light wings upon balmy
    flowers,
And court the fair-eyed dew to take me to her shining
    tent.
The weeping virgin, trembling kneels before the risen
    sun,
Till we arise link'd in a golden band and never part,
But walk united, bearing food to all our tender flowers."

"Dost thou, O little Cloud? I fear that I am not like
    thee,
For I walk thro' the vales of Har, and smell the sweetest
    flowers.
But I feed not the little flowers; I hear the warbling
    birds,
But I feed not the warbling birds; they fly and seek their
    food.
But Thel delights in these no more, because I fade
    away,
And all shall say: 'Without a use this shining woman
    liv'd,
Or did she only live to be at death the food of worms?'"

The Cloud reclin'd upon his airy throne and answer'd
    thus,

"Then if thou art the food of worms, O virgin of the
    skies,
How great thy use, how great thy blessing! every thing
    that lives
Lives not alone nor for itself: fear not, and I will call
The weak worm from its lowly bed, and thou shalt hear
    its voice.
Come forth, worm of the silent valley, to thy pensive
    queen."

The helpless worm arose, and sat upon the Lilly's leaf:
And the bright Cloud sail'd on, to find his partner in the
    vale.

### III

Then Thel astonish'd view'd the Worm upon its dewy
    bed.

"Art thou a Worm? image of weakness, art thou but a
    Worm?
I see thee like an infant wrapped in the Lilly's leaf.
Ah, weep not, little voice! thou canst not speak, but
    thou canst weep.
Is this a Worm? I see thee lay helpless and naked, weep-
    ing,
And none to answer, none to cherish thee with mother's
    smiles."

The Clod of Clay heard the Worm's voice and rais'd her
    pitying head;
She bow'd over the weeping infant, and her life exhal'd
In milky fondness: then on Thel she fix'd her humble
    eyes.

"O beauty of the vales of Har, we live not for ourselves.
Thou seest me the meanest thing, and so I am indeed,
My bosom of itself is cold, and of itself is dark;
But he, that loves the lowly, pours his oil upon my head
And kisses me, and binds his nuptial bands around my
    breast,
And says: 'Thou mother of my children, I have lovèd
    thee,
And I have given thee a crown that none can take
    away.'
But how this is, sweet maid, I know not, and I cannot
    know.
I ponder, and I cannot ponder; yet I live and love."

The daughter of beauty wip'd her pitying tears with her
    white veil,
And said: "Alas! I knew not this, and therefore did I
    weep.
That God would love a Worm I knew, and punish the
    evil foot
That wilful bruis'd its helpless form; but that he cher-
    ish'd it
With milk and oil I never knew: and therefore did I
    weep;
And I complain'd in the mild air, because I fade away,
And lay me down in thy cold bed, and leave my shining
    lot."

"Queen of the vales," the matron Clay answer'd, "I
    heard thy sighs,
And all thy moans flew o'er my roof, but I have call'd
    them down.
Wilt thou, O Queen, enter my house? 'tis given thee to
    enter
And to return: fear nothing, enter with thy virgin feet."

## IV

The eternal gates' terrific porter lifted the northern bar.
Thel enter'd in and saw the secrets of the land unknown.
She saw the couches of the dead, and where the fibrous
  roots
Of every heart on earth infixes deep its restless twists,
A land of sorrows and of tears where never smile was
  seen.

She wander'd in the land of clouds thro' valleys dark,
  list'ning
Dolours and lamentations; waiting oft beside a dewy
  grave
She stood in silence, list'ning to the voices of the ground,
Till to her own grave plot she came, and there she sat
  down,
And heard this voice of sorrow breathèd from the hollow
  pit.

"Why cannot the Ear be closed to its own destruction,
Or the glist'ning Eye to the poison of a smile?
Why are Eyelids stor'd with arrows ready drawn,
Where a thousand fighting men in ambush lie;
Or an Eye of gifts and graces show'ring fruits and
  coined gold?
Why a Tongue impress'd with honey from every wind?
Why an Ear, a whirlpool fierce to draw creations in?
Why a Nostril wide inhaling terror, trembling, and
  affright?
Why a tender curb upon the youthful burning boy?
Why a little curtain of flesh on the bed of our desire?"

The Virgin started from her seat, and with a shriek
Fled back unhinder'd till she came into the vales of Har.

# Robert Burns

(1759–1796)

## The Jolly Beggars: A Cantata

### RECITATIVO

When lyart leaves bestrow the yird,
Or wavering like the bauckie-bird,
  Bedim cauld Boreas' blast;
When hailstanes drive wi' bitter skyte,
And infant frosts begin to bite,
  In hoary cranreuch drest;
Ae night at e'en a merry core
  O' randie, gangrel bodies
In Poosie Nansie's held the splore,
  To drink their orra duddies:
    Wi' quaffing and laughing,
      They ranted and they sang;
    Wi' jumping an' thumping,
      The vera girdle rang.

First, neist the fire, in auld red rags,
Ane sat, weel brac'd wi' mealy bags,
  And knapsack a' in order;
His doxy lay within his arm,
Wi' usquebae an' blankets warm—
  She blinket on her sodger:
An' ay he gies the tozie drab
  The tither skelpin' kiss,
While she held up her greedy gab

Just like an aumous dish.
　　Ilk smack still, did crack still,
　　　Just like a cadger's whip,
　　Then staggering and swaggering
　　　He roar'd this ditty up—


### AIR

*Tune—"Soldiers' Joy"*

I am a son of Mars who have been in many wars,
And show my cuts and scars wherever I come;
This here was for a wench, and that other in a trench,
When welcoming the French at the sound of the drum.
　　　　　*Lal de daudle, etc.*

My 'prenticeship I pass'd where my leader breath'd his
　　last,
When the bloody die was cast on the heights of Abram;
I served out my trade when the gallant game was play'd,
And the Moro low was laid at the sound of the drum.

I lastly was with Curtis, among the floating batt'ries,
And there I left for witness an arm and a limb:
Yet let my country need me, with Eliott to head me,
I'd clatter on my stumps at the sound of a drum.

And now tho' I must beg with a wooden arm and leg,
And many a tatter'd rag hanging over my bum,
I'm as happy with my wallet, my bottle and my callet,
As when I us'd in scarlet to follow a drum.

What tho' with hoary locks, I must stand the winter
　　shocks,
Beneath the woods and rocks oftentimes for a home?
When the t'other bag I sell, and the t'other bottle tell,
I could meet a troop of hell, at the sound of the drum.

## RECITATIVO

He ended; and the kebars sheuk,
　　Aboon the chorus roar;
While frighted rattons backward leuk,
　　And seek the benmost bore;
A fairy fiddler frae the neuk,
　　He skirl'd out *Encore!*
But up arose the martial chuck
　　And laid the loud uproar.

## AIR

### Tune—"Soldier Laddie"

I once was a maid, tho' I cannot tell when,
And still my delight is in proper young men;
Some one of a troop of dragoons was my daddie,
No wonder I'm fond of a sodger laddie.
　　　　　　　　　*Sing, Lal de lal, etc.*

The first of my loves was a swaggering blade,
To rattle the thundering drum was his trade;
His leg was so tight, and his cheek was so ruddy,
Transported I was with my sodger laddie.

But the godly old chaplain left him in the lurch,
The sword I forsook for the sake of the church;
He ventur'd the *soul*, and I risked the *body*,
'Twas then I prov'd false to my sodger laddie.

Full soon I grew sick of my sanctified sot,
The regiment at large for a husband I got;
From the gilded spontoon to the fife I was ready,
I asked no more but a sodger laddie.

But the peace it reduc'd me to beg in despair,
Till I met my old boy at Cunningham fair;

His rags regimental they flutter'd so gaudy,
My heart it rejoic'd at my sodger laddie.

And now I have liv'd—I know not how long,
And still I can join in a cup or a song;
But whilst with both hands I can hold the glass steady,
Here's to thee, my hero, my sodger laddie!

## RECITATIVO

Poor Merry-Andrew in the neuk
 Sat guzzling wi' a tinkler-hizzie;
They mind't na wha the chorus teuk,
 Between themselves they were sae busy.
 At length, wi' drink and courting dizzy,
He stoitered up an' made a face;
 Then turn'd, an' laid a smack on Grizzy,
Syne tun'd his pipes wi' grace grimace.

## AIR

*Tune—"Auld Sir Symon"*

Sir Wisdom's a fool when he's fou,
 Sir Knave is a fool in a session;
He's there but a 'prentice I trow,
 But I am a fool by profession.

My grannie she bought me a beuk,
 An' I held awa to the school;
I fear I my talent misteuk,
 But what will ye hae of a fool?

For drink I would venture my neck;
 A hizzie's the half o' my craft;
But what could ye other expect,
 Of ane that's avowedly daft?

I ance was tied up like a stirk,
   For civilly swearing and quaffing;
I ance was abused i' the kirk,
   For touzling a lass i' my daffin.

Poor Andrew that tumbles for sport,
   Let naebody name wi' a jeer;
There's even, I'm tauld, i' the Court,
   A tumbler ca'd the Premier.

Observ'd ye yon reverend lad
   Mak faces to tickle the mob?
He rails at our mountebank squad—
   It's rivalship just i' the job!

And now my conclusion I'll tell,
   For faith! I'm confoundedly dry:
The chiel that's a fool for himsel';
   Gude Lord! he's far dafter than I.

## RECITATIVO

Then neist outspak a raucle carlin,
Wha kent fu' weel to cleek the sterling,
For mony a pursie she had hooked,
And had in mony a well been ducked.
Her love had been a Highland laddie,
But weary fa' the waefu' woodie!
Wi' sighs and sobs she thus began
To wail her braw John Highlandman.

## AIR

*Tune—"Oh an ye were dead, Gudeman"*

A Highland lad my love was born,
The Lalland laws he held in scorn;
But he still was faithfu' to his clan,
My gallant braw John Highlandman.

### CHORUS

*Sing, hey my braw John Highlandman!*
*Sing, ho my braw John Highlandman!*
*There's not a lad in a' the lan'*
*Was match for my John Highlandman.*

With his philibeg an' tartan plaid,
An' gude claymore down by his side,
The ladies' hearts he did trepan,
My gallant braw John Highlandman.
                    *Sing, hey, etc.*

We ranged a' from Tweed to Spey,
An' liv'd like lords and ladies gay;
For a Lalland face he feared none,
My gallant braw John Highlandman.

They banish'd him beyond the sea,
But ere the bud was on the tree,
Adown my cheeks the pearls ran,
Embracing my John Highlandman.

But, oh! they catch'd him at the last,
And bound him in a dungeon fast;
My curse upon them every one!
They've hang'd my braw John Highlandman.

And now a widow, I must mourn
The pleasures that will ne'er return;
No comfort but a hearty can,
When I think on John Highlandman.

### RECITATIVO

A pigmy scraper, wi' his fiddle,
Wha us'd to trysts and fairs to driddle,
Her strappin limb and gausy middle

(He reach'd nae higher)
Had hol'd his heartie like a riddle,
    An' blawn't on fire.

Wi' hand on haunch, an' upward e'e,
He croon'd his gamut, one, two, three,
Then in an Arioso key,
    The wee Apollo
Set off wi' *Allegretto* glee
    His *giga* solo.

## AIR

*Tune—"Whistle owre the lave o't"*

Let me ryke up to dight that tear,
An' go wi' me to be my dear,
An' then your every care and fear
    May whistle owre the lave o't.

### CHORUS

*I am a fiddler to my trade,*
*An' a' the tunes that e're I play'd,*
*The sweetest still to wife or maid,*
    *Was whistle owre the lave o't.*

At kirns and weddings we'se be there,
An' oh! sae nicely's we will fare;
We'll bouse about till Daddie Care
    Sing whistle owre the lave o't.
                *I am, etc.*

Sae merrily the banes we'll pyke,
An' sun oursels about the dyke,
An' at our leisure, when we like,
    We'll whistle owre the lave o't.

But bless me wi' your heaven o' charms,
And while I kittle hair on thairms,
Hunger, cauld, an' a' sic harms,
 May whistle owre the lave o't.


### RECITATIVO

Her charms had struck a sturdy caird,
 As weel as poor Gutscraper;
He taks the fiddler by the beard,
 And draws a rusty rapier.—
He swoor by a' was swearing worth,
 To speet him like a pliver,
Unless he would from that time forth,
 Relinquish her forever.
Wi' ghastly e'e, poor tweedle-dee
 Upon his hunkers bended,
And pray'd for grace wi' ruefu' face,
 And so the quarrel ended.
But though his little heart did grieve,
 When round the tinker prest her,
He feign'd to snirtle in his sleeve,
 When thus the caird address'd her.


### AIR

*Tune—"Clout the Caudron."*

My bonie lass, I work in brass,
 A tinker is my station;
I've travell'd round all Christian ground
 In this my occupation.
I've ta'en the gold, I've been enroll'd
 In many a noble squadron;
But vain they search'd, when off I march'd
 To go and clout the caudron.
     *I've ta'en the gold, etc.*

Despise that shrimp, that wither'd imp,
  Wi' a' his noise and caprin',
An' tak' a share wi' those that bear
  The budget an' the apron.
An' by that stowp! my faith an' houpe,
  An' by that dear Keilbagie,
If e'er ye want, or meet wi' scant,
  May I ne'er weet my craigie.
                    *An' by that stowp, etc.*

### RECITATIVO

The caird prevail'd—the unblushing fair
  In his embraces sunk,
Partly wi' love o'ercome sae sair,
  An' partly she was drunk.
Sir Violino, with an air
  That show'd a man of spunk,
Wish'd *unison* between the pair,
  An' made the bottle clunk
        To their health that night.

But urchin Cupid shot a shaft
  That play'd a dame a shavie,
The fiddler rak'd her fore and aft,
  Behint the chicken cavie,
Her lord, a wight o' Homer's craft,
  Tho' limping wi' the spavie,
He hirpl'd up, and lap like daft,
  An shor'd them Dainty Davie
        O' boot that night.

He was a care-defying blade
  As ever Bacchus listed,
Tho' Fortune sair upon him laid,
  His heart she ever miss'd it.

He had no wish but—to be glad,
  Nor want but—when he thirsted;
He hated nought but—to be sad,
  And thus the Muse suggested
    His sang that night.

### AIR

*Tune—"For a' that, an' a' that."*

I am a bard of no regard,
  Wi' gentle folks, an' a' that;
But Homer-like, the glowrin byke,
  Frae town to town I draw that.

### CHORUS

*For a' that, an' a' that,*
  *An' twice as muckle's a' that;*
*I've lost but ane, I've twa behin',*
  *I've wife enough for a' that.*

I never drank the Muses' stank,
  Castalia's burn, an' a' that;
But there it streams, and richly reams,
  My Helicon I ca' that,
            *For a' that, etc.*

Great love I bear to a' the fair,
  Their humble slave, an' a' that;
But lordly will, I hold it still
  A mortal sin to thraw that.

In raptures sweet, this hour we meet,
  Wi' mutual love an' a' that;
But for how lang the flee may stang,
  Let inclination law that.

Their tricks and craft have put me daft,
  They've ta'en me in, an' a' that;

But clear your decks, and here's the *sex!*
I like the jads for a' that.

> *For a' that, an' a' that,*
>    *An' twice as muckle's a' that;*
> *My dearest bluid, to do them guid,*
>    *They're welcome till't for a' that.*

### RECITATIVO

So sung the bard—and Nansie's wa's
   Shook with a thunder of applause,
Re-echo'd from each mouth;
   They toom'd their pocks, an' pawn'd their duds,
They scarcely left to co'er their fuds,
   To quench their lowin drouth.
Then owre again, the jovial thrang,
   The poet did request,
To loose his pack an' wale a sang,
   A ballad o' the best:
      He rising, rejoicing,
         Between his twa Deborahs,
     Looks round him, an' found them
       Impatient for the chorus.

### AIR

*Tune—"Jolly Mortals, fill your Glasses"*

See! the smoking bowl before us,
   Mark our jovial ragged ring!
Round and round take up the chorus,
   And in raptures let us sing.

### CHORUS

> *A fig for those by law protected!*
> *Liberty's a glorious feast!*

*Courts for cowards were erected,*
    *Churches built to please the priest.*

What is title? what is treasure?
    What is reputation's care?
If we lead a life of pleasure,
    'Tis no matter how or where!
            *A fig, etc.*

With the ready trick and fable,
    Round we wander all the day;
And at night, in barn or stable,
    Hug our doxies on the hay.

Does the train-attended carriage
    Through the country lighter rove?
Does the sober bed of marriage
    Witness brighter scenes of love?

Life is all a *variorum,*
    We regard not how it goes;
Let them cant about *decorum*
    Who have characters to lose.

Here's to budgets, bags and wallets!
    Here's to all the wandering train!
Here's our ragged brats and callets!
    One and all cry out, Amen!

        *A fig for those by law protected!*
            *Liberty's a glorious feast!*
        *Courts for cowards were erected,*
            *Churches built to please the priest.*

## Address to the Deil

> O Prince! O Chief of many throned pow'rs!
> That led th' embattl'd seraphim to war!
> —MILTON.

O thou! whatever title suit thee—
Auld Hornie, Satan, Nick, or Clootie
Wha in yon cavern grim an' sootie,
       Clos'd under hatches,
Spairges about the brunstane cootie,
       To scaud poor wretches!

Hear me, Auld Hangie, for a wee,
An' let poor damned bodies be;
I'm sure sma' pleasure it can gie,
       Ev'n to a deil,
To skelp an' scaud poor dogs like me,
       An' hear us squeel.

Great is thy pow'r, an' great thy fame;
Far kend an' noted is thy name;
An' tho' yon lowin heugh's thy hame,
       Thou travels far;
An' faith! thou's neither lag, nor lame,
       Nor blate, nor scaur.

Whyles, ranging like a roarin lion,
For prey, a' holes an' corners trying;
Whyles, on the strong-wing'd tempest flyin,
       Tirlin the kirks;
Whyles, in the human bosom pryin,
       Unseen thou lurks.

I've heard my rev'rend graunie say,
In lanely glens ye like to stray;

Or where auld ruin'd castles gray
      Nod to the moon,
Ye fright the nightly wand'rer's way
      Wi' eldritch croon.

When twilight did my graunie summon,
To say her pray'rs, douce, honest woman!
Aft yont the dyke she's heard you bummin,
      Wi' eerie drone;
Or, rustlin thro' the boortrees comin,
      Wi' heavy groan.

Ae dreary, windy, winter night,
The star shot down wi' sklentin' light,
Wi' you mysel I gat a fright:
      Ayont the lough,
Ye, like a rash-buss, stood in sight,
      Wi' waving sugh.

The cudgel in my nieve did shake,
Each bristl'd hair stood like a stake,
When wi' an eldritch, stoor "quaick, quaick,"
      Amang the springs,
Awa ye squatter'd like a drake,
      On whistling wings.

Let warlocks grim, an' wither'd hags,
Tell how wi' you, on ragweed nags,
They skim the muirs an' dizzy crags,
      Wi' wicked speed;
And in kirkyards renew their leagues
      Owre howkit dead.

Thence, countra wives, wi' toil an' pain,
May plunge an' plunge the kirn in vain;
For O! the yellow treasure's taen
      By witching skill;

An' dawtet, twal-pint hawkie's gaen  
　　　As yell's the bill.

Thence, mystic knots mak great abuse  
On young guidmen, fond, keen, an' croose;  
When the best wark-lume i' the house,  
　　　By cantrip wit,  
Is instant made no worth a louse,  
　　　Just at the bit.

When thowes dissolve the snawy hoord,  
An' float the jinglin icy-boord,  
Then, water-kelpies haunt the foord,  
　　　By your direction,  
An' nighted trav'llers are allur'd  
　　　To their destruction.

And aft your moss-traversing spunkies  
Decoy the wight that late an' drunk is;  
The bleezin, curst, mischievous monkies  
　　　Delude his eyes,  
Till in some miry slough he sunk is,  
　　　Ne'er mair to rise.

When Masons' mystic word an' grip  
In storms an' tempests raise you up,  
Some cock or cat your rage maun stop,  
　　　Or, strange to tell!  
The youngest brother ye wad whip  
　　　Aff straight to hell.

Lang syne in Eden's bonie yard,  
When youthfu' lovers first were pair'd,  
An' all the soul of love they shar'd,  
　　　The raptur'd hour,  
Sweet on the fragrant, flow'ry swaird,  
　　　In shady bow'r:

Then you, ye auld, snick-drawing dog!
Ye cam to Paradise incog,
An' play'd on man a cursed brogue
      (Black be your fa'!),
An' gied the infant warld a shog,
      'Maist ruin'd a'.

D' ye mind that day when in a bizz,
Wi' reeket duds, an' reestet gizz,
Ye did present your smoutie phiz
      'Mang better folk,
An' sklented on the man of Uzz
      Your spitefu' joke?

An' how ye gat him i' your thrall,
An' brak him out o' house an' hal',
While scabs an' botches did him gall,
      Wi' bitter claw;
An' lows'd his ill-tongu'd, wicked scaul,
      Was warst ava?

But a' your doings to rehearse,
Your wily snares an' fetchin fierce,
Sin' that day Michael did you pierce,
      Down to this time,
Wad ding a Lallan tongue, or Erse,
      In prose or rhyme.

An' now, Auld Cloots, I ken ye're thinkin,
A certain bardie's rantin, drinkin,
Some luckless hour will send him linkin
      To your black pit:
But, faith! he'll turn a corner jinkin,
      An' cheat you yet.

But, fare you weel, Auld Nickie-ben!
Oh, wad ye tak a thought an' men'!

Ye aiblins might—I dinna ken—
          Still hae a stake:
I'm wae to think upo' yon den,
          Ev'n for your sake!


## Holy Willie's Prayer

And send the godly in a pet to pray.—POPE

### ARGUMENT

*Holy Willie was a rather oldish bachelor elder, in the parish of Mauchline, and much and justly famed for that polemical chattering which ends in tippling orthodoxy, and for that spiritualized bawdry which refines to liquorish devotion. In a sessional process with a gentleman in Mauchline—a Mr. Gavin Hamilton—Holy Willie and his priest, Father Auld, after full hearing in the Presbytery of Ayr, came off but second best, owing partly to the oratorical powers of Mr. Robert Aiken, Mr. Hamilton's counsel; but chiefly to Mr. Hamilton's being one of the most irreproachable and truly respectable characters in the country. On losing his process, the Muse overheard him at his devotions as follows—*

O Thou that in the Heavens does dwell,
Wha, as it pleases best Thysel,
Sends ane to Heaven an' ten to Hell
          A' for Thy glory,
And no for onie guid or ill
          They've done before Thee!

I bless and praise Thy matchless might,
When thousands Thou hast left in night,
That I am here before Thy sight,
          For gifts an' grace
A burning and a shining light
          To a' this place.

What was I, or my generation,
That I should get sic exaltation?
I, wha deserv'd most just damnation
            For broken laws
Sax thousand years ere my creation,
            Thro' Adam's cause!

When from my mither's womb I fell,
Thou might hae plung'd me deep in Hell,
To gnash my gooms, and weep, and wail
            In burning lakes,
Whare damned devils roar and yell,
            Chain'd to their stakes.

Yet I am here, a chosen sample,
To show Thy grace is great and ample:
I'm here a pillar o' Thy temple,
            Strong as a rock,
A guide, a buckler, and example
            To a' Thy flock.

But yet, O Lord! confess I must;
At times I'm fash'd wi' fleshly lust;
An' sometimes, too, in warldly trust,
            Vile self gets in;
But Thou remembers we are dust,
            Defiled wi' sin.

O Lord! yestreen, Thou kens, wi' Meg—
Thy pardon I sincerely beg—
Oh may 't ne'er be a living plague
            To my dishonour!
An' I'll ne'er lift a lawless leg
            Again upon her.

Besides, I farther maun avow—
Wi' Leezie's lass, three times, I trow—

But, Lord, that Friday I was fou,
     When I cam near her,
Or else, Thou kens, Thy servant true
     Wad never steer her.

Maybe Thou lets this fleshly thorn
Buffet Thy servant e'en and morn,
Lest he ower proud and high should turn
     That he's sae gifted:
If sae, Thy han' maun e'en be borne
     Until Thou lift it.

Lord, bless Thy chosen in this place,
For here Thou has a chosen race!
But God confound their stubborn face
     An' blast their name,
Wha bring Thy elders to disgrace
     An' open shame!

Lord, mind Gau'n Hamilton's deserts:
He drinks, an' swears, an' plays at cartes,
Yet has sae monie takin arts
     Wi' great and sma',
Frae God's ain priest the people's hearts
     He steals awa.

And when we chasten'd him therefore,
Thou kens how he bred sic a splore,
And set the warld in a roar
     O' laughin at us:
Curse Thou his basket and his store,
     Kail an' potatoes!

Lord, hear my earnest cry and pray'r,
Against that Presbyt'ry of Ayr!
Thy strong right hand, Lord, mak it bare
     Upo' their heads!

Lord, visit them, and dinna spare,
        For their misdeeds!

O Lord, my God! that glib-tongu'd Aiken,
My vera heart and flesh are quakin,
To think how we stood sweatin, shakin,
        An' piss'd wi' dread,
While he, wi' hingin lip an' snakin,
        Held up his head.

Lord, in Thy day o' vengeance try him!
Lord, visit him wha did employ him!
And pass not in Thy mercy by them,
        Nor hear their pray'r,
But for Thy people's sake destroy them,
        An' dinna spare!

But, Lord, remember me and mine
Wi' mercies temporal and divine,
That I for grace an' gear may shine
        Excell'd by nane;
And a' the glory shall be Thine—
        Amen, Amen!


## Tam Samson's Elegy

"An honest man's the noblest work of God."—POPE.

*When this worthy old sportsman went out, last muirfowl season, he supposed it was to be, in Ossian's phrase, "the last of his fields," and expressed an ardent wish to die and be buried in the muirs. On this hint the author composed his elegy and epitaph.*—R. B., 1787.

Has auld Kilmarnock seen the deil?
Or great Mackinlay thrawn his heel?
Or Robertson again grown weel,

To preach an' read?
"Na, waur than a'!" cries ilka chiel,
     "Tam Samson's dead!"

Kilmarnock lang may grunt an' grane,
An' sigh, an' sab, an' greet her lane,
An' cleed her bairns, man, wife, an' wean,
     In mourning weed;
To Death she's dearly pay'd the kane—
     Tam Samson's dead!

The Brethren, o' the mystic level
May hing their head in woefu' bevel,
While by their nose the tears will revel,
     Like ony bead;
Death's gien the Lodge an unco devel;
     Tam Samson's dead!

When Winter muffles up his cloak,
And binds the mire like a rock;
When to the loughs the curlers flock,
     Wi' gleesome speed,
Wha will they station at the cock?
     Tam Samson's dead!

He was the king o' a' the core,
To guard, or draw, or wick a bore,
Or up the rink like Jehu roar,
     In time o' need;
But now he lags on Death's hog-score—
     Tam Samson's dead!

Now safe the stately sawmont sail,
And trouts bedropp'd wi' crimson hail,
And eels, weel-ken'd for souple tail,
     And geds for greed,
Since, dark in Death's fish-creel, we wail
     Tam Samson's dead!

Rejoice, ye birring paitricks a';
Ye cookie muircocks, crowsely craw;
Ye maukins, cock your fud fu' braw
                    Withouten dread;
Your mortal fae is now awa;
                    Tam Samson's dead!

That waeful morn be ever mourn'd,
Saw him in shooting graith adorn'd,
While pointers round impatient burn'd,
                    Frae couples free'd;
But och! he gaed and ne'er return'd!
                    Tam Samson's dead!

In vain auld age his body batters,
In vain the gout his ancles fetters,
In vain the burns come down like waters,
                    An acre braid!
Now ev'ry auld wife, greetin, clatters
                    "Tam Samson's dead!"

Owre mony a weary hag he limpit,
An' aye the tither shot he thumpit,
Till coward Death behind him jumpit,
                    Wi' deadly feid;
Now he proclaims with tout o' trumpet,
                    "Tam Samson's dead!"

When at his heart he felt the dagger,
He reel'd his wonted bottle-swagger,
But yet he drew the mortal trigger,
                    With well-aim'd heed;
"L—d, five!" he cry'd, an' owre did stagger—
                    Tam Samson's dead!

Ilk hoary hunter mourn'd a brither;
Ilk sportsman youth bemoan'd a father;

Yon auld gray stane, amang the heather,
            Marks out his head;
Whare Burns has wrote, in rhyming blether,
            "Tam Samson's dead!"

There, low he lies in lasting rest;
Perhaps upon his mould'ring breast
Some spitefu' muirfowl bigs her nest
            To hatch an' breed:
Alas! nae mair he'll them molest!
            Tam Samson's dead!

When August winds the heather wave,
And sportsmen wander by yon grave,
Three volleys let his memory crave,
            O' pouther an' lead,
Till Echo answer frae her cave,
            "Tam Samson's dead!"

Heav'n rest his saul whare'er he be!
Is th' wish o' mony mae than me:
He had twa fauts, or maybe three,
            Yet what remead?
Ae social, honest man want we:
            Tam Samson's dead!

### THE EPITAPH

Tam Samson's weel-worn clay here lies:
Ye canting zealots, spare him!
If honest worth in Heaven rise,
Ye'll mend or ye win near him.

### PER CONTRA

Go, Fame, an' canter like a filly
Thro' a' the streets an' neuks o' Killie;
Tell ev'ry social honest billie

To cease his grievin;
For, yet unskaith'd by Death's gleg gullie,
Tam Samson's leevin!


## Open the Door to Me, Oh!

Oh, open the door, some pity to shew,
Oh, open the door to me, oh!
Tho' thou hast been false, I'll ever prove true,
Oh, open the door to me, oh!

Cauld is the blast upon my pale cheek,
But caulder thy love for me, oh!
The frost that freezes the life at my heart,
Is nought to my pains fra thee, oh!

The wan moon is setting behind the white wave,
And time is setting with me, oh!
False friends, false love, farewell! for mair
I'll ne'er trouble them, nor thee, oh!

She has open'd the door, she has open'd it wide;
She sees his pale corse on the plain, oh!
My true love! she cried, and sank down by his side,
Never to rise again, oh!


## The Poet's Welcome
## to His Love-begotten Daughter

Thou's welcome, wean! mishanter fa' me,
If ought of thee, or of thy mammy,
Shall ever daunton me, or awe me,

My sweet wee lady,
Or if I blush when thou shalt ca' me
Tit-ta or daddy.

Wee image of my bonnie Betty,
I fatherly will kiss and daut thee,
As dear an' near my heart I set thee
Wi' as guid will,
As a' the priests had seen me get thee
That's out o' hell.

What tho' they ca' me fornicator,
An' tease my name in kintra clatter:
The mair they talk I'm kent the better,
E'en let them clash;
An auld wife's tongue's a feckless matter
To gie ane fash.

Welcome, my bonnie, sweet wee dochter—
Tho' ye come here a wee unsought for,
An' tho' your comin' I hae fought for
Baith kirk an' queir;
Yet, by my faith, ye're no unwrought for!
That I shall swear!

Sweet fruit o' mony a merry dint,
My funny toil is now a' tint,
Sin' thou came to the warl asklent,
Which fools may scoff at;
In my last plack thy part's be in't—
The better half o't.

An' if thou be what I wad hae thee,
An' tak the counsel I shall gie thee,
A lovin' father I'll be to thee,
If thou be spar'd;

Thro' a' thy childish years I'll ee thee,
    An' think't weel war'd.

Tho' I should be the waur bested,
Thou's be as braw an' bienly clad,
An' thy young years as nicely bred
        Wi' education,
As ony brat o' wedlock's bed
        In a' thy station.

Gude grant that thou may aye inherit
Thy mither's person, grace an' merit,
An' thy poor worthless daddy's spirit,
        Without his failins;
'Twill please me mair to see and hear o't
        Than stockit mailins.

## A Red, Red Rose

Oh my luve is like a red, red rose,
    That's newly sprung in June:
Oh my luve is like the melodie,
    That's sweetly play'd in tune.

As fair art thou, my bonie lass,
    So deep in luve am I;
And I will luve thee still, my dear,
    Till a' the seas gang dry.

Till a' the seas gang dry, my dear,
    And the rocks melt wi' the sun;
And I will luve thee still, my dear,
    While the sands o' life shall run.

And fare thee weel, my only luve!
And fare thee weel a while!
And I will come again, my luve,
Tho' it were ten thousand mile!


## Ye flowery banks

Ye flowery banks o' bonie Doon,
    How can ye blume sae fair?
How can ye chant, ye little birds,
    And I sae fu' o' care?

Thou'll break my heart, thou bonie bird
    That sings upon the bough;
Thou minds me o' the happy days
    When my fause luve was true.

Thou'll break my heart, thou bonie bird,
    That sings beside thy mate;
For sae I sat, and sae I sang,
    And wist na o' my fate.

Aft hae I rov'd by bonie Doon,
    To see the woodbine twine,
And ilka bird sang o' its luve,
    And sae did I o' mine.

Wi' lightsome heart I pu'd a rose,
    Frae aff its thorny tree;
And my fause luver staw my rose,
    But left the thorn wi' me.

## Simmer's a pleasant time

*Tune—"Ay Waukin O"*

Simmer's a pleasant time,
    Flow'rs of ev'ry colour;
The water rins o'er the heugh,
    And I long for my true lover.
        Ay waukin O,
            Waukin still and wearie:
        Sleep I can get nane
            For thinking on my dearie.

When I sleep I dream,
    When I wauk I'm eerie;
Sleep I can get nane
    For thinking on my dearie.

Lanely night comes on,
    A' the lave are sleepin';
I think on my bonnie lad,
    And I bleer my een with greetin'.
        Ay waukin O,
            Waukin still and wearie;
        Sleep I can get nane
            For thinking on my dearie.

## O whistle, and I'll come to you, my lad

*O whistle, and I'll come to you, my lad,*
*O whistle, and I'll come to you, my lad;*
*Tho' father and mother and a' should gae mad,*
*O whistle, and I'll come to you, my lad.*

But warily tent, when ye come to court me,
And come na unless the back-yett be a-jee;
Syne up the back-stile, and let naebody see,
And come, as ye were na coming to me,
And come, as ye were na coming to me.

At kirk, or at market, whene'er ye meet me,
Gang by me as tho' ye car'd na a flee;
But steal me a blink o' your bonie black e'e,
Yet look as ye were na looking at me,
Yet look as ye were na looking at me.

Ay vow and protest that ye care na for me,
And whyles ye may lightly my beauty a wee;
But court na anither, tho' joking ye be,
For fear that she wyle your fancy frae me,
For fear that she wyle your fancy frae me.


## It was a' for our rightfu' king

It was a' for our rightfu' king
    We left fair Scotland's strand;
It was a' for our rightfu' king,
    We e'er saw Irish land, my dear,
        We e'er saw Irish land.

Now a' is done that men can do,
    And a' is done in vain:
My Love and Native Land fareweel,
    For I maun cross the main, my dear,
        For I maun cross the main.

He turn'd him right and round about,
    Upon the Irish shore,

And gae his bridle reins a shake,
   With, adieu for evermore, my dear,
    With, adieu for evermore!

The soger frae the wars returns,
   The sailor frae the main,
But I hae parted frae my Love,
   Never to meet again, my dear,
    Never to meet again.

When day is gane, and night is come,
   And a' folk bound to sleep;
I think on him that's far awa,
   The lee-lang night, and weep, my dear,
    The lee-lang night and weep.

## Ae fond kiss

Ae fond kiss, and then we sever!
Ae farewell, and then forever!
Deep in heart-wrung tears I'll pledge thee,
Warring sighs and groans I'll wage thee.
Who shall say that Fortune grieves him
While the star of hope she leaves him?
Me, nae cheerfu' twinkle lights me;
Dark despair around benights me.

I'll ne'er blame my partial fancy;
Naething could resist my Nancy;
But to see her was to love her;
Love but her, and love forever.
Had we never lov'd sae kindly,
Had we never lov'd sae blindly,
Never met—or never parted—
We had ne'er been broken-hearted.

Fare thee weel, thou first and fairest!
Fare thee weel, thou best and dearest!
Thine be ilka joy and treasure,
Peace, enjoyment, love, and pleasure!
Ae fond kiss, and then we sever;
Ae farewell, alas, forever!
Deep in heart-wrung tears I'll pledge thee,
Warring sighs and groans I'll wage thee!

# George Crabbe

(1754–1832)

FROM *The Village*

## VILLAGE LIFE

*The Subject proposed—Remarks upon Pastoral Poetry—A
Tract of Country near the Coast described—An impoverished
Borough—Smugglers and their Assistants—Rude Manners of
the Inhabitants—Ruinous Effects of a high Tide—The Vil-
lage Life more generally considered: Evils of it—The youth-
ful Labourer—The old Man: his Soliloquy—The Parish
Workhouse: its Inhabitants—The sick Poor: their Apothecary
—The dying Pauper—The Village Priest.*

The Village Life, and every care that reigns
O'er youthful peasants and declining swains;
What labour yields, and what, that labour past,
Age, in its hour of languor, finds at last;
What form the real picture of the poor,
Demand a song—the Muse can give no more.
   Fled are those times, when, in harmonious strains,
The rustic poet praised his native plains:
No shepherds now, in smooth alternate verse,
Their country's beauty or their nymphs' rehearse;
Yet still for these we frame the tender strain,
Still in our lays fond Corydons complain,
And shepherds' boys their amorous pains reveal,
The only pains, alas! they never feel.
   On Mincio's banks, in Caesar's bounteous reign,
If Tityrus found the Golden Age again,

Must sleepy bards the flattering dream prolong,
Mechanic echoes of the Mantuan song?
From Truth and Nature shall we widely stray,
Where Virgil, not where Fancy, leads the way?

　Yes, thus the Muses sing of happy swains,
Because the Muses never knew their pains:
They boast their peasants' pipes; but peasants now
Resign their pipes and plod behind the plough;
And few, amid the rural-tribe, have time
To number syllables, and play with rhyme;
Save honest Duck, what son of verse could share
The poet's rapture, and the peasant's care?
Or the great labours of the field degrade,
With the new peril of a poorer trade?

　From this chief cause these idle praises spring,
That themes so easy few forbear to sing;
For no deep thought the trifling subjects ask:
To sing of shepherds is an easy task.
The happy youth assumes the common strain,
A nymph his mistress, and himself a swain;
With no sad scenes he clouds his tuneful prayer,
But all, to look like her, is painted fair.

　I grant indeed that fields and flocks have charms
For him that grazes or for him that farms;
But when amid such pleasing scenes I trace
The poor laborious natives of the place,
And see the mid-day sun, with fervid ray,
On their bare heads and dewy temples play;
While some, with feebler heads and fainter hearts,
Deplore their fortune, yet sustain their parts:
Then shall I dare these real ills to hide
In tinsel trappings of poetic pride?

　No; cast by Fortune on a frowning coast,
Which neither groves nor happy valleys boast;
Where other cares than those the Muse relates,

And other shepherds dwell with other mates;
By such examples taught, I paint the Cot,
As Truth will paint it, and as Bards will not:
Nor you, ye poor, of letter'd scorn complain,
To you the smoothest song is smooth in vain;
O'ercome by labour, and bow'd down by time,
Feel you the barren flattery of a rhyme?
Can poets soothe you, when you pine for bread,
By winding myrtles round your ruin'd shed?
Can their light tales your weighty griefs o'erpower,
Or glad with airy mirth the toilsome hour?

    Lo! where the heath, with withering brake grown o'er.
Lends the light turf that warms the neighbouring poor;
From thence a length of burning sand appears,
Where the thin harvest waves its wither'd ears;
Rank weeds, that every art and care defy,
Reign o'er the land, and rob the blighted rye:
There thistles stretch their prickly arms afar,
And to the ragged infant threaten war;
There poppies nodding, mock the hope of toil;
There the blue bugloss paints the sterile soil;
Hardy and high, above the slender sheaf,
The slimy mallow waves her silky leaf;
O'er the young shoot the charlock throws a shade,
And clasping tares cling round the sickly blade;
With mingled tints the rocky coasts abound,
And a sad splendour vainly shines around.
So looks the nymph whom wretched arts adorn,
Betray'd by man, then left for man to scorn;
Whose cheek in vain assumes the mimic rose,
While her sad eyes the troubled breast disclose;
Whose outward splendour is but folly's dress,
Exposing most, when most it gilds distress.

    Here joyless roam a wild amphibious race,
With sullen wo display'd in every face;

Who, far from civil arts and social fly,
And scowl at strangers with suspicious eye.

Here too the lawless merchant of the main
Draws from his plough th' intoxicated swain;
Want only claim'd the labour of the day,
But vice now steals his nightly rest away.

Where are the swains, who, daily labour done,
With rural games play'd down the setting sun;
Who struck with matchless force the bounding ball,
Or made the pond'rous quoit obliquely fall;
While some huge Ajax, terrible and strong,
Engaged some artful stripling of the throng,
And fell beneath him, foil'd, while far around
Hoarse triumph rose, and rocks return'd the sound?
Where now are these?—Beneath yon cliff they stand,
To show the freighted pinnace where to land;
To load the ready steed with guilty haste,
To fly in terror o'er the pathless waste,
Or, when detected, in their straggling course,
To foil their foes by cunning or by force;
Or, yielding part (which equal knaves demand),
To gain a lawless passport through the land.

Here, wand'ring long, amid these frowning fields,
I sought the simple life that Nature yields;
Rapine and Wrong and Fear usurp'd her place,
And a bold, artful, surly, savage race;
Who, only skill'd to take the finny tribe,
The yearly dinner, or septennial bribe,
Wait on the shore, and, as the waves run high,
On the tost vessel bend their eager eye,
Which to their coast directs its vent'rous way;
Theirs, or the ocean's, miserable prey.

As on their neighbouring beach yon swallows stand,
And wait for favouring winds to leave the land,
While still for flight the ready wing is spread:

So waited I the favouring hour, and fled—
Fled from these shores where guilt and famine reign,
And cried, Ah! hapless they who still remain;
Who still remain to hear the ocean roar,
Whose greedy waves devour the lessening shore;
Till some fierce tide, with more imperious sway,
Sweeps the low hut and all it holds away;
When the sad tenant weeps from door to door,
And begs a poor protection from the poor!

But these are scenes where Nature's niggard hand
Gave a spare portion to the famish'd land;
Hers is the fault, if here mankind complain
Of fruitless toil and labour spent in vain;
But yet in other scenes more fair in view,
Where Plenty smiles—alas! she smiles for few—
And those who taste not, yet behold her store,
Are as the slaves that dig the golden ore,—
The wealth around them makes them doubly poor.

Or will you deem them amply paid in health,
Labour's fair child, that languishes with wealth?
Go then! and see them rising with the sun,
Through a long course of daily toil to run;
See them beneath the dog-star's raging heat,
When the knees tremble and the temples beat;
Behold them, leaning on their scythes, look o'er
The labour past, and toils to come explore;
See them alternate suns and showers engage,
And hoard up aches and anguish for their age;
Through fens and marshy moors their steps pursue,
When their warm pores imbibe the evening dew;
Then own that labour may as fatal be
To these thy slaves, as thine excess to thee.

Amid this tribe too oft a manly pride
Strives in strong toil the fainting heart to hide;
There may you see the youth of slender frame

Contend with weakness, weariness, and shame;
Yet, urged along, and proudly loth to yield,
He strives to join his fellows of the field.
Till long-contending nature droops at last,
Declining health rejects his poor repast,
His cheerless spouse the coming danger sees,
And mutual murmurs urge the slow disease.

Yet grant them health, 'tis not for us to tell,
Though the head droops not, that the heart is well;
Or will you praise that homely, healthy fare,
Plenteous and plain, that happy peasants share!
Oh! trifle not with wants you cannot feel,
Nor mock the misery of a stinted meal;
Homely, not wholesome, plain, not plenteous, such
As you who praise would never deign to touch.

Ye gentle souls, who dream of rural ease,
Whom the smooth stream and smoother sonnet please;
Go! if the peaceful cot your praises share,
Go look within, and ask if peace be there;
If peace be his—that drooping weary sire,
Or theirs, that offspring round their feeble fire;
Or hers, that matron pale, whose trembling hand
Turns on the wretched hearth th' expiring brand!

Nor yet can Time itself obtain for these
Life's latest comforts, due respect and ease;
For yonder see that hoary swain, whose age
Can with no cares except his own engage;
Who, propp'd on that rude staff, looks up to see
The bare arms broken from the withering tree,
On which, a boy, he climb'd the loftiest bough,
Then his first joy, but his sad emblem now.

He once was chief in all the rustic trade;
His steady hand the straightest furrow made;
Full many a prize he won, and still is proud
To find the triumphs of his youth allow'd;

A transient pleasure sparkles in his eyes,
He hears and smiles, then thinks again and sighs:
For now he journeys to his grave in pain;
The rich disdain him; nay, the poor disdain:
Alternate masters now their slave command,
Urge the weak efforts of his feeble hand,
And, when his age attempts its task in vain,
With ruthless taunts, of lazy poor complain.

    Oft may you see him, when he tends the sheep,
His winter-charge, beneath the hillock weep;
Oft hear him murmur to the winds that blow
O'er his white locks and bury them in snow,
When, roused by rage and muttering in the morn,
He mends the broken hedge with icy thorn:—

    "Why do I live, when I desire to be
At once from life and life's long labour free?
Like leaves in spring, the young are blown away,
Without the sorrows of a slow decay;
I, like yon wither'd leaf, remain behind,
Nipp'd by the frost, and shivering in the wind;
There it abides till younger buds come on,
As I, now all my fellow-swains are gone;
Then, from the rising generation thrust,
It falls, like me, unnoticed to the dust.

    "These fruitful fields, these numerous flocks I see,
Are others' gain, but killing cares to me;
To me the children of my youth are lords,
Cool in their looks, but hasty in their words:
Wants of their own demand their care; and who
Feels his own want and succours others too?
A lonely, wretched man, in pain I go,
None need my help, and none relieve my wo;
Then let my bones beneath the turf be laid,
And men forget the wretch they would not aid."

    Thus groan the old, till, by disease oppress'd,

They taste a final wo, and then they rest.

Theirs is yon house that holds the parish-poor,
Whose walls of mud scarce bear the broken door;
There, where the putrid vapours, flagging, play,
And the dull wheel hums doleful through the day;—
There children dwell who know no parents' care;
Parents, who know no children's love, dwell there!
Heartbroken matrons on their joyless bed,
Forsaken wives, and mothers never wed;
Dejected widows with unheeded tears,
And crippled age with more than childhood fears;
The lame, the blind, and, far the happiest they!
The moping idiot and the madman gay.
Here too the sick their final doom receive,
Here brought, amid the scenes of grief, to grieve,
Where the loud groans from some sad chamber flow,
Mix'd with the clamours of the crowd below;
Here, sorrowing, they each kindred sorrow scan,
And the cold charities of man to man:
Whose laws indeed for ruin'd age provide,
And strong compulsion plucks the scrap from pride;
But still that scrap is bought with many a sigh,
And pride embitters what it can't deny.

Say ye, oppress'd by some fantastic woes,
Some jarring nerve that baffles your repose;
Who press the downy couch, while slaves advance
With timid eye, to read the distant glance;
Who with sad prayers the weary doctor tease,
To name the nameless ever-new disease;
Who with mock patience dire complaints endure,
Which real pain, and that, alone, can cure;
How would ye bear in real pain to lie,
Despised, neglected, left alone to die?
How would ye bear to draw your latest breath,
Where all that's wretched paves the way for death?

Such is that room which one rude beam divides,
And naked rafters form the sloping sides;
Where the vile bands that bind the thatch are seen,
And lath and mud are all that lie between;
Save one dull pane, that, coarsely patch'd, gives way
To the rude tempest, yet excludes the day:
Here, on a matted flock, with dust o'erspread,
The drooping wretch reclines his languid head;
For him no hand the cordial cup applies,
Or wipes the tear that stagnates in his eyes;
No friends with soft discourse his pain beguile,
Or promise hope till sickness wears a smile.

But soon a loud and hasty summons calls,
Shakes the thin roof, and echoes round the walls;
Anon, a figure enters, quaintly neat,
All pride and business, bustle and conceit;
With looks unalter'd by these scenes of wo,
With speed that, entering, speaks his haste to go,
He bids the gazing throng around him fly,
And carries fate and physic in his eye:
A potent quack, long versed in human ills,
Who first insults the victim whom he kills;
Whose murd'rous hand a drowsy Bench protect,
And whose most tender mercy is neglect.

Paid by the parish for attendance here,
He wears contempt upon his sapient sneer;
In haste he seeks the bed where Misery lies,
Impatience mark'd in his averted eyes;
And, some habitual queries hurried o'er,
Without reply, he rushes on the door:
His drooping patient, long inured to pain,
And long unheeded, knows remonstrance vain;
He ceases now the feeble help to crave
Of man; and silent sinks into the grave.

But ere his death some pious doubts arise,

Some simple fears, which "bold bad" men despise:
Fain would he ask the parish-priest to prove
His title certain to the joys above;
For this he sends the murmuring nurse, who calls
The holy stranger to these dismal walls;
And doth not he, the pious man, appear,
He, "passing rich with forty pounds a year"?
Ah! no; a shepherd of a different stock,
And far unlike him, feeds this little flock:
A jovial youth, who thinks his Sunday's task
As much as God or man can fairly ask;
The rest he gives to loves and labours light,
To fields the morning, and to feasts the night:
None better skill'd the noisy pack to guide,
To urge their chase, to cheer them or to chide;
A sportsman keen, he shoots through half the day,
And, skill'd at whist, devotes the night to play:
Then, while such honours bloom around his head,
Shall he sit sadly by the sick man's bed,
To raise the hope he feels not, or with zeal
To combat fears that e'en the pious feel?

Now once again the gloomy scene explore,
Less gloomy now; the bitter hour is o'er,
The man of many sorrows sighs no more.—
Up yonder hill, behold how sadly slow
The bier moves winding from the vale below;
There lie the happy dead, from trouble free,
And the glad parish pays the frugal fee:
No more, O Death! thy victim starts to hear
Churchwarden stern, or kingly overseer;
No more the farmer claims his humble bow,
Thou art his lord, the best of tyrants thou!

Now to the church behold the mourners come,
Sedately torpid and devoutly dumb;
The village children now their games suspend,

To see the bier that bears their ancient friend;
For he was one in all their idle sport,
And like a monarch ruled their little court;
The pliant bow he form'd, the flying ball,
The bat, the wicket, were his labours all;
Him now they follow to his grave, and stand
Silent and sad, and gazing, hand in hand;
While bending low, their eager eyes explore
The mingled relics of the parish poor:
The bell tolls late, the moping owl flies round,
Fear marks the flight and magnifies the sound;
The busy priest, detain'd by weightier care,
Defers his duty till the day of prayer;
And, waiting long, the crowd retire distress'd,
To think a poor man's bones should lie unbless'd.

                                        (Book I, *entire*)


FROM *The Borough*


PETER GRIMES

——Was a sordid soul,
 Such as does murder for a meed;
Who but for fear knows no control,
Because his conscience, sear'd and foul,
 Feels not the import of the deed;
One whose brute feeling ne'er aspires
Beyond his own more brute desires.
                —Scott, *Marmion*, canto ii.

Methought the souls of all that I had murder'd
Came to my tent, and every one did threat.
    —Shakespeare, *Richard III*, Act V, scene iii.

The times have been,
That when the brains were out, the man would die,

And there an end; but now they rise again,
With twenty mortal murders on their crowns,
And push us from our stools.
    —SHAKESPEARE, *Macbeth*, Act III, scene iv.

*The Father of Peter a Fisherman—Peter's early Conduct—*
*His Grief for the old Man—He takes an Apprentice—The*
*Boy's Suffering and Fate—A second Boy: how he died—*
*Peter acquitted—A third Apprentice—A Voyage by Sea: the*
*Boy does not return—Evil Report on Peter: he is tried and*
*threatened—Lives alone—His Melancholy and incipient Mad-*
*ness—Is observed and visited—He escapes and is taken: is*
*lodged in a Parish-house: Women attend and watch him—*
*He speaks in a Delirium: grows more collected—His Account*
*of his Feelings and visionary Terrors previous to his Death.*

Old Peter Grimes made fishing his employ;
His wife he cabin'd with him and his boy,
And seem'd that life laborious to enjoy.
To town came quiet Peter with his fish,
And had of all a civil word and wish.
He left his trade upon the sabbath-day,
And took young Peter in his hand to pray:
But soon the stubborn boy from care broke loose,
At first refused, then added his abuse:
His father's love he scorn'd, his power defied,
But being drunk, wept sorely when he died.

Yes! then he wept, and to his mind there came
Much of his conduct, and he felt the shame,—
How he had oft the good old man reviled,
And never paid the duty of a child;
How, when the father in his Bible read,
He in contempt and anger left the shed;
"It is the word of life," the parent cried;
—"This is the life itself," the boy replied;
And while old Peter in amazement stood,
Gave the hot spirit to his boiling blood:—

How he, with oath and furious speech, began
To prove his freedom and assert the man;
And when the parent check'd his impious rage,
How he had cursed the tyranny of age;—
Nay, once had dealt the sacrilegious blow
On his bare head, and laid his parent low;
The father groan'd—"If thou art old," said he,
"And hast a son—thou wilt remember me:
Thy mother left me in a happy time,
Thou kill'dst not her—Heav'n spares the double crime."
   On an inn-settle, in his maudlin grief,
This he revolved, and drank for his relief.

   Now lived the youth in freedom, but debarr'd
From constant pleasure, and he thought it hard;
Hard that he could not every wish obey,
But must awhile relinquish ale and play;
Hard! that he could not to his cards attend,
But must acquire the money he would spend.

   With greedy eye he look'd on all he saw,
He knew not justice, and he laugh'd at law;
On all he mark'd he stretch'd his ready hand;
He fish'd by water, and he filch'd by land:
Oft in the night has Peter dropp'd his oar,
Fled from his boat and sought for prey on shore;
Oft up the hedge-row glided, on his back
Bearing the orchard's produce in a sack,
Or farm-yard load, tugg'd fiercely from the stack;
And as these wrongs to greater numbers rose,
The more he look'd on all men as his foes.

   He built a mud-wall'd hovel, where he kept
His various wealth, and there he oft-times slept;
But no success could please his cruel soul,
He wish'd for one to trouble and control;
He wanted some obedient boy to stand
And bear the blow of his outrageous hand;

And hoped to find in some propitious hour
A feeling creature subject to his power.

Peter had heard there were in London then,—
Still have they being!—workhouse-clearing men,
Who, undisturb'd by feelings just or kind,
Would parish-boys to needy tradesmen bind:
They in their want a trifling sum would take,
And toiling slaves of piteous orphans make.

Such Peter sought, and when a lad was found,
The sum was dealt him, and the slave was bound.
Some few in town observed in Peter's trap
A boy, with jacket blue and woollen cap;
But none inquired how Peter used the rope,
Or what the bruise, that made the stripling stoop;
None could the ridges on his back behold,
None sought him shiv'ring in the winter's cold;
None put the question,—"Peter, dost thou give
The boy his food?—What, man! the lad must live:
Consider, Peter, let the child have bread,
He'll serve thee better if he's stroked and fed."
None reason'd thus—and some, on hearing cries,
Said calmly, "Grimes is at his exercise."

Pinn'd, beaten, cold, pinch'd, threaten'd, and
    abused—
His efforts punish'd and his food refused,—
Awake tormented,—soon aroused from sleep,—
Struck if he wept, and yet compell'd to weep,
The trembling boy dropp'd down and strove to pray,
Received a blow, and trembling turn'd away,
Or sobb'd and hid his piteous face;—while he,
The savage master, grinn'd in horrid glee:
He'd now the power he ever loved to show,
A feeling being subject to his blow.

Thus lived the lad, in hunger, peril, pain,
His tears despised, his supplications vain:

Compell'd by fear to lie, by need to steal,
His bed uneasy and unbless'd his meal,
For three sad years the boy his tortures bore,
And then his pains and trials were no more.

"How died he, Peter?" when the people said,
He growl'd—"I found him lifeless in his bed";
Then tried for softer tone, and sigh'd, "Poor Sam is
    dead."
Yet murmurs were there, and some questions ask'd,—
How he was fed, how punish'd, and how task'd?
Much they suspected, but they little proved,
And Peter pass'd untroubled and unmoved.

Another boy with equal ease was found,
The money granted, and the victim bound;
And what his fate?—One night it chanced he fell
From the boat's mast and perish'd in her well,
Where fish were living kept, and where the boy
(So reason'd men) could not himself destroy:—

"Yes! so it was," said Peter, "in his play,
(For he was idle both by night and day,)
He climb'd the main-mast and then fell below";—
Then show'd his corpse and pointed to the blow:
"What said the jury?"—they were long in doubt,
But sturdy Peter faced the matter out:
So they dismiss'd him, saying at the time,
"Keep fast your hatchway when you've boys who climb."
This hit the conscience, and he colour'd more
Than for the closest questions put before.

Thus all his fears the verdict set aside,
And at the slave-shop Peter still applied.

Then came a boy, of manners soft and mild,—
Our seamen's wives with grief beheld the child;
All thought (the poor themselves) that he was one
Of gentle blood, some noble sinner's son,
Who had, belike, deceived some humble maid,

Whom he had first seduced and then betray'd:—
However this, he seem'd a gracious lad,
In grief submissive and with patience sad.

Passive he labour'd, till his slender frame
Bent with his loads, and he at length was lame:
Strange that a frame so weak could bear so long
The grossest insult and the foulest wrong;
But there were causes—in the town they gave
Fire, food, and comfort, to the gentle slave;
And though stern Peter, with a cruel hand,
And knotted rope, enforced the rude command,
Yet he consider'd what he'd lately felt,
And his vile blows with selfish pity dealt.

One day such draughts the cruel fisher made,
He could not vend them in his borough-trade,
But sail'd for London-mart: the boy was ill,
But ever humbled to his master's will;
And on the river, where they smoothly sail'd,
He strove with terror and awhile prevail'd;
But new to danger on the angry sea,
He clung affrighten'd to his master's knee:
The boat grew leaky and the wind was strong,
Rough was the passage and the time was long;
His liquor fail'd, and Peter's wrath arose,—
No more is known—the rest we must suppose,
Or learn of Peter;—Peter says, he "spied
The stripling's danger and for harbour tried;
Meantime the fish, and then th' apprentice died."

The pitying women raised a clamour round,
And weeping said, "Thou hast thy 'prentice drown'd."

Now the stern man was summon'd to the hall,
To tell his tale before the burghers all:
He gave th' account; profess'd the lad he loved,
And kept his brazen features all unmoved.

The mayor himself with tone severe replied,—

"Henceforth with thee shall never boy abide;
Hire thee a freeman, whom thou durst not beat,
But who, in thy despite, will sleep and eat:
Free thou art now!—again shouldst thou appear,
Thou'lt find thy sentence, like thy soul, severe."

   Alas! for Peter not a helping hand,
So was he hated, could he now command;
Alone he row'd his boat, alone he cast
His nets beside, or made his anchor fast;
To hold a rope or hear a curse was none,—
He toil'd and rail'd; he groan'd and swore alone.

   Thus by himself compell'd to live each day,
To wait for certain hours the tide's delay;
At the same times the same dull views to see,
The bounding marsh-bank and the blighted tree;
The water only, when the tides were high,
When low, the mud half-cover'd and half-dry;
The sun-burnt tar that blisters on the planks,
And bank-side stakes in their uneven ranks;
Heaps of entangled weeds that slowly float,
As the tide rolls by the impeded boat.

   When tides were neap, and, in the sultry day,
Through the tall bounding mud-banks made their way,
Which on each side rose swelling, and below
The dark warm flood ran silently and slow;
There anchoring, Peter chose from man to hide,
There hang his head, and view the lazy tide
In its hot slimy channel slowly glide;
Where the small eels that left the deeper way
For the warm shore, within the shallows play;
Where gaping muscles, left upon the mud,
Slope their slow passage to the fallen flood:—
Here dull and hopeless he'd lie down and trace
How sidelong crabs had scrawl'd their crooked race;
Or sadly listen to the tuneless cry

Of fishing gull or clanging golden-eye;
What time the sea-birds to the marsh would come,
And the loud bittern, from the bull-rush home,
Gave from the salt-ditch side the bellowing boom:
He nursed the feelings these dull scenes produce,
And loved to stop beside the opening sluice;
Where the small stream, confined in narrow bound,
Ran with a dull, unvaried, sadd'ning sound;
Where all, presented to the eye or ear,
Oppress'd the soul with misery, grief, and fear.

Besides these objects, there were places three,
Which Peter seem'd with certain dread to see;
When he drew near them he would turn from each,
And loudly whistle till he pass'd the reach.

A change of scene to him brought no relief;
In town, 'twas plain, men took him for a thief:
The sailors' wives would stop him in the street,
And say, "Now, Peter, thou'st no boy to beat";
Infants at play, when they perceived him, ran,
Warning each other—"That's the wicked man";
He growl'd an oath, and in an angry tone
Cursed the whole place and wish'd to be alone.

Alone he was, the same dull scenes in view,
And still more gloomy in his sight they grew:
Though man he hated, yet employ'd alone
At bootless labour, he would swear and groan,
Cursing the shoals that glided by the spot,
And gulls that caught them when his arts could not.

Cold nervous tremblings shook his sturdy frame,
And strange disease—he couldn't say the name;
Wild were his dreams, and oft he rose in fright,
Waked by his view of horrors in the night,—
Horrors that would the sternest minds amaze,
Horrors that demons might be proud to raise:
And though he felt forsaken, grieved at heart,

To think he lived from all mankind apart;
Yet, if a man approach'd, in terrors he would start.

A winter pass'd since Peter saw the town,
And summer-lodgers were again come down;
These, idly curious, with their glasses spied
The ships in bay as anchor'd for the tide,—
The river's craft,—the bustle of the quay,—
And sea-port views, which landmen love to see.

One, up the river, had a man and boat
Seen day by day, now anchor'd, now afloat;
Fisher he seem'd, yet used no net nor hook;
Of sea-fowl swimming by no heed he took,
But on the gliding waves still fix'd his lazy look:
At certain stations he would view the stream,
As if he stood bewilder'd in a dream,
Or that some power had chain'd him for a time,
To feel a curse or meditate on crime.

This known, some curious, some in pity went,
And others question'd—"Wretch, dost thou repent?"
He heard, he trembled, and in fear resign'd
His boat: new terror fill'd his restless mind;
Furious he grew, and up the country ran,
And there they seized him—a distemper'd man:—
Him we received, and to a parish-bed,
Follow'd and cursed, the groaning man was led.

Here when they saw him, whom they used to shun,
A lost, lone man, so harass'd and undone,
Our gentle females, ever prompt to feel,
Perceived compassion on their anger steal;
His crimes they could not from their memories blot,
But they were grieved, and trembled at his lot.

A priest too came, to whom his words are told;
And all the signs they shudder'd to behold.

"Look! look!" they cried; "his limbs with horror shake,
And as he grinds his teeth, what noise they make!

How glare his angry eyes, and yet he's not awake:
See! what cold drops upon his forehead stand,
And how he clenches that broad bony hand."

The priest attending, found he spoke at times
As one alluding to his fears and crimes:
"It was the fall," he mutter'd, "I can show
The manner how—I never struck a blow":—
And then aloud—"Unhand me, free my chain;
On oath, he fell—it struck him to the brain:—
Why ask my father?—that old man will swear
Against my life; besides, he wasn't there:—
What, all agreed?—Am I to die to-day?—
My Lord, in mercy, give me time to pray."

Then, as they watch'd him, calmer he became,
And grew so weak he couldn't move his frame,
But murmuring spake,—while they could see and hear
The start of terror and the groan of fear;
See the large dew-beads on his forehead rise,
And the cold death-drop glaze his sunken eyes;
Nor yet he died, but with unwonted force
Seem'd with some fancied being to discourse:
He knew not us, or with accustom'd art
He hid the knowledge, yet exposed his heart;
'Twas part confession and the rest defence,
A madman's tale, with gleams of waking sense.

"I'll tell you all," he said, "the very day
When the old man first placed them in my way:
My father's spirit—he who always tried
To give me trouble, when he lived and died—
When he was gone, he could not be content
To see my days in painful labour spent,
But would appoint his meetings, and he made
Me watch at these, and so neglect my trade.

" 'Twas one hot noon, all silent, still, serene,
No living being had I lately seen;

I paddled up and down and dipp'd my net,
But (such his pleasure) I could nothing get,—
A father's pleasure, when his toil was done,
To plague and torture thus an only son!
And so I sat and look'd upon the stream,
How it ran on, and felt as in a dream:
But dream it was not; no!—I fix'd my eyes
On the mid stream and saw the spirits rise;
I saw my father on the water stand,
And hold a thin pale boy in either hand;
And there they glided ghastly on the top
Of the salt flood, and never touch'd a drop:
I would have struck them, but they knew th' intent,
And smiled upon the oar, and down they went.

"Now, from that day, whenever I began
To dip my net, there stood the hard old man—
He and those boys: I humbled me and pray'd
They would be gone;—they heeded not, but stay'd:
Nor could I turn, nor would the boat go by,
But gazing on the spirits, there was I:
They bade me leap to death, but I was loth to die:
And every day, as sure as day arose,
Would these three spirits meet me ere the close;
To hear and mark them daily was my doom,
And 'Come,' they said, with weak, sad voices, 'come.'
To row away with all my strength I try'd,
But there were they, hard by me in the tide,
The three unbodied forms—and 'Come,' still 'come,'
    they cried.

"Fathers should pity—but this old man shook
His hoary locks, and froze me by a look:
Thrice, when I struck them, through the water came
A hollow groan, that weaken'd all my frame:
'Father!' said I, 'have mercy':—He replied,
I know not what—the angry spirit lied,—

'Didst thou not draw thy knife?' said he:—'Twas true,
But I had pity and my arm withdrew:
He cried for mercy which I kindly gave,
But he has no compassion in his grave.

  "There were three places, where they ever rose,—
The whole long river has not such as those,—
Places accursed, where, if a man remain,
He'll see the things which strike him to the brain;
And there they made me on my paddle lean,
And look at them for hours;—accursed scene!
When they would glide to that smooth eddy-space,
Then bid me leap and join them in the place;
And at my groans each little villain sprite
Enjoy'd my pains and vanish'd in delight.

  "In one fierce summer-day, when my poor brain
Was burning hot and cruel was my pain,
Then came this father-foe, and there he stood
With his two boys again upon the flood;
There was more mischief in their eyes, more glee
In their pale faces when they glared at me:
Still did they force me on the oar to rest,
And when they saw me fainting and oppress'd,
He, with his hand, the old man, scoop'd the flood,
And there came flame about him mix'd with blood;
He bade me stoop and look upon the place,
Then flung the hot-red liquor in my face;
Burning it blazed, and then I roar'd for pain,
I thought the demons would have turn'd my brain.

  "Still there they stood, and forced me to behold
A place of horrors—they cannot be told—
Where the flood open'd, there I heard the shriek
Of tortured guilt—no earthly tongue can speak:
'All days alike! for ever!' did they say,
'And unremitted torments every day'—

Yes, so they said":—But there he ceased and gazed
On all around, affrighten'd and amazed;
And still he tried to speak, and look'd in dread
Of frighten'd females gathering round his bed;
Then dropp'd exhausted and appear'd at rest,
Till the strong foe the vital powers possess'd:
Then with an inward, broken voice he cried,
"Again they come," and mutter'd as he died.

(*Letter xxii, entire*)

## FROM *Sir Eustace Grey*

*Scene—A mad-house*
*Persons—Visitor, Physician, and Patient*

### PHYSICIAN

Peace, peace, my friend; these subjects fly;
Collect thy thoughts—go calmly on.—

### PATIENT

And shall I then the fact deny?
    I was,—thou know'st,—I was begone,
Like him who fill'd the eastern throne,
    To whom the Watcher cried aloud;
That royal wretch of Babylon,
    Who was so guilty and so proud.

Like him, with haughty, stubborn mind,
    I, in my state, my comforts sought;
Delight and praise I hoped to find,
    In what I builded, planted, bought!
Oh! arrogance! by misery taught—
    Soon came a voice! I felt it come;

"Full be his cup, with evil fraught,
 Demons his guides, and death his doom!"

Then was I cast from out my state;
 Two fiends of darkness led my way;
They waked me early, watch'd me late,
 My dread by night, my plague by day!
Oh! I was made their sport, their play,
 Through many a stormy troubled year;
And how they used their passive prey
 Is sad to tell:—but you shall hear.

And first, before they sent me forth,
 Through this unpitying world to run,
They robb'd Sir Eustace of his worth,
 Lands, manors, lordships, every one;
So was that gracious man undone,
 Was spurn'd as vile, was scorn'd as poor,
Whom every former friend would shun,
 And menials drove from every door.

Then those ill-favour'd Ones, whom none
 But my unhappy eyes could view,
Led me, with wild emotion, on,
 And, with resistless terror, drew.
Through lands we fled, o'er seas we flew,
 And halted on a boundless plain;
Where nothing fed, nor breathed, nor grew,
 But silence ruled the still domain.

Upon that boundless plain, below,
 The setting sun's last rays were shed,
And gave a mild and sober glow,
 Where all were still, asleep, or dead;
Vast ruins in the midst were spread,
 Pillars and pediments sublime,

Where the grey moss had form'd a bed,
  And clothed the crumbling spoils of time.

There was I fix'd, I know not how,
  Condemn'd for untold years to stay:
Yet years were not;—one dreadful *now*
  Endured no change of night or day;
The same mild evening's sleeping ray
  Shone softly-solemn and serene,
And all that time I gazed away,
  The setting sun's sad rays were seen.

At length a moment's sleep stole on,—
  Again came my commission'd foes;
Again through sea and land we're gone,
  No peace, no respite, no repose:
Above the dark broad sea we rose,
  We ran through bleak and frozen land;
I had no strength their strength t' oppose,
  An infant in a giant's hand.

They placed me where those streamers play,
  Those nimble beams of brilliant light;
It would the stoutest heart dismay,
  To see, to feel, that dreadful sight:
So swift, so pure, so cold, so bright,
  They pierced my frame with icy wound,
And all that half-year's polar night,
  Those dancing streamers wrapp'd me round.

Slowly that darkness pass'd away,
  When down upon the earth I fell,—
Some hurried sleep was mine by day;
  But, soon as toll'd the evening bell,
They forced me on, where ever dwell
  Far-distant men in cities fair,

Cities of whom no trav'lers tell,
  Nor feet but mine were wanderers there.

Their watchmen stare, and stand aghast,
  As on we hurry through the dark;
The watch-light blinks as we go past,
  The watch-dog shrinks and fears to bark;
The watch-tower's bell sounds shrill; and, hark!
  The free wind blows—we've left the town—
A wide sepulchral-ground I mark,
  And on a tombstone place me down.

What monuments of mighty dead!
  What tombs of various kinds are found!
And stones erect their shadows shed
  On humble graves, with wickers bound;
Some risen fresh, above the ground,
  Some level with the native clay,
What sleeping millions wait the sound,
  "Arise, ye dead, and come away!"

Alas! they stay not for that call;
  Spare me this wo! ye demons, spare!—
They come! the shrouded shadows all,—
  'Tis more than mortal brain can bear;
Rustling they rise, they sternly glare
  At man upheld by vital breath;
Who, led by wicked fiends, should dare
  To join the shadowy troops of death!

Yes, I have felt all man can feel,
  Till he shall pay his nature's debt;
Ills that no hope has strength to heal,
  No mind the comfort to forget:
Whatever cares the heart can fret,
  The spirits wear, the temper gall,

Wo, want, dread, anguish, all beset
  My sinful soul!—together all!

Those fiends upon a shaking fen
  Fix'd me, in dark tempestuous night;
There never trod the foot of men,
  There flock'd the fowl in wint'ry flight;
There danced the moor's deceitful light
  Above the pool where sedges grow;
And when the morning-sun shone bright,
  It shone upon a field of snow.

They hung me on a bough so small,
  The rook could build her nest no higher;
They fix'd me on the trembling ball
  That crowns the steeple's quiv'ring spire;
They set me where the seas retire,
  But drown with their returning tide;
And made me flee the mountain's fire,
  When rolling from its burning side.

I've hung upon the ridgy steep
  Of cliffs, and held the rambling brier;
I've plunged below the billowy deep,
  Where air was sent me to respire;
I've been where hungry wolves retire;
  And (to complete my woes) I've ran
Where Bedlam's crazy crew conspire
  Against the life of reasoning man.

I've furl'd in storms the flapping sail,
  By hanging from the topmast-head;
I've served the vilest slaves in jail,
  And pick'd the dunghill's spoil for bread;
I've made the badger's hole my bed,
  I've wander'd with a gipsy crew;

I've dreaded all the guilty dread,
  And done what they would fear to do.

On sand, where ebbs and flows the flood,
  Midway they placed and bade me die;
Propp'd on my staff, I stoutly stood
  When the swift waves came rolling by;
And high they rose, and still more high,
  Till my lips drank the bitter brine;
I sobb'd convulsed, then cast mine eye,
  And saw the tide's re-flowing sign.

And then, my dreams were such as nought
  Could yield but my unhappy case;
I've been of thousand devils caught,
  And thrust into that horrid place,
Where reign dismay, despair, disgrace;
  Furies with iron fangs were there,
To torture that accursed race,
  Doom'd to dismay, disgrace, despair.

Harmless I was; yet hunted down
  For treasons, to my soul unfit;
I've been pursued through many a town,
  For crimes that petty knaves commit;
I've been adjudged t' have lost my wit,
  Because I preach'd so loud and well;
And thrown into the dungeon's pit,
  For trampling on the pit of hell.

Such were the evils, man of sin,
  That I was fated to sustain;
And add to all, without—within,
  A soul defiled with every stain
That man's reflecting mind can pain;
  That pride, wrong, rage, despair, can make;

In fact, they'd nearly touch'd my brain,
  And reason on her throne would shake.

But pity will the vilest seek,
  If punish'd guilt will not repine,—
I heard a heavenly teacher speak,
  And felt the SUN OF MERCY shine:
I hail'd the light! the birth divine!
  And then was seal'd among the few;
Those angry fiends beheld the sign,
  And from me in an instant flew.

Come hear how thus the charmers cry
  To wandering sheep, the strays of sin,
While some the wicket-gate pass by,
  And some will knock and enter in:
Full joyful 'tis a soul to win,
  For he that winneth souls is wise;
Now hark! the holy strains begin,
  And thus the sainted preacher cries:—

"Pilgrim, burthen'd with thy sin,
Come the way to Zion's gate,
There, till Mercy let thee in,
Knock and weep and watch and wait.
  Knock!—He knows the sinner's cry:
  Weep!—He loves the mourner's tears:
  Watch!—for saving grace is nigh:
  Wait,—till heavenly light appears.

"Hark! it is the Bridegroom's voice;
Welcome, pilgrim, to thy rest;
Now within the gate rejoice,
Safe and seal'd and bought and bless'd!
  Safe—from all the lures of vice,
  Seal'd—by signs the chosen know,

Bought—by love and life the price,
Bless'd—the mighty debt to owe.

"Holy Pilgrim! what for thee
In a world like this remain?
From thy guarded breast shall flee
Fear and shame, and doubt and pain.
  Fear—the hope of Heaven shall fly,
  Shame—from glory's view retire,
  Doubt—in certain rapture die,
  Pain—in endless bliss expire."

But though my day of grace was come,
  Yet still my days of grief I find;
The former clouds' collected gloom
  Still sadden the reflecting mind;
The soul, to evil things consign'd,
  Will of their evil some retain;
The man will seem to earth inclined,
  And will not look erect again.

Thus, though elect, I feel it hard
  To lose what I possess'd before,
To be from all my wealth debarr'd,—
  The brave Sir Eustace is no more:
But old I wax and passing poor,
  Stern, rugged men my conduct view;
They chide my wish, they bar my door,
  'Tis hard—I weep—you see I do.—

Must you, my friends, no longer stay?
  Thus quickly all my pleasures end;
But I'll remember, when I pray,
  My kind physician and his friend;
And those sad hours, you deign to spend
  With me, I shall requite them all;

Sir Eustace for his friends shall send,
   And thank their love at Greyling Hall.

### VISITOR

The poor Sir Eustace!—Yet his hope
   Leads him to think of joys again;
And when his earthly visions droop,
   His views of heavenly kind remain:—
But whence that meek and humbled strain
   That spirit wounded, lost, resign'd?
Would not so proud a soul disdain
   The madness of the poorest mind?

(Lines 156–403)

# Philip Freneau
(1752–1832)

## FROM *The House of Night*

By some sad means, when Reason holds no sway,
Lonely I rov'd at midnight o'er a plain
Where murmuring streams and mingling rivers flow
Far to their springs, or seek the sea again.

Sweet vernal May! tho' then thy woods in bloom
Flourish'd, yet nought of this could Fancy see,
No wild pinks bless'd the meads, no green the fields,
And naked seem'd to stand each lifeless tree:

Dark was the sky, and not one friendly star
Shone from the zenith or horizon, clear,
Mist sate upon the woods, and darkness rode
In her black chariot, with a wild career.

And from the woods the late resounding note
Issued of the loquacious Whip-poor-will,
Hoarse, howling dogs, and nightly roving wolves
Clamour'd from far off cliffs invisible.

Rude, from the wide extended Chesapeke
I heard the winds the dashing waves assail,
And saw from far, by picturing fancy form'd,
The black ship travelling through the noisy gale.

At last, by chance and guardian fancy led,
I reach'd a noble dome, rais'd fair and high,
And saw the light from upper windows flame,
Presage of mirth and hospitality.

And by that light around the dome appear'd
A mournful garden of autumnal hue,
Its lately pleasing flowers all drooping stood
Amidst high weeds that in rank plenty grew.

The Primrose there, the violet darkly blue,
Daisies and fair Narcissus ceas'd to rise,
Gay spotted pinks their charming bloom withdrew.
And Polyanthus quench'd its thousand dyes.

No pleasant fruit or blossom gaily smil'd,
Nought but unhappy plants or trees were seen,
The yew, the myrtle, and the church-yard elm,
The cypress, with its melancholy green.

There cedars dark, the osier, and the pine,
Shorn tamarisks, and weeping willows grew,
The poplar tall, the lotos, and the lime,
And Pyracantha did her leaves renew.

The poppy there, companion to repose,
Display'd her blossoms that began to fall,
And here the purple amaranthus rose
With mint strong-scented, for the funeral.

And here and there with laurel shrubs between
A tombstone lay, inscrib'd with strains of woe,
And stanzas sad, throughout the dismal green,
Lamented for the dead that slept below.

(Stanzas 6–17)

## The Wild Honeysuckle

Fair flower, that dost so comely grow,
Hid in this silent, dull retreat,
Untouched thy honied blossoms blow,
Unseen thy little branches greet:
    No roving foot shall crush thee here,
    No busy hand provoke a tear.

By Nature's self in white arrayed,
She bade thee shun the vulgar eye,
And planted here the guardian shade,
And sent soft waters murmuring by;
    Thus quietly thy summer goes,
    Thy days declining to repose.

Smit with those charms, that must decay,
I grieve to see your future doom;
They died—nor were those flowers more gay,
The flowers that did in Eden bloom;
    Unpitying frosts, and Autumn's power
    Shall leave no vestige of this flower.

From morning suns and evening dews
At first thy little being came:
If nothing once, you nothing lose,
For when you die you are the same;
    The space between, is but an hour,
    The frail duration of a flower.

## The Indian Burying Ground

In spite of all the learned have said,
    I still my old opinion keep;
The posture, that we give the dead,
    Points out the soul's eternal sleep.

Not so the ancients of these lands—
    The Indian, when from life released,
Again is seated with his friends,
    And shares again the joyous feast.

His imaged birds, and painted bowl,
    And venison, for a journey dressed,
Bespeak the nature of the soul,
    Activity, that knows no rest.

His bow, for action ready bent,
    And arrows, with a head of stone,
Can only mean that life is spent,
    And not the old ideas gone.

Thou, stranger, that shalt come this way,
    No fraud upon the dead commit—
Observe the swelling turf, and say
    They do not lie, but here they sit.

Here still a lofty rock remains,
    On which the curious eye may trace
(Now wasted, half by wearing rains)
    The fancies of a ruder race.

Here still an aged elm aspires,
    Beneath whose far-projecting shade

(And which the shepherd still admires)
  The children of the forest played!

There oft a restless Indian queen
  (Pale Shebah, with her braided hair)
And many a barbarous form is seen
  To chide the man that lingers there.

By midnight moons, o'er moistening dews;
  In habit for the chase arrayed,
The hunter still the deer pursues,
  The hunter and the deer, a shade!

And long shall timorous fancy see
  The painted chief, and pointed spear,
And Reason's self shall bow the knee
  To shadows and delusions here.

# The Adventures of Simon Swaugum, a Village Merchant

### Written in 1768

### PRELIMINARY PARTICULARS

Sprung from a race that had long till'd the soil,
And first disrobed it of its native trees,
He wish'd to heir their lands, but not their toil,
And thought the ploughman's life no life of ease;—
  "Tis wrong (said he) these pretty hands to wound
With felling oaks, or delving in the ground:
I, who at least have forty pounds in cash
And in a country store might cut a dash,
Why should I till these barren fields (he said)

ſ wно have learnt to cypher, write and read,
These fields that shrubs, and weeds, and brambles bear,
That pay me not, and only bring me care!"
  Some thoughts had he, long while, to quit the sod,
In sea-port towns to try his luck in trade,
But, then, their ways of living seem'd most odd—
For dusty streets to leave his native shade,
From grassy plats to pebbled walks removed—
The more he thought of them, the less he loved:
The city springs he could not drink, and still
Preferr'd the fountain near some bushy hill:
  And yet no splendid objects there were seen,
No distant hills, in gaudy colours clad,
Look where you would, the prospect was but mean,
Scrub oaks, and scatter'd pines, and willows sad—
Banks of a shallow river, stain'd with mud;
A stream, where never swell'd the tide of flood,
Nor lofty ship her topsails did unloose,
Nor sailor sail'd, except in long canoes.
  It would have puzzled Faustus, to have told,
What did attach him to this paltry spot;
Where even the house he heir'd was very old,
And all its outworks hardly worth a groat:
Yet so it was, the fancy took his brain
A country shop might here some custom gain:
Whiskey, he knew, would always be in vogue,
While there are country squires to take a cogue,
Laces and lawns would draw each rural maid,
And one must have her shawl, and one her shade.—


### THE SHOP DESCRIBED
### AND THE MERCHANT'S OUTSET

Hard by the road a pigmy building stood,
Thatch'd was its roof, and earthen were its floors;

So small its size, that, in a jesting mood,
It might be call'd a house turn'd out of doors—
Yet here, adjacent to an agèd oak,
Full fifty years old dad his hams did smoke,
Nor ceas'd the trade, 'till worn with years and spent,
To Pluto's smoke-house he, himself, was sent.
   Hither our merchant turn'd his curious eye,
And mused awhile upon this sable shell;
   "Here father smoked his hogs (he said) and why
In truth, may not our garret do as well?"
So, down he took his hams and bacon flitches,
Resolv'd to fill the place with other riches;
From every hole and cranny brush'd the soot,
And fixt up shelves throughout the crazy hut;
A counter, too, most cunningly was plann'd,
Behind whose breast-work none but he might stand,
Excepting now and then, by special grace,
Some brother merchant from some other place.
   Now, muster'd up his cash, and said his prayers,
In Sunday suit he rigs himself for town,
Two raw-boned steeds (design'd for great affairs)
Are to the waggon hitch'd, old Bay and Brown;
Who ne'er had been before a league from home,
But now are doom'd full many a mile to roam,
Like merchant-ships, a various freight to bring
Of ribbons, lawns, and many a tawdry thing.
Molasses too, blest sweet, was not forgot,
And island Rum, that every taste delights,
And teas, for maid and matron, must be bought,
Rosin and catgut strings for fiddling wights—
But why should I his invoice here repeat?
'Twould be like counting grains in pecks of wheat.
Half Europe's goods were on his invoice found,
And all was to be bought with forty pound!
   Soon as the early dawn proclaim'd the day,

He cock'd his hat with pins, and comb'd his hair:
Curious it was, and laughable to see
The village-merchant, mounted in his chair:
Shelves, piled with lawns and linens, in his head,
Coatings and stuffs, and cloths, and scarlets red—
All that would suit man, woman, girl, or boy;
Muslins and muslinets, jeans, grograms, corduroy.
    Alack! said I, he little, little dreams
That all the cash he guards with studious care—
His cash! the mother of a thousand schemes,
Will hardly buy a load of earthen ware!
But why should I excite the hidden tear
By whispering truths ungrateful to his ear;
Still let him travel on, with scheming pate,
As disappointment never comes too late.—


### HIS JOURNEY TO THE METROPOLIS;
### AND MERCANTILE TRANSACTIONS

Through woods obscure and rough perplexing ways,
Slow and alone, he urged the clumsy wheel;
Now stopping short, to let his horses graze,
Now treating them with straw and Indian meal:
At length a lofty steeple caught his eye,
"Higher (thought he) than ever kite did fly:—
But so it is, these churchmen are so proud
They ever will be climbing to a cloud;
Bound on a sky-blue cruise, they always rig
The longest steeple, and the largest wig."
    Now safe arrived upon the pebbled way,
Where well-born steeds the rattling coaches trail,
Where shops on shops are seen—and ladies gay
Walk with their curtains some, and some their veil;
Where sons of art their various labors shew
And one cries fish! and one cries muffins ho!

Amaz'd, alike, the merchant, and his pair
Of scare-crow steeds, did nothing else but stare;
So new was all the scene, that, smit with awe,
They grinn'd, and gaz'd, and gap'd at all they saw,
And often stopp'd, to ask at every door,
"Sirs, can you tell us where's the cheapest store!"
    "The cheapest store (a sly retailer said)
Cheaper than cheap, guid faith, I have to sell;
Here are some colour'd cloths that never fade:
No other shop can serve you half so well;
Wanting some money now, to pay my rent,
I'll sell them at a loss of ten per cent.—
Hum-hums are here—and muslins—what you please—
Bandanas, baftas, pullcats, India teas;
Improv'd by age, and now grown very old,
And given away, you may depend—not sold!"
    Lured by the bait the wily shopman laid,
He gave his steeds their mess of straw and meal,
Then gazing round the shop, thus, cautious said,
"Well, if you sell so cheap, I think we'll deal;
But pray remember, 'tis for goods I'm come,
For, as to polecats, we've enough at home—
Full forty pounds I have, and that in gold
(Enough to make a trading man look bold);
Unrig your shelves, and let me take a peep;
'Tis odds I leave them bare, you sell so cheap."
    The city merchant stood, with lengthen'd jaws;
And stared awhile, then made this short reply—
    "You clear my shelves! (he said)—this trunk of gauze
Is more than all your forty pounds can buy:—
On yonder board, whose burthen seems so small
That one man's pocket might contain it all,
More value lies, than you and all your race
From Adam down, could purchase or possess."
    Convinced, he turn'd him to another street,

Where humbler shopmen from the crowd retreat;
Here caught his eye coarse callicoes and crape,
Pipes and tobacco, ticklenburghs and tape.
Pitchers and pots, of value not so high
But he might sell, and forty pounds would buy.

Some jugs, some pots, some fifty ells of tape,
A keg of wine, a cask of low proof rum,
Bung'd close—for fear the spirit should escape
That many a sot was waiting for at home;
A gross of pipes, a case of home-made gin,
Tea, powder, shot—small parcels he laid in;
Molasses, too, for swichell-loving wights,
(Swichell, that wings Sangrado's boldest flights,
When bursting forth the wild ideas roll,
Flash'd from that farthing-candle, call'd his soul:)
All these he bought, and would have purchased more,
To furnish out his Lilliputian store;
But cash fell short—and they who smiled while yet
The cash remain'd, now took a serious fit:—
No more the shop-girl could his talk endure,
But, like her cat, sat sullen and demure.—
The dull retailer found no more to say,
But shook his head, and wish'd to sneak away,
Leaving his house-dog, now, to make reply,
And watch the counter with a lynx's eye.—
Our merchant took the hint, and off he went,
Resolv'd to sell at twenty-five per cent.

## THE MERCHANT'S RETURN

Returning far o'er many a hill and stone
And much in dread his earthen ware would break,
Thoughtful he rode, and uttering many a groan
Lest at some worm-hole vent his cask should leak—
His cask, that held the joys of rural squire

Which even, 'twas said, the parson did admire,
And valued more than all the dusty pages
That Calvin penn'd, and fifty other sages—
Once high in fame—beprais'd in verse and prose,
But now unthumb'd, enjoy a sweet repose.

    At dusk of eve he reach'd his old abode,
Around him quick his anxious townsmen came,
One ask'd what luck had happ'd him on the road,
And one ungear'd the mud-bespatter'd team.
While on his cask each glanced a loving eye,
Patient, to all he gave a brisk reply—
Told all that had befallen him on his way,
What wonders in the town detain'd his stay—
"Houses as high as yonder white-oak tree
And boats of monstrous size that go to sea,
Streets throng'd with busy folk, like swarming hive;
The Lord knows how they all contrive to live—
No ploughs I saw, no hoes, no care, no charge,
In fact, they all are gentlemen at large,
And goods so thick on every window lie,
They all seem born to sell—and none to buy."


### THE CATASTROPHE,
### OR THE BROKEN MERCHANT

Alack-a-day! on life's uncertain road
How many plagues, what evils must befal;—
Jove has on none unmingled bliss bestow'd,
But disappointment is the lot of all:
Thieves rob our stores, in spite of locks and keys,
Cats steal our cream, and rats infest our cheese,
The gayest coat a grease-spot may assail,
Or Susan pin a dish-clout to its tail.—

    Our village-merchant (trust me) had his share
Of vile mis-haps—for now, the goods unpackt,

Discover'd, what might make a deacon swear,
Jugs, cream-pots, pipes, and grog-bowls sadly crackt—
A general groan throughout the crowd was heard;
Most pitied him, and some his ruin fear'd;
Poor wight! 'twas sad to see him fret and chafe,
While each enquir'd, "Sir, is the rum-cask safe?"

Alas! even that some mischief had endured;—
One rascal hoop had started near the chine!
Then curiously the bung-hole they explored,
With stem of pipe, the leakage to define—
Five gallons must be charged to loss and gain!—
"—Five gallons! (cry'd the merchant, writh'd with
    pain)
Now may the cooper never see full flask,
But still be driving at an empty cask—
Five gallons might have mellowed down the squire
And made the captain strut a full inch higher;
Five gallons might have prompted many a song,
And made a frolic more than five days long:
Five gallons now are lost, and—sad to think,
That when they leak'd—no soul was there to drink!"

Now, slightly treated with a proof-glass dram,
Each neighbor took his leave, and went to bed,
All but our merchant: he, with grief o'ercome,
Revolv'd strange notions in his scheming head—
"For losses such as these, (thought he) 'tis meant,
That goods are sold at twenty-five per cent:
No doubt these trading men know what is just,
'Tis twenty-five times what they cost at first!"

So rigging off his shelves by light of candle,
The dismal smoke-house walls began to shine:
Here, stood his tea-pots—some without a handle—
A broken jar—and there his keg of wine;
Pipes, many a dozen, ordered in a row;
Jugs, mugs, and grog-bowls—less for sale than show:

The leaky cask, replenish'd from the well,
Roll'd to its birth—but we no tales will tell.—

Catching the eye in elegant display,
All was arranged and snug, by break of day:
The blue dram-bottle, on the counter plac'd,
Stood, all prepared for him that buys to taste;—
Sure bait! by which the man of cash is taken,
As rats are caught by cheese or scraps of bacon.

Now from all parts the rural people ran,
With ready cash, to buy what might be bought:
One went to choose a pot, and one a pan,
And they that had no pence their produce brought,
A hog, a calf, safe halter'd by the neck;
Potatoes (Ireland's glory) many a peck;
Bacon and cheese, of real value more
Than India's gems, or all Potosi's ore.

Some questions ask'd, the folks began to stare—
No soul would purchase, pipe, or pot, or pan:
Each shook his head—hung back—"Your goods so dear!
"In fact (said they) the devil's in the man!
"Rum ne'er shall meet my lips (cry'd honest Sam)
In shape of toddy, punch, grog, sling, or dram";
"No cash of mine you'll get (said pouting Kate)
While gauze is valued at so dear a rate."

Thus things dragg'd on for many a tedious day;
No custom came; and nought but discontent
Gloom'd through the shop.—"Well, let them have their
        way,
(The merchant said) I'll sell at cent per cent,
By which, 'tis plain, I scarce myself can save,
For cent per cent is just the price I gave."

"Now! (cry'd the squire who still had kept his pence)
Now, Sir, you reason like a man of sense!
Custom will now from every quarter come;
In joyous streams shall flow the inspiring rum,

'Till every soul in pleasing dreams be sunk,
And even our Socrates himself—is drunk!"
   Soon were the shelves disburthen'd of their load;
In three short hours the kegs of wine ran dry—
Swift from its tap even dull molasses flow'd;
Each saw the rum cask wasting, with a sigh—
The farce concluded, as it was foreseen—
With empty shelves—long trust—and law suits keen—
The woods resounding with a curse on trade,—
An empty purse—sour looks—and hanging head.—

## THE PUNCHEON'S EULOGY

"Here lies a worthy corpse (Sangrado said)
Its debt to Commerce now, no doubt, is paid.—
Well—'twas a vile disease that kill'd it, sure,
A quick consumption, that no art could cure!
Thus shall we all, when life's vain dream is out,
Be lodg'd in corners dark, or kick'd about!
Time is the tapster of our race below,
That turns the key, and bids the juices flow:
Quitting my books, henceforth be mine the task
To moralize upon this empty cask—
Thank heaven we've had the taste—so far 'twas well;
And still, thro' mercy, may enjoy the smell!"

# Fitz-Greene Halleck

(1790–1867)

## On the Death of Joseph Rodman Drake

> The good die first,
> And they, whose hearts are dry as summer dust,
> Burn to the socket.
> —WORDSWORTH

Green be the turf above thee,
　Friend of my better days!
None knew thee but to love thee,
　Nor named thee but to praise.

Tears fell, when thou wert dying,
　From eyes unused to weep,
And long where thou art lying,
　Will tears the cold turf steep.

When hearts, whose truth was proven,
　Like thine, are laid in earth,
There should a wreath be woven
　To tell the world their worth;

And I, who woke each morrow
　To clasp thy hand in mine,
Who shared thy joy and sorrow,
　Whose weal and wo were thine;

It should be mine to braid it
　Around thy faded brow,
But I've in vain essayed it,
　And feel I cannot now.

While memory bids me weep thee,
    Nor thoughts nor words are free,
The grief is fixed too deeply
    That mourns a man like thee.


## The Field of the Grounded Arms

### SARATOGA

Strangers! your eyes are on that valley fixed
Intently, as we gaze on vacancy,
    When the mind's wings o'erspread
    The spirit-world of dreams.

True, 'tis a scene of loveliness—the bright
Green dwelling of the summer's first-born Hours,
    Whose wakened leaf and bud
    Are welcoming the morn.

And morn returns the welcome, sun and cloud
Smile on the green earth from their home in heaven,
    Even as a mother smiles
    Above her cradled boy,

And wreath their light and shade o'er plain and mountain,
O'er sleepless seas of grass whose waves are flowers,
    The river's golden shores,
    The forests of dark pines.

The song of the wild bird is on the wind,
The hum of the wild bee, the music wild
    Of waves upon the bank,
    Of leaves upon the bough.

But all is song and beauty in the land,
Beneath her skies of June; then journey on,

A thousand scenes like this
Will greet you ere the eve.

Ye linger yet—ye see not, hear not now
The sunny smile, the music of to-day,
  Your thoughts are wandering up,
  Far up the stream of time;

And boyhood's lore and fireside listened tales
Are rushing on your memories, as ye breathe
  That valley's storied name,
  FIELD OF THE GROUNDED ARMS.

Strangers no more, a kindred "pride of place,"
Pride in the gift of country and of name,
  Speaks in your eye and step—
  Ye tread your native land.

And your high thoughts are on her glory's day,
The solemn sabbath of the week of battle,
  Whose tempests bowed to earth
  Her foeman's banner here.

The forest leaves lay scattered cold and dead,
Upon the withered grass that autumn morn,
  When, with as withered hearts
  And hopes as dead and cold,

A gallant army formed their last array
Upon that field, in silence and deep gloom,
  And at their conqueror's feet
  Laid their war-weapons down.

Sullen and stern, disarmed but not dishonored;
Brave men, but brave in vain, they yielded there:
  The soldier's trial task
  Is not alone "to die."

Honor to chivalry! the conqueror's breath
Stains not the ermine of his foeman's fame,
　　Nor mocks his captive's doom—
　　The bitterest cup of war.

But be that bitterest cup the doom of all
Whose swords are lightning flashes in the cloud
　　Of the Invader's wrath,
　　Threatening a gallant land.

His armies' trumpet-tones wake not alone
Her slumbering echoes; from a thousand hills
　　Her answering voices shout,
　　And her bells ring to arms!

Then danger hovers o'er the Invader's march,
On raven wings, hushing the song of fame,
　　And glory's hues of beauty
　　Fade from the cheek of death.

A foe is heard in every rustling leaf,
A fortress seen in every rock and tree,
　　The eagle eye of art
　　Is dim and powerless then,

And war becomes a people's joy, the drum
Man's merriest music, and the field of death
　　His couch of happy dreams,
　　After life's harvest home.

He battles heart and arm, his own blue sky
Above him, and his own green land around,
　　Land of his father's grave,
　　His blessing and his prayers,

Land where he learned to lisp a mother's name,
The first beloved in life, the last forgot,
　　Land of his frolic youth,
　　Land of his bridal eve,

Land of his children—vain your columned **strength,**
Invaders! vain your battles' steel and fire!
   Choose ye the morrow's doom,—
   A prison or a grave.

And such were Saratoga's victors—such
The Yeomen-Brave, whose deeds and death have given
   A glory to her skies,
   A music to her name.

In honorable life her fields they trod,
In honorable death they sleep below;
   Their sons' proud feelings here
   Their noblest monuments.

# Sir Walter Scott

(1771–1832)

## The Eve of Saint John

The Baron of Smaylho'me rose with day,
   He spurred his courser on,
Without stop or stay, down the rocky way,
   That leads to Brotherstone.

He went not with the bold Buccleuch
   His banner broad to rear;
He went not 'gainst the English yew
   To lift the Scottish spear.

Yet his plate-jack was braced and his helmet was laced,
   And his vaunt-brace of proof he wore;
At his saddle-gerthe was a good steel sperthe,
   Full ten pound weight and more.

The baron returned in three days' space,
   And his looks were sad and sour;
And weary was his courser's pace
   As he reached his rocky tower.

He came not from where Ancram Moor
   Ran red with English blood;
Where the Douglas true and the bold Buccleuch
   'Gainst keen Lord Evers stood.

Yet was his helmet hacked and hewed,
   His acton pierced and tore,

113

His axe and his dagger with blood imbrued,—
  But it was not English gore.

He lighted at the Chapellage,
  He held him close and still;
And he whistled thrice for his little foot-page,
  His name was English Will.

"Come thou hither, my little foot-page,
  Come hither to my knee;
Though thou art young and tender of age,
  I think thou art true to me.

"Come, tell me all that thou hast seen,
  And look thou tell me true!
Since I from Smaylho'me tower have been,
  What did thy lady do?"

"My lady, each night, sought the lonely light
  That burns on the wild Watchfold;
For from height to height the beacons bright
  Of the English foemen told.

"The bittern clamored from the moss,
  The wind blew loud and shrill;
Yet the craggy pathway she did cross
  To the eiry Beacon Hill.

"I watched her steps, and silent came
  Where she sat her on a stone;—
No watchman stood by the dreary flame,
  It burnèd all alone.

"The second night I kept her in sight
  Till to the fire she came,
And, my Mary's might! an armèd knight
  Stood by the lonely flame.

"And many a word that warlike lord
    Did speak to my lady there;
But the rain fell fast and loud blew the blast,
    And I heard not what they were.

"The third night there the sky was fair,
    And the mountain-blast was still,
As again I watched the secret pair
    On the lonesome Beacon Hill.

"And I heard her name the midnight hour,
    And name this holy eve;
And say, 'Come this night to thy lady's bower;
    Ask no bold baron's leave.

" 'He lifts his spear with the bold Buccleuch;
    His lady is all alone;
The door she'll undo to her knight so true
    On the eve of good Saint John.'

" 'I cannot come; I must not come;
    I dare not come to thee;
On the eve of Saint John I must wander alone:
    In thy bower I may not be.'

" 'Now, out on thee, faint-hearted knight!
    Thou shouldst not say me nay;
For the eve is sweet, and when lovers meet
    Is worth the whole summer's day.

" 'And I'll chain the blood-hound, and the warder shall
        not sound,
    And rushes shall be strewed on the stair;
So, by the black rood-stone and by holy Saint John,
    I conjure thee, my love, to be there!'

" 'Though the blood-hound be mute and the rush be-
        neath my foot,

And the warder his bugle should not blow,
Yet there sleepeth a priest in the chamber to the east,
 And my footstep he would know.'

" 'O, fear not the priest who sleepeth to the east,
 For to Dryburgh the way he has ta'en;
And there to say mass, till three days do pass,
 For the soul of a knight that is slayne.'

"He turned him around and grimly he frowned;
 Then he laughed right scornfully—
'He who says the mass-rite for the soul of that knight
 May as well say mass for me:

" 'At the lone midnight hour when bad spirits have
  power
 In thy chamber will I be.'—
With that he was gone and my lady left alone,
 And no more did I see."

Then changed, I trow, was that bold baron's brow
 From the dark to the blood-red high;
"Now, tell me the mien of the knight thou hast seen,
 For, by Mary, he shall die!"

"His arms shone full bright in the beacon's red light;
 His plume it was scarlet and blue;
On his shield was a hound in a silver leash bound,
 And his crest was a branch of the yew."

"Thou liest, thou liest, thou little foot-page,
 Loud dost thou lie to me!
For that knight is cold and low laid in the mould,
 All under the Eildon-tree."

"Yet hear but my word, my noble lord!
 For I heard her name his name;

And that lady bright, she called the knight
  Sir Richard of Coldinghame."

The bold baron's brow then changed, I trow,
  From high blood-red to pale—
"The grave is deep and dark—and the corpse is stiff and
    stark—
  So I may not trust thy tale.

"Where fair Tweed flows round holy Melrose,
  And Eildon slopes to the plain,
Full three nights ago by some secret foe
  That gay gallant was slain.

"The varying light deceived thy sight,
  And the wild winds drowned the name;
For the Dryburgh bells ring and the white monks do
    sing
  For Sir Richard of Coldinghame!"

He passed the court-gate and he oped the tower-gate,
  And he mounted the narrow stair,
To the bartizan-seat where, with maids that on her wait,
  He found his lady fair.

That lady sat in mournful mood;
  Looked over hill and vale;
Over Tweed's fair flood and Mertoun's wood,
  And all down Teviotdale.

"Now hail, now hail, thou lady bright!"
  "Now hail, thou baron true!
What news, what news, from Ancram fight?
  What news from the bold Buccleuch?"

"The Ancram moor is red with gore,
  For many a Southern fell;
And Buccleuch has charged us evermore
  To watch our beacons well."

The lady blushed red, but nothing she said:
 Nor added the baron a word:
Then she stepped down the stair to her chamber fair,
 And so did her moody lord.

In sleep the lady mourned, and the baron tossed and
  turned,
 And oft to himself he said,—
"The worms around him creep, and his bloody grave is
  deep—
 It cannot give up the dead!"

It was near the ringing of matin-bell,
 The night was well-nigh done,
When a heavy sleep on that baron fell,
 On the eve of good Saint John.

The lady looked through the chamber fair,
 By the light of a dying flame;
And she was aware of a knight stood there—
 Sir Richard of Coldinghame!

"Alas! away, away!" she cried,
 "For the holy Virgin's sake!"
"Lady, I know who sleeps by thy side;
 But, lady, he will not awake.

"By Eildon-tree for long nights three
 In bloody grave have I lain;
The mass and the death-prayer are said for me,
 But, lady, they are said in vain.

"By the baron's brand, near Tweed's fair strand,
 Most foully slain I fell;
And my restless spirit on the beacon's height
 For a space is doomed to dwell.

"At our trysting-place, for a certain space,
 I must wander to and fro;

But I had not had power to come to thy bower
　Hadst thou not conjured me so."

Love mastered fear—her brow she crossed;
　"How, Richard, hast thou sped?
And art thou saved or art thou lost?"
　The vision shook his head!

"Who spilleth life shall forfeit life;
　So bid thy lord believe:
That lawless love is guilt above,
　This awful sign receive."

He laid his left palm on an oaken beam,
　His right upon her hand;
The lady shrunk and fainting sunk,
　For it scorched like a fiery brand.

The sable score of fingers four
　Remains on that board impressed;
And forevermore that lady wore
　A covering on her wrist.

There is a nun in Dryburgh bower
　Ne'er looks upon the sun;
There is a monk in Melrose tower
　He speaketh word to none.

That nun who ne'er beholds the day,
　That monk who speaks to none—
That nun was Smaylho'me's lady gay,
　That monk the bold baron.

## FROM *Marmion*

### SONG

Where shall the lover rest,
  Whom the fates sever
From his true maiden's breast,
  Parted forever?
Where, through groves deep and high,
  Sounds the far billow,
Where early violets die,
  Under the willow.

CHORUS. *Eleu loro, etc.* Soft shall be his pillow.

There, through the summer day,
  Cool streams are laving;
There, while the tempests sway,
  Scarce are boughs waving;
There thy rest shalt thou take,
  Parted forever,
Never again to wake,
  Never, O never!

CHORUS. *Eleu loro, etc.* Never, O never!

Where shall the traitor rest,
  He the deceiver,
Who could win maiden's breast,
  Ruin and leave her?
In the lost battle,

Borne down by the flying,
Where mingles war's rattle
    With groans of the dying.

CHORUS. *Eleu loro, etc*. There shall he be lying.


Her wing shall the eagle flap
    O'er the false-hearted;
His warm blood the wolf shall lap,
    Ere life be parted.
Shame and dishonor sit
    By his grave ever;
Blessing shall hallow it,—
    Never, O never!


CHORUS. *Eleu loro, etc*. Never, O never!

(Canto iii, lines 148–83)


### THE BATTLE

By this, though deep the evening fell,
Still rose the battle's deadly swell,
For still the Scots around their king,
Unbroken, fought in desperate ring.
Where's now their victor vaward wing,
    Where Huntley, and where Home?—
Oh! for a blast of that dread horn,
On Fontarabian echoes borne,
    That to King Charles did come,
When Rowland brave, and Olivier,
And every paladin and peer,
    On Roncesvalles died!
Such blasts might warn them, not in vain,
To quit the plunder of the slain

And turn the doubtful day again,
　　While yet on Flodden side
Afar the Royal Standard flies,
And round it toils and bleeds and dies
　　Our Caledonian pride!
In vain the wish—for far away,
While spoil and havoc mark their way,
Near Sibyl's Cross the plunderers stray.—
"O lady," cried the monk, "away!"
　　And placed her on her steed,
And led her to the chapel fair
　　Of Tilmouth upon Tweed.
There all the night they spent in prayer,
And at the dawn of morning there
She met her kinsman, Lord Fitz-Clare.

But as they left the darkening heath
More desperate grew the strife of death.
The English shafts in volleys hailed,
In headlong charge their horse assailed;
Front, flank, and rear, the squadrons sweep
To break the Scottish circle deep
　　That fought around their king.
But yet, though thick the shafts as snow,
Though charging knights like whirlwinds go,
Though billmen ply the ghastly blow,
　　Unbroken was the ring;
The stubborn spearmen still made good
Their dark impenetrable wood,
Each stepping where his comrade stood
　　The instant that he fell.
No thought was there of dastard flight;
Linked in the serried phalanx tight,
Groom fought like noble, squire like knight,
　　As fearlessly and well,

Till utter darkness closed her wing
O'er their thin host and wounded king.
Then skilful Surrey's sage commands
Led back from strife his shattered bands;
   And from the charge they drew,
As mountain-waves from wasted lands
   Sweep back to ocean blue.
Then did their loss his foemen know;
Their king, their lords, their mightiest low,
They melted from the field, as snow,
When streams are swoln and southwinds blow,
   Dissolves in silent dew.
Tweed's echoes heard the ceaseless plash,
   While many a broken band
Disordered through her currents dash,
   To gain the Scottish land;
To town and tower, to down and dale,
To tell red Flodden's dismal tale,
And raise the universal wail.
Tradition, legend, tune, and song
Shall many an age that wail prolong;
Still from the sire the son shall hear
Of the stern strife and carnage drear
   Of Flodden's fatal field,
Where shivered was fair Scotland's spear
   And broken was her shield!
                 (*Canto vi, lines 993–1066*)

# FROM *The Lady of the Lake*

### THE WESTERN WAVES OF EBBING DAY

   The western waves of ebbing day
   Rolled o'er the glen their level way;
   Each purple peak, each flinty spire,

Was bathed in floods of living fire.
But not a setting beam could glow
Within the dark ravines below,
Where twined the path in shadow hid,
Round many a rocky pyramid,
Shooting abruptly from the dell
Its thunder-splintered pinnacle;
Round many an insulated mass,
The native bulwarks of the pass,
Huge as the tower which builders vain
Presumptuous piled on Shinar's plain.
The rocky summits, split and rent,
Formed turret, dome, or battlement,
Or seemed fantastically set
With cupola or minaret,
Wild crests as pagod ever decked,
Or mosque of Eastern architect.
Nor were these earth-born castles bare,
Nor lacked they many a banner fair;
For, from their shivered brows displayed,
Far o'er the unfathomable glade,
All twinkling with the dewdrop sheen,
The brier-rose fell in streamers green,
And creeping shrubs, of thousand dyes,
Waved in the west-wind's summer sighs.

Boon nature scattered, free and wild,
Each plant or flower, the mountain's child.
Here eglantine embalmed the air,
Hawthorn and hazel mingled there;
The primrose pale, and violet flower,
Found in each cliff a narrow bower;
Fox-glove and night-shade, side by side,
Emblems of punishment and pride,
Grouped their dark hues with every stain

The weather-beaten crags retain.
With boughs that quaked at every breath,
Gray birch and aspen wept beneath;
Aloft, the ash and warrior oak
Cast anchor in the rifted rock;
And, higher yet, the pine-tree hung
His shattered trunk, and frequent flung,
Where seemed the cliffs to meet on high,
His boughs athwart the narrowed sky.
Highest of all, where white peaks glanced,
Where glist'ning streamers waved and danced,
The wanderer's eye could barely view
The summer heaven's delicious blue;
So wondrous wild, the whole might seem
The scenery of a fairy dream.

Onward, amid the copse 'gan peep
A narrow inlet, still and deep,
Affording scarce such breadth of brim
As served the wild duck's brood to swim.
Lost for a space, through thickets veering,
But broader when again appearing,
Tall rocks and tufted knolls their face
Could on the dark-blue mirror trace;
And farther as the hunter strayed,
Still broader sweep its channels made.
The shaggy mounds no longer stood,
Emerging from entangled wood,
But, wave-encircled, seemed to float,
Like castle girdled with its moat;
Yet broader floods extending still
Divide them from their parent hill,
Till each, retiring, claims to be
An islet in an inland sea.

And now, to issue from the glen,
No pathway meets the wanderer's ken.
Unless he climb, with footing nice,
A far projecting precipice.
The broom's tough roots his ladder made,
The hazel saplings lent their aid;
And thus an airy point he won,
Where, gleaming with the setting sun,
One burnished sheet of living gold,
Loch Katrine lay beneath him rolled;
In all her length far winding lay,
With promontory, creek, and bay,
And islands that, empurpled bright,
Floated amid the livelier light,
And mountains, that like giants stand,
To sentinel enchanted land.
High on the south, huge Benvenue
Down to the lake in masses threw
Crags, knolls, and mountains, confusedly hurled,
The fragments of an earlier world;
A wildering forest feathered o'er
His ruined sides and summit hoar,
While on the north, through middle air,
Ben-an heaved high his forehead bare.

(Canto i, lines 184–277)

## BOAT SONG

Hail to the Chief who in triumph advances!
    Honored and blessed be the ever-green Pine!
Long may the tree, in his banner that glances,
    Flourish, the shelter and grace of our line!
        Heaven sent it happy dew,
        Earth lend it sap anew,
    Gayly to bourgeon and broadly to grow,
        While every Highland glen

Sends our shout back again,
"Roderigh Vich Alpine dhu, ho! ieroe!"

Ours is no sapling, chance-sown by the fountain,
  Blooming at Beltane, in winter to fade;
When the whirlwind has stripped every leaf on the
    mountain,
  The more shall Clan-Alpine exult in her shade.
    Moored in the rifted rock,
    Proof to the tempest's shock,
  Firmer he roots him the ruder it blow;
    Menteith and Breadalbane, then,
    Echo his praise again,
  "Roderigh Vich Alpine dhu, ho! ieroe!"

Proudly our pibroch has thrilled in Glen Fruin,
  And Bannochar's groans to our slogan replied;
Glen-Luss and Ross-dhu, they are smoking in ruin,
  And the best of Loch Lomond lie dead on her side.
    Widow and Saxon maid
    Long shall lament our raid,
  Think of Clan-Alpine with fear and with woe;
    Lennox and Leven-glen
    Shake when they hear again,
  "Roderigh Vich Alpine dhu, ho! ieroe!"

Row, vassals, row, for the pride of the Highlands!
  Stretch to your oars for the ever-green Pine!
O that the rosebud that graces yon islands
  Were wreathed in a garland around him to twine!
    O that some seedling gem,
    Worthy such noble stem,
  Honored and blessed in their shadow might grow!
    Loud should Clan-Alpine then
    Ring from her deepmost glen,
  "Roderigh Vich Alpine dhu, ho! ieroe!"

                              (*Canto ii, lines 399–438*)

## *Pibroch of Donuil Dhu*

Pibroch of Donuil Dhu,
  Pibroch of Donuil,
Wake thy wild voice anew,
  Summon Clan Conuil.
Come away, come away,
  Hark to the summons!
Come in your war array,
  Gentles and commons.

Come from deep glen and
  From mountains so rocky,
The war-pipe and pennon
  Are at Inverlochy.
Come every hill-plaid and
  True heart that wears one,
Come every steel blade and
  Strong hand that bears one.

Leave untended the herd,
  The flock without shelter;
Leave the corpse uninterred,
  The bride at the altar;
Leave the deer, leave the steer,
  Leave nets and barges:
Come with your fighting gear,
  Broadswords and targes.

Come as the winds come when
  Forests are rended;
Come as the waves come when
  Navies are stranded:
Faster come, faster come,

    Faster and faster,
Chief, vassal, page and groom,
    Tenant and master.

Fast they come, fast they come;
    See how they gather!
Wide waves the eagle plume,
    Blended with heather.
Cast your plaids, draw your blades,
    Forward each man set!
Pibroch of Donuil Dhu,
    Knell for the onset!


## Proud Maisie

Proud Maisie is in the wood
    Walking so early;
Sweet Robin sits on the bush,
    Singing so rarely.

"Tell me, thou bonny bird,
    When shall I marry me?"—
"When six braw gentlemen
    Kirkward shall carry ye."

"Who makes the bridal bed,
    Birdie, say truly?"—
"The gray-headed sexton
    That delves the grave duly.

"The glow-worm o'er grave and stone
    Shall light thee steady,
The owl from the steeple sing,
    'Welcome, proud lady.'"

# Samuel Taylor Coleridge

(1772–1834)

## Phantom

All look and likeness caught from earth,
All accident of kin and birth,
Had pass'd away. There was no trace
Of aught on that illumined face,
Upraised beneath the rifted stone
But of one spirit all her own;—
She, she herself, and only she,
Shone through her body visibly.

## The Rime of the Ancient Mariner

### IN SEVEN PARTS

### PART THE FIRST

*An ancient Mar-
iner meeteth
three Gallants
bidden to a
wedding-feast,
and detaineth
one.*

It is an ancient Mariner
And he stoppeth one of three.
"By thy long grey beard and glittering
eye,
Now wherefore stopp'st thou me?

The Bridegroom's doors are opened wide,
And I am next of kin;
The guests are met, the feast is set:
May'st hear the merry din."

130

He holds him with his skinny hand,
There was a ship, quoth he.
"Hold off! unhand me, grey-beard loon!"
Eftsoons his hand dropt he.

*The Wedding-Guest is spellbound by the eye of the old seafaring man, and constrained to hear his tale.*

He holds him with his glittering eye—
The Wedding-Guest stood still,
And listens like a three years' child:
The Mariner hath his will.

The Wedding-Guest sat on a stone:
He cannot choose but hear;
And thus spake on that ancient man,
The bright-eyed Mariner.

The ship was cheered, the harbor
    cleared,
Merrily did we drop
Below the kirk, below the hill,
Below the lighthouse top.

*The Mariner tells how the ship sailed southward with a good wind and fair weather, till it reached the Line.*

The Sun came up upon the left,
Out of the sea came he!
And he shone bright, and on the right
Went down into the sea.

Higher and higher every day,
Till over the mast at noon—
The Wedding-Guest here beat his breast,
For he heard the loud bassoon.

*The Wedding-Guest heareth the bridal music; but the Mariner continueth his tale.*

The bride hath paced into the hall,
Red as a rose is she;
Nodding their heads before her goes
The merry minstrelsy.

The Wedding-Guest he beat his breast,
Yet he cannot choose but hear;

And thus spake on that ancient man,
The bright-eyed Mariner.

*The ship driven by a storm toward the south pole.*

And now the storm-blast came, and he
Was tyrannous and strong:
He struck with his o'ertaking wings,
And chased us south along.

With sloping masts and dipping prow,
As who pursued with yell and blow
Still treads the shadow of his foe
And forward bends his head,
The ship drove fast, loud roared the blast,
And southward aye we fled.

And now there came both mist and snow,
And it grew wondrous cold:
And ice, mast-high, came floating by,
As green as emerald.

*The land of ice, and of fearful sounds, where no living thing was to be seen.*

And through the drifts the snowy clifts
Did send a dismal sheen:
Nor shapes of men nor beasts we ken—
The ice was all between.

The ice was here, the ice was there,
The ice was all around:
It cracked and growled, and roared and
    howled,
Like noises in a swound!

*Till a great sea-bird, called the Albatross, came through the snow-fog, and was received with great joy and hospitality.*

At length did cross an Albatross:
Through the fog it came;
As if it had been a Christian soul,
We hailed it in God's name.

It ate the food it ne'er had eat,
And round and round it flew.

The ice did split with a thunder-fit;
The helmsman steered us through!

*And lo! the Albatross proveth a bird of good omen, and followeth the ship as it returned northward through fog and floating ice.*

And a good south wind sprung up behind;
The Albatross did follow,
And every day, for food or play,
Came to the mariners' hollo!

In mist or cloud, on mast or shroud,
It perched for vespers nine;
Whiles all the night, through fog-smoke white,
Glimmered the white Moon-shine.

*The ancient Mariner inhospitably killeth the pious bird of good omen.*

"God save thee, ancient Mariner!
From the fiends, that plague thee thus!—
Why look'st thou so?"—With my cross-bow
I shot the Albatross.

## PART THE SECOND

The Sun now rose upon the right:
Out of the sea came he,
Still hid in mist, and on the left
Went down into the sea.

And the good south wind still blew behind,
But no sweet bird did follow,
Nor any day for food or play
Came to the mariners' hollo!

*His shipmates cry out against the ancient Mariner, for killing the bird of good luck.*

And I had done a hellish thing,
And it would work 'em woe:
For all averred, I had killed the bird
That made the breeze to blow.

"Ah, wretch!" said they, "the bird to slay,
That made the breeze to blow!"

*But when the
fog cleared off,
they justify the
same, and thus
make themselves
accomplices in
the crime.*

Nor dim nor red, like God's own head,
The glorious Sun uprist:
Then all averred, I had killed the bird
That brought the fog and mist.
" 'Twas right," said they, "such birds to
    slay,
That bring the fog and mist."

*The fair breeze
continues; the
ship enters the
Pacific Ocean,
and sails north-
ward, even till it
reaches the Line.*

The fair breeze blew, the white foam
    flew,
The furrow followed free;
We were the first that ever burst
Into that silent sea.

Down dropt the breeze, the sails dropt
    down,

*The ship hath
been suddenly
becalmed.*

'Twas sad as sad could be;
And we did speak only to break
The silence of the sea!

All in a hot and copper sky,
The bloody Sun, at noon,
Right up above the mast did stand,
No bigger than the Moon.

Day after day, day after day,
We stuck, nor breath nor motion;
As idle as a painted ship
Upon a painted ocean.

*And the Alba-
tross begins to
be avenged.*

Water, water, every where,
And all the boards did shrink;
Water, water, every where,
Nor any drop to drink.

The very deep did rot: O Christ!
That ever this should be!
Yea, slimy things did crawl with legs
Upon the slimy sea.

About, about, in reel and rout
The death-fires danced at night;
The water, like a witch's oils,
Burnt green, and blue, and white.

*A Spirit had followed them; one of the invisible inhabitants of this planet, neither departed souls nor angels; concerning whom the learned Jew, Josephus, and the Platonic Constantinopolitan, Michael Psellus, may be consulted. They are very numerous, and there is no climate or element without one or more.*

And some in dreams assurèd were
Of the Spirit that plagued us so;
Nine fathom deep he had followed us
From the land of mist and snow.

And every tongue, through utter drought,
Was withered at the root;
We could not speak, no more than if
We had been choked with soot.

*The shipmates, in their sore distress, would fain throw the whole guilt on the ancient Mariner: in sign whereof they hang the dead sea-bird round his neck.*

Ah! well-a-day! what evil looks
Had I from old and young!
Instead of the cross, the Albatross
About my neck was hung.

## PART THE THIRD

There passed a weary time. Each throat
Was parched, and glazed each eye.
A weary time! a weary time!

*The ancient Mariner beholdeth a sign in the element afar off.*

How glazed each weary eye,
When looking westward, I beheld
A something in the sky.

At first it seemed a little speck,
And then it seemed a mist;
It moved and moved, and took at last
A certain shape, I wist.

A speck, a mist, a shape, I wist!
And still it neared and neared:
As if it dodged a water-sprite,
It plunged and tacked and veered.

*At its nearer ap-*
*proach, it seem-*
*eth him to be a*
*ship; and at a*
*dear ransom he*
*freeth his speech*
*from the bonds*
*of thirst.*

With throats unslaked, with black lips
　　baked,
We could nor laugh nor wail;
Through utter drought all dumb we stood!
I bit my arm, I sucked the blood,
And cried, A sail! a sail!

With throats unslaked, with black lips
　　baked,
Agape they heard me call:

*A flash of joy;*

Gramercy! they for joy did grin,
And all at once their breath drew in,
As they were drinking all.

*And horror fol-*
*lows. For can it*
*be a ship that*
*comes onward*
*without wind or*
*tide?*

See! see! (I cried) she tacks no more!
Hither to work us weal;
Without a breeze, without a tide,
She steadies with upright keel!

The western wave was all a-flame.
The day was well-nigh done!
Almost upon the western wave
Rested the broad bright Sun;
When that strange shape drove suddenly
Betwixt us and the Sun.

*It seemeth him*
*but the skeleton*
*of a ship.*

And straight the Sun was flecked with
　　bars,
(Heaven's Mother send us grace!)

As if through a dungeon-grate he peered
With broad and burning face.

Alas! (thought I, and my heart beat loud)
How fast she nears and nears!
Are those *her* sails that glance in the Sun,
Like restless gossameres?

*And its ribs are seen as bars on the face of the setting Sun. The Spectre-Woman and her Death-mate, and no other on board the skeleton-ship.*

Are those *her* ribs through which the Sun
Did peer, as through a grate?
And is that Woman all her crew?
Is that a Death? and are there two?
Is Death that woman's mate?

*Like vessel, like crew!*

*Her* lips were red, *her* looks were free,
Her locks were yellow as gold:
Her skin was as white as leprosy,
The Night-mare Life-in-Death was she,
Who thicks man's blood with cold.

*Death and Life-in-Death have diced for the ship's crew, and she (the latter) winneth the ancient Mariner.*

The naked hulk alongside came,
And the twain were casting dice;
"The game is done! I've won! I've won!"
Quoth she, and whistles thrice.

*No twilight within the courts of the Sun.*

The Sun's rim dips; the stars rush out:
At one stride comes the dark;
With far-heard whisper, o'er the sea,
Off shot the spectre-bark.

*At the rising of the Moon,*

We listened and looked sideways up!
Fear at my heart, as at a cup,
My life-blood seemed to sip!
The stars were dim, and thick the night,
The steersman's face by his lamp gleamed
　　white;
From the sails the dew did drip—

Till clomb above the eastern bar
The hornèd Moon, with one bright star
Within the nether tip.

*One after an-*
*other,*

One after one, by the star-dogged Moon,
Too quick for groan or sigh,
Each turned his face with a ghastly pang,
And cursed me with his eye.

*His shipmates*
*drop down dead.*

Four times fifty living men,
(And I heard nor sigh nor groan)
With heavy thump, a lifeless lump,
They dropped down one by one.

*But Life-in-*
*Death begins her*
*work on the an-*
*cient Mariner.*

The souls did from their bodies fly,—
They fled to bliss or woe!
And every soul, it passed me by,
Like the whizz of my cross-bow!

## PART THE FOURTH

*The Wedding-*
*Guest feareth*
*that a Spirit is*
*talking to him;*

"I fear thee, ancient Mariner!
I fear thy skinny hand!
And thou art long, and lank, and brown,
As is the ribbed sea-sand.

I fear thee and thy glittering eye,
And thy skinny hand, so brown."—

*But the ancient*
*Mariner assureth*
*him of his bodily*
*life, and pro-*
*ceedeth to relate*
*his horrible pen-*
*ance.*

Fear not, fear not, thou Wedding-Guest!
This body dropt not down.

Alone, alone, all, all alone,
Alone on a wide wide sea!
And never a saint took pity on
My soul in agony.

*He despiseth the*
*creatures of the*
*calm.*

The many men, so beautiful!
And they all dead did lie:

And a thousand thousand slimy things
Lived on; and so did I.

*And envieth that they should live, and so many lie dead.*

I looked upon the rotting sea,
And drew my eyes away;
I looked upon the rotting deck,
And there the dead men lay.

I looked to heaven, and tried to pray;
But or ever a prayer had gusht,
A wicked whisper came, and made
My heart as dry as dust.

I closed my lids, and kept them close,
And the balls like pulses beat;
For the sky and the sea, and the sea and
    the sky
Lay like a load on my weary eye,
And the dead were at my feet.

*But the curse liveth for him in the eye of the dead men.*

The cold sweat melted from their limbs,
Nor rot nor reek did they:
The look with which they looked on me
Had never passed away.

An orphan's curse would drag to hell
A spirit from on high;
But oh! more horrible than that
Is the curse in a dead man's eye!
Seven days, seven nights, I saw that curse,
And yet I could not die.

*In his loneliness and fixedness he yearneth towards the journeying Moon, and the stars that still sojourn, yet still move onward; and everywhere*

The moving Moon went up the sky
And no where did abide:
Softly she was going up,
And a star or two beside—

Her beams bemocked the sultry main,
Like April hoar-frost spread;

*the blue sky be-*
*longs to them,*
*and is their ap-*
*pointed rest, and*
*their native*

But where the ship's huge shadow lay,
The charmèd water burnt alway
A still and awful red.

*country and their own natural homes, which they enter unannounced,*
*as lords that are certainly expected and yet there is a silent joy at their*
*arrival.*

*By the light of*
*the Moon he be-*
*holdeth God's*
*creatures of the*
*great calm.*

Beyond the shadow of the ship,
I watched the water-snakes:
They moved in tracks of shining white,
And when they reared, the elfish light
Fell off in hoary flakes.

Within the shadow of the ship
I watched their rich attire:
Blue, glossy green, and velvet black,
They coiled and swam; and every track
Was a flash of golden fire.

*Their beauty*
*and their happi-*
*ness.*

O happy living things! no tongue
Their beauty might declare:
A spring of love gushed from my heart,

*He blesseth them*
*in his heart.*

And I blessed them unaware:
Sure my kind saint took pity on me,
And I blessed them unaware.

*The spell begins*
*to break.*

The self-same moment I could pray;
And from my neck so free
The Albatross fell off, and sank
Like lead into the sea.

## PART THE FIFTH

Oh sleep! it is a gentle thing,
Beloved from pole to pole!
To Mary Queen the praise be given!

She sent the gentle sleep from Heaven,
That slid into my soul.

*By grace of the
holy Mother, the
ancient Mariner
is refreshed with
rain.*

The silly buckets on the deck,
That had so long remained,
I dreamt that they were filled with dew;
And when I awoke, it rained.

My lips were wet, my throat was cold,
My garments all were dank;
Sure I had drunken in my dreams,
And still my body drank.

I moved, and could not feel my limbs:
I was so light—almost
I thought that I had died in sleep,
And was a blessèd ghost.

*He heareth
sounds and seeth
strange sights
and commotions
in the sky and
the element.*

And soon I heard a roaring wind:
It did not come anear;
But with its sound it shook the sails,
That were so thin and sere.

The upper air burst into life!
And a hundred fire-flags sheen,
To and fro they were hurried about!
And to and fro, and in and out,
The wan stars danced between.

And the coming wind did roar more loud,
And the sails did sigh like sedge;
And the rain poured down from one black
   cloud;
The Moon was at its edge.

The thick black cloud was cleft, and still
The Moon was at its side:
Like waters shot from some high crag,

The lightning fell with never a jag,
A river steep and wide.

*The bodies of
the ship's crew
are inspired and
the ship moves
on;*

The loud wind never reached the ship,
Yet now the ship moved on!
Beneath the lightning and the Moon
The dead men gave a groan.

They groaned, they stirred, they all up-
rose,
Nor spake, nor moved their eyes;
It had been strange, even in a dream,
To have seen those dead men rise.

The helmsman steered, the ship moved
on;
Yet never a breeze up-blew;
The mariners all 'gan work the ropes,
Where they were wont to do;
They raised their limbs like lifeless tools—
We were a ghastly crew.

The body of my brother's son
Stood by me, knee to knee:
The body and I pulled at one rope,
But he said nought to me.

"I fear thee, ancient Mariner!"
Be calm, thou Wedding-Guest!

*But not by the
souls of the men,
nor by dæmons
of earth or mid-
dle air, but by a
blessed troop of
angelic spirits,
sent down by
the invocation of
the guardian
saint.*

'Twas not those souls that fled in pain,
Which to their corses came again,
But a troop of spirits blest:

For when it dawned—they dropped their
arms,
And clustered round the mast;
Sweet sounds rose slowly through their
mouths,
And from their bodies passed.

Around, around, flew each sweet sound,
Then darted to the Sun;
Slowly the sounds came back again,
Now mixed, now one by one.

Sometimes a-dropping from the sky
I heard the sky-lark sing;
Sometimes all little birds that are,
How they seemed to fill the sea and air
With their sweet jargoning!

And now 'twas like all instruments,
Now like a lonely flute;
And now it is an angel's song,
That makes the heavens be mute.

It ceased; yet still the sails made on
A pleasant noise till noon,
A noise like of a hidden brook
In the leafy month of June,
That to the sleeping woods all night
Singeth a quiet tune.

Till noon we quietly sailed on,
Yet never a breeze did breathe:
Slowly and smoothly went the ship,
Moved onward from beneath.

*The lonesome Spirit from the south pole carries on the ship as far as the Line, in obedience to the angelic troop, but still requireth vengeance.*

Under the keel nine fathom deep,
From the land of mist and snow,
The spirit slid: and it was he
That made the ship to go.
The sails at noon left off their tune,
And the ship stood still also.

The Sun, right up above the mast,
Had fixed her to the ocean:

But in a minute she 'gan stir,
With a short uneasy motion—
Backwards and forwards half her length
With a short uneasy motion.

Then like a pawing horse let go,
She made a sudden bound:
It flung the blood into my head,
And I fell down in a swound.

*The Polar
Spirit's fellow-
dæmons, the in-
visible inhabit-
ants of the ele-
ment, take part
in his wrong;
and two of them
relate, one to the
other, that pen-
ance long and
heavy for the
ancient Mariner
hath been ac-
corded to the
Polar Spirit, who
returneth south-
ward.*

How long in that same fit I lay,
I have not to declare;
But ere my living life returned,
I heard and in my soul discerned
Two voices in the air.

"Is it he?" quoth one, "Is this the man?
By him who died on cross,
With his cruel bow he laid full low
The harmless Albatross.

The spirit who bideth by himself
In the land of mist and snow,
He loved the bird that loved the man
Who shot him with his bow."

The other was a softer voice,
As soft as honey-dew:
Quoth he, "The man hath penance done,
And penance more will do."

### PART THE SIXTH

#### FIRST VOICE

"But tell me, tell me! speak again,
Thy soft response renewing—
What makes that ship drive on so fast?
What is the ocean doing?"

SECOND VOICE

"Still as a slave before his lord,
The ocean hath no blast;
His great bright eye most silently
Up to the Moon is cast—

If he may know which way to go;
For she guides him smooth or grim.
See, brother, see! how graciously
She looketh down on him."

FIRST VOICE

*The Mariner
hath been cast
into a trance; for
the angelic
power causeth
the vessel to
drive northward
faster than hu-
man life could
endure.*

"But why drives on that ship so fast,
Without or wave or wind?"

SECOND VOICE

"The air is cut away before,
And closes from behind.

Fly, brother, fly! more high, more high!
Or we shall be belated:
For slow and slow that ship will go,
When the Mariner's trance is abated."

*The supernatural
motion is re-
tarded; the
Mariner awakes,
and his penance
begins anew.*

I woke, and we were sailing on
As in a gentle weather:
'Twas night, calm night, the Moon was
    high;
The dead men stood together.

All stood together on the deck,
For a charnel-dungeon fitter:
All fixed on me their stony eyes,
That in the Moon did glitter.

The pang, the curse, with which they
    died,
Had never passed away:

I could not draw my eyes from theirs,
Nor turn them up to pray.

*The curse is finally expiated.*

And now this spell was snapt: once more
I viewed the ocean green,
And looked far forth, yet little saw
Of what had else been seen—

Like one, that on a lonesome road
Doth walk in fear and dread,
And having once turned round walks on
And turns no more his head;
Because he knows, a frightful fiend
Doth close behind him tread.

But soon there breathed a wind on me,
Nor sound nor motion made:
Its path was not upon the sea,
In ripple or in shade.

It raised my hair, it fanned my cheek
Like a meadow-gale of spring—
It mingled strangely with my fears,
Yet it felt like a welcoming.

Swiftly, swiftly flew the ship,
Yet she sailed softly too:
Sweetly, sweetly blew the breeze—
On me alone it blew.

*And the ancient Mariner beholdeth his native country.*

Oh! dream of joy! is this indeed
The light-house top I see?
Is this the hill? is this the kirk?
Is this mine own countree?

We drifted o'er the harbor-bar,
And I with sobs did pray—

O let me be awake, my God!
Or let me sleep alway.

The harbor-bay was clear as glass,
So smoothly it was strewn!
And on the bay the moonlight lay,
And the shadow of the Moon.

The rock shone bright, the kirk no less,
That stands above the rock:
The moonlight steeped in silentness
The steady weathercock.

*The angelic spirits leave the dead bodies,*

And the bay was white with silent light,
Till rising from the same,
Full many shapes, that shadows were,
In crimson colors came.

*And appear in their own forms of light.*

A little distance from the prow
Those crimson shadows were:
I turned my eyes upon the deck—
Oh, Christ! what saw I there!

Each corse lay flat, lifeless and flat,
And, by the holy rood!
A man all light, a seraph-man,
On every corse there stood.

This seraph-band, each waved his hand:
It was a heavenly sight!
They stood as signals to the land,
Each one a lovely light;

This seraph-band, each waved his hand,
No voice did they impart—
No voice; but oh! the silence sank
Like music on my heart.

But soon I heard the dash of oars,
I heard the Pilot's cheer;
My head was turned perforce away,
And I saw a boat appear.

The Pilot, and the Pilot's boy.
I heard them coming fast:
Dear Lord in Heaven! it was a joy
The dead men could not blast.

I saw a third—I heard his voice:
It is the Hermit good!
He singeth loud his godly hymns
That he makes in the wood.
He'll shrieve my soul, he'll wash away
The Albatross's blood.

## PART THE SEVENTH

*The Hermit of the Wood*

This Hermit good lives in that wood
Which slopes down to the sea.
How loudly his sweet voice he rears!
He loves to talk with marineres
That come from a far countree.

He kneels at morn, and noon, and eve—
He hath a cushion plump:
It is the moss that wholly hides
The rotted old oak-stump.

The skiff-boat neared: I heard them talk,
"Why this is strange, I trow!
Where are those lights so many and fair,
That signal made but now?"

*Approacheth the ship with wonder.*

"Strange, by my faith!" the Hermit said—
"And they answered not our cheer!

The planks looked warped! and see those
    sails
How thin they are and sere!
I never saw aught like to them,
Unless perchance it were

Brown skeletons of leaves that lag
My forest-brook along;
When the ivy-tod is heavy with snow,
And the owlet whoops to the wolf below,
That eats the she-wolf's young."

"Dear Lord! it hath a fiendish look—
(The Pilot made reply)
I am a-feared"—"Push on, push on!"
Said the Hermit cheerily.

The boat came closer to the ship,
But I nor spake nor stirred;
The boat came close beneath the ship,
And straight a sound was heard.

*The ship sud-*
*denly sinketh.*

Under the water it rumbled on,
Still louder and more dread:
It reached the ship, it split the bay;
The ship went down like lead.

*The ancient*
*Mariner is saved*
*in the Pilot's*
*boat.*

Stunned by that loud and dreadful sound,
Which sky and ocean smote,
Like one that hath been seven days
    drowned
My body lay afloat;
But swift as dreams, myself I found
Within the Pilot's boat.

Upon the whirl, where sank the ship,
The boat spun round and round;

And all was still, save that the hill
Was telling of the sound.

I moved my lips—the Pilot shrieked
And fell down in a fit;
The holy Hermit raised his eyes,
And prayed where he did sit.

I took the oars: the Pilot's boy,
Who now doth crazy go,
Laughed loud and long, and all the while
His eyes went to and fro.
"Ha! ha!" quoth he, "full plain I see,
The Devil knows how to row."

And now, all in my own countree,
I stood on the firm land!
The Hermit stepped forth from the boat,
And scarcely he could stand.

*The ancient Mariner earnestly entreateth the Hermit to shrieve him; and the penance of life falls on him.*

"O shrieve me, shrieve me, holy man!"
The Hermit crossed his brow.
"Say quick," quoth he, "I bid thee say—
What manner of man art thou?"

Forthwith this frame of mine was
    wrenched
With a woeful agony,
Which forced me to begin my tale;
And then it left me free.

*And ever and anon throughout his future life an agony constraineth him to travel from land to land;*

Since then, at an uncertain hour,
That agony returns:
And till my ghastly tale is told,
This heart within me burns.

I pass, like night, from land to land;
I have strange power of speech;

That moment that his face I see,
I know the man that must hear me:
To him my tale I teach.

What loud uproar bursts from that door!
The wedding-guests are there:
But in the garden-bower the bride
And bride-maids singing are:
And hark the little vesper bell,
Which biddeth me to prayer!

O Wedding-Guest! this soul hath been
Alone on a wide wide sea:
So lonely 'twas, that God himself
Scarce seemèd there to be.

O sweeter than the marriage-feast,
'Tis sweeter far to me,
To walk together to the kirk
With a goodly company!—

To walk together to the kirk,
And all together pray,
While each to his great Father bends,
Old men, and babes, and loving friends,
And youths and maidens gay!

Farewell, farewell! but this I tell
To thee, thou Wedding-Guest!
He prayeth well, who loveth well
Both man and bird and beast.

*And to teach, by his own example, love and reverence to all things that God made and loveth.* He prayeth best, who loveth best
All things both great and small;
For the dear God who loveth us,
He made and loveth all.

The Mariner, whose eye is bright,
Whose beard with age is hoar,

Is gone: and now the Wedding-Guest
Turned from the bridegroom's door.

He went like one that hath been stunned,
And is of sense forlorn:
A sadder and a wiser man,
He rose the morrow morn.

# Kubla Khan: or, A Vision in a Dream

## A FRAGMENT

*In the summer of the year 1797, the Author, then in ill-health, had retired to a lonely farm-house between Porlock and Linton, on the Exmoor confines of Somerset and Devonshire. In consequence of a slight indisposition, an anodyne had been prescribed, from the effect of which he fell asleep in his chair at the moment he was reading the following sentence, or words of the same substance, in Purchas's* Pilgrimage: *"Here the Khan Kubla commanded a palace to be built, and a stately garden thereunto: and thus ten miles of fertile ground were inclosed with a wall." The Author continued for about three hours in a profound sleep, at least of the external senses, during which time he has the most vivid confidence, that he could not have composed less than from two to three hundred lines; if that indeed can be called composition in which all the images rose up before him as things, with a parallel production of the correspondent expressions, without any sensation or consciousness of effort. On awaking he appeared to himself to have a distinct recollection of the whole, and taking his pen, ink, and paper, instantly and eagerly wrote down the lines that are here preserved. At this moment he was unfortunately called out by a person on business from Porlock, and detained by him above an hour, and on his return to his room, found, to his no small surprise and mortification, that though he still retained some vague and dim recollection of the general purport of the vision, yet, with the exception of some eight or ten scattered lines and images, all the rest had passed away like the images on the surface of a stream into which a stone had been cast, but, alas! without the after restoration of the latter:*

> Then all the charm
> Is broken—all that phantom-world so fair,
> Vanishes, and a thousand circlets spread,
> And each mis-shape[s] the other. Stay awhile,
> Poor youth! who scarcely dar'st lift up thine eyes—
> The stream will soon renew its smoothness, soon
> The visions will return! And lo! he stays,
> And soon the fragments dim of lovely forms
> Come trembling back, unite, and now once more
> The pool becomes a mirror.

[From "The Picture"]

*Yet from the still surviving recollections in his mind, the Author has frequently purposed to finish for himself what had been originally, as it were, given to him Αὔριον ἄδιον ἄσω: but the to-morrow is yet to come.*

In Xanadu did Kubla Khan
A stately pleasure-dome decree:
Where Alph, the sacred river, ran
Through caverns measureless to man
   Down to a sunless sea.
So twice five miles of fertile ground
With walls and towers were girdled round:
And there were gardens bright with sinuous rills,
Where blossomed many an incense-bearing tree;
And here were forests ancient as the hills,
Enfolding sunny spots of greenery.

But oh! that deep romantic chasm which slanted
Down the green hill athwart a cedarn cover!
A savage place! as holy and enchanted
As e'er beneath a waning moon was haunted

By woman wailing for her demon-lover!
And from this chasm, with ceaseless turmoil seething,
As if this earth in fast thick pants were breathing,
A mighty fountain momently was forced:
Amid whose swift half-intermitted burst
Huge fragments vaulted like rebounding hail,
Or chaffy grain beneath the thresher's flail:
And 'mid these dancing rocks at once and ever
It flung up momently the sacred river.
Five miles meandering with a mazy motion
Through wood and dale the sacred river ran,
Then reached the caverns measureless to man,
And sank in tumult to a lifeless ocean:
And 'mid this tumult Kubla heard from far
Ancestral voices prophesying war!
    The shadow of the dome of pleasure
    Floated midway on the waves;
    Where was heard the mingled measure
    From the fountain and the caves.
It was a miracle of rare device,
A sunny pleasure-dome with caves of ice!

    A damsel with a dulcimer
    In a vision once I saw:
    It was an Abyssinian maid,
    And on her dulcimer she played,
    Singing of Mount Abora.
Could I revive within me
    Her symphony and song,
    To such a deep delight 'twould win me,
That with music loud and long,
I would build that dome in air,
That sunny dome! those caves of ice!
And all who heard should see them there,
And all should cry, Beware! Beware!

His flashing eyes, his floating hair!
Weave a circle round him thrice,
And close your eyes with holy dread,
For he on honey-dew hath fed,
And drunk the milk of Paradise.


## Dejection: An Ode

Late, late yestreen I saw the new Moon,
With the old Moon in her arms:
And I fear, I fear, my Master dear!
We shall have a deadly storm.
            *Ballad of Sir Patrick Spence.*

Well! If the Bard was weather-wise, who made
   The grand old ballad of Sir Patrick Spence,
   This night, so tranquil now, will not go hence
Unroused by winds, that ply a busier trade
Than those which mold yon cloud in lazy flakes,
Or the dull sobbing draft, that moans and rakes
Upon the strings of this Æolian lute,
      Which bettter far were mute.
   For lo! the new-moon winter-bright!
   And overspread with phantom light,
   (With swimming phantom light o'erspread
   But rimmed and circled by a silver thread)
I see the old moon in her lap, foretelling
   The coming-on of rain and squally blast.
And oh! that even now the gust were swelling,
   And the slant night-shower driving loud and fast!
Those sounds which oft have raised me, whilst they
      awed,
      And sent my soul abroad,

Might now perhaps their wonted impulse give,
Might startle this dull pain, and make it move and live!

A grief without a pang, void, dark, and drear,
  A stifled, drowsy, unimpassioned grief,
  Which finds no natural outlet, no relief,
    In word, or sigh, or tear—
O Lady! in this wan and heartless mood,
To other thoughts by yonder throstle wooed,
  All this long eve, so balmy and serene,
Have I been gazing on the western sky,
  And its peculiar tint of yellow green:
And still I gaze—and with how blank an eye!
And those thin clouds above, in flakes and bars,
That give away their motion to the stars;
Those stars, that glide behind them or between,
Now sparkling, now bedimmed, but always seen:
Yon crescent Moon, as fixed as if it grew
In its own cloudless, starless lake of blue;
I see them all so excellently fair,
I see, not feel, how beautiful they are!

    My genial spirits fail;
    And what can these avail
To lift the smothering weight from off my breast?
    It were a vain endeavor,
    Though I should gaze forever
On that green light that lingers in the west:
I may not hope from outward forms to win
The passion and the life, whose fountains are within.

O Lady! we receive but what we give,
And in our life alone does Nature live:
Ours is her wedding garment, ours her shroud!
  And would we aught behold, of higher worth,
Than that inanimate cold world allowed

To the poor loveless ever-anxious crowd,
    Ah! from the soul itself must issue forth
A light, a glory, a fair luminous cloud
    Enveloping the Earth—
And from the soul itself must there be sent
    A sweet and potent voice, of its own birth,
Of all sweet sounds the life and element!

O pure of heart! thou need'st not ask of me
What this strong music in the soul may be!
What, and wherein it doth exist,
This light, this glory, this fair luminous mist,
This beautiful and beauty-making power.
    Joy, virtuous lady! Joy that ne'er was given,
Save to the pure, and in their purest hour,
Life, and Life's effluence, cloud at once and shower,
Joy, Lady! is the spirit and the power,
Which wedding Nature to us gives in dower
    A new Earth and new Heaven,
Undreamt of by the sensual and the proud—
Joy is the sweet voice, Joy the luminous cloud—
    We in ourselves rejoice!
And thence flows all that charms or ear or sight,
    All melodies the echoes of that voice,
All colors a suffusion from that light.

There was a time when, though my path was rough,
    This joy within me dallied with distress,
And all misfortunes were but as the stuff
    Whence Fancy made me dreams of happiness:
For hope grew round me, like the twining vine,
And fruits, and foliage, not my own, seemed mine.
But now afflictions bow me down to earth:
Nor care I that they rob me of my mirth;
    But oh! each visitation
Suspends what nature gave me at my birth,

My shaping spirit of Imagination.
For not to think of what I needs must feel,
    But to be still and patient, all I can;
And haply by abstruse research to steal
    From my own nature all the natural man—
    This was my sole resource, my only plan:
Till that which suits a part infects the whole,
And now is almost grown the habit of my soul.


Hence, viper thoughts, that coil around my mind
      Reality's dark dream!
I turn from you, and listen to the wind,
    Which long has raved unnoticed. What a scream
Of agony by torture lengthened out
That lute sent forth! Thou Wind, that rav'st without,
Bare crag, or mountain-tairn, or blasted tree,
Or pine-grove whither woodman never clomb,
Or lonely house, long held the witches' home,
    Methinks were fitter instruments for thee,
Mad Lutanist! who in this month of showers,
Of dark-brown gardens, and of peeping flowers,
Mak'st Devils' yule, with worse than wintry song,
The blossoms, buds, and timorous leaves among.
    Thou Actor, perfect in all tragic sounds!
Thou mighty Poet, e'en to frenzy bold!
      What tell'st thou now about?
     'Tis of the rushing of an host in rout,
With groans, of trampled men, with smarting
      wounds—
At once they groan with pain, and shudder with the
      cold!
But hush! there is a pause of deepest silence!
And all that noise, as of a rushing crowd,
With groans, and tremulous shudderings—all is over—
    It tells another tale, with sounds less deep and loud!

A tale of less affright,
And tempered with delight,
As Otway's self had framed the tender lay,—
'Tis of a little child
Upon a lonesome wild,
Not far from home, but she hath lost her way:
And now moans low in bitter grief and fear,
And now screams loud, and hopes to make her mother
        hear.

'Tis midnight, but small thoughts have I of sleep:
Full seldom may my friend such vigils keep!
Visit her, gentle Sleep! with wings of healing,
    And may this storm be but a mountain-birth,
May all the stars hang bright above her dwelling,
    Silent as though they watched the sleeping Earth!
        With light heart may she rise,
        Gay fancy, cheerful eyes,
    Joy lift her spirit, joy attune her voice;
To her may all things live, from pole to pole,
Their life the eddying of her living soul!
    O simple spirit, guided from above,
Dear Lady! friend devoutest of my choice,
Thus mayest thou ever, evermore rejoice.


## This Lime-Tree Bower My Prison

### ADDRESSED TO CHARLES LAMB,
### OF THE INDIA HOUSE, LONDON

*In the June of 1797 some long-expected friends paid a visit
to the author's cottage; and on the morning of their arrival,
he met with an accident, which disabled him from walking
during the whole time of their stay. One evening, when they*

*had left him for a few hours, he composed the following lines in the garden-bower.*

Well, they are gone, and here must I remain,
This lime-tree bower my prison! I have lost
Beauties and feelings, such as would have been
Most sweet to my remembrance even when age
Had dimmed mine eyes to blindness! They, meanwhile,
Friends, whom I never more may meet again,
On springy heath, along the hill-top edge,
Wander in gladness, and wind down, perchance,
To that still roaring dell, of which I told;
The roaring dell, o'erwooded, narrow, deep,
And only speckled by the mid-day sun;
Where its slim trunk the ash from rock to rock
Flings arching like a bridge;—that branchless ash,
Unsunned and damp, whose few poor yellow leaves
Ne'er tremble in the gale, yet tremble still,
Fanned by the water-fall! and there my friends
Behold the dark green file of long lank weeds,
That all at once (a most fantastic sight!)
Still nod and drip beneath the dripping edge
Of the blue clay-stone.

        Now, my friends emerge
Beneath the wide wide Heaven—and view again
The many-steepled tract magnificent
Of hilly fields and meadows, and the sea,
With some fair bark, perhaps, whose sails light up
The slip of smooth clear blue betwixt two Isles
Of purple shadow! Yes! they wander on
In gladness all; but thou, methinks, most glad,
My gentle-hearted Charles! for thou hast pined
And hungered after Nature, many a year,
In the great City pent, winning thy way
With sad yet patient soul, through evil and pain

And strange calamity! Ah! slowly sink
Behind the western ridge, thou glorious Sun!
Shine in the slant beams of the sinking orb,
Ye purple heath-flowers! richlier burn, ye clouds!
Live in the yellow light, ye distant groves!
And kindle, thou blue Ocean! So my friend
Struck with deep joy, may stand, as I have stood,
Silent with swimming sense; yea, gazing round
On the wide landscape, gaze till all doth seem
Less gross than bodily, and of such hues
As veil the Almighty Spirit, when yet he makes
Spirits perceive his presence.

                    A delight
Comes sudden on my heart, and I am glad
As I myself were there! Nor in this bower,
This little lime-tree bower, have I not marked
Much that has soothed me. Pale beneath the blaze
Hung the transparent foliage; and I watched
Some broad and sunny leaf, and loved to see
The shadow of the leaf and stem above
Dappling its sunshine! And that walnut-tree
Was richly tinged, and a deep radiance lay
Full on the ancient ivy, which usurps
Those fronting elms, and now, with blackest mass
Makes their dark branches gleam a lighter hue
Through the late twilight: and though now the bat
Wheels silent by, and not a swallow twitters,
Yet still the solitary humble-bee
Sings in the bean-flower! Henceforth I shall know
That Nature ne'er deserts the wise and pure;
No plot so narrow, be but Nature there,
No waste so vacant, but may well employ
Each faculty of sense, and keep the heart
Awake to Love and Beauty! and sometimes

'Tis well to be bereft of promised good,
That we may lift the soul, and contemplate
With lively joy the joys we cannot share.
My gentle-hearted Charles! when the last rook
Beat its straight path along the dusky air
Homewards, I blest it! deeming its black wing
(Now a dim speck, now vanishing in light)
Had crossed the mighty Orb's dilated glory,
While thou stood'st gazing; or, when all was still,
Flew creeking o'er thy head, and had a charm
For thee, my gentle-hearted Charles, to whom
No sound is dissonant which tells of Life.

## Frost at Midnight

The frost performs its secret ministry,
Unhelped by any wind. The owlet's cry
Came loud—and hark, again! loud as before.
The inmates of my cottage, all at rest,
Have left me to that solitude, which suits
Abstruser musings: save that at my side
My cradled infant slumbers peacefully.
'Tis calm indeed! so calm, that it disturbs
And vexes meditation with its strange
And extreme silentncss. Sea, hill, and wood,
This populous village! Sea, and hill, and wood,
With all the numberless goings-on of life,
Inaudible as dreams! the thin blue flame
Lies on my low-burnt fire, and quivers not;
Only that film, which fluttered on the grate,
Still flutters there, the sole unquiet thing.
Methinks, its motion in this hush of nature
Gives it dim sympathies with me who live,

Making it a companionable form,
Whose puny flaps and freaks the idling Spirit
By its own moods interprets, everywhere
Echo or mirror seeking of itself,
And makes a toy of Thought.

                     But O! how oft,
How oft, at school, with most believing mind,
Presageful, have I gazed upon the bars,
To watch that fluttering stranger! and as oft
With unclosed lids, already had I dreamt
Of my sweet birth-place, and the old church-tower,
Whose bells, the poor man's only music, rang
From morn to evening, all the hot Fair-day,
So sweetly, that they stirred and haunted me
With a wild pleasure, falling on mine ear
Most like articulate sounds of things to come!
So gazed I, till the soothing things, I dreamt,
Lulled me to sleep, and sleep prolonged my dreams!
And so I brooded all the following morn,
Awed by the stern preceptor's face, mine eye
Fixed with mock study on my swimming book:
Save if the door half opened, and I snatched
A hasty glance, and still my heart leaped up,
For still I hoped to see the *stranger's* face,
Townsman, or aunt, or sister more beloved,
My playmate when we both were clothed alike!

Dear Babe, that sleepest cradled by my side,
Whose gentle breathings, heard in this deep calm,
Fill up the interspersèd vacancies
And momentary pauses of the thought!
My babe so beautiful! it thrills my heart
With tender gladness, thus to look at thee,
And think that thou shalt learn far other lore,
And in far other scenes! For I was reared

In the great city, pent 'mid cloisters dim,
And saw nought lovely but the sky and stars.
But *thou,* my babe! shalt wander like a breeze
By lakes and sandy shores, beneath the crags
Of ancient mountain, and beneath the clouds,
Which image in their bulk both lakes and shores
And mountain crags: so shalt thou see and hear
The lovely shapes and sounds intelligible
Of that eternal language, which thy God
Utters, who from eternity doth teach
Himself in all, and all things in himself.
Great universal Teacher! he shall mold
Thy spirit, and by giving make it ask.

Therefore all seasons shall be sweet to thee,
Whether the summer clothe the general earth
With greenness, or the redbreast sit and sing
Betwixt the tufts of snow on the bare branch
Of mossy apple-tree, while the nigh thatch
Smokes in the sun-thaw; whether the evedrops fall
Heard only in the trances of the blast,
Or if the secret ministry of frost
Shall hang them up in silent icicles,
Quietly shining to the quiet Moon.

# William Wordsworth

(1770–1850)

## There was a Boy

There was a Boy; ye knew him well, ye cliffs
And islands of Winander!—many a time,
At evening, when the earliest stars began
To move along the edges of the hills,
Rising or setting, would he stand alone,
Beneath the trees, or by the glimmering lake;
And there, with fingers interwoven, both hands
Pressed closely palm to palm and to his mouth
Uplifted, he, as through an instrument,
Blew mimic hootings to the silent owls,
That they might answer him.—And they would shout
Across the watery vale, and shout again,
Responsive to his call,—with quivering peals,
And long halloos, and screams, and echoes loud
Redoubled and redoubled; concourse wild
Of jocund din! And, when there came a pause
Of silence such as baffled his best skill:
Then, sometimes, in that silence, while he hung
Listening, a gentle shock of mild surprise
Has carried far into his heart the voice
Of mountain-torrents; or the visible scene
Would enter unawares into his mind
With all its solemn imagery, its rocks,
Its woods, and that uncertain heaven received
Into the bosom of the steady lake.

   This boy was taken from his mates, and died
In childhood, ere he was full twelve years old.
Pre-eminent in beauty is the vale
Where he was born and bred: the church-yard hangs
Upon a slope above the village-school;
And, through that church-yard when my way has led
On summer-evenings, I believe that there
A long half-hour together I have stood
Mute—looking at the grave in which he lies!


## To H. C.

### SIX YEARS OLD

O Thou! whose fancies from afar are brought;
Who of thy words dost make a mock apparel,
And fittest to unutterable thought
The breeze-like motion and the self-born carol:
Thou faery voyager! that dost float
In such clear water, that thy boat
May rather seem
To brood on air than on an earthly stream;
Suspended in a stream as clear as sky,
Where earth and heaven do make one imagery;
O blessed vision! happy child!
Thou art so exquisitely wild,
I think of thee with many fears
For what may be thy lot in future years.
   I thought of times when Pain might be thy guest,
Lord of thy house and hospitality;
And Grief, uneasy lover! never rest
But when she sate within the touch of thee.
O too industrious folly!
O vain and causeless melancholy!

Nature will either end thee quite;
Or, lengthening out thy season of delight,
Preserve for thee, by individual right,
A young lamb's heart among the full-grown flocks.
What hast thou to do with sorrow,
Or the injuries of to-morrow?
Thou art a dew-drop, which the morn brings forth,
Ill fitted to sustain unkindly shocks,
Or to be trailed along the soiling earth;
A gem that glitters while it lives,
And no forewarning gives;
But, at the touch of wrong, without a strife
Slips in a moment out of life.


## *It is a beauteous evening, calm and free*

It is a beauteous evening, calm and free,
The holy time is quiet as a Nun
Breathless with adoration; the broad sun
Is sinking down in its tranquillity;
The gentleness of heaven broods o'er the Sea:
Listen! the mighty Being is awake,
And doth with his eternal motion make
A sound like thunder—everlastingly.
Dear Child! dear Girl! that walkest with me here,
If thou appear untouched by solemn thought,
Thy nature is not therefore less divine:
Thou liest in Abraham's bosom all the year;
And worshipp'st at the Temple's inner shrine,
God being with thee when we know it not.

## *The world is too much with us*

The world is too much with us; late and soon,
Getting and spending, we lay waste our powers:
Little we see in Nature that is ours;
We have given our hearts away, a sordid boon!
This Sea that bares her bosom to the moon;
The winds that will be howling at all hours,
And are up-gathered now like sleeping flowers;
For this, for everything, we are out of tune;
It moves us not.—Great God! I'd rather be
A Pagan suckled in a creed outworn;
So might I, standing on this pleasant lea,
Have glimpses that would make me less forlorn;
Have sight of Proteus rising from the sea;
Or hear old Triton blow his wreathèd horn.

## *Composed upon Westminster Bridge*
### *September 3, 1802*

Earth has not anything to show more fair:
Dull would he be of soul who could pass by
A sight so touching in its majesty:
This City now doth, like a garment, wear
The beauty of the morning; silent, bare,
Ships, towers, domes, theatres, and temples lie
Open unto the fields, and to the sky;
All bright and glittering in the smokeless air.
Never did sun more beautifully steep

In his first splendour, valley, rock, or hill;
Ne'er saw I, never felt, a calm so deep!
The river glideth at his own sweet will:
Dear God! the very houses seem asleep;
And all that mighty heart is lying still!


## London, 1802

Milton! thou shouldst be living at this hour:
England hath need of thee: she is a fen
Of stagnant waters: altar, sword, and pen,
Fireside, the heroic wealth of hall and bower,
Have forfeited their ancient English dower
Of inward happiness. We are selfish men;
Oh! raise us up, return to us again;
And give us manners, virtue, freedom, power.
Thy soul was like a Star, and dwelt apart;
Thou hadst a voice whose sound was like the sea:
Pure as the naked heavens, majestic, free,
So didst thou travel on life's common way,
In cheerful godliness; and yet thy heart
The lowliest duties on herself did lay.


## Where lies the Land

Where lies the Land to which yon Ship must go?
Fresh as a lark mounting at break of day,
Festively she puts forth in trim array;
Is she for tropic suns, or polar snow?
What boots the enquiry?—Neither friend nor foe

She cares for; let her travel where she may,
She finds familiar names, a beaten way
Ever before her, and a wind to blow.
Yet still I ask, what haven is her mark?
And, almost as it was when ships were rare,
(From time to time, like Pilgrims, here and there
Crossing the waters) doubt, and something dark,
Of the old Sea some reverential fear,
Is with me at thy farewell, joyous Bark!


## Ruth

When Ruth was left half desolate,
Her Father took another Mate;
And Ruth, not seven years old,
A slighted child, at her own will
Went wandering over dale and hill,
In thoughtless freedom, bold.

And she had made a pipe of straw,
And music from that pipe could draw
Like sounds of winds and floods;
Had built a bower upon the green,
As if she from her birth had been
An infant of the woods.

Beneath her father's roof, alone
She seemed to live; her thoughts her own;
Herself her own delight;
Pleased with herself, nor sad, nor gay;
And, passing thus the live-long day,
She grew to woman's height.

There came a Youth from Georgia's shore—
A military casque he wore,

With splendid feathers drest;
He brought them from the Cherokees;
The feathers nodded in the breeze,
And made a gallant crest.

From Indian blood you deem him sprung:
But no! he spake the English tongue,
And bore a soldier's name;
And, when America was free
From battle and from jeopardy,
He 'cross the ocean came.

With hues of genius on his cheek
In finest tones the Youth could speak:
—While he was yet a boy,
The moon, the glory of the sun,
And streams that murmur as they run,
Had been his dearest joy.

He was a lovely Youth! I guess
The panther in the wilderness
Was not so fair as he;
And, when he chose to sport and play,
No dolphin ever was so gay
Upon the tropic sea.

Among the Indians he had fought
And with him many tales he brought
Of pleasure and of fear;
Such tales as told to any maid
By such a Youth, in the green shade,
Were perilous to hear.

He told of girls—a happy rout!
Who quit their fold with dance and shout,
Their pleasant Indian town,
To gather strawberries all day long;

Returning with a choral song
When daylight is gone down.

He spake of plants that hourly change
Their blossoms, through a boundless range
Of intermingling hues;
With budding, fading, faded flowers
They stand the wonder of the bowers
From morn to evening dews.

He told of the magnolia, spread
High as a cloud, high over head!
The cypress and her spire;
—Of flowers that with one scarlet gleam
Cover a hundred leagues, and seem
To set the hills on fire.

The Youth of green savannas spake,
And many an endless, endless lake,
With all its fairy crowds
Of islands, that together lie
As quietly as spots of sky
Among the evening clouds.

"How pleasant," then he said, "it were,
A fisher or a hunter there,
In sunshine or in shade
To wander with an easy mind;
And build a household fire, and find
A home in every glade!

"What days and what bright years! Ah me!
Our life were life indeed, with thee
So passed in quiet bliss,
And all the while," said he, "to know
That we were in a world of woe,
On such an earth as this!"

And then he sometimes interwove
Fond thoughts about a father's love:
"For there," said he, "are spun
Around the heart such tender ties,
That our own children to our eyes
Are dearer than the sun.

"Sweet Ruth! and could you go with me
My helpmate in the woods to be,
Our shed at night to rear;
Or run, my own adopted bride,
A silvan huntress at my side,
And drive the flying deer!

"Beloved Ruth!"—No more he said.
The wakeful Ruth at midnight shed
A solitary tear.
She thought again—and did agree
With him to sail across the sea,
And drive the flying deer.

"And now, as fitting is and right,
We in the church our faith will plight,
A husband and a wife."
Even so they did; and I may say
That to sweet Ruth that happy day
Was more than human life.

Through dream and vision did she sink,
Delighted all the while to think
That on those lonesome floods
And green savannas, she should share
His board with lawful joy, and bear
His name in the wild woods.

But, as you have before been told,
This Stripling, sportive, gay, and bold,

And, with his dancing crest,
So beautiful, through savage lands
Had roamed about, with vagrant bands
Of Indians in the West.

The wind, the tempest roaring high,
The tumult of a tropic sky,
Might well be dangerous food
For him, a Youth to whom was given
So much of earth—so much of heaven,
And such impetuous blood.

Whatever in those climes he found
Irregular in sight or sound
Did to his mind impart
A kindred impulse, seemed allied
To his own powers, and justified
The workings of his heart.

Nor less, to feed voluptuous thought,
The beauteous forms of nature wrought,
Fair trees and gorgeous flowers;
The breezes their own languor lent;
The stars had feelings, which they sent
Into those favored bowers.

Yet, in his worst pursuits I ween
That sometimes there did intervene
Pure hopes of high intent;
For passions linked to forms so fair
And stately needs must have their share
Of noble sentiment.

But ill he lived, much evil saw,
With men to whom no better law
Nor better life was known;
Deliberately, and undeceived,

Those wild men's vices he received,
And gave them back his own.

His genius and his moral frame
Were thus impaired, and he became
The slave of low desires—
A Man who without self-control
Would seek what the degraded soul
Unworthily admires.

And yet he with no feigned delight
Had wooed the Maiden, day and night
Had loved her, night and morn.
What could he less than love a Maid
Whose heart with so much nature played?
So kind and so forlorn!

Sometimes, most earnestly, he said,
"O Ruth! I have been worse than dead;
False thoughts, thoughts bold and vain,
Encompassed me on every side
When I, in confidence and pride,
Had crossed the Atlantic main.

"Before me shone a glorious world—
Fresh as a banner bright, unfurled
To music suddenly.
I looked upon those hills and plains,
And seemed as if let loose from chains,
To live at liberty.

"No more of this; for now, by thee
Dear Ruth! more happily set free
With nobler zeal I burn;
My soul from darkness is released,
Like the whole sky when to the east
The morning doth return."

Full soon that better mind was gone;
No hope, no wish remained, not one,—
They stirred him now no more;
New objects did new pleasure give,
And once again he wished to live
As lawless as before.

Meanwhile, as thus with him it fared,
They for the voyage were prepared,
And went to the sea-shore,
But, when they thither came, the Youth
Deserted his poor Bride, and Ruth
Could never find him more.

God help thee, Ruth!—Such pains she had,
That she in half a year was mad,
And in a prison housed;
And there, with many a doleful song
Made of wild words, her cup of wrong
She fearfully caroused.

Yet sometimes milder hours she knew,
Nor wanted sun, nor rain, nor dew,
Nor pastimes of the May;
—They all were with her in her cell;
And a clear brook with cheerful knell
Did o'er the pebbles play.

When Ruth three seasons thus had lain,
There came a respite to her pain;
She from her prison fled;
But of the Vagrant none took thought;
And where it liked her best she sought
Her shelter and her bread.

Among the fields she breathed again;
The master-current of her brain

Ran permanent and free;
And, coming to the Banks of Tone,
There did she rest; and dwell alone
Under the greenwood tree.

The engines of her pain, the tools
That shaped her sorrow, rocks and pools,
And airs that gently stir
The vernal leaves—she loved them still;
Nor ever taxed them with the ill
Which had been done to her.

A barn her *winter* bed supplies;
But, till the warmth of summer skies
And summer days is gone
(And all do in this tale agree),
She sleeps beneath the greenwood tree,
And other home hath none.

An innocent life, yet far astray!
And Ruth will, long before her day,
Be broken down and old.
Sore aches she needs must have! but less
Of mind than body's wretchedness,
From damp, and rain, and cold.

If she is prest by want of food,
She from her dwelling in the wood
Repairs to a road-side;
And there she begs at one steep place
Where up and down with easy pace
The horsemen-travellers ride.

That oaten pipe of hers is mute,
Or thrown away; but with a flute
Her loneliness she cheers:
This flute, made of a hemlock stalk,

At evening in his homeward walk
The Quantock woodman hears.

I, too, have passed her on the hills
Setting her little water-mills
By spouts and fountains wild—
Such small machinery as she turned
Ere she had wept, ere she had mourned,
A young and happy Child!

Farewell! and when thy days are told,
Ill-fated Ruth, in hallowed mould
Thy corpse shall buried be,
For thee a funeral bell shall ring,
And all the congregation sing
A Christian psalm for thee.

## Resolution and Independence

There was a roaring in the wind all night;
The rain came heavily and fell in floods;
But now the sun is rising calm and bright;
The birds are singing in the distant woods;
Over his own sweet voice the Stock-dove broods;
The Jay makes answer as the Magpie chatters;
And all the air is filled with pleasant noise of waters.

All things that love the sun are out of doors;
The sky rejoices in the morning's birth;
The grass is bright with rain-drops;—on the moors
The hare is running races in her mirth;
And with her feet she from the plashy earth
Raises a mist, that, glittering in the sun,
Runs with her all the way, wherever she doth run.

I was a Traveller then upon the moor;
I saw the hare that raced about with joy;
I heard the woods and distant waters roar;
Or heard them not, as happy as a boy:
The pleasant season did my heart employ:
My old remembrances went from me wholly;
And all the ways of men, so vain and melancholy.

But, as it sometimes chanceth, from the might
Of joy in minds that can no further go,
As high as we have mounted in delight
In our dejection do we sink as low;
To me that morning did it happen so;
And fears and fancies thick upon me came;
Dim sadness—and blind thoughts, I knew not, nor could
    name.

I heard the sky-lark warbling in the sky;
And I bethought me of the playful hare:
Even such a happy Child of earth am I;
Even as these blissful creatures do I fare;
Far from the world I walk, and from all care;
But there may come another day to me—
Solitude, pain of heart, distress, and poverty.

My whole life I have lived in pleasant thought,
As if life's business were a summer mood;
As if all needful things would come unsought
To genial faith, still rich in genial good;
But how can He expect that others should
Build for him, sow for him, and at his call
Love him, who for himself will take no heed at all?

I thought of Chatterton, the marvellous Boy,
The sleepless Soul that perished in his pride;
Of Him who walked in glory and in joy
Following his plough, along the mountain-side:

By our own spirits are we deified:
We Poets in our youth begin in gladness;
But thereof come in the end despondency and madness.

Now, whether it were by peculiar grace,
A leading from above, a something given,
Yet it befell that, in this lonely place,
When I with these untoward thoughts had striven,
Beside a pool bare to the eye of heaven
I saw a Man before me unawares:
The oldest man he seemed that ever wore grey hairs.

As a huge stone is sometimes seen to lie
Couched on the bald top of an eminence;
Wonder to all who do the same espy,
By what means it could thither come, and whence;
So that it seems a thing endued with sense:
Like a sea-beast crawled forth, that on a shelf
Of rock or sand reposeth, there to sun itself;

Such seemed this man, not all alive nor dead,
Nor all asleep—in his extreme old age:
His body was bent double, feet and head
Coming together in life's pilgrimage;
As if some dire constraint of pain, or rage
Of sickness felt by him in times long past,
A more than human weight upon his frame had cast.

Himself he propped, limbs, body, and pale face,
Upon a long grey staff of shaven wood:
And, still as I drew near with gentle pace,
Upon the margin of that moorish flood
Motionless as a cloud the old Man stood,
That heareth not the loud winds when they call;
And moveth all together, if it move at all.

At length, himself unsettling, he the pond
Stirred with his staff, and fixedly did look

Upon the muddy water, which he conned,
As if he had been reading in a book:
And now a stranger's privilege I took;
And, drawing to his side, to him did say,
"This morning gives us promise of a glorious day."

A gentle answer did the old Man make,
In courteous speech which forth he slowly drew:
And him with further words I thus bespake,
"What occupation do you there pursue?
This is a lonesome place for one like you."
Ere he replied, a flash of mild surprise
Broke from the sable orbs of his yet-vivid eyes.

His words came feebly, from a feeble chest,
But each in solemn order followed each,
With something of a lofty utterance drest—
Choice word and measured phrase, above the reach
Of ordinary men; a stately speech;
Such as grave Livers do in Scotland use,
Religious men, who give to God and man their dues.

He told that to these waters he had come
To gather leeches, being old and poor:
Employment hazardous and wearisome!
And he had many hardships to endure:
From pond to pond he roamed, from moor to moor;
Housing, with God's good help, by choice or chance;
And in this way he gained an honest maintenance.

The old Man still stood talking by my side;
But now his voice to me was like a stream
Scarce heard; nor word from word could I divide;
And the whole body of the Man did seem
Like one whom I had met with in a dream;
Or like a man from some far region sent,
To give me human strength, by apt admonishment.

My former thoughts returned: the fear that kills;
And hope that is unwilling to be fed:
Cold, pain, and labour, and all fleshly ills;
And mighty Poets in their misery dead.
—Perplexed, and longing to be comforted,
My question eagerly did I renew,
"How is it that you live, and what is it you do?"

He with a smile did then his words repeat;
And said that, gathering leeches, far and wide
He travelled; stirring thus about his feet
The waters of the pools where they abide.
"Once I could meet with them on every side;
But they have dwindled long by slow decay;
Yet still I persevere, and find them where I may."

While he was talking thus, the lonely place,
The old Man's shape, and speech—all troubled me:
In my mind's eye I seemed to see him pace
About the weary moors continually,
Wandering about alone and silently.
While I these thoughts within myself pursued,
He, having made a pause, the same discourse renewed.

And soon with this he other matter blended,
Cheerfully uttered, with demeanour kind,
But stately in the main; and, when he ended,
I could have laughed myself to scorn to find
In that decrepit Man so firm a mind.
"God," said I, "be my help and stay secure;
I'll think of the Leech-gatherer on the lonely moor!"

## The Affliction of Margaret

Where art thou, my beloved Son,
Where art thou, worse to me than dead?
Oh find me, prosperous or undone!
Or, if the grave be now thy bed,
Why am I ignorant of the same
That I may rest; and neither blame
Nor sorrow may attend thy name?

Seven years, alas! to have received
No tidings of an only child;
To have despaired, have hoped, believed,
And been for evermore beguiled;
Sometimes with thoughts of very bliss!
I catch at them, and then I miss;
Was ever darkness like to this?

He was among the prime in worth,
An object beauteous to behold;
Well born, well bred; I sent him forth
Ingenuous, innocent, and bold:
If things ensued that wanted grace,
As hath been said, they were not base;
And never blush was on my face.

Ah! little doth the young-one dream,
When full of play and childish cares,
What power is in his wildest scream,
Heard by his mother unawares!
He knows it not, he cannot guess;
Years to a mother bring distress;
But do not make her love the less.

Neglect me! no, I suffered long
From that ill thought; and, being blind,
Said, "Pride shall help me in my wrong:
Kind mother have I been, as kind
As ever breathed": and that is true;
I've wet my path with tears like dew,
Weeping for him when no one knew.

My Son, if thou be humbled, poor,
Hopeless of honour and of gain,
Oh! do not dread thy mother's door;
Think not of me with grief and pain:
I now can see with better eyes;
And worldly grandeur I despise,
And fortune with her gifts and lies.

Alas! the fowls of heaven have wings,
And blasts of heaven will aid their flight;
They mount—how short a voyage brings
The wanderers back to their delight!
Chains tie us down by land and sea;
And wishes, vain as mine, may be
All that is left to comfort thee.

Perhaps some dungeon hears thee groan,
Maimed, mangled by inhuman men;
Or thou upon a desert thrown
Inheritest the lion's den;
Or hast been summoned to the deep,
Thou, thou and all thy mates, to keep
An incommunicable sleep.

I look for ghosts; but none will force
Their way to me: 'tis falsely said
That there was ever intercourse
Between the living and the dead;
For, surely, then I should have sight

Of him I wait for day and night,
With love and longings infinite.

My apprehensions come in crowds;
I dread the rustling of the grass;
The very shadows of the clouds
Have power to shake me as they pass:
I question things and do not find
One that will answer to my mind;
And all the world appears unkind.

Beyond participation lie
My troubles, and beyond relief:
If any chance to heave a sigh,
They pity me, and not my grief.
Then come to me, my Son, or send
Some tidings that my woes may end;
I have no other earthly friend!

## Three years she grew in sun and shower

Three years she grew in sun and shower,
Then Nature said, "A lovelier flower
On earth was never sown;
This Child I to myself will take;
She shall be mine, and I will make
A Lady of my own.

"Myself will to my darling be
Both law and impulse: and with me
The Girl, in rock and plain,
In earth and heaven, in glade and bower,
Shall feel an overseeing power
To kindle or restrain.

"She shall be sportive as the fawn
That wild with glee across the lawn,
Or up the mountain springs;
And hers shall be the breathing balm,
And hers the silence and the calm
Of mute insensate things.

"The floating clouds their state shall lend
To her; for her the willow bend;
Nor shall she fail to see
Even in the motions of the Storm
Grace that shall mould the Maiden's form
By silent sympathy.

"The stars of midnight shall be dear
To her; and she shall lean her ear
In many a secret place
Where rivulets dance their wayward round,
And beauty born of murmuring sound
Shall pass into her face.

"And vital feelings of delight
Shall rear her form to stately height,
Her virgin bosom swell;
Such thoughts to Lucy I will give
While she and I together live
Here in this happy dell."

Thus Nature spake—The work was done—
How soon my Lucy's race was run!
She died, and left to me
This heath, this calm, and quiet scene;
The memory of what has been,
And never more will be.

## A slumber did my spirit seal

A slumber did my spirit seal;
   I had no human fears:
She seemed a thing that could not feel
   The touch of earthly years.

No motion has she now, no force;
   She neither hears nor sees;
Rolled round in earth's diurnal course,
   With rocks, and stones, and trees.  — return to nature

## She was a Phantom of delight

She was a Phantom of delight
When first she gleamed upon my sight;
A lovely Apparition, sent
To be a moment's ornament;
Her eyes as stars of Twilight fair;
Like Twilight's, too, her dusky hair;
But all things else about her drawn
From May-time and the cheerful Dawn;
A dancing Shape, an Image gay,
To haunt, to startle, and way-lay.

I saw her upon nearer view,
A Spirit, yet a Woman too!
Her household motions light and free,
And steps of virgin-liberty;
A countenance in which did meet

Sweet records, promises as sweet;
A Creature not too bright or good
For human nature's daily food;
For transient sorrows, simple wiles,
Praise, blame, love, kisses, tears, and smiles.

And now I see with eye serene
The very pulse of the machine;
A Being breathing thoughtful breath,
A Traveller between life and death;
The reason firm, the temperate will,
Endurance, foresight, strength, and skill;
A perfect Woman, nobly planned,
To warn, to comfort, and command;
And yet a Spirit still, and bright
With something of angelic light.

## Stepping Westward

*While my Fellow-traveller and I were walking by the side of Loch Ketterine, one fine evening after sunset, in our road to a Hut where, in the course of our Tour, we had been hospitably entertained some weeks before, we met, in one of the loneliest parts of that solitary region, two well-dressed Women, one of whom said to us, by way of greeting, "What, you are stepping westward?"*

"What, you are stepping westward?"—"Yea."
—'Twould be a *wildish* destiny,
If we, who thus together roam
In a strange Land, and far from home,
Were in this place the guests of Chance:
Yet who would stop, or fear to advance,
Though home or shelter he had none,
With such a sky to lead him on?

The dewy ground was dark and cold;
Behind, all gloomy to behold;
And stepping westward seemed to be
A kind of *heavenly* destiny:
I liked the greeting; 'twas a sound
Of something without place or bound;
And seemed to give me spiritual right
To travel through that region bright.

The voice was soft, and she who spake
Was walking by her native lake:
The salutation had to me
The very sound of courtesy:
Its power was felt; and while my eye
Was fixed upon the glowing Sky,
The echo of the voice enwrought
A human sweetness with the thought
Of travelling through the world that lay
Before me in my endless way.

## The Solitary Reaper

Behold her, single in the field,
Yon solitary Highland Lass!
Reaping and singing by herself;
Stop here, or gently pass!
Alone she cuts and binds the grain,
And sings a melancholy strain;
O listen! for the Vale profound
Is overflowing with the sound.

No Nightingale did ever chaunt
More welcome notes to weary bands
Of travellers in some shady haunt,

Among Arabian sands:
A voice so thrilling ne'er was heard
In spring-time from the Cuckoo-bird,
Breaking the silence of the seas
Among the farthest Hebrides.

Will no one tell me what she sings?—
Perhaps the plaintive numbers flow
For old, unhappy, far-off things,
And battles long ago:
Or is it some more humble lay,
Familiar matter of today?
Some natural sorrow, loss, or pain,
That has been, and may be again?

Whate'er the theme, the Maiden sang
As if her song could have no ending;
I saw her singing at her work,
And o'er the sickle bending;—
I listened, motionless and still;
And, as I mounted up the hill,
The music in my heart I bore,
Long after it was heard no more.

## A Complaint

There is a change—and I am poor;
Your love hath been, nor long ago,
A fountain at my fond heart's door,
Whose only business was to flow;
And flow it did; not taking heed
Of its own bounty, or my need.

What happy moments did I count!
Blest was I then all bliss above!

Now, for that consecrated fount
Of murmuring, sparkling, living love,
What have I? shall I dare to tell?
A comfortless and hidden well.

A well of love—it may be deep—
I trust it is,—and never dry:
What matter? if the waters sleep
In silence and obscurity.
—Such change, and at the very door
Of my fond heart, hath made me poor.


## Great men have been among us

Great men have been among us; hands that penned
And tongues that uttered wisdom—better none:
The later Sidney, Marvel, Harrington,
Young Vane, and others who called Milton friend.
These moralists could act and comprehend:
They knew how genuine glory was put on;
Taught us how rightfully a nation shone
In splendour: what strength was, that would not bend
But in magnanimous meekness. France, 'tis strange,
Hath brought forth no such souls as we had then.
Perpetual emptiness! unceasing change!
No single volume paramount, no code,
No master spirit, no determined road;
But equally a want of books and men!

## Mutability

From low to high doth dissolution climb,
And sink from high to low, along a scale
Of awful notes, whose concord shall not fail;
A musical but melancholy chime,
Which they can hear who meddle not with crime,
Nor avarice, nor over-anxious care.
Truth fails not; but her outward forms that bear
The longest date do melt like frosty rime,
That in the morning whitened hill and plain
And is no more; drop like the tower sublime
Of yesterday, which royally did wear
His crown of weeds, but could not even sustain
Some casual shout that broke the silent air,
Or the unimaginable touch of Time.

## Lines Composed a Few Miles
## Above Tintern Abbey

### ON REVISITING THE BANKS OF THE WYE
### DURING A TOUR, *July 13, 1798*

Five years have past; five summers, with the length
Of five long winters! and again I hear
These waters, rolling from their mountain-springs
With a soft inland murmur.—Once again
Do I behold these steep and lofty cliffs,
That on a wild secluded scene impress
Thoughts of more deep seclusion; and connect

The landscape with the quiet of the sky.
The day is come when I again repose
Here, under this dark sycamore, and view
These plots of cottage-ground, these orchard-tufts,
Which at this season, with their unripe fruits,
Are clad in one green hue, and lose themselves
'Mid groves and copses. Once again I see
These hedge-rows, hardly hedge-rows, little lines
Of sportive wood run wild; these pastoral farms,
Green to the very door; and wreaths of smoke
Sent up, in silence from among the trees!
With some uncertain notice, as might seem
Of vagrant dwellers in the houseless woods,
Or of some Hermit's cave, where by his fire
The Hermit sits alone.

                    These beauteous forms
Through a long absence, have not been to me
As is a landscape to a blind man's eye:
But oft, in lonely rooms, and 'mid the din
Of towns and cities, I have owed to them
In hours of weariness, sensations sweet,
Felt in the blood, and felt along the heart;
And passing even into my purer mind,
With tranquil restoration:—feelings too
Of unremembered pleasure: such, perhaps,
As have no slight or trivial influence
On that best portion of a good man's life.
His little, nameless, unremembered acts
Of kindness and of love. Nor less, I trust,
To them I may have owed another gift,
Of aspect more sublime; that blessed mood,
In which the burthen of the mystery,
In which the heavy and the weary weight
Of all this unintelligible world,

Is lightened:—that serene and blessed mood,
In which the affections gently lead us on,—
Until, the breath of this corporeal frame
And even the motion of our human blood
Almost suspended, we are laid asleep
In body, and become a living soul:
While with an eye made quiet by the power       *Death like*
Of harmony, and the deep power of joy,
We see into the life of things.       *meditative insight*
                              If this
Be but a vain belief, yet, oh! how oft
In darkness and amid the many shapes
Of joyless daylight; when the fretful stir
Unprofitable, and the fever of the world,
Have hung upon the beatings of my heart—
How oft, in spirit, have I turned to thee,
O sylvan Wye! thou wanderer thro' the woods,
How often has my spirit turned to thee!

And now, with gleams of half-extinguished thought,
With many recognitions dim and faint,       *Present*
And somewhat of a sad perplexity,
The picture of the mind revives again:
While here I stand, not only with the sense
Of present pleasure, but with pleasing thoughts
That in this moment there is life and food
For future years. And so I dare to hope,
Though changed, no doubt, from what I was when first
I came among these hills; when like a roe
I bounded o'er the mountains, by the sides
Of the deep rivers, and the lonely streams,       *animal-like*
Wherever nature led: more like a man       *unselfconscious*
Flying from something that he dreads, than one
Who sought the thing he loved. For nature then
(The coarser pleasures of my boyish days,

And their glad animal movements all gone by)
To me was all in all.—I cannot paint
What then I was. The sounding cataract
Haunted me like a passion: the tall rock,
The mountain, and the deep and gloomy wood,
Their colours and their forms, were then to me
An appetite; a feeling and a love,
That had no need of a remoter charm,
By thought supplied, nor any interest
Unborrowed from the eye.—That time is past,
And all its aching joys are now no more,
And all its dizzy raptures. Not for this
Faint I, nor mourn nor murmur; other gifts
Have followed; for such loss, I would believe,
Abundant recompense. For I have learned
To look on nature, not as in the hour
Of thoughtless youth; but hearing oftentimes
The still, sad music of humanity,
Nor harsh nor grating, though of ample power
To chasten and subdue. And I have felt
A presence that disturbs me with the joy
Of elevated thoughts; a sense sublime
Of something far more deeply interfused,
Whose dwelling is the light of setting suns,
And the round ocean and the living air,
And the blue sky, and in the mind of man;
A motion and a spirit, that impels
All thinking things, all objects of all thought,
And rolls through all things. Therefore am I still
A lover of the meadows and the woods,
And mountains; and of all that we behold
From this green earth; of all the mighty world
Of eye, and ear,—both what they half create,
And what perceive; well pleased to recognise
In nature and the language of the sense,

The anchor of my purest thoughts, the nurse,
The guide, the guardian of my heart, and soul
Of all my moral being.
                         Nor perchance,
If I were not thus taught, should I the more
Suffer my genial spirits to decay:
For thou art with me here upon the banks
Of this fair river; thou my dearest Friend,
My dear, dear Friend; and in thy voice I catch
The language of my former heart, and read
My former pleasures in the shooting lights
Of thy wild eyes. Oh! yet a little while
May I behold in thee what I was once,
My dear, dear Sister! and this prayer I make,
Knowing that Nature never did betray
The heart that loved her; 'tis her privilege,
Through all the years of this our life, to lead
From joy to joy: for she can so inform
The mind that is within us, so impress
With quietness and beauty, and so feed
With lofty thoughts, that neither evil tongues,
Rash judgments, nor the sneers of selfish men,
Nor greetings where no kindness is, nor all
The dreary intercourse of daily life,
Shall e'er prevail against us, or disturb
Our cheerful faith, that all which we behold
Is full of blessings. Therefore let the moon
Shine on thee in thy solitary walk;
And let the misty mountain-winds be free
To blow against thee: and, in after years,
When these wild ecstasies shall be matured
Into a sober pleasure; when thy mind
Shall be a mansion for all lovely forms,
Thy memory be as a dwelling-place
For all sweet sounds and harmonies; oh! then,

If solitude, or fear, or pain, or grief,
Should be thy portion, with what healing thoughts
Of tender joy wilt thou remember me,
And these my exhortations! Nor, perchance—
If I should be where I no more can hear
Thy voice, nor catch from thy wild eyes these gleams
Of past existence—wilt thou then forget
That on the banks of this delightful stream
We stood together, and that I, so long
A worshipper of Nature, hither came
Unwearied in that service: rather say
With warmer love—oh! with far deeper zeal
Of holier love. Nor wilt thou then forget,
That after many wanderings, many years
Of absence, these steep woods and lofty cliffs,
And this green pastoral landscape, were to me
More dear, both for themselves and for thy sake!

## Ode: Intimations of Immortality
## from Recollections of Early Childhood

*The Child is father of the Man;*
*And I could wish my days to be*
*Bound each to each by natural piety.*

There was a time when meadow, grove, and stream,
The earth, and every common sight,
  To me did seem
  Apparelled in celestial light,
The glory and the freshness of a dream.
It is not now as it hath been of yore;—
  Turn wheresoe'er I may,
  By night or day,
The things which I have seen I now can see no more.

The Rainbow comes and goes,
And lovely is the Rose,
The Moon doth with delight
Look round her when the heavens are bare,
Waters on a starry night
Are beautiful and fair;
The sunshine is a glorious birth;
But yet I know, where'er I go,
That there hath past away a glory from the earth.

Now, while the birds thus sing a joyous song,
And while the young lambs bound
As to the tabor's sound,
To me alone there came a thought of grief:
A timely utterance gave that thought relief,
And I again am strong:
The cataracts blow their trumpets from the steep;
No more shall grief of mine the season wrong;
I hear the Echoes through the mountains throng,
The Winds come to me from the fields of sleep.
And all the earth is gay;
Land and sea
Give themselves up to jollity,
And with the heart of May
Doth every Beast keep holiday;—
Thou Child of Joy,
Shout round me, let me hear thy shouts, thou happy
Shepherd-boy!

Ye blessèd Creatures, I have heard the call
Ye to each other make; I see
The heavens laugh with you in your jubilee;
My heart is at your festival,
My head hath its coronal,
The fulness of your bliss, I feel—I feel it all.
Oh evil day! if I were sullen

While Earth herself is adorning,
    This sweet May-morning,
And the Children are culling
    On every side,
In a thousand valleys far and wide,
Fresh flowers; while the sun shines warm,
And the Babe leaps up on his Mother's arm:—
    I hear, I hear, with joy I hear!
    —But there's a Tree, of many, one,
A single Field which I have looked upon,
Both of them speak of something that is gone:
    The Pansy at my feet
    Doth the same tale repeat:
Whither is fled the visionary gleam?
Where is it now, the glory and the dream?

Our birth is but a sleep and a forgetting:
The Soul that rises with us, our life's Star,
    Hath had elsewhere its setting,
    And cometh from afar:
Not in entire forgetfulness,
And not in utter nakedness,
But trailing clouds of glory do we come
    From God, who is our home:
Heaven lies about us in our infancy!
Shades of the prison-house begin to close
    Upon the growing Boy,
But He beholds the light, and whence it flows,
    He sees it in his joy;
The Youth, who daily farther from the east
    Must travel, still is Nature's Priest,
    And by the vision splendid
    Is on his way attended;
At length the Man perceives it die away,
And fade into the light of common day.

Earth fills her lap with pleasures of her own;
Yearnings she hath in her own natural kind,
And, even with something of a Mother's mind,
    And no unworthy aim,
    The homely Nurse doth all she can
To make her Foster-child, her Inmate Man,
    Forget the glories he hath known,
And that imperial palace whence he came.

Behold the Child among his new-born blisses,
A six years' Darling of a pigmy size!
See, where 'mid work of his own hand he lies,
Fretted by sallies of his mother's kisses,
With light upon him from his father's eyes!
See, at his feet, some little plan or chart,
Some fragment from his dream of human life,
Shaped by himself with newly-learned art;
    A wedding or a festival,
    A mourning or a funeral;
     And this hath now his heart,
    And unto this he frames his song:
     Then will he fit his tongue
To dialogues of business, love, or strife;
    But it will not be long
    Ere this be thrown aside,
    And with new joy and pride
The little Actor cons another part;
Filling from time to time his "humorous stage"
With all the Persons, down to palsied Age,
That Life brings with her in her equipage;
    As if his whole vocation
    Were endless imitation.

Thou, whose exterior semblance doth belie
    Thy Soul's immensity;
Thou best Philosopher, who yet dost keep

Thy heritage, thou Eye among the blind,
That, deaf and silent, read'st the eternal deep,
Haunted for ever by the eternal mind,—
    Mighty Prophet! Seer blest!
    On whom those truths do rest,
Which we are toiling all our lives to find,
In darkness lost, the darkness of the grave;
Thou, over whom thy Immortality
Broods like the Day, a Master o'er a Slave,
A Presence which is not to be put by;
Thou little Child, yet glorious in the might
Of heaven-born freedom on thy being's height,
Why with such earnest pains dost thou provoke
The years to bring the inevitable yoke,
Thus blindly with thy blessedness at strife?
Full soon thy Soul shall have her earthly freight,     *Mortality*
And custom lie upon thee with a weight,
Heavy as frost, and deep almost as life!

    O joy! that in our embers
    Is something that doth live,
    That nature yet remembers
    What was so fugitive!
The thought of our past years in me doth breed
Perpetual benediction: not indeed
For that which is most worthy to be blest;
Delight and liberty, the simple creed
Of Childhood, whether busy or at rest,
With new-fledged hope still fluttering in his breast:—
    Not for these I raise
    The song of thanks and praise;
But for those obstinate questionings
Of sense and outward things,
Fallings from us, vanishings;
Blank misgivings of a Creature

Moving about in worlds not realised,
High instincts before which our mortal Nature
Did tremble like a guilty Thing surprised:
    But for those first affections,
    Those shadowy recollections,
  Which, be they what they may,
Are yet the fountain-light of all our day,
Are yet a master-light of all our seeing;
    Uphold us, cherish, and have power to make
Our noisy years seem moments in the being
Of the eternal Silence: truths that wake,
        To perish never:
Which neither listlessness, nor mad endeavour,
      Nor Man nor Boy,
Nor all that is at enmity with joy,
Can utterly abolish or destroy.
      Hence in a season of calm weather
       Though inland far we be,
Our Souls have sight of that immortal sea
      Which brought us hither,
      Can in a moment travel thither,
And see the Children sport upon the shore,
And hear the mighty waters rolling evermore.

Then sing, ye Birds, sing, sing a joyous song!
      And let the young Lambs bound
      As to the tabor's sound!
We in thought will join your throng,
      Ye that pipe and ye that play,
      Ye that through your hearts to-day
      Feel the gladness of the May!
What though the radiance which was once so bright
Be now for ever taken from my sight,
    Though nothing can bring back the hour
Of splendour in the grass, of glory in the flower;

We will grieve not, rather find
Strength in what remains behind;
In the primal sympathy
Which having been must ever be;
In the soothing thoughts that spring
Out of human suffering;
In the faith that looks through death,
In years that bring the philosophic mind.

And O, ye Fountains, Meadows, Hills, and Groves,
Forebode not any severing of our loves!
Yet in my heart of hearts I feel your might;
I only have relinquished one delight
To live beneath your more habitual sway.
I love the Brooks which down their channels fret,
Even more than when I tripped lightly as they;
The innocent brightness of a new-born Day
                    Is lovely yet;
The Clouds that gather round the setting sun
Do take a sober colouring from an eye
That hath kept watch o'er man's mortality;
Another race hath been, and other palms are won,
Thanks to the human heart by which we live,
Thanks to its tenderness, its joys, and fears,
To me the meanest flower that blows can give
Thoughts that do often lie too deep for tears.

FROM *The Prelude*

## OR, GROWTH OF A POET'S MIND

*An Autobiographical Poem*
*(1850 version)*

## INTRODUCTION—CHILDHOOD AND
## SCHOOL-TIME

Fair seed-time had my soul, and I grew up
Fostered alike by beauty and by fear:
Much favoured in my birth-place, and no less
In that belovèd Vale to which erelong
We were transplanted;—there were we let loose
For sports of wider range. Ere I had told
Ten birth-days, when among the mountain slopes
Frost, and the breath of frosty wind, had snapped
The last autumnal crocus, 'twas my joy
With store of springes o'er my shoulder hung
To range the open heights where woodcocks run
Along the smooth green turf. Through half the night,
Scudding away from snare to snare, I plied
That anxious visitation;—moon and stars
Were shining o'er my head. I was alone,
And seemed to be a trouble to the peace
That dwelt among them. Sometimes it befell
In these night wanderings, that a strong desire
O'erpowered my better reason, and the bird
Which was the captive of another's toil
Became my prey; and when the deed was done
I heard among the solitary hills
Low breathings coming after me, and sounds

Of undistinguishable motion, steps
Almost as silent as the turf they trod.

   Nor less when spring had warmed the cultured Vale,   Winter →
Moved we as plunderers where the mother-bird                        Spring
Had in high places built her lodge; though mean
Our object and inglorious, yet the end
Was not ignoble. Oh! when I have hung
Above the raven's nest, by knots of grass
And half-inch fissures in the slippery rock
But ill sustained, and almost—so it seemed—
Suspended by the blast that blew amain,
Shouldering the naked crag, oh, at that time
While on the perilous ridge I hung alone,
With what strange utterance did the loud, dry wind
Blow through my ear! the sky seemed not a sky
Of earth—and with what motion moved the clouds!

   Dust as we are, the immortal spirit grows
Like harmony in music; there is a dark
Inscrutable workmanship that reconciles
Discordant elements, makes them cling together
In one society. How strange that all
The terrors, pains, and early miseries,
Regrets, vexations, lassitudes interfused
Within my mind, should e'er have borne a part,
And that a needful part, in making up
The calm existence that is mine when I
Am worthy of myself! Praise to the end!
Thanks to the means which Nature deigned to employ;
Whether her fearless visitings, or those
That came with soft alarm, like hurtless light
Opening the peaceful clouds; or she may use
Severer interventions, ministry
More palpable, as best might suit her aim.

Summer    One summer evening (led by her) I found
A little boat tied to a willow tree
Within a rocky cove, its usual home.
Straight I unloosed her chain, and stepping in
Pushed from the shore. It was an act of stealth
And troubled pleasure, nor without the voice
Of mountain echoes did my boat move on;
Leaving behind her still, on either side,
Small circles glittering idly in the moon,
Until they melted all into one track
Of sparkling light. But now, like one who rows,
Proud of his skill, to reach a chosen point
With an unswerving line, I fixed my view
Upon the summit of a craggy ridge,
The horizon's utmost boundary; far above
Was nothing but the stars and the gray sky.
She was an elfin pinnace; lustily
I dipped my oars into the silent lake,
And, as I rose upon the stroke, my boat
Went heaving through the water like a swan;
When, from behind that craggy steep till then
The horizon's bound, a huge peak, black and huge,
As if with voluntary power instinct
Upreared its head. I struck and struck again,
And growing still in stature the grim shape
Towered up between me and the stars, and still,
For so it seemed, with purpose of its own
And measured motion like a living thing,
Strode after me. With trembling oars I turned,
And through the silent water stole my way
Back to the covert of the willow tree;
There in her mooring-place I left my bark,—
And through the meadows homeward went, in grave
And serious mood; but after I had seen
That spectacle, for many days, my brain

Worked with a dim and undetermined sense
Of unknown modes of being; o'er my thoughts
There hung a darkness, call it solitude
Or blank desertion. No familiar shapes
Remained, no pleasant images of trees,
Of sea or sky, no colors of green fields;
But huge and mighty forms, that do not live
Like living men, moved slowly through the mind
By day, and were a trouble to my dreams.

    Wisdom and Spirit of the universe!
Thou Soul that art the eternity of thought,
That givest to forms and images a breath
And everlasting motion, not in vain
By day or starlight thus from my first dawn
Of childhood didst thou intertwine for me
The passions that build up our human soul;
Not with the mean and vulgar works of man,
But with high objects, with enduring things—
With life and nature—purifying thus
The elements of feeling and of thought,
And sanctifying, by such discipline,
Both pain and fear, until we recognize
A grandeur in the beatings of the heart.
Nor was this fellowship vouchsafed to me
With stinted kindness. In November days,
When vapors rolling down the valley made
A lonely scene more lonesome, among woods,
At noon and 'mid the calm of summer nights,
When, by the margin of the trembling lake,
Beneath the gloomy hills homeward I went
In solitude, such intercourse was mine;
Mine was it in the fields both day and night,
And by the waters, all the summer long.

    And in the frosty season, when the sun

Fall →
Winter

Was set, and visible for many a mile
The cottage windows blazed through twilight gloom,
I heeded not their summons: happy time
It was indeed for all of us—for me
It was a time of rapture! Clear and loud
The village clock tolled six,—I wheeled about,
Proud and exulting like an untired horse
That cares not for his home. All shod with steel,
We hissed along the polished ice in games
Confederate, imitative of the chase
And woodland pleasures,—the resounding horn,
The pack loud chiming, and the hunted hare.
So through the darkness and the cold we flew,
And not a voice was idle; with the din
Smitten, the precipices rang aloud;
The leafless trees and every icy crag
Tinkled like iron; while far distant hills
Into the tumult sent an alien sound
Of melancholy not unnoticed, while the stars
Eastward were sparkling clear, and in the west
The orange sky of evening died away.
Not seldom from the uproar I retired
Into a silent bay, or sportively
Glanced sideway, leaving the tumultuous throng,
To cut across the reflex of a star
That fled, and, flying still before me, gleamed
Upon the glassy plain; and oftentimes,
When we had given our bodies to the wind,
And all the shadowy banks on either side
Came sweeping through the darkness, spinning still
The rapid line of motion, then at once
Have I, reclining back upon my heels,
Stopped short; yet still the solitary cliffs
Wheeled by me—even as if the earth had rolled
With visible motion her diurnal round!

Behind me did they stretch in solemn train,
Feebler and feebler, and I stood and watched
Till all was tranquil as a dreamless sleep.

   Ye Presences of Nature in the sky
And on the earth! Ye Visions of the hills!
And Souls of lonely places! can I think
A vulgar hope was yours when ye employed
Such ministry, when ye through many a year
Haunting me thus among my boyish sports,
On caves and trees, upon the woods and hills,
Impressed upon all forms the characters
Of danger or desire; and thus did make
The surface of the universal earth
With triumph and delight, with hope and fear,
Work like a sea?
          Not uselessly employed,
Might I pursue this theme through every change
Of exercise and play, to which the year    > year
Did summon us in his delightful round.

                  (Book I, lines 301–478)


## SUMMER VACATION

               Yet in spite
Of pleasure won, and knowledge not withheld,
There was an inner falling off—I loved,
Loved deeply all that had been loved before,
More deeply even than ever: but a swarm
Of heady schemes jostling each other, gawds,
And feast and dance, and public revelry,
And sports and games (too grateful in themselves,
Yet in themselves less grateful, I believe,
Than as they were a badge glossy and fresh
Of manliness and freedom) all conspired

To lure my mind from firm habitual quest
Of feeding pleasures, to depress the zeal
And damp those yearnings which had once been mine—
A wild, unworldly-minded youth, given up
To his own eager thoughts. It would demand
Some skill, and longer time than may be spared
To paint these vanities, and how they wrought
In haunts where they, till now, had been unknown.
It seemed the very garments that I wore
Preyed on my strength, and stopped the quiet stream
Of self-forgetfulness.

                    Yes, that heartless chase
Of trivial pleasures was a poor exchange
For books and nature at that early age.
'Tis true, some casual knowledge might be gained
Of character or life; but at that time,
Of manners put to school I took small note,
And all my deeper passions lay elsewhere.
Far better had it been to exalt the mind
By solitary study, to uphold
Intense desire through meditative peace;
And yet, for chastisement of these regrets,
The memory of one particular hour
Doth here rise up against me. 'Mid a throng
Of maids and youths, old men, and matrons staid,
A medley of all tempers, I had passed
The night in dancing, gaiety, and mirth,
With din of instruments and shuffling feet,
And glancing forms, and tapers glittering,
And unaimed prattle flying up and down;
Spirits upon the stretch, and here and there
Slight shocks of young love-liking interspersed,
Whose transient pleasure mounted to the head,
And tingled through the veins. Ere we retired,
The cock had crowed, and now the eastern sky

Was kindling, not unseen, from humble copse
And open field, through which the pathway wound,
And homeward led my steps. Magnificent
The morning rose, in memorable pomp,
Glorious as e'er I had beheld—in front,
The sea lay laughing at a distance; near,
The solid mountains shone, bright as the clouds,
Grain-tinctured, drenched in empyrean light;
And in the meadows and the lower grounds
Was all the sweetness of a common dawn—
Dews, vapors, and the melody of birds,
And laborers going forth to till the fields.
Ah! need I say, dear Friend! that to the brim
My heart was full; I made no vows, but vows
Were then made for me; bond unknown to me
Was given, that I should be, else sinning greatly,
A dedicated Spirit. On I walked
In thankful blessedness, which yet survives.

                          (*Book IV, lines 276–338*)


## BOOKS

Whereupon I told,
That once in the stillness of a summer's noon,
While I was seated in a rocky cave
By the sea-side, perusing, so it chanced,
The famous history of the errant knight
Recorded by Cervantes, these same thoughts
Beset me, and to height unusual rose,
While listlessly I sate, and having closed
The book, had turned my eyes toward the wide sea.
On poetry and geometric truth,
And their high privilege of lasting life,
From all internal injury exempt,
I mused; upon these chiefly: and at length,

My senses yielding to the sultry air,
Sleep seized me, and I passed into a dream.
I saw before me stretched a boundless plain
Of sandy wilderness, all black and void,
And as I looked around, distress and fear
Came creeping over me, when at my side,
Close at my side, an uncouth shape appeared
Upon a dromedary, mounted high,
He seemed an Arab of the Bedouin tribes:
A lance he bore, and underneath one arm
A stone, and in the opposite hand a shell
Of a surpassing brightness. At the sight
Much I rejoiced, not doubting but a guide
Was present, one who with unerring skill
Would through the desert lead me; and while yet
I looked and looked, self-questioned what this freight
Which the new-comer carried through the waste
Could mean, the Arab told me that the stone
(To give it in the language of the dream)
Was "Euclid's Elements"; and "This," said he,
"Is something of more worth"; and at the word
Stretched forth the shell, so beautiful in shape,
In colour so resplendent, with command
That I should hold it to my ear. I did so,
And heard that instant in an unknown tongue,
Which yet I understood, articulate sounds,
A loud prophetic blast of harmony;
An Ode, in passion uttered, which foretold
Destruction to the children of the earth
By deluge, now at hand. No sooner ceased
The song, than the Arab with calm look declared
That all would come to pass of which the voice
Had given forewarning, and that he himself
Was going then to bury those two books:

The one that held acquaintance with the stars,
And wedded soul to soul in purest bond
Of reason, undisturbed by space or time;
The other that was a god, yea many gods,
Had voices more than all the winds, with power
To exhilarate the spirit, and to soothe,
Through every clime, the heart of human kind.
While this was uttering, strange as it may seem,
I wondered not, although I plainly saw
The one to be a stone, the other a shell;
Nor doubted once but that they both were books,
Having a perfect faith in all that passed.
Far stronger, now, grew the desire I felt
To cleave unto this man; but when I prayed
To share his enterprise, he hurried on
Reckless of me: I followed, not unseen,
For oftentimes he cast a backward look,
Grasping his twofold treasure.—Lance in rest,
He rode, I keeping pace with him; and now
He, to my fancy, had become the knight
Whose tale Cervantes tells; yet not the knight,
But was an Arab of the desert too;
Of these was neither, and was both at once.
His countenance, meanwhile, grew more disturbed;
And, looking backwards when he looked, mine eyes
Saw, over half the wilderness diffused,
A bed of glittering light: I asked the cause:
"It is," said he, "the waters of the deep
Gathering upon us"; quickening then the pace
Of the unwieldy creature he bestrode,
He left me: I called after him aloud;
He heeded not; but, with his twofold charge
Still in his grasp, before me, full in view,
Went hurrying o'er the illimitable waste,

With the fleet waters of a drowning world
In chase of him; whereat I waked in terror,
And saw the sea before me, and the book,
In which I had been reading, at my side.

(Book V, lines 56–140)

### CAMBRIDGE AND THE ALPS

The melancholy slackening that ensued
Upon those tidings by the peasant given
Was soon dislodged. Downwards we hurried fast,
And, with the half-shaped road which we had missed,
Entered a narrow chasm. The brook and road
Were fellow-travellers in this gloomy strait,
And with them did we journey several hours
At a slow pace. The immeasurable height
Of woods decaying, never to be decayed,
The stationary blasts of waterfalls,
And in the narrow rent at every turn
Winds thwarting winds, bewildered and forlorn,
The torrent shooting from the clear blue sky,
The rocks that muttered close upon our ears,
Black drizzling crags that spake by the way-side
As if a voice were in them, the sick sight
And giddy prospect of the raving stream,
The unfettered clouds and region of the Heavens,
Tumult and peace, the darkness and the light—
Were all like workings of one mind, the features
Of the same face, blossoms upon one tree;
Characters of the great Apocalypse,
The types and symbols of Eternity,
Of first, and last, and midst, and without end.

(Book VI, lines 617–40)

## RESIDENCE IN LONDON

As the black storm upon the mountain-top
Sets off the sunbeam in the valley, so
That huge fermenting mass of human-kind
Serves as a solemn background, or relief,
To single forms and objects, whence they draw,
For feeling and contemplative regard,
More than inherent liveliness and power.
How oft, amid those overflowing streets,
Have I gone forward with the crowd, and said
Unto myself, "The face of every one
That passes by me is a mystery!"
Thus have I looked, nor ceased to look, oppressed
By thoughts of what and whither, when and how,
Until the shapes before my eyes became
A second-sight procession, such as glides
Over still mountains, or appears in dreams;
And once, far-travelled in such mood, beyond
The reach of common indication, lost
Amid the moving pageant, I was smitten
Abruptly, with the view (a sight not rare)
Of a blind Beggar, who, with upright face,
Stood, propped against a wall, upon his chest
Wearing a written paper, to explain
His story, whence he came, and who he was.
Caught by the spectacle my mind turned round
As with the might of waters; an apt type
This label seemed of the utmost we can know,
Both of ourselves and of the universe;
And, on the shape of that unmoving man,
His steadfast face and sightless eyes, I gazed,
As if admonished from another world.

Though reared upon the base of outward things,
Structures like these the excited spirit mainly
Builds for herself; scenes different there are,
Full-formed, that take, with small internal help,
Possession of the faculties,—the peace
That comes with night; the deep solemnity
Of nature's intermediate hours of rest,
When the great tide of human life stands still;
The business of the day to come, unborn,
Of that gone by, locked up, as in the grave;
The blended calmness of the heavens and earth,
Moonlight and stars, and empty streets, and sounds
Unfrequent as in deserts; at late hours
Of winter evenings, when unwholesome rains
Are falling hard, with people yet astir,
The feeble salutation from the voice
Of some unhappy woman, now and then
Heard as we pass, when no one looks about,
Nothing is listened to. But these, I fear,
Are falsely catalogued; things that are, are not,
As the mind answers to them, or the heart
Is prompt, or slow, to feel. What say you, then,
To times, when half the city shall break out
Full of one passion, vengeance, rage, or fear?
To executions, to a street on fire,
Mobs, riots, or rejoicings? From these sights
Take one,—that ancient festival, the Fair,
Holden where martyrs suffered in past time,
And named of St. Bartholomew; there, see
A work completed to our hands, that lays,
If any spectacle on earth can do,
The whole creative powers of man asleep!—
For once, the Muse's help will we implore,
And she shall lodge us, wafted on her wings,
Above the press and danger of the crowd,

Upon some showman's platform. What a shock
For eyes and ears! what anarchy and din,
Barbarian and infernal,—a phantasma,
Monstrous in color, motion, shape, sight, sound!
Below, the open space, through every nook
Of the wide area, twinkles, is alive
With heads; the midway region, and above,
Is thronged with staring pictures and huge scrolls,
Dumb proclamations of the Prodigies;
With chattering monkeys dangling from their poles,
And children whirling in their round-abouts;
With those that stretch the neck and strain the eyes,
And crack the voice in rivalship, the crowd
Inviting; with buffoons against buffoons
Grimacing, writhing, screaming,—him who grinds
The hurdy-gurdy, at the fiddle weaves,
Rattles the salt-box, thumps the kettle-drum,
And him who at the trumpet puffs his cheeks,
The silver-collared Negro with his timbrel,
Equestrians, tumblers, women, girls, and boys,
Blue-breeched, pink-vested, with high-towering
        plumes.—
All movables of wonder, from all parts,
Are here— Albinos, painted Indians, Dwarfs,
The Horse of knowledge, and the learned Pig,
The Stone-eater, the man that swallows fire,
Giants, Ventriloquists, the Invisible Girl,
The Bust that speaks and moves its goggling eyes,
The Wax-work, Clock-work, all the marvellous craft
Of modern Merlins, Wild Beasts, Puppet-shows,
All out-o'-the-way, far-fetched, perverted things,
All freaks of nature, all Promethean thoughts
Of man, his dulness, madness, and their feats
All jumbled up together, to compose
A Parliament of Monsters. Tents and Booths

Meanwhile, as if the whole were one vast mill,
Are vomiting, receiving on all sides,
Men, women, three-years' children, babes in arms.

Oh, blank confusion! true epitome
Of what the mighty city is herself,
To thousands upon thousands of her sons,
Living amid the same perpetual whirl
Of trivial objects, melted and reduced
To one identity, by differences
That have no law, no meaning, and no end—
Oppression, under which even highest minds
Must labor, whence the strongest are not free.

(Book VII, lines 619–730)

## RESIDENCE IN FRANCE

Cheered with this hope, to Paris I returned,
And ranged, with ardour heretofore unfelt,
The spacious city, and in progress passed
The prison where the unhappy Monarch lay,
Associate with his children and his wife
In bondage; and the palace, lately stormed
With roar of cannon by a furious host.
I crossed the square (an empty area then!)
Of the Carrousel, where so late had lain
The dead, upon the dying heaped, and gazed
On this and other spots, as doth a man
Upon a volume whose contents he knows
Are memorable, but from him locked up,
Being written in a tongue he cannot read,
So that he questions the mute leaves with pain,
And half upbraids their silence. But that night
I felt most deeply in what world I was,
What ground I trod on, and what air I breathed.

High was my room and lonely, near the roof
Of a large mansion or hotel, a lodge
That would have pleased me in more quiet times;
Nor was it wholly without pleasure then.
With unextinguished taper I kept watch,
Reading at intervals; the fear gone by
Pressed on me almost like a fear to come.
I thought of those September massacres,
Divided from me by one little month,
Saw them and touched: the rest was conjured up
From tragic fictions or true history,
Remembrances and dim admonishments.
The horse is taught his manage, and no star
Of wildest course but treads back his own steps;
For the spent hurricane the air provides
As fierce a successor; the tide retreats
But to return out of its hiding-place
In the great deep; all things have second birth;
The earthquake is not satisfied at once;
And in this way I wrought upon myself,
Until I seemed to hear a voice that cried,
To the whole city, "sleep no more." The trance
Fled with the voice to which it had given birth;
But vainly comments of a calmer mind
Promised soft peace and sweet forgetfulness.
The place, all hushed and silent as it was,
Appeared unfit for the repose of night,
Defenceless as a wood where tigers roam.

(Book X, lines 48-93)


### RESIDENCE IN FRANCE (CONTINUED)

O pleasant exercise of hope and joy!
For mighty were the auxiliars which then stood
Upon our side, us who were strong in love!

Bliss was it in that dawn to be alive,
But to be young was very Heaven! O times,
In which the meagre, stale, forbidding ways
Of custom, law, and statute, took at once
The attraction of a country in romance!
When Reason seemed the most to assert her rights
When most intent on making of herself
A prime enchantress—to assist the work,
Which then was going forward in her name!
Not favored spots alone, but the whole Earth,
The beauty wore of promise—that which sets
(As at some moments might not be unfelt
Among the bowers of Paradise itself)
The budding rose above the rose full blown.
What temper at the prospect did not wake
To happiness unthought of? The inert
Were roused, and lively natures rapt away!
They who had fed their childhood upon dreams,
The play-fellows of fancy, who had made
All powers of swiftness, subtilty, and strength
Their ministers,—who in lordly wise had stirred
Among the grandest objects of the sense,
And dealt with whatsoever they found there
As if they had within some lurking right
To wield it;—they, too, who of gentle mood
Had watched all gentle motions, and to these
Had fitted their own thoughts, schemers more mild,
And in the region of their peaceful selves;—
Now was it that *both* found, the meek and lofty
Did both find, helpers to their heart's desire,
And stuff at hand, plastic as they could wish,—
Were called upon to exercise their skill,
Not in Utopia,—subterranean fields,—
Or some secreted island, Heaven knows where!

But in the very world, which is the world
Of all of us,—the place where, in the end,
We find our happiness, or not at all!

(*Book XI, lines 105-14*)


## IMAGINATION AND TASTE, HOW IMPAIRED AND RESTORED

There are in our existence spots of time,
That with distinct pre-eminence retain
A renovating virtue, whence—depressed
By false opinion and contentious thought,
Or aught of heavier or more deadly weight,
In trivial occupations, and the round
Of ordinary intercourse—our minds
Are nourished and invisibly repaired;
A virtue, by which pleasure is enhanced,
That penetrates, enables us to mount,
When high, more high, and lifts us up when fallen.
This efficacious spirit chiefly lurks
Among those passages of life that give
Profoundest knowledge to what point, and how,
The mind is lord and master—outward sense
The obedient servant of her will. Such moments
Are scattered everywhere, taking their date
From our first childhood. I remember well,
That once, while yet my inexperienced hand
Could scarcely hold a bridle, with proud hopes
I mounted, and we journeyed towards the hills:
An ancient servant of my father's house
Was with me, my encourager and guide:
We had not travelled long, ere some mischance
Disjoined me from my comrade; and, through fear
Dismounting, down the rough and stony moor

I led my horse, and, stumbling on, at length
Came to a bottom, where in former times
A murderer had been hung in iron chains.
The gibbet-mast had moldered down, the bones
And iron case were gone; but on the turf,
Hard by, soon after that fell deed was wrought,
Some unknown hand had carved the murderer's name.
The monumental letters were inscribed
In times long past; but still, from year to year
By superstition of the neighborhood,
The grass is cleared away, and to this hour
The characters are fresh and visible:
A casual glance had shown them, and I fled,
Faltering and faint, and ignorant of the road:
Then, reascending the bare common, saw
A naked pool that lay beneath the hills,
The beacon on the summit, and, more near,
A girl, who bore a pitcher on her head,
And seemed with difficult steps to force her way
Against the blowing wind. It was, in truth,
An ordinary sight; but I should need
Colors and words that are unknown to man,
To paint the visionary dreariness
Which, while I looked all round for my lost guide,
Invested moorland waste and naked pool,
The beacon crowning the lone eminence,
The female and her garments vexed and tossed
By the strong wind. When, in the blessèd hours
Of early love, the loved one at my side,
I roamed, in daily presence of this scene,
Upon the naked pool and dreary crags,
And on the melancholy beacon, fell
A spirit of pleasure and youth's golden gleam;
And think ye not with radiance more sublime
For these remembrances, and for the power

They had left behind? So feeling comes in aid
Of feeling, and diversity of strength
Attends us, if but once we have been strong.
Oh! mystery of man, from what a depth
Proceed thy honors. I am lost, but see
In simple childhood something of the base
On which thy greatness stands; but this I feel,
That from thyself it comes, that thou must give,
Else never canst receive. The days gone by
Return upon me almost from the dawn
Of life: the hiding-places of man's power
Open; I would approach them, but they close.
I see by glimpses now; when age comes on,
May scarcely see at all; and I would give,
While yet we may, as far as words can give,
Substance and life to what I feel, enshrining,
Such is my hope, the spirit of the Past
For future restoration—yet another
Of these memorials:—

     One Christmas-time,
On the glad eve of its dear holidays,
Feverish, and tired, and restless, I went forth
Into the fields, impatient for the sight
Of those led palfreys that should bear us home;
My brothers and myself. There rose a crag,
That, from the meeting-point of two highways
Ascending, overlooked them both, far stretched;
Thither, uncertain on which road to fix
My expectation, thither I repaired,
Scout-like, and gained the summit; 'twas a day
Tempestuous, dark, and wild, and on the grass
I sate half-sheltered by a naked wall;
Upon my right hand couched a single sheep,
Upon my left a blasted hawthorn stood;
With those companions at my side, I watched,

Straining my eyes intensely, as the mist
Gave intermitting prospect of the copse
And plain beneath. Ere we to school returned,—
That dreary time,—ere we had been ten days
Sojourners in my father's house, he died,
And I and my three brothers, orphans then,
Followed his body to the grave. The event,
With all the sorrow that it brought, appeared
A chastisement; and when I called to mind
That day so lately past, when from the crag
I looked in such anxiety of hope;
With trite reflections of morality,
Yet in the deepest passion, I bowed low
To God, Who thus corrected my desires;
And, afterwards, the wind and sleety rain,
And all the business of the elements,
The single sheep, and the one blasted tree,
And the bleak music from that old stone wall,
The noise of wood and water, and the mist
That on the line of each of those two roads
Advanced in such indisputable shapes;
All these were kindred spectacles and sounds
To which I oft repaired, and thence would drink,
As at a fountain; and on winter nights,
Down to this very time, when storm and rain
Beat on my roof, or, haply, at noon-day,
While in a grove I walk, whose lofty trees,
Laden with summer's thickest foliage, rock
In a strong wind, some working of the spirit,
Some inward agitations thence are brought,
Whate'er their office, whether to beguile
Thoughts over busy in the course they took,
Or animate an hour of vacant ease.

(Book XII, lines 208–335)

## CONCLUSION

It was a close, warm, breezeless summer night,
Wan, dull, and glaring, with a dripping fog
Low-hung and thick that covered all the sky;
But, undiscouraged, we began to climb
The mountain-side. The mist soon girt us round,
And, after ordinary travellers' talk
With our conductor, pensively we sank
Each into commerce with his private thoughts.
Thus did we breast the ascent, and by myself
Was nothing either seen or heard that checked
Those musings or diverted, save that once
The shepherd's lurcher, who, among the crags,
Had to his joy unearthed a hedgehog, teased
His coiled-up prey with barkings turbulent.
This small adventure, for even such it seemed
In that wild place and at the dead of night,
Being over and forgotten, on we wound
In silence as before. With forehead bent
Earthward, as if in opposition set
Against an enemy, I panted up
With eager pace, and no less eager thoughts.
Thus might we wear a midnight hour away,
Ascending at loose distance each from each,
And I, as chanced, the foremost of the band;
When at my feet the ground appeared to brighten,
And with a step or two seemed brighter still;
Nor was time given to ask or learn the cause,
For instantly a light upon the turf
Fell like a flash, and lo! as I looked up,
The moon hung naked in a firmament
Of azure without cloud, and at my feet
Rested a silent sea of hoary mist.

A hundred hills their dusky backs upheaved
All over this still ocean; and beyond,
Far, far beyond the solid vapors stretched,
In headlands, tongues, and promontory shapes,
Into the main Atlantic, that appeared
To dwindle, and give up his majesty,
Usurped upon far as the sight could reach.
Not so the ethereal vault; encroachment none
Was there, nor loss; only the inferior stars
Had disappeared, or shed a fainter light
In the clear presence of the full-orbed moon,
Who, from her sovereign elevation, gazed
Upon the billowy ocean, as it lay
All meek and silent, save that through a rift—
Not distant from the shore whereon we stood,
A fixed, abysmal, gloomy, breathing place—
Mounted the roar of waters, torrents, streams
Innumerable, roaring with one voice!
Heard over earth and sea, and, in that hour,
For so it seemed, felt by the starry heavens.

When into air had partially dissolved
That vision, given to spirits of the night
And three chance human wanderers, in calm thought
Reflected, it appeared to me the type
Of a majestic intellect, its acts
And its possessions, what it has and craves,
What in itself it is, and would become.
There I beheld the emblem of a mind
That feeds upon infinity, that broods
Over the dark abyss, intent to hear
Its voices issuing forth to silent light
In one continuous stream; a mind sustained
By recognitions of transcendent power,
In sense conducting to ideal form,

In soul of more than mortal privilege.
One function, above all, of such a mind
Had Nature shadowed there, by putting forth,
'Mid circumstances awful and sublime,
That mutual domination which she loves
To exert upon the face of outward things,
So molded, joined, abstracted, so endowed
With interchangeable supremacy,
That men, least sensitive, see, hear, perceive,
And cannot choose but feel. The power, which all
Acknowledge when thus moved, which Nature thus
To bodily sense exhibits, is the express
Resemblance of that glorious faculty
That higher minds bear with them as their own.
This is the very spirit in which they deal
With the whole compass of the universe:
They from their native selves can send abroad
Kindred mutations; for themselves create
A like existence; and, whene'er it dawns
Created for them, catch it, or are caught
By its inevitable mastery,
Like angels stopped upon the wing by sound
Of harmony from Heaven's remotest spheres.
Them the enduring and the transient both
Serve to exalt; they build up greatest things
From least suggestions; ever on the watch,
Willing to work and to be wrought upon,
They need not extraordinary calls
To rouse them; in a world of life they live,
By sensible impressions not enthralled,
But by their quickening impulse made more prompt
To hold fit converse with the spiritual world,
And with the generations of mankind
Spread over time, past, present, and to come,
Age after age, till time shall be no more.

Such minds are truly from the Deity,
For they are Powers; and hence the highest bliss
That flesh can know is theirs—the consciousness
Of Whom they are, habitually infused
Through every image and through every thought,
And all affections by communion raised
From earth to heaven, from human to divine;
Hence endless occupation for the soul,
Whether discursive or intuitive;
Hence cheerfulness for acts of daily life,
Emotions which best foresight need not fear,
Most worthy then of trust when most intense.
Hence, amid ills that vex and wrongs that crush
Our hearts—if here the words of Holy Writ
May with fit reverence be applied—that peace
Which passeth understanding, that repose
In moral judgments which from this pure source
Must come, or will by man be sought in vain.

(Book XIV, lines 11-129)

# Hartley Coleridge

(1796–1849)

## Long time a child, and still a child, when years

Long time a child, and still a child, when years
Had painted manhood on my cheek, was I,—
For yet I lived like one not born to die;
A thriftless prodigal of smiles and tears,
No hope I needed, and I knew no fears.
But sleep, though sweet, is only sleep, and waking,
I waked to sleep no more, at once o'ertaking
The vanguard of my age, with all arrears
Of duty on my back. Nor child, nor man,
Nor youth, nor sage, I find my head is grey,
For I have lost the race I never ran:
A rathe December blights my lagging May;
And still I am a child, tho' I be old,
Time is my debtor for my years untold.

## To a Deaf and Dumb Little Girl

Like a loose island on the wide expanse,
Unconscious floating on the fickle sea,
Herself her all, she lives in privacy;
Her waking life as lonely as a trance,
Doom'd to behold the universal dance,

And never hear the music which expounds
The solemn step, coy slide, the merry bounds,
The vague, mute language of the countenance.
In vain for her I smooth my antic rhyme;
She cannot hear it. All her little being
Concentred in her solitary seeing—
What can she know of beauty or sublime?
And yet methinks she looks so calm and good,
God must be with her in her solitude!

## Lines ——

I have been cherish'd and forgiven
    By many tender-hearted,
'Twas for the sake of one in Heaven
    Of *him* that is departed.

Because I bear my Father's name
    I am not quite despised,
My little legacy of fame
    I've not yet realized.

And yet if you should praise myself
    I'll tell you, I had rather
You'd give your love to me, poor elf,
    Your praise to my great father.

# William Cullen Bryant

(1794–1878)

## To a Waterfowl

Whither, midst falling dew,
While glow the heavens with the last steps of day,
Far, through their rosy depths, dost thou pursue
   Thy solitary way?

Vainly the fowler's eye
Might mark thy distant flight to do thee wrong,
As, darkly seen against the crimson sky,
   Thy figure floats along.

Seek'st thou the plashy brink
Of weedy lake, or marge of river wide,
Or where the rocking billows rise and sink
   On the chafed ocean-side?

There is a Power whose care
Teaches thy way along that pathless coast—
The desert and illimitable air—
   Lone wandering, but not lost.

All day thy wings have fanned,
At that far height, the cold, thin atmosphere,
Yet stoop not, weary, to the welcome land,
   Though the dark night is near.

And soon that toil shall end;
Soon shalt thou find a summer home, and rest,

And scream among thy fellows; reeds shall bend,
  Soon, o'er thy sheltered nest.

Thou'rt gone, the abyss of heaven
Hath swallowed up thy form; yet, on my heart
Deeply has sunk the lesson thou hast given,
  And shall not soon depart.

He who, from zone to zone,
Guides through the boundless sky thy certain flight,
In the long way that I must tread alone,
  Will lead my steps aright.

## Summer Wind

It is a sultry day; the sun has drunk
The dew that lay upon the morning grass;
There is no rustling in the lofty elm
That canopies my dwelling, and its shade
Scarce cools me. All is silent, save the faint
And interrupted murmur of the bee,
Settling on the sick flowers, and then again
Instantly on the wing. The plants around
Feel the too potent fervors: the tall maize
Rolls up its long green leaves; the clover droops
Its tender foliage, and declines its blooms.
But far in the fierce sunshine tower the hills,
With all their growth of woods, silent and stern,
As if the scorching heat and dazzling light
Were but an element they loved. Bright clouds,
Motionless pillars of the brazen heaven—
Their bases on the mountains—their white tops
Shining in the far ether—fire the air
With a reflected radiance, and make turn

The gazer's eye away. For me, I lie
Languidly in the shade, where the thick turf,
Yet virgin from the kisses of the sun,
Retains some freshness, and I woo the wind
That still delays his coming. Why so slow,
Gentle and voluble spirit of the air?
Oh, come and breathe upon the fainting earth
Coolness and life. Is it that in his caves
He hears me? See, on yonder woody ridge,
The pine is bending his proud top, and now
Among the nearer groves, chestnut and oak
Are tossing their green boughs about. He comes;
Lo, where the grassy meadow runs in waves!
The deep distressful silence of the scene
Breaks up with mingling of unnumbered sounds
And universal motion. He is come,
Shaking a shower of blossoms from the shrubs,
And bearing on their fragrance; and he brings
Music of birds, and rustling of young boughs,
And sound of swaying branches, and the voice
Of distant waterfalls. All the green herbs
Are stirring in his breath; a thousand flowers,
By the road-side and the borders of the brook,
Nod gayly to each other; glossy leaves
Are twinkling in the sun, as if the dew
Were on them yet, and silver waters break
Into small waves and sparkle as he comes.

## The Prairies

These are the gardens of the Desert, these
The unshorn fields, boundless and beautiful,
For which the speech of England has no name—

The Prairies. I behold them for the first,
And my heart swells, while the dilated sight
Takes in the encircling vastness. Lo! they stretch,
In airy undulations, far away,
As if the ocean, in his gentlest swell,
Stood still, with all his rounded billows fixed,
And motionless forever.—Motionless?—
No—they are all unchained again. The clouds
Sweep over with their shadows, and, beneath,
The surface rolls and fluctuates to the eye;
Dark hollows seem to glide along and chase
The sunny ridges. Breezes of the South!
Who toss the golden and the flame-like flowers,
And pass the prairie-hawk that, poised on high,
Flaps his broad wings, yet moves not—ye have played
Among the palms of Mexico and vines
Of Texas, and have crisped the limpid brooks
That from the fountains of Sonora glide
Into the calm Pacific—have ye fanned
A nobler or a lovelier scene than this?
Man hath no power in all this glorious work:
The hand that built the firmament hath heaved
And smoothed these verdant swells, and sown their
    slopes
With herbage, planted them with island groves,
And hedged them round with forests. Fitting floor
For this magnificent temple of the sky—
With flowers whose glory and whose multitude
Rival the constellations! The great heavens
Seem to stoop down upon the scene in love,—
A nearer vault, and of a tenderer blue,
Than that which bends above our eastern hills.

　　As o'er the verdant waste I guide my steed,
Among the high rank grass that sweeps his sides

The hollow beating of his footstep seems
A sacrilegious sound. I think of those
Upon whose rest he tramples. Are they here—
The dead of other days?—and did the dust
Of these fair solitudes once stir with life
And burn with passion? Let the mighty mounds
That overlook the rivers, or that rise
In the dim forest crowded with old oaks,
Answer. A race, that long has passed away,
Built them;—a disciplined and populous race
Heaped, with long toil, the earth, while yet the Greek
Was hewing the Pentelicus to forms
Of symmetry, and rearing on its rock
The glittering Parthenon. These ample fields
Nourished their harvests, here their herds were fed,
When haply by their stalls the bison lowed,
And bowed his manèd shoulder to the yoke.
All day this desert murmured with their toils,
Till twilight blushed, and lovers walked, and wooed
In a forgotten language, and old tunes,
From instruments of unremembered form,
Gave the soft winds a voice. The red man came—
The roaming hunter tribes, warlike and fierce,
And the mound-builders vanished from the earth.
The solitude of centuries untold
Has settled where they dwelt. The prairie-wolf
Hunts in their meadows, and his fresh-dug den
Yawns by my path. The gopher mines the ground
Where stood the swarming cities. All is gone;
All—save the piles of earth that hold their bones,
The platforms where they worshipped unknown gods,
The barriers which they builded from the soil
To keep the foe at bay—till o'er the walls
The wild beleaguerers broke, and, one by one,
The strongholds of the plain were forced, and heaped

With corpses. The brown vultures of the wood
Flocked to those vast uncovered sepulchres,
And sat unscared and silent at their feast.
Haply some solitary fugitive,
Lurking in marsh and forest, till the sense
Of desolation and of fear became
Bitterer than death, yielded himself to die.
Man's better nature triumphed then. Kind words
Welcomed and soothed him; the rude conquerors
Seated the captive with their chiefs; he chose
A bride among their maidens, and at length
Seemed to forget—yet ne'er forgot—the wife
Of his first love, and her sweet little ones,
Butchered, amid their shrieks, with all his race.

Thus change the forms of being. Thus arise
Races of living things, glorious in strength,
And perish, as the quickening breath of God
Fills them, or is withdrawn. The red man, too,
Has left the blooming wilds he ranged so long,
And, nearer to the Rocky Mountains, sought
A wilder hunting-ground. The beaver builds
No longer by these streams, but far away,
On waters whose blue surface ne'er gave back
The white man's face—among Missouri's springs,
And pools whose issues swell the Oregon—
He rears his little Venice. In these plains
The bison feeds no more. Twice twenty leagues
Beyond remotest smoke of hunter's camp,
Roams the majestic brute, in herds that shake
The earth with thundering steps—yet here I meet
His ancient footprints stamped beside the pool.

Still this great solitude is quick with life.
Myriads of insects, gaudy as the flowers
They flutter over, gentle quadrupeds,

And birds, that scarce have learned the fear of man,
Are here, and sliding reptiles of the ground,
Startlingly beautiful. The graceful deer
Bounds to the wood at my approach. The bee,
A more adventurous colonist than man,
With whom he came across the eastern deep,
Fills the savannas with his murmurings,
And hides his sweets, as in the golden age,
Within the hollow oak. I listen long
To his domestic hum, and think I hear
The sound of that advancing multitude
Which soon shall fill these deserts. From the ground
Comes up the laugh of children, the soft voice
Of maidens, and the sweet and solemn hymn
Of Sabbath worshippers. The low of herds
Blends with the rustling of the heavy grain
Over the dark brown furrows. All at once
A fresher wind sweeps by, and breaks my dream,
And I am in the wilderness alone.

# Walter Savage Landor

(1775–1864)

## Lately our poets

Lately our poets loiter'd in green lanes,
Content to catch the ballads of the plains;
I fancied I had strength enough to climb
A loftier station at no distant time,
And might securely from intrusion doze
Upon the flowers thro' which Ilissus flows.
In those pale olive grounds all voices cease,
And from afar dust fills the paths of Greece.
My slumber broken and my doublet torn,
I find the laurel also bears a thorn.

## Rose Aylmer

Ah what avails the sceptred race,
    Ah what the form divine!
What, every virtue, every grace!
    Rose Aylmer, all were thine.

Rose Aylmer, whom these wakeful eyes
    May weep, but never see,
A night of sorrows and of sighs
    I consecrate to thee.

## Ianthe

Past ruin'd Ilion Helen lives,
  Alcestis rises from the shades;
Verse calls them forth; 'tis verse that gives
  Immortal youth to mortal maids.

Soon shall Oblivion's deepening veil
  Hide all the peopled hills you see,
The gay, the proud, while lovers hail
  In distant ages you and me.

The tear for fading beauty check,
  For passing glory cease to sigh;
One form shall rise above the wreck,
  One name, Ianthe, shall not die.

## Graceful Acacia

Graceful Acacia! slender, brittle,
  I think I know the like of thee;
But thou art tall and she is little . . .
  What God shall call her his own tree?
Some God must be the last to change her;
  From him alone she will not flee;
O may he fix to earth the ranger,
  And may he lend her shade to me!

## To Our House-Dog Captain

Captain! we often heretofore
Have boxt behind the coach-house door,
When thy strong paws were rear'd against
My ribs and bosom, badly fenced:
None other dared to try thy strength,
And hurl thee side-long at full length,
But we well knew each other's mind,
And paid our little debts in kind.
I often braved with boyish fist
The vanquisht bull's antagonist,
And saw unsheath'd thy tiny teeth
And the dark cell that oped beneath.
Thou wert like others of the strong,
But only more averse from wrong;
Reserved and proud perhaps, but just,
And strict and constant to thy trust,
Somewhat inclement to the poor,
Suspecting each for evil-doer,
But hearing reason when I spoke,
And letting go the ragged cloak.
Thee dared I; but I never dar'd
To drive the pauper from the yard.

## Dirce

Stand close around, ye Stygian set,
 With Dirce in one boat conveyed!
Or Charon, seeing, may forget
 That he is old and she a shade.

## Death stands above me

Death stands above me, whispering low
   I know not what into my ear:
Of his strange language all I know
   Is, there is not a word of fear.


## Age

Death, tho I see him not, is near
And grudges me my eightieth year.
Now, I would give him all these last
For one that fifty have run past.
Ah! he strikes all things, all alike,
But bargains: those he will not strike.


## Izaac Walton, Cotton, and William Oldways

*Walton.* Whenever I am beside a river or rivulet on a sunny
day . . . I am readier to live and less unready to die.

   Son Cotton! these light idle brooks,
Peeping into so many nooks,
Yet have not for their idlest wave
The leisure you may think they have:
No, not the little ones that run
And hide behind the first big stone,

When they have squirted in the eye
Of their next neighbour passing by;
Nor yonder curly sideling fellow
Of tones than Pan's own flute more mellow,
Who learns his tune and tries it over
As girl who fain would please her lover.
Something has each of them to say . . .
He says it, and then runs away,
And says it in another place . . .
Continuing the unthrifty chase.
    We have as many tales to tell,
And look as gay and run as well,
But leave another to pursue
What we had promised we would do,
Till, in the order God has fated,
One after one precipitated,
Whether we *would* on, or would *not* on,
Just like these idle waves, son Cotton!


## Mimnermus incert.

Mimnermus . . . Take however the verses . . . Certainly
they are his best. (*Aspasia to Cleone.*)

    I wish not Thasos rich in mines,
Nor Naxos girt around with vines,
Nor Crete nor Samos, the abodes
Of those who govern men and Gods,
Nor wider Lydia, where the sound
Of tymbrels shakes the thymy ground,
And with white feet and with hoofs cloven
The dedal dance is spun and woven:
Meanwhile each prying younger thing
Is sent for water to the spring,

Under where red Priapus rears
His club amid the junipers;
In this whole world enough for me
Is any spot the Gods decree;
Albeit the pious and the wise
Would tarry where, like mulberries,
In the first hour of ripeness fall
The tender creatures, one and all.
To take what falls with even mind
Jove wills, and we must be resign'd.


## Ternissa! you are fled

Ternissa! you are fled!
  I say not to the dead,
But to the happy ones who rest below:
  For surely, surely, where
  Your voice and graces are,
Nothing of death can any feel or know.
  Girls who delight to dwell
  Where grows most asphodel,
Gather to their calm breasts each word you speak:
  The mild Persephone
  Places you on her knee,
And your cool palm smoothes down stern Pluto's cheek.


## Dull is my verse

Dull is my verse: not even thou
  Who movest many cares away
From this lone breast and weary brow,

Canst make, as once, its fountain play;
No, nor those gentle words that now
Support my heart to hear thee say:
"The bird upon its lonely bough
Sings sweetest at the close of day."

# Thomas Moore

(1779–1852)

## The Meeting of the Waters

There is not in the wide world a valley so sweet,
As that vale in whose bosom the bright waters meet;
Oh! the last rays of feeling and life must depart
Ere the bloom of that valley shall fade from my heart.

Yet it *was* not that Nature had shed o'er the scene
Her purest of crystal and brightest of green;
'Twas *not* her soft magic of streamlet or hill,
Oh! no—it was something more exquisite still.

'Twas that friends, the beloved of my bosom, were near,
Who made every dear scene of enchantment more dear,
And who felt how the best charms of Nature improve,
When we see them reflected from looks that we love.

Sweet vale of Avoca! how calm could I rest
In thy bosom of shade, with the friends I love best,
Where the storms that we feel in this cold world should
    cease,
And our hearts, like thy waters, be mingled in peace.


## Believe me, if all those endearing young charms

Believe me, if all those endearing young charms,
    Which I gaze on so fondly to-day,
Were to change by to-morrow, and fleet in my arms,

Like fairy-gifts fading away,
Thou wouldst still be ador'd, as this moment thou art
Let thy loveliness fade as it will,
And around the dear ruin each wish of my heart
    Would entwine itself verdantly still.

It is not while beauty and youth are thine own,
    And thy cheeks unprofan'd by a tear,
That the fervor and faith of a soul can be known,
    To which time will but make thee more dear;
No, the heart that has truly lov'd never forgets,
    But as truly loves on to the close,
As the sun-flower turns on her god, when he sets,
    The same look which she turn'd when he rose.

## Ill Omens

When daylight was yet sleeping under the billow,
    And stars in the heavens still lingering shone,
Young Kitty, all blushing, rose up from her pillow,
    The last time she e'er was to press it alone.
For the youth whom she treasured her heart and her
        soul in,
    Had promised to link the last tie before noon;
And when once the young heart of a maiden is stolen,
    The maiden herself will steal after it soon.

As she look'd in the glass which a woman ne'er misses
    Nor ever wants time for a sly glance or two,
A butterfly, fresh from the night flower's kisses,
    Flew over the mirror and shaded her view.
Enraged with the insect for hiding her graces,
    She brushed him—he fell, alas! never to rise—
"Ah! such," said the girl, "is the pride of our faces,
    For which the soul's innocence too often dies."

While she stole through the garden, where heart's-ease
    was growing,
  She cull'd some, and kiss'd off its night-fallen dew;
And a rose further on look'd so tempting and glowing,
  That, spite of her haste, she must gather it too;
But, while o'er the roses too carelessly leaning,
  Her zone flew in two and the heart's-ease was lost:
"Ah! this means," said the girl (and she sighed at its
    meaning)
  "That love is scarce worth the repose it will cost!"


## At the mid hour of night

*Air—"Molly, my Dear"*

At the mid hour of night, when stars are weeping, I fly
To the lone vale we loved when life was warm in thine
    eye,
  And I think that if spirits can steal from the regions
    of air
  To revisit past scenes of delight, thou wilt come to
    me there,
And tell me our love is remember'd, even in the sky!

Then I sing the wild song it once was rapture to hear!
When our voices, commingling, breathed like one on the
    ear,
  And, as Echo far off through the vale my sad orison
    rolls,
  I think, oh, my love! 'tis thy voice from the kingdom
    of souls,
Faintly answering still the notes that once were so dear.

## Oft, in the stilly night

Oft, in the stilly night,
  Ere Slumber's chain has bound me,
Fond Memory brings the light
  Of other days around me;
    The smiles, the tears,
    Of boyhood's years,
  The words of love then spoken;
    The eyes that shone,
    Now dimm'd and gone,
  The cheerful hearts now broken!
Thus, in the stilly night,
  Ere Slumber's chain has bound me,
Sad Memory brings the light
  Of other days around me.

When I remember all
  The friends so link'd together,
I've seen around me fall,
  Like leaves in wintry weather;
    I feel like one,
    Who treads alone
  Some banquet-hall deserted,
    Whose lights are fled,
    Whose garlands dead,
  And all but he departed!
Thus, in the stilly night,
  Ere Slumber's chain has bound me,
Sad Memory brings the light
  Of other days around me.

## 'Tis the last rose of summer

*Air—"Groves of Blarney"*

'Tis the last rose of summer,
  Left blooming alone;
All her lovely companions
  Are faded and gone;
No flower of her kindred,
  No rose-bud is nigh,
To reflect back her blushes,
  Or give sigh for sigh!

I'll not leave thee, thou lone one!
  To pine on the stem;
Since the lovely are sleeping,
  Go, sleep thou with them.
Thus kindly I scatter
  Thy leaves o'er the bed,
Where thy mates of the garden
  Lie scentless and dead.

So soon may *I* follow,
  When friendships decay,
And from Love's shining circle
  The gems drop away!
When true hearts lie wither'd,
  And fond ones are flown,
Oh! who would inhabit
  This bleak world alone?

## To ladies' eyes

To ladies' eyes a round, boy,
   We can't refuse, we can't refuse;
Though bright eyes so abound, boy,
   'Tis hard to choose, 'tis hard to choose.
For thick as stars that lighten
   Yon airy bowers, yon airy bowers,
The countless eyes that brighten
   This earth of ours, this earth of ours.
But fill the cup—where'er, boy,
   Our choice may fall, our choice may fall,
We're sure to find Love there, boy,
   So drink them all! so drink them all!

Some looks there are so holy,
   They seem but given, they seem but given,
As splendid beacons solely,
   To light to heaven, to light to heaven.
While some—oh! ne'er believe them—
   With tempting ray, with tempting ray,
Would lead us (God forgive them!)
   The other way, the other way.
But fill the cup—where'er, boy,
   Our choice may fall, our choice may fall,
We're sure to find Love there, boy,
   So drink them all! so drink them all!

In some, as in a mirror,
   Love seems portrayed, Love seems portrayed;
But shun the flattering error,
   'Tis but his shade, 'tis but his shade.
Himself has fixed his dwelling

In eyes we know, in eyes we know,
And lips—but this is telling,
So here they go! so here they go!
Fill up, fill up—where'er, boy,
Our choice may fall, our choice may fall,
We're sure to find Love there, boy,
So drink them all! so drink them all!


## They may rail at this life

They may rail at this life—from the hour I began it,
I've found it a life full of kindness and bliss;
And until they can show me some happier planet,
More social and bright, I'll content me with this.
As long as the world has such lips and such eyes,
As before me this moment enraptured I see,
They may say what they will of the orbs in the skies,
But this earth is the planet for you, love, and me.

In Mercury's star, where each minute can bring them
New sunshine and wit from the fountain on high,
Though the nymphs may have livelier poets to sing
them,
They've none, even there, more enamoured than I.
And as long as this harp can be wakened to love,
And that eye its divine inspiration shall be,
They may talk as they will of their Edens above,
But this earth is the planet for you, love, and me.

In that star of the west, by whose shadowy splendor
At twilight so often we've roamed through the dew,
There are maidens, perhaps, who have bosoms as tender,
And look, in their twilights, as lovely as you.
But though they were even more bright than the queen

Of that isle they inhabit in heaven's blue sea,
As I never those fair young celestials have seen,
  Why,—this earth is the planet for you, love, and me.

As for those chilly orbs on the verge of creation,
  Where sunshine and smiles must be equally rare,
Did they want a supply of cold hearts for that station,
  Heaven knows we have plenty on earth we could
    spare.
Oh! think what a world we should have of it here,
  If the haters of peace, of affection, and glee,
Were to fly up to Saturn's comfortless sphere,
  And leave earth to such spirits as you, love, and me.


## I wish I was by that dim Lake

*Air—"I wish I was on yonder Hill"*

I wish I was by that dim Lake,
Where sinful souls their farewell take
Of this vain world, and half-way lie
In death's cold shadow, ere they die.
There, there, far from thee,
Deceitful world, my home should be;
Where, come what might of gloom and pain,
False hope should ne'er deceive again.

The lifeless sky, the mournful sound
Of unseen waters falling round;
The dry leaves, quiv'ring o'er my head,
Like man, unquiet ev'n when dead!
These, ay, these shall wean
My soul from life's deluding scene,
And turn each thought, o'ercharged with gloom,
Like willows, downward tow'rds the tomb.

As they, who to their couch at night
Would win repose, first quench the light,
So must the hopes, that keep this breast
Awake, be quench'd, ere it can rest.
Cold, cold, this heart must grow,
Unmoved by either joy or woe,
Like freezing founts, where all that's thrown
Within their current turns to stone.

# George Gordon, Lord Byron

(1788–1824)

## So, we'll go no more a roving

So, we'll go no more a roving
  So late into the night,
Though the heart be still as loving,
  And the moon be still as bright.

For the sword outwears its sheath,
  And the soul wears out the breast,
And the heart must pause to breathe,
  And Love itself have rest.

Though the night was made for loving,
  And the day returns too soon,
Yet we'll go no more a roving
  By the light of the moon.

## She walks in beauty

She walks in beauty, like the night
  Of cloudless climes and starry skies;
And all that's best of dark and bright
  Meet in her aspect and her eyes:
Thus mellow'd to that tender light
  Which heaven to gaudy day denies.

One shade the more, one ray the less,
   Had half impair'd the nameless grace
Which waves in every raven tress,
   Or softly lightens o'er her face;
Where thoughts serenely sweet express
   How pure, how dear their dwelling-place.

And on that cheek, and o'er that brow,
   So soft, so calm, yet eloquent,
The smiles that win, the tints that glow,
   But tell of days in goodness spent,
A mind at peace with all below,
   A heart whose love is innocent!

## And thou art dead

*"Heu, quanto minus est cum reliquis versari quam tui meminisse!"*

And thou art dead, as young and fair
   As aught of mortal birth;
And form so soft, and charms so rare,
   Too soon return'd to Earth!
Though Earth received them in her bed,
And o'er the spot the crowd may tread
   In carelessness or mirth,
There is an eye which could not brook
A moment on that grave to look.

I will not ask where thou liest low,
   Nor gaze upon the spot;
There flowers or weeds at will may grow,
   So I behold them not:
It is enough for me to prove
That what I loved, and long must love,

Like common earth can rot;
To me there needs no stone to tell,
'Tis nothing that I loved so well.

Yet did I love thee to the last
    As fervently as thou,
Who didst not change through all the past,
    And canst not alter now.
The love where Death has set his seal,
Nor age can chill, nor rival steal,
    Nor falsehood disavow:
And, what were worse, thou canst not see
Or wrong, or change, or fault in me.

The better days of life were ours;
    The worst can be but mine:
The sun that cheers, the storm that lowers,
    Shall never more be thine.
The silence of that dreamless sleep
I envy now too much to weep;
    Nor need I to repine
That all those charms have pass'd away,
I might have watch'd through long decay.

The flower in ripen'd bloom unmatch'd
    Must fall the earliest prey;
Though by no hand untimely snatch'd,
    The leaves must drop away:
And yet it were a greater grief
To watch it withering, leaf by leaf,
    Than see it pluck'd to-day;
Since earthly eye but ill can bear
To trace the change to foul from fair.

I know not if I could have borne
    To see thy beauties fade;
The night that follow'd such a morn

Had worn a deeper shade.
The day without a cloud hath pass'd,
And thou wert lovely to the last;
   Extinguish'd, not decay'd;
As stars that shoot along the sky
Shine brightest as they fall from high.

As once I wept, if I could weep,
   My tears might well be shed,
To think I was not near to keep
   One vigil o'er thy bed;
To gaze, how fondly! on thy face,
To fold thee in a faint embrace,
   Uphold thy drooping head;
And show that love, however vain,
Nor thou nor I can feel again.

Yet how much less it were to gain,
   Though thou has left me free,
The loveliest things that still remain,
   Than thus remember thee!
The all of thine that cannot die
Through dark and dread Eternity
   Returns again to me,
And more thy buried love endears
Than aught, except its living years.

## Fare thee well

Alas! they had been friends in Youth;
But whispering tongues can poison truth;
And constancy lives in realms above;
And Life is thorny; and youth is vain;

And to be wroth with one we love,
Doth work like madness in the brain;

      •     •     •

But never either found another
To free the hollow heart from paining—
They stood aloof, the scars remaining,
Like cliffs, which had been rent asunder;
A dreary sea now flows between,
But neither heat, nor frost, nor thunder,
Shall wholly do away, I ween,
The marks of that which once hath been.
               —COLERIDGE, *Christabel.*

Fare thee well! and if for ever,
   Still for ever, fare thee well:
Even though unforgiving, never
   'Gainst thee shall my heart rebel.

Would that breast were bared before thee
   Where thy head so oft hath lain,
While that placid sleep came o'er thee
   Which thou ne'er canst know again:

Would that breast, by thee glanced over,
   Every inmost thought could show!
Then thou wouldst at last discover
   'Twas not well to spurn it so.

Though the world for this commend thee—
   Though it smile upon the blow,
Even its praises must offend thee,
   Founded on another's woe:

Though my many faults defaced me,
   Could no other arm be found,
Than the one which once embraced me,
   To inflict a cureless wound?

Yet, oh yet, thyself deceive not;
   Love may sink by slow decay,

But by sudden wrench, believe not
   Hearts can thus be torn away:

Still thine own its life retaineth,
   Still must mine, though bleeding, beat;
And the undying thought which paineth
   Is—that we no more may meet.

These are words of deeper sorrow
   Than the wail above the dead;
Both shall live, but every morrow
   Wake us from a widow'd bed.

And when thou wouldst solace gather,
   When our child's first accents flow,
Wilt thou teach her to say "Father!"
   Though his care she must forego?

When her little hands shall press thee,
   When her lip to thine is press'd,
Think of him whose prayer shall bless thee,
   Think of him thy love had bless'd!

Should her lineaments resemble
   Those thou never more may'st see,
Then thy heart will softly tremble
   With a pulse yet true to me.

All my faults perchance thou knowest,
   All my madness none can know;
All my hopes, where'er thou goest,
   Wither, yet with *thee* they go.

Every feeling hath been shaken;
   Pride, which not a world could bow,
Bows to thee—by thee forsaken,
   Even my soul forsakes me now:

But 'tis done—all words are idle—
   Words from me are vainer still;

But the thoughts we cannot bridle
  Force their way without the will.

Fare thee well!—thus disunited,
  Torn from every nearer tie.
Sear'd in heart, and lone, and blighted,
  More than this I scarce can die.


## Darkness

I had a dream, which was not all a dream.
The bright sun was extinguish'd, and the stars
Did wander darkling in the eternal space,
Rayless, and pathless, and the icy earth
Swung blind and blackening in the moonless air;
Morn came and went—and came, and brought no day,
And men forgot their passions in the dread
Of this their desolation; and all hearts
Were chill'd into a selfish prayer for light:
And they did live by watchfires—and the thrones,
The palaces of crowned kings—the huts,
The habitations of all things which dwell,
Were burnt for beacons; cities were consumed,
And men were gather'd round their blazing homes
To look once more into each other's face;
Happy were those who dwelt within the eye
Of the volcanos, and their mountain-torch:
A fearful hope was all the world contain'd;
Forests were set on fire—but hour by hour
They fell and faded—and the crackling trunks
Extinguish'd with a crash—and all was black.
The brows of men by the despairing light
Wore an unearthly aspect, as by fits
The flashes fell upon them; some lay down

And hid their eyes and wept; and some did rest
Their chins upon their clenchèd hands, and smiled;
And others hurried to and fro, and fed
Their funeral piles with fuel, and look'd up
With mad disquietude on the dull sky,
The pall of a past world; and then again
With curses cast them down upon the dust,
And gnash'd their teeth and howl'd: the wild birds
    shriek'd
And, terrified, did flutter on the ground,
And flap their useless wings; the wildest brutes
Came tame and tremulous; and vipers crawl'd
And twined themselves among the multitude,
Hissing, but stingless—they were slain for food.
And War, which for a moment was no more,
Did glut himself again:—a meal was bought
With blood, and each sate sullenly apart
Gorging himself in gloom: no love was left;
All earth was but one thought—and that was death,
Immediate and inglorious; and the pang
Of famine fed upon all entrails—men
Died, and their bones were tombless as their flesh;
The meagre by the meagre were devour'd,
Even dogs assail'd their masters, all save one,
And he was faithful to a corse, and kept
The birds and beasts and famish'd men at bay,
Till hunger clung them, or the dropping dead
Lured their lank jaws; himself sought out no food,
But with a piteous and perpetual moan,
And a quick desolate cry, licking the hand
Which answer'd not with a caress—he died.
The crowd was famish'd by degrees; but two
Of an enormous city did survive,
And they were enemies: they met beside
The dying embers of an altar-place

Where had been heap'd a mass of holy things
For an unholy usage; they raked up,
And shivering scraped with their cold skeleton hands
The feeble ashes, and their feeble breath
Blew for a little life, and made a flame
Which was a mockery; then they lifted up
Their eyes as it grew lighter, and beheld
Each other's aspects—saw, and shriek'd, and died—
Even of their mutual hideousness they died,
Unknowing who he was upon whose brow
Famine had written Fiend. The world was void,
The populous and the powerful was a lump
Seasonless, herbless, treeless, manless, lifeless,
A lump of death—a chaos of hard clay.
The rivers, lakes, and ocean all stood still,
And nothing stirr'd within their silent depths;
Ships sailorless lay rotting on the sea,
And their masts fell down piecemeal: as they dropp'd
They slept on the abyss without a surge—
The waves were dead; the tides were in their grave,
The Moon, their mistress, had expired before;
The winds were wither'd in the stagnant air,
And the clouds perish'd; Darkness had no need
Of aid from them—She was the Universe.

FROM *Childe Harold's Pilgrimage*

[*Lake Leman*]

Lake Leman woos me with its crystal face,
The mirror where the stars and mountains view
The stillness of their aspect in each trace
Its clear depth yields of their far height and hue:

There is too much of man here, to look through
With a fit mind the might which I behold;
But soon in me shall Loneliness renew
Thoughts hid, but not less cherish'd than of old,
Ere mingling with the herd had penn'd me in their fold.

To fly from, need not be to hate, mankind:
All are not fit with them to stir and toil,
Nor is it discontent to keep the mind
Deep in its fountain, lest it overboil
In the hot throng, where we become the spoil
Of our infection, till too late and long
We may deplore and struggle with the coil,
In wretched interchange of wrong for wrong
Midst a contentious world, striving where none are
    strong.

There, in a moment we may plunge our years
In fatal penitence, and in the blight
Of our own soul turn all our blood to tears,
And colour things to come with hues of Night;
The race of life becomes a hopeless flight
To those that walk in darkness: on the sea
The boldest steer but where their ports invite;
But there are wanderers o'er Eternity
Whose bark drives on and on, and anchor'd ne'er shall
    be.

Is it not better, then, to be alone,
And love Earth only for its earthly sake?
By the blue rushing of the arrowy Rhone,
Or the pure bosom of its nursing lake,
Which feeds it as a mother who doth make
A fair but froward infant her own care,
Kissing its cries away as these awake;—
Is it not better thus our lives to wear,
Than join the crushing crowd, doom'd to inflict or bear?

I live not in myself, but I become
Portion of that around me; and to me
High mountains are a feeling, but the hum
Of human cities torture: I can see
Nothing to loathe in nature, save to be
A link reluctant in a fleshly chain,
Class'd among creatures, when the soul can flee,
And with the sky, the peak, the heaving plain
Of ocean, or the stars, mingle, and not in vain.

And thus I am absorb'd, and this is life:
I look upon the peopled desert past,
As on a place of agony and strife,
Where, for some sin, to sorrow I was cast,
To act and suffer, but remount at last
With a fresh pinion; which I feel to spring,
Though young, yet waxing vigorous as the blast
Which it would cope with, on delighted wing,
Spurning the clay-cold bonds which round our being
    cling.

And when, at length, the mind shall be all free
From what it hates in this degraded form,
Reft of its carnal life, save what shall be
Existent happier in the fly and worm,—
When elements to elements conform,
And dust is as it should be, shall I not
Feel all I see, less dazzling, but more warm?
The bodiless thought? the Spirit of each spot?
Of which, even now, I share at times the immortal lot?

Are not the mountains, waves, and skies, a part
Of me and of my soul, as I of them?
Is not the love of these deep in my heart
With a pure passion? should I not contemn
All objects, if compared with these? and stem

A tide of suffering, rather than forego
Such feelings for the hard and worldly phlegm
Of those whose eyes are only turn'd below,
Gazing upon the ground, with thoughts which dare not
    glow?

(Canto iii, stanzas 68–75)

### [The Ocean]

Oh! that the Desert were my dwelling-place,
With one fair Spirit for my minister,
That I might all forget the human race,
And, hating no one, love but only her!
Ye elements!—in whose ennobling stir
I feel myself exalted—Can ye not
Accord me such a being? Do I err
In deeming such inhabit many a spot?
Though with them to converse can rarely be our lot.

There is a pleasure in the pathless woods,
There is a rapture on the lonely shore,
There is society, where none intrudes,
By the deep Sea, and music in its roar:
I love not Man the less, but Nature more,
From these our interviews, in which I steal
From all I may be, or have been before,
To mingle with the Universe, and feel
What I can ne'er express, yet cannot all conceal.

Roll on, thou deep and dark blue Ocean—roll!
Ten thousand fleets sweep over thee in vain;
Man marks the earth with ruin—his control
Stops with the shore; upon the watery plain
The wrecks are all thy deed, nor doth remain
A shadow of man's ravage, save his own,
When, for a moment, like a drop of rain,

He sinks into thy depths with bubbling groan,
Without a grave, unknell'd, uncoffin'd, and unknown.

His steps are not upon thy paths,—thy fields
Are not a spoil for him,—thou dost arise
And shake him from thee; the vile strength he wields
For earth's destruction thou dost all despise,
Spurning him from thy bosom to the skies,
And send'st him, shivering in thy playful spray
And howling, to his Gods, where haply lies
His petty hope in some near port or bay,
And dashest him again to earth:—there let him lay.

The armaments which thunderstrike the walls
Of rock-built cities, bidding nations quake,
And monarchs tremble in their capitals,
The oak leviathans, whose huge ribs make
Their clay creator the vain title take
Of lord of thee, and arbiter of war—
These are thy toys, and, as the snowy flake,
They melt into the yeast of waves, which mar
Alike the Armada's pride or spoils of Trafalgar.

Thy shores are empires, changed in all save thee—
Assyria, Greece, Rome, Carthage, what are they?
Thy waters wash'd them power while they were free,
And many a tyrant since; their shores obey
The stranger, slave, or savage; their decay
Has dried up realms to deserts:—not so thou;—
Unchangeable, save to thy wild waves' play,
Time writes no wrinkle on thine azure brow:
Such as creation's dawn beheld, thou rollest now.

Thou glorious mirror, where the Almighty's form
Glasses itself in tempests; in all time,—
Calm or convulsed, in breeze, or gale, or storm,
Icing the pole, or in the torrid ciime

Dark-heaving—boundless, endless, and sublime,
The image of eternity, the throne
Of the Invisible; even from out thy slime
The monsters of the deep are made; each zone
Obeys thee; thou goest forth, dread, fathomless, alone.

And I have loved thee, Ocean! and my joy
Of youthful sports was on thy breast to be
Borne, like thy bubbles, onward: from a boy
I wanton'd with thy breakers—they to me
Were a delight; and if the freshening sea
Made them a terror—'twas a pleasing fear,
For I was as it were a child of thee,
And trusted to thy billows far and near,
And laid my hand upon thy mane—as I do here.

(Canto iv, stanzas 177–84)

## FROM *Don Juan*

### [*Donna Julia*]

Happy the nations of the moral North!
    Where all is virtue, and the winter season
Sends sin, without a rag on, shivering forth
    ('Twas snow that brought St. Anthony to reason);
Where juries cast up what a wife is worth,
    By laying whate'er sum, in mulct, they please on
The lover, who must pay a handsome price,
Because it is a marketable vice.

Alfonso was the name of Julia's lord,
    A man well looking for his years, and who
Was neither much beloved nor yet abhorr'd:
    They lived together as most people do,
Suffering each other's foibles by accord,

And not exactly either *one* or *two*;
Yet he was jealous, though he did not show it,
For jealousy dislikes the world to know it.

Julia was—yet I never could see why—
  With Donna Inez quite a favourite friend;
Between their tastes there was small sympathy,
  For not a line had Julia ever penn'd:
Some people whisper (but, no doubt, they lie,
  For malice still imputes some private end)
That Inez had, ere Don Alfonso's marriage,
Forgot with him her very prudent carriage;

And that still keeping up the old connection,
  Which time had lately render'd much more chaste,
She took his lady also in affection,
  And certainly this course was much the best:
She flatter'd Julia with her sage protection,
  And complimented Don Alfonso's taste;
And if she could not (who can?) silence scandal,
At least she left it a more slender handle.

I can't tell whether Julia saw the affair
  With other people's eyes, or if her own
Discoveries made, but none could be aware
  Of this, at least no symptom e'er was shown;
Perhaps she did not know, or did not care,
  Indifferent from the first, or callous grown:
I'm really puzzled what to think or say,
She kept her counsel in so close a way.

Juan she saw, and, as a pretty child,
  Caress'd him often—such a thing might be
Quite innocently done, and harmless styled,
  When she had twenty years, and thirteen he;
But I am not so sure I should have smiled
  When he was sixteen, Julia twenty-three;

These few short years make wondrous alterations,
Particularly amongst sun-burnt nations.

Whate'er the cause might be, they had become
   Changed; for the dame grew distant, the youth shy,
Their looks cast down, their greetings almost dumb,
   And much embarrassment in either eye;
There surely will be little doubt with some
   That Donna Julia knew the reason why,
But as for Juan, he had no more notion
Than he who never saw the sea of ocean.

Yet Julia's very coldness still was kind,
   And tremulously gentle her small hand
Withdrew itself from his, but left behind
   A little pressure, thrilling, and so bland
And slight, so very slight, that to the mind
   'Twas but a doubt; but ne'er magician's wand
Wrought change with all Armida's fairy art
Like what this light touch left on Juan's heart.

And if she met him, though she smiled no more,
   She look'd a sadness sweeter than her smile,
As if her heart had deeper thoughts in store
   She must not own, but cherish'd more the while
For that compression in its burning core;
   Even innocence itself has many a wile,
And will not dare to trust itself with truth,
And love is taught hypocrisy from youth.

But passion most dissembles, yet betrays
   Even by its darkness; as the blackest sky
Foretells the heaviest tempest, it displays
   Its workings through the vainly guarded eye,
And in whatever aspect it arrays
   Itself, 'tis still the same hypocrisy;

Coldness or anger, even disdain or hate,
Are masks it often wears, and still too late.

Then there were sighs, the deeper for suppression,
   And stolen glances, sweeter for the theft,
And burning blushes, though for no transgression,
   Tremblings when met, and restlessness when left;
All these are little preludes to possession,
   Of which young passion cannot be bereft,
And merely tend to show how greatly love is
Embarrass'd at first starting with a novice.

Poor Julia's heart was in an awkward state;
   She felt it going, and resolved to make
The noblest efforts for herself and mate,
   For honour's, pride's, religion's, virtue's sake.
Her resolutions were most truly great,
   And almost might have made a Tarquin quake;
She pray'd the Virgin Mary for her grace,
As being the best judge of a lady's case.

She vow'd she never would see Juan more,
   And next day paid a visit to his mother,
And look'd extremely at the opening door,
   Which, by the Virgin's grace, let in another;
Grateful she was, and yet a little sore—
   Again it opens, it can be no other,
'Tis surely Juan now—No! I'm afraid
That night the Virgin was no further pray'd.

She now determined that a virtuous woman
   Should rather face and overcome temptation,
That flight was base and dastardly, and no man
   Should ever give her heart the least sensation;
That is to say, a thought beyond the common
   Preference, that we must feel upon occasion,

For people who are pleasanter than others,
But then they only seem so many brothers.

And even if by chance—and who can tell?
   The devil's so very sly—she should discover
That all within was not so very well,
   And, if still free, that such or such a lover
Might please perhaps, a virtuous wife can quell
   Such thoughts, and be the better when they're over;
And if the man should ask, 'tis but denial:
I recommend young ladies to make trial.

And then there are such things as love divine,
   Bright and immaculate, unmix'd and pure,
Such as the angels think so very fine,
   And matrons, who would be no less secure,
Platonic, perfect, "just such love as mine":
   Thus Julia said—and thought so, to be sure;
And so I'd have her think, were I the man
On whom her reveries celestial ran.

Such love is innocent, and may exist
   Between young persons without any danger.
A hand may first, and then a lip be kist;
   For my part, to such doings I'm a stranger,
But *hear* these freedoms form the utmost list
   Of all o'er which such love may be a ranger:
If people go beyond, 'tis quite a crime,
But not my fault—I tell them all in time.

Love, then, but love within its proper limits,
   Was Julia's innocent determination
In young Don Juan's favour, and to him its
   Exertion might be useful on occasion;
And, lighted at too pure a shrine to dim its
   Ethereal lustre, with what sweet persuasion

He might be taught, by love and her together—
I really don't know what, nor Julia either.

Fraught with this fine intention, and well fenced
    In mail of proof—her purity of soul,
She, for the future of her strength convinced,
    And that her honour was a rock, or mole,
Exceeding sagely from that hour dispensed
    With any kind of troublesome control;
But whether Julia to the task was equal
Is that which must be mention'd in the sequel.

Her plan she deem'd both innocent and feasible,
    And, surely, with a stripling of sixteen
Not scandal's fangs could fix on much that's seizable,
    Or if they did so, satisfied to mean
Nothing but what was good, her breast was peaceable:
    A quiet conscience makes one so serene!
Christians have burnt each other, quite persuaded
That all the Apostles would have done as they did.

And if in the mean time her husband died,
    But Heaven forbid that such a thought should cross
Her brain, though in a dream! (and then she sigh'd)
    Never could she survive that common loss;
But just suppose that moment should betide,
    I only say suppose it—*inter nos*.
(This should be *entre nous*, for Julia thought
In French, but then the rhyme would go for nought.)

I only say, suppose this supposition:
    Juan being then grown up to a man's estate
Would fully suit a widow of condition,
    Even seven years hence it would not be too late;
And in the interim (to pursue this vision)
    The mischief, after all, could not be great,

For he would learn the rudiments of love,
I mean the seraph way of those above.

So much for Julia. Now we'll turn to Juan.
 Poor little fellow! he had no idea
Of his own case, and never hit the true one;
 In feelings quick as Ovid's Miss Medea,
He puzzled over what he found a new one,
 But not as yet imagined it could be a
Thing quite in course, and not at all alarming,
Which, with a little patience, might grow charming.

Silent and pensive, idle, restless, slow,
 His home deserted for the lonely wood,
Tormented with a wound he could not know,
 His, like all deep grief, plunged in solitude:
I'm fond myself of solitude or so,
 But then, I beg it may be understood,
By solitude I mean a Sultan's, not
A hermit's, with a haram for a grot.

"Oh Love! in such a wilderness as this,
 Where transport and security entwine,
Here is the empire of thy perfect bliss,
 And here thou art a god indeed divine."
The bard I quote from does not sing amiss,
 With the exception of the second line,
For that same twining "transport and security"
Are twisted to a phrase of some obscurity.

The poet meant, no doubt, and thus appeals
 To the good sense and senses of mankind,
The very thing which everybody feels,
 As all have found on trial, or may find,
That no one likes to be disturb'd at meals
 Or love.—I won't say more about "entwined"

Or "transport," as we knew all that before,
But beg "Security" will bolt the door.

Young Juan wander'd by the glassy brooks,
    Thinking unutterable things; he threw
Himself at length within the leafy nooks
    Where the wild branch of the cork forest grew;
There poets find materials for their books,
    And every now and then we read them through,
So that their plan and prosody are eligible,
Unless, like Wordsworth, they prove unintelligible.

He, Juan (and not Wordsworth), so pursued
    His self-communion with his own high soul,
Until his mighty heart, in its great mood,
    Had mitigated part, though not the whole
Of its disease; he did the best he could
    With things not very subject to control,
And turn'd, without perceiving his condition,
Like Coleridge, into a metaphysician.

He thought about himself, and the whole earth,
    Of man the wonderful, and of the stars,
And how the deuce they ever could have birth;
    And then he thought of earthquakes, and of wars,
How many miles the moon might have in girth,
    Of air-balloons, and of the many bars
To perfect knowledge of the boundless skies;—
And then he thought of Donna Julia's eyes.

In thoughts like these true wisdom may discern
    Longings sublime, and aspirations high,
Which some are born with, but the most part learn
    To plague themselves withal, they know not why:
'Twas strange that one so young should thus concern
    His brain about the action of the sky;

If *you* think 'twas philosophy that this did,
I can't help thinking puberty assisted.

He pored upon the leaves, and on the flowers,
   And heard a voice in all the winds; and then
He thought of wood-nymphs and immortal bowers,
   And how the goddesses came down to men:
He miss'd the pathway, he forgot the hours,
   And when he look'd upon his watch again,
He found how much old Time had been a winner—
He also found that he had lost his dinner.

Sometimes he turn'd to gaze upon his book,
   Boscan, or Garcilasso;—by the wind
Even as the page is rustled while we look,
   So by the poesy of his own mind
Over the mystic leaf his soul was shook,
   As if 'twere one whereon magicians bind
Their spells, and give them to the passing gale
According to some good old woman's tale.

Thus would he while his lonely hours away
   Dissatisfied, nor knowing what he wanted;
Nor glowing reverie, nor poet's lay,
   Could yield his spirit that for which it panted,
A bosom whereon he his head might lay,
   And hear the heart beat with the love it granted,
With—several other things, which I forget,
Or which, at least, I need not mention yet.

Those lonely walks, and lengthening reveries,
   Could not escape the gentle Julia's eyes;
She saw that Juan was not at his ease;
   But that which chiefly may, and must surprise,
Is, that the Donna Inez did not tease
   Her only son with question or surmise;

Whether it was she did not see, or would not,
Or, like all very clever people, could not.

This may seem strange, but yet 'tis very common;
  For instance—gentlemen, whose ladies take
Leave to o'erstep the written rights of woman,
  And break the — Which commandment is't they
    break?
(I have forgot the number, and think no man
  Should rashly quote, for fear of a mistake.)
I say, when these same gentlemen are jealous,
They make some blunder, which their ladies tell us.

A real husband always is suspicious,
  But still no less suspects in the wrong place,
Jealous of some one who had no such wishes,
  Or pandering blindly to his own disgrace,
By harbouring some dear friend extremely vicious;
  The last indeed's infallibly the case:
And when the spouse and friend are gone off wholly,
He wonders at their vice, and not his folly.

Thus parents also are at times short-sighted;
  Though watchful as the lynx, they ne'er discover,
The while the wicked world beholds delighted,
  Young Hopeful's mistress, or Miss Fanny's lover,
Till some confounded escapade has blighted
  The plan of twenty years, and all is over;
And then the mother cries, the father swears,
And wonders why the devil he got heirs.

But Inez was so anxious, and so clear
  Of sight, that I must think, on this occasion,
She had some other motive much more near
  For leaving Juan to this new temptation;
But what that motive was, I shan't say here;
  Perhaps to finish Juan's education,

Perhaps to open Don Alfonso's eyes,
In case he thought his wife too great a prize.

It was upon a day, a summer's day;—
   Summer's indeed a very dangerous season,
And so is spring about the end of May;
   The sun, no doubt, is the prevailing reason;
But whatsoe'er the cause is, one may say,
   And stand convicted of more truth than treason,
That there are months which nature grows more merry
    in,—
March has its hares, and May must have its heroine.

'Twas on a summer's day—the sixth of June:—
   I like to be particular in dates,
Not only of the age, and year, but moon;
   They are a sort of post-house, where the Fates
Change horses, making history change its tune,
   Then spur away o'er empires and o'er states,
Leaving at last not much besides chronology,
Excepting the post-obits of theology.

'Twas on the sixth of June, about the hour
   Of half-past six—perhaps still nearer seven—
When Julia sate within as pretty a bower
   As e'er held houri in that heathenish heaven
Described by Mahomet, and Anacreon Moore,
   To whom the lyre and laurels have been given,
With all the trophies of triumphant song—
He won them well, and may he wear them long!

She sate, but not alone; I know not well
   How this same interview had taken place,
And even if I knew, I should not tell—
   People should hold their tongues in any case;
No matter how or why the thing befell,
   But there were she and Juan, face to face—

When two such faces are so, 'twould be wise,
But very difficult, to shut their eyes.

How beautiful she look'd! her conscious heart
   Glow'd in her cheek, and yet she felt no wrong.
Oh Love! how perfect is thy mystic art,
   Strengthening the weak, and trampling on the strong,
How self-deceitful is the sagest part
   Of mortals whom thy lure hath led along—
The precipice she stood on was immense,
So was her creed in her own innocence.

She thought of her own strength, and Juan's youth,
   And of the folly of all prudish fears,
Victorious virtue, and domestic truth,
   And then of Don Alfonso's fifty years:
I wish these last had not occurr'd, in sooth,
   Because that number rarely much endears,
And through all climes, the snowy and the sunny,
Sounds ill in love, whate'er it may in money.

When people say, "I've told you *fifty* times."
   They mean to scold, and very often do;
When poets say, "I've written *fifty* rhymes,"
   They make you dread that they'll recite them too;
In gangs of *fifty*, thieves commit their crimes;
   At *fifty* love for love is rare, 'tis true,
But then, no doubt, it equally as true is,
A good deal may be bought for *fifty* Louis.

Julia had honour, virtue, truth, and love
   For Don Alfonso; and she inly swore,
By all the vows below to powers above,
   She never would disgrace the ring she wore,
Nor leave a wish which wisdom might reprove;
   And while she ponder'd this, besides much more,

One hand on Juan's carelessly was thrown,
Quite by mistake—she thought it was her own;

Unconsciously she lean'd upon the other,
    Which play'd within the tangles of her hair;
And to contend with thoughts she could not smother
    She seem'd, by the distraction of her air.
'Twas surely very wrong in Juan's mother
    To leave together this imprudent pair,
She who for many years had watch'd her son so—
I'm very certain *mine* would not have done so.

The hand which still held Juan's, by degrees
    Gently, but palpably confirm'd its grasp,
As if it said, "Detain me, if you please";
    Yet there's no doubt she only meant to clasp
His fingers with a pure Platonic squeeze;
    She would have shrunk as from a toad, or asp,
Had she imagined such a thing could rouse
A feeling dangerous to a prudent spouse.

I cannot know what Juan thought of this,
    But what he did, is much what you would do;
His young lip thank'd it with a grateful kiss,
    And then, abash'd at its own joy, withdrew
In deep despair, lest he had done amiss,—
    Love is so very timid when 'tis new:
She blush'd, and frown'd not, but she strove to speak,
And held her tongue, her voice was grown so weak.

The sun set, and up rose the yellow moon:
    The devil's in the moon for mischief; they
Who call'd her CHASTE, methinks, began too soon
    Their nomenclature; there is not a day,
The longest, not the twenty-first of June,
    Sees half the business in a wicked way

On which three single hours of moonshine smile—
And then she looks so modest all the while.

There is a dangerous silence in that hour,
  A stillness, which leaves room for the full soul
To open all itself, without the power
  Of calling wholly back its self-control;
The silver light which, hallowing tree and tower,
  Sheds beauty and deep softness o'er the whole,
Breathes also to the heart, and o'er it throws
A loving languor, which is not repose.

And Julia sate with Juan, half embraced
  And half retiring from the glowing arm,
Which trembled like the bosom where 'twas placed;
  Yet still she must have thought there was no harm,
Or else 'twere easy to withdraw her waist;
  But then the situation had its charm,
And then—God knows what next—I can't go on;
I'm almost sorry that I e'er begun.

Oh Plato! Plato! you have paved the way,
  With your confounded fantasies, to more
Immoral conduct by the fancied sway
  Your system feigns o'er the controlless core
Of human hearts, than all the long array
  Of poets and romancers:—You're a bore,
A charlatan, a coxcomb—and have been,
At best, no better than a go-between.

And Julia's voice was lost, except in sighs,
  Until too late for useful conversation;
The tears were gushing from her gentle eyes,
  I wish, indeed, they had not had occasion,
But who, alas! can love, and then be wise?
  Not that remorse did not oppose temptation;

A little still she strove, and much repented,
And whispering "I will ne'er consent"—consented.

'Tis said that Xerxes offer'd a reward
  To those who could invent him a new pleasure:
Methinks the requisition's rather hard,
  And must have cost his majesty a treasure:
For my part, I'm a moderate-minded bard,
  Fond of a little love (which I call leisure);
I care not for new pleasures, as the old
Are quite enough for me, so they but hold.

Oh Pleasure! you're indeed a pleasant thing,
  Although one must be damn'd for you, no doubt:
I make a resolution every spring
  Of reformation, ere the year run out,
But somehow, this my vestal vow takes wing,
  Yet still, I trust, it may be kept throughout:
I'm very sorry, very much ashamed,
And mean, next winter, to be quite reclaim'd.

Here my chaste Muse a liberty must take—
  Start not! still chaster reader—she'll be nice hence-
forward, and there is no great cause to quake;
  This liberty is a poetic licence,
Which some irregularity may make
  In the design, and as I have a high sense
Of Aristotle and the Rules, 'tis fit
To beg his pardon when I err a bit.

This licence is to hope the reader will
  Suppose from June the sixth (the fatal day
Without whose epoch my poetic skill
  For want of facts would all be thrown away),
But keeping Julia and Don Juan still
  In sight, that several months have pass'd; we'll say

'Twas in November, but I'm not so sure
About the day—the era's more obscure.

We'll talk of that anon.—'Tis sweet to hear
    At midnight on the blue and moonlit deep
The song and oar of Adria's gondolier,
    By distance mellow'd, o'er the waters sweep;
'Tis sweet to see the evening star appear;
    'Tis sweet to listen as the night-winds creep
From leaf to leaf; 'tis sweet to view on high
The rainbow, based on ocean, span the sky.

'Tis sweet to hear the watch-dog's honest bark
    Bay deep-mouth'd welcome as we draw near home;
'Tis sweet to know there is an eye will mark
    Our coming, and look brighter when we come;
'Tis sweet to be awaken'd by the lark,
    Or lull'd by falling waters; sweet the hum
Of bees, the voice of girls, the song of birds,
The lisp of children, and their earliest words.

Sweet is the vintage, when the showering grapes
    In Bacchanal profusion reel to earth,
Purple and gushing: sweet are our escapes
    From civic revelry to rural mirth;
Sweet to the miser are his glittering heaps,
    Sweet to the father is his first-born's birth,
Sweet is revenge—especially to women,
Pillage to soldiers, prize-money to seamen.

Sweet is a legacy, and passing sweet
    The unexpected death of some old lady
Or gentleman of seventy years complete,
    Who've made "us youth" wait too—too long already
For an estate, or cash, or country seat,
    Still breaking, but with stamina so steady

That all the Israelites are fit to mob its
Next owner for their double-damn'd post-obits.

'Tis sweet to win, no matter how, one's laurels,
   By blood or ink! 'tis sweet to put an end
To strife; 'tis sometimes sweet to have our quarrels,
   Particularly with a tiresome friend:
Sweet is old wine in bottles, ale in barrels;
   Dear is the helpless creature we defend
Against the world; and dear the schoolboy spot
We ne'er forget, though there we are forgot.

But sweeter still than this, than these, than all,
   Is first and passionate love—it stands alone,
Like Adam's recollection of his fall;
   The tree of knowledge has been pluck'd—all's
      known—
And life yields nothing further to recall
   Worthy of this ambrosial sin, so shown,
No doubt in fable, as the unforgiven
Fire which Prometheus filch'd for us from heaven.

                    (Canto *i*, stanzas 64–127)

### [Gulbeyaz]

Gulbeyaz, for the first time in her days,
   Was much embarrass'd, never having met
In all her life with aught save prayers and praise;
   And as she also risk'd her life to get
Him whom she meant to tutor in love's ways
   Into a comfortable tête-à-tête,
To lose the hour would make her quite a martyr,
And they had wasted now almost a quarter.

I also would suggest the fitting time,
   To gentlemen in any such like case,
That is to say—in a meridian clime,

With us there is more law given to the chase
But here a small delay forms a great crime:
    So recollect that the extremest grace
Is just two minutes for your declaration—
A moment more would hurt your reputation.

Juan's was good; and might have been still better,
    But he had got Haidée into his head:
However strange, he could not yet forget her,
    Which made him seem exceedingly ill-bred.
Gulbeyaz, who look'd on him as her debtor
    For having had him to her palace led,
Began to blush up to the eyes, and then
Grow deadly pale, and then blush back again.

At length, in an imperial way, she laid
    Her hand on his, and bending on him eyes,
Which needed not an empire to persuade,
    Look'd into his for love, where none replies:
Her brow grew black, but she would not upbraid,
    That being the last thing a proud woman tries;
She rose, and pausing one chaste moment, threw
Herself upon his breast, and there she grew.

This was an awkward test, as Juan found,
    But he was steel'd by sorrow, wrath, and pride:
With gentle force her white arms he unwound,
    And seated her all drooping by his side,
Then rising haughtily he glanced around,
    And looking coldly in her face, he cried,
"The prison'd eagle will not pair, nor I
Serve a Sultana's sensual phantasy.

"Thou ask'st, if I can love? be this the proof
    How much I *have* loved—that I love not *thee!*
In this vile garb, the distaff, web, and woof,
    Were fitter for me: Love is for the free!

I am not dazzled by this splendid roof;
  Whate'er thy power, and great it seems to be,
Heads bow, knees bend, eyes watch around a throne,
And hands obey—our hearts are still our own."

This was a truth to us extremely trite;
  Not so to her, who ne'er had heard such things:
She deem'd her least command must yield delight,
  Earth being only made for queens and kings.
If hearts lay on the left side or the right
  She hardly knew, to such perfection brings
Legitimacy its born votaries, when
Aware of their due royal rights o'er men.

Besides, as has been said, she was so fair
  As even in a much humbler lot had made
A kingdom or confusion anywhere,
  And also, as may be presumed, she laid
Some stress on charms, which seldom are, if e'er,
  By their possessors thrown into the shade:
She thought hers gave a double "right divine";
And half of that opinion's also mine.

Remember, or (if you cannot) imagine,
  Ye! who have kept your chastity when young,
While some more desperate dowager has been waging
  Love with you, and been in the dog-days stung
By your refusal, recollect her raging!
  Or recollect all that was said or sung
On such a subject; then suppose the face
Of a young downright beauty in this case.

Suppose,—but you already have supposed,
  The spouse of Potiphar, the Lady Booby,
Phædra, and all which story has disclosed
  Of good examples; pity that so few by
Poets and private tutors are exposed,

To educate—ye youth of Europe—you by!
But when you have supposed the few we know,
You can't suppose Gulbeyaz' angry brow.

A tigress robb'd of young, a lioness,
　Or any interesting beast of prey
Are similes at hand for the distress
　Of ladies who cannot have their own way;
But though my turn will not be served with less,
　These don't express one half what I should say:
For what is stealing young ones, few or many,
To cutting short their hopes of having any?

The love of offspring's nature's general law,
　From tigresses and cubs to ducks and ducklings;
There's nothing whets the beak, or arms the claw,
　Like an invasion of their babes and sucklings;
And all who have seen a human nursery, saw
　How mothers love their children's squalls and chuck-
　　　lings;
This strong extreme effect (to tire no longer
Your patience) shows the cause must still be stronger.

If I said fire flash'd from Gulbeyaz' eyes,
　'Twere nothing—for her eyes flash'd always fire;
Or said her cheeks assumed the deepest dyes,
　I should but bring disgrace upon the dyer,
So supernatural was her passion's rise;
　For ne'er till now she knew a check'd desire:
Even ye who know what a check'd woman is
(Enough, God knows!) would much fall short of this.

Her rage was but a minute's, and 'twas well—
　A moment's more had slain her; but the while
It lasted 'twas like a short glimpse of hell:
　Nought's more sublime than energetic bile,
Though horrible to see, yet grand to tell,

Like ocean warring 'gainst a rocky isle;
And the deep passions flashing through her form
Made her a beautiful embodied storm.

A vulgar tempest 'twere to a typhoon
  To match a common fury with her rage,
And yet she did not want to reach the moon,
  Like moderate Hotspur on the immortal page;
Her anger pitch'd into a lower tune,
  Perhaps the fault of her soft sex and age—
Her wish was but to "kill, kill, kill," like Lear's,
And then her thirst of blood was quench'd in tears.

A storm it raged, and like the storm it pass'd,
  Pass'd without words—in fact she could not speak;
And then her sex's shame broke in at last,
  A sentiment till then in her but weak,
But now it flow'd in natural and fast,
  As water through an unexpected leak;
For she felt humbled—and humiliation
Is sometimes good for people in her station.

It teaches them that they are flesh and blood,
  It also gently hints to them that others,
Although of clay, are yet not quite of mud;
  That urns and pipkins are but fragile brothers,
And works of the same pottery, bad or good,
  Though not all born of the same sires and mothers;
It teaches—Heaven knows only what it teaches,
But sometimes it may mend, and often reaches.

Her first thought was to cut off Juan's head;
  Her second, to cut only his—acquaintance;
Her third, to ask him where he had been bred;
  Her fourth, to rally him into repentance;
Her fifth, to call her maids and go to bed;

Her sixth, to stab herself; her seventh, to sentence
The lash to Baba:—but her grand resource
Was to sit down again, and cry of course.

She thought to stab herself, but then she had
  The dagger close at hand, which made it awkward;
For Eastern stays are little made to pad,
  So that a poniard pierces if 'tis stuck hard:
She thought of killing Juan—but, poor lad!
  Though he deserved it well for being so backward,
The cutting off his head was not the art
Most likely to attain her aim—his heart.

Juan was moved: he had made up his mind
  To be impaled, or quarter'd as a dish
For dogs, or to be slain with pangs refined,
  Or thrown to lions, or made baits for fish,
And thus heroically stood resign'd,
  Rather than sin—except to his own wish:
But all his great preparatives for dying
Dissolved like snow before a woman crying.

As through his palms Bob Acres' valour oozed,
  So Juan's virtue ebb'd, I know not how;
And first he wonder'd why he had refused;
  And then, if matters could be made up now;
And next his savage virtue he accused,
  Just as a friar may accuse his vow,
Or as a dame repents her of her oath,
Which mostly ends in some small breach of both.

So he began to stammer some excuses;
  But words are not enough in such a matter,
Although you borrow'd all that e'er the muses
  Have sung, or even a Dandy's dandiest chatter.
Or all the figures Castlereagh abuses;
  Just as a languid smile began to flatter

His peace was making, but before he ventured
Further, old Baba rather briskly enter'd.

(Canto v, stanzas 122–43)

### [*Lady Adeline Amundeville*]

I now mean to be serious;—it is time,
   Since laughter now-a-days is deem'd too serious.
A jest at Vice by Virtue's call'd a crime,
   And critically held as deleterious:
Besides, the sad's a source of the sublime,
   Although when long a little apt to weary us;
And therefore shall my lay soar high and solemn,
As an old temple dwindled to a column.

The Lady Adeline Amundeville
   ('Tis an old Norman name, and to be found
In pedigrees, by those who wander still
   Along the last fields of that Gothic ground)
Was high-born, wealthy by her father's will,
   And beauteous, even where beauties most abound,
In Britain—which of course true patriots find
The goodliest soil of body and of mind.

I'll not gainsay them; it is not my cue;
   I'll leave them to their taste, no doubt the best:
An eye's an eye, and whether black or blue,
   Is no great matter, so 'tis in request,
'Tis nonsense to dispute about a hue—
   The kindest may be taken as a test.
The fair sex should be always fair; and no man
Till thirty, should perceive there's a plain woman.

And after that serene and somewhat dull
   Epoch, that awkward corner turn'd for days
More quiet, when our moon's no more at full,
   We may presume to criticise or praise;

Because indifference begins to lull
   Our passions, and we walk in wisdom's ways;
Also because the figure and the face
Hint, that 'tis time to give the younger place.

I know that some would fain postpone this era,
   Reluctant as all placemen to resign
Their post; but theirs is merely a chimera,
   For they have pass'd life's equinoctial line:
But then they have their claret and Madeira
   To irrigate the dryness of decline;
And county meetings, and the parliament,
And debt, and what not, for their solace sent.

And is there not religion, and reform,
   Peace, war, the taxes, and what's called the "Nation"?
The struggle to be pilots in a storm?
   The landed and the monied speculation?
The joys of mutual hate to keep them warm,
   Instead of love, that mere hallucination?
Now hatred is by far the longest pleasure;
Men love in haste, but they detest at leisure.

Rough Johnson, the great moralist, profess'd,
   Right honestly, "he liked an honest hater!"—
The only truth that yet has been confest
   Within these latest thousand years or later.
Perhaps the fine old fellow spoke in jest:—
   For my part, I am but a mere spectator,
And gaze where'er the palace or the hovel is,
Much in the mode of Goethe's Mephistopheles;

But neither love nor hate in much excess;
   Though 'twas not once so. If I sneer sometimes,
It is because I cannot well do less,
   And now and then it also suits my rhymes.
I should be very willing to redress

Men's wrongs, and rather check than punish crimes,
Had not Cervantes, in that too true tale
Of Quixote, shown how all such efforts fail.

Of all tales 'tis the saddest—and more sad,
　　Because it makes us smile: his hero's right,
And still pursues the right;—to curb the bad
　　His only object, and 'gainst odds to fight
His guerdon: 'tis his virtue makes him mad!
　　But his adventures form a sorry sight;—
A sorrier still is the great moral taught
By that real epic unto all who have thought.

Redressing injury, revenging wrong,
　　To aid the damsel and destroy the caitiff;
Opposing singly the united strong,
　　From foreign yoke to free the helpless native:—
Alas! must noblest views, like an old song,
　　Be for mere fancy's sport a theme creative,
A jest, a riddle, Fame through thick and thin sought!
And Socrates himself but Wisdom's Quixote?

Cervantes smiled Spain's chivalry away;
　　A single laugh demolish'd the right arm
Of his own country;—seldom since that day
　　Has Spain had heroes. While Romance could charm,
The world gave ground before her bright array;
　　And therefore have his volumes done such harm,
That all their glory, as a composition,
Was dearly purchased by his land's perdition.

I'm "at my old lunes"—digression, and forget
　　The Lady Adeline Amundeville;
The fair most fatal Juan ever met,
　　Although she was not evil nor meant ill;
But Destiny and Passion spread the net
　　(Fate is a good excuse for our own will),

And caught them;—what do they *not* catch, methinks?
But I'm not Œdipus, and life's a Sphinx.

I tell the tale as it is told, nor dare
   To venture a solution: "Davus sum!"
And now I will proceed upon the pair.
   Sweet Adeline, amidst the gay world's hum,
Was the Queen-Bee, the glass of all that's fair;
   Whose charms made all men speak, and women
     dumb.
The last's a miracle, and such was reckon'd,
And since that time there has not been a second.

Chaste was she, to detraction's desperation,
   And wedded unto one she had loved well—
A man known in the councils of the nation,
   Cool, and quite English, imperturbable,
Though apt to act with fire upon occasion,
   Proud of himself and her: the world could tell
Nought against either, and both seem'd secure—
She in her virtue, he in his hauteur.

It chanced some diplomatical relations,
   Arising out of business, often brought
Himself and Juan in their mutual stations
   Into close contact. Though reserved, nor caught
By specious seeming, Juan's youth, and patience,
   And talent, on his haughty spirit wrought,
And form'd a basis of esteem, which ends
In making men what courtesy calls friends.

And thus Lord Henry, who was cautious as
   Reserve and pride could make him, and full slow
In judging men—when once his judgment was
   Determined, right or wrong, on friend or foe,
Had all the pertinacity pride has,
   Which knows no ebb to its imperious flow,

And loves or hates, disdaining to be guided,
Because its own good pleasure hath decided.

His friendships, therefore, and no less aversions,
    Though oft well founded, which confirm'd but more
His prepossessions, like the laws of Persians
    And Medes, would ne'er revoke what went before.
His feelings had not those strange fits, like tertians,
    Of common likings, which make some deplore
What they should laugh at—the mere ague still
Of men's regard, the fever or the chill.

" 'Tis not in mortals to command success:
    But *do you more*, Sempronius—*don't* deserve it,"
And take my word, you won't have any less.
    Be wary, watch the time, and always serve it;
Give gently way, when there's too great a press;
    And for your conscience only learn to nerve it,
For, like a racer, or a boxer training,
'Twill make, if proved, vast efforts without paining.

Lord Henry also liked to be superior,
    As most men do, the little or the great;
The very lowest find out an inferior,
    At least they think so, to exert their state
Upon: for there are very few things wearier
    Than solitary Pride's oppressive weight,
Which mortals generously would divide,
By bidding others carry while they ride.

In birth, in rank, in fortune likewise equal,
    O'er Juan he could no distinction claim;
In years he had the advantage of time's sequel;
    And, as he thought, in country much the same—
Because bold Britons have a tongue and free quill,
    At which all modern nations vainly aim;

And the Lord Henry was a great debater,
So that few members kept the house up later.

These were advantages: and then he thought—
   It was his foible, but by no means sinister—
That few or none more than himself had caught
   Court mysteries, having been himself a minister:
He liked to teach that which he had been taught,
   And greatly shone whenever there had been a stir;
And reconciled all qualities which grace man,
Always a patriot, and sometimes a placeman.

He liked the gentle Spaniard for his gravity;
   He almost honour'd him for his docility;
Because, though young, he acquiesced with suavity,
   Or contradicted but with proud humility.
He knew the world, and would not see depravity
   In faults which sometimes show the soil's fertility,
If that the weeds 'erlive not the first crop—
For then they are very difficult to stop.

And then he talk'd with him about Madrid,
   Constantinople, and such distant places;
Where people always did as they were bid,
   Or did what they should not with foreign graces.
Of coursers also spake they: Henry rid
   Well, like most Englishmen, and loved the races;
And Juan, like a true-born Andalusian,
Could back a horse, as despots ride a Russian.

And thus acquaintance grew, at noble routs,
   And diplomatic dinners, or at other—
For Juan stood well both with Ins and Outs,
   As in freemasonry a higher brother.
Upon his talent Henry had no doubts;
   His manner show'd him sprung from a high mother;

And all men like to show their hospitality
To him whose breeding matches with his quality.

At Blank-Blank Square;—for we will break no squares
   By naming streets: since men are so censorious,
And apt to sow an author's wheat with tares,
   Reaping allusions private and inglorious,
Where none were dreamt of, unto love's affairs,
   Which were, or are, or are to be notorious,
That therefore do I previously declare,
Lord Henry's mansion was in Blank-Blank Square.

Also there bin another pious reason
   For making squares and streets anonymous;
Which is, that there is scarce a single season
   Which doth not shake some very splendid house
With some slight heart-quake of domestic treason—
   A topic scandal doth delight to rouse:
Such I might stumble over unawares,
Unless I knew the very chastest squares.

'Tis true, I might have chosen Piccadilly,
   A place where peccadillos are unknown;
But I have motives, whether wise or silly,
   For letting that pure sanctuary alone.
Therefore I name not square, street, place, until I
   Find one where nothing naughty can be shown,
A vestal shrine of innocence of heart:
Such are—but I have lost the London Chart.

At Henry's mansion then, in Blank-Blank Square,
   Was Juan a recherché, welcome guest,
As many other noble scions were;
   And some who had but talent for their crest;
Or wealth, which is a passport everywhere;
   Or even mere fashion, which indeed's the best

Recommendation; and to be well drest
Will very often supersede the rest.

And since "there's safety in a multitude
    Of counsellors," as Solomon has said,
Or some one for him, in some sage, grave mood;—
    Indeed we see the daily proof display'd
In senates, at the bar, in wordy feud,
    Where'er collective wisdom can parade,
Which is the only cause that we can guess
Of Britain's present wealth and happiness;—

But as "there's safety" grated in the number
    "Of counsellors" for men,—thus for the sex
A large acquaintance lets not Virtue slumber;
    Or should it shake, the choice will more perplex—
Variety itself will more encumber.
    'Midst many rocks we guard more against wrecks;
And thus with women: howsoe'er it shocks some's
Self-love, there's safety in a crowd of coxcombs.

But Adeline had not the least occasion
    For such a shield, which leaves but little merit
To virtue proper, or good education.
    Her chief resource was in her own high spirit,
Which judged mankind at their due estimation;
    And for coquetry, she disdain'd to wear it:
Secure of admiration, its impression
Was faint as of an every-day possession.

To all she was polite without parade;
    To some she show'd attention of that kind
Which flatters, but is flattery convey'd
    In such a sort as cannot leave behind
A trace unworthy either wife or maid;—
    A gentle, genial courtesy of mind,

To those who were, or pass'd for meritorious,
Just to console sad glory for being glorious;

Which is in all respects, save now and then,
   A dull and desolate appendage. Gaze
Upon the shades of those distinguish'd men
   Who were or are the puppet-shows of praise,
The praise of persecution. Gaze again
   On the most favour'd; and amidst the blaze
Of sunset halos o'er the laurel-brow'd,
What can ye recognize?—a gilded cloud.

There also was of course in Adeline
   That calm patrician polish in the address,
Which ne'er can pass the equinoctial line
   Of anything which nature would express;
Just as a mandarin finds nothing fine,—
   At least his manner suffers not to guess,
That anything he views can greatly please.
Perhaps we have borrow'd this from the Chinese—

Perhaps from Horace: his *"Nil admirari"*
   Was what he call'd the "Art of Happiness";
An art on which the artists greatly vary,
   And have not yet attain'd to much success.
However, 'tis expedient to be wary:
   Indifference certes don't produce distress;
And rash enthusiasm in good society
Were nothing but a moral inebriety.

But Adeline was not indifferent: for
   (*Now* for a common-place!) beneath the snow,
As a volcano holds the lava more
   Within—*et cætera*. Shall I go on?—No
I hate to hunt down a tired metaphor,
   So let the often-used volcano go.

Poor thing! How frequently, by me and others,
It hath been stirr'd up till its smoke quite smothers!

I'll have another figure in a trice:—
   What say you to a bottle of champagne?
Frozen into a very vinous ice,
   Which leaves few drops of that immortal rain,
Yet in the very centre, past all price,
   About a liquid glassful will remain;
And this is stronger than the strongest grape
Could e'er express in its expanded shape:

'Tis the whole spirit brought to a quintessence;
   And thus the chilliest aspects may concentre
A hidden nectar under a cold presence.
   And such are many—though I only meant her
From whom I now deduce these moral lessons,
   On which the Muse has always sought to enter.
And your cold people are beyond all price,
When once you've broken their confounded ice.

But after all they are a North-West Passage
   Unto the glowing India of the soul;
And as the good ships sent upon that message
   Have not exactly ascertain'd the Pole
(Though Parry's efforts look a lucky presage),
   Thus gentlemen may run upon a shoal;
For if the Pole's not open, but all frost
(A chance still), 'tis a voyage or vessel lost.

And young beginners may as well commence
   With quiet cruising o'er the ocean woman;
While those who are not beginners should have sense
   Enough to make for port, ere Time shall summon
With his grey signal-flag; and the past tense,
   The dreary *"Fuimus"* of all things human,

Must be declined, while life's thin thread's spun out
Between the gaping heir and gnawing gout.

But heaven must be diverted; its diversion
  Is sometimes truculent—but never mind:
The world upon the whole is worth the assertion
  (If but for comfort) that all things are kind:
And that same devilish doctrine of the Persian,
  Of the two principles, but leaves behind
As many doubts as any other doctrine
Has ever puzzled Faith withal, or yoked her in.

The English winter—ending in July,
  To recommence in August—now was done.
'Tis the postilion's paradise: wheels fly;
  On roads, east, south, north, west, there is a run.
But for post-horses who finds sympathy?
  Man's pity for himself, or for his son,
Always premising that said son at college
Has not contracted much more debt than knowledge.

The London winter's ended in July—
  Sometimes a little later. I don't err
In this: whatever other blunders lie
  Upon my shoulders, here I must aver
My Muse a glass of weatherology;
  For parliament is our barometer:
Let radicals its other acts attack,
Its sessions form our only almanack.

When its quicksilver's down at zero,—lo!
  Coach, chariot, luggage, baggage, equipage!
Wheels whirl from Carlton palace to Soho,
  And happiest they who horses can engage;
The turnpikes glow with dust; and Rotten Row
  Sleeps from the chivalry of this bright age;

And tradesmen, with long bills and longer faces,
Sigh—as the postboys fasten on the traces.

They and their bills, "Arcadians both," are left
   To the Greek kalends of another session.
Alas! to them of ready cash bereft,
   What hope remains? Of *hope* the full possession
Or generous draft, conceded as a gift,
   At a long date—till they can get a fresh one—
Hawk'd about at a discount, small or large;
Also the solace of an overcharge.

But these are trifles. Downward flies my lord,
   Nodding beside my lady in his carriage.
Away! away! "Fresh horses!" are the word,
   And changed as quickly as hearts after marriage;
The obsequious landlord hath the change restored;
   The postboys have no reason to disparage
Their fee; but ere the water'd wheels may hiss hence,
The ostler pleads too for a reminiscence.

'Tis granted; and the valet mounts the dickey—
   That gentleman of lords and gentlemen;
Also my lady's gentlewoman, tricky,
   Trick'd out, but modest more than poet's pen
Can paint,—"*Cosi viaggino i Ricchi!*"
   (Excuse a foreign slipslop now and then,
If but to show I've travell'd: and what's travel,
Unless it teaches one to quote and cavil?)

The London winter and the country summer
   Were well nigh over. 'Tis perhaps a pity,
When nature wears the gown that doth become her.
   To lose those best months in a sweaty city,
And wait until the nightingale grows dumber,
   Listening debates not very wise or witty,

Ere patriots their true *country* can remember;—
But there's no shooting (save grouse) till September.

I've done with my tirade. The world was gone;
    The twice two thousand, for whom earth was made,
Were vanish'd to be what they call alone—
    That is, with thirty servants for parade,
As many guests, or more; before whom groan
    As many covers, duly, daily laid.
Let none accuse old England's hospitality—
Its quantity is but condensed to quality.

Lord Henry and the Lady Adeline
    Departed like the rest of their compeers,
The peerage, to a mansion very fine;
    The Gothic Babel of a thousand years.
None than themselves could boast a longer line,
    Where time through heroes and through beauties
        steers;
And oaks as olden as their pedigree
Told of their sires, a tomb in every tree.

A paragraph in every paper told
    Of their departure: such is modern fame:
'Tis pity that it takes no further hold
    Than an advertisement, or much the same;
When, ere the ink be dry, the sound grows cold.
    The Morning Post was foremost to proclaim—
"Departure, for his country seat, to-day,
Lord H. Amundeville and Lady A.

"We understand the splendid host intends
    To entertain, this autumn, a select
And numerous party of his noble friends;
    'Midst whom we have heard, from sources quite
        correct,
The Duke of D—— the shooting season spends,

With many more by rank and fashion deck'd;
Also a foreigner of high condition,
The envoy of the secret Russian mission."

And thus we see—who doubts the Morning Post?
  (Whose articles are like the "Thirty-nine,"
Which those most swear to who believe them most)—
  Our gay Russ Spaniard was ordain'd to shine,
Deck'd by the rays reflected from his host,
  With those who, Pope says, "greatly daring dine."—
'Tis odd, but true,—last war the News abounded
More with these dinners than the kill'd or wounded;—

As thus: "On Thursday there was a grand dinner;
  Present, Lords A.B.C."—Earls, dukes, by name
Announced with no less pomp than victory's winner:
  Then underneath, and in the very same
Column: date, "Falmouth. There has lately been here
  The Slap-dash regiment, so well known to fame,
Whose loss in the late action we regret:
The vacancies are fill'd up—see Gazette."

To Norman Abbey whirl'd the noble pair,—
  An old, old monastery once, and now
Still older mansion,—of a rich and rare
  Mix'd Gothic, such as artists all allow
Few specimens yet left us can compare
  Withal: it lies perhaps a little low,
Because the monks preferr'd a hill behind,
To shelter their devotion from the wind.

It stood embosom'd in a happy valley,
  Crown'd by high woodlands, where the Druid oak
Stood, like Caractacus, in act to rally
  His host, with broad arms 'gainst the thunderstroke;
And from beneath his boughs were seen to sally
  The dappled foresters—as day awoke,

The branching stag swept down with all his herd,
To quaff a brook which murmur'd like a bird.

Before the mansion lay a lucid lake,
    Broad as transparent, deep, and freshly fed
By a river, which its soften'd way did take
    In currents through the calmer water spread
Around: the wildfowl nestled in the brake
    And sedges, brooding in their liquid bed:
The woods sloped downwards to its brink, and stood
With their green faces fix'd upon the flood.

Its outlet dash'd into a deep cascade,
    Sparkling with foam, until again subsiding,
Its shriller echoes—like an infant made
    Quiet—sank into softer ripples, gliding
Into a rivulet; and thus allay'd,
    Pursued its course, now gleaming, and now hiding
Its windings through the woods; now clear, now blue,
According as the skies their shadows threw.

A glorious remnant of the Gothic pile
    (While yet the church was Rome's) stood half apart
In a grand arch, which once screen'd many an aisle.
    These last had disappear'd—a loss to art:
The first yet frown'd superbly o'er the soil,
    And kindled feelings in the roughest heart,
Which mourn'd the power of time's or tempest's march,
In gazing on that venerable arch.

Within a niche, nigh to its pinnacle,
    Twelve saints had once stood sanctified in stone;
But these had fallen, not when the friars fell,
    But in the war which struck Charles from his throne,
When each house was a fortalice—as tell
    The annals of full many a line undone,—

The gallant cavaliers, who fought in vain
For those who knew not to resign or reign.

But in a higher niche, alone, but crown'd,
 The Virgin-Mother of the God-born Child,
With her Son in her blessed arms, look'd round,
 Spared by some chance when all beside was spoil'd;
She made the earth below seem holy ground.
 This may be superstition, weak or wild,
But even the faintest relics of a shrine
Of any worship wake some thoughts divine.

A mighty window, hollow in the centre,
 Shorn of its glass of thousand colourings,
Through which the deepen'd glories once could enter,
 Streaming from off the sun like seraph's wings,
Now yawns all desolate: now loud, now fainter,
 The gale sweeps through its fretwork, and oft sings
The owl his anthem, where the silenced quire
Lie with their hallelujahs quench'd like fire.

But in the noontide of the moon, and when
 The wind is winged from one point of heaven,
There moans a strange unearthly sound, which then
 Is musical—a dying accent driven
Through the huge arch, which soars and sinks again.
 Some deem it but the distant echo given
Back to the night wind by the waterfall,
And harmonised by the old choral wall:

Others, that some original shape, or form
 Shaped by decay perchance, hath given the power
(Though less than that of Memnon's statue, warm
 In Egypt's rays, to harp at a fix'd hour)
To this grey ruin, with a voice to charm
 Sad, but serene, it sweeps o'er tree or tower;

The cause I know not, nor can solve; but such
The fact:—I've heard it,—once perhaps too much.

Amidst the court a Gothic fountain play'd,
   Symmetrical, but deck'd with carvings quaint—
Strange faces, like to men in masquerade,
   And here perhaps a monster, there a saint:
The spring gush'd through grim mouths of granite
     made,
   And sparkled into basins, where it spent
Its little torrent in a thousand bubbles,
Like man's vain glory, and his vainer troubles.

The mansion's self was vast and venerable,
   With more of the monastic than has been
Elsewhere preserved: the cloisters still were stable,
   The cells, too, and refectory, I ween:
An exquisite small chapel had been able,
   Still unimpair'd, to decorate the scene;
The rest had been reform'd, replaced, or sunk,
And spoke more of the baron than the monk.

Huge halls, long galleries, spacious chambers, join'd
   By no quite lawful marriage of the arts,
Might shock a connoisseur; but when combined,
   Form'd a whole which, irregular in parts,
Yet left a grand impression on the mind,
   At least of those whose eyes are in their hearts:
We gaze upon a giant for his stature,
Nor judge at first if all be true to nature.

Steel barons, molten the next generation
   To silken rows of gay and garter'd earls,
Glanced from the walls in goodly preservation:
   And Lady Marys blooming into girls,
With fair long locks, had also kept their station:
   And countesses mature in robes and pearls:

Also some beauties of Sir Peter Lely,
Whose drapery hints we may admire them freely.

Judges in very formidable ermine
   Were there, with brows that did not much invite
The accused to think their lordships would determine
   His cause by leaning much from might to right:
Bishops, who had not left a single sermon:
   Attorneys-general, awful to the sight,
As hinting more (unless our judgments warp us)
Of the "Star Chamber" than of "Habeas Corpus."

Generals, some all in armour, of the old
   And iron time, ere lead had ta'en the lead;
Others in wigs of Marlborough's martial fold,
   Huger than twelve of our degenerate breed:
Lordlings, with staves of white or keys of gold:
   Nimrods, whose canvas scarce contain'd the steed;
And here and there some stern high patriot stood,
Who could not get the place for which he sued.

But ever and anon, to soothe your vision,
   Fatigued with these hereditary glories,
There rose a Carlo Dolce or a Titian,
   Or wilder group of savage Salvatore's:
Here danced Albano's boys, and here the sea shone
   In Vernet's ocean lights; and there the stories
Of martyrs awed, as Spagnoletto tainted
His brush with all the blood of all the sainted.

Here sweetly spread a landscape of Lorraine;
   There Rembrandt made his darkness equal light,
Or gloomy Caravaggio's gloomier stain
   Bronzed o'er some lean and stoic anchorite:—
But, lo! a Teniers woos, and not in vain,
   Your eyes to revel in a livelier sight:

His bell-mouth'd goblet makes me feel quite Danish
Or Dutch with thirst—What, ho! a flask of Rhenish.

O reader! if that thou canst read,—and know,
   'Tis not enough to spell, or even to read,
To constitute a reader; there must go
   Virtues of which both you and I have need.
Firstly, begin with the beginning—(though
   That clause is hard); and secondly, proceed;
Thirdly commence not with the end—or, sinning
In this sort, end at last with the beginning.

But reader, thou hast patient been of late,
   While I, without remorse of rhyme, or fear,
Have built and laid out ground at such a rate,
   Dan Phœbus takes me for an auctioneer.
That poets were so from their earliest date,
   By Homer's "Catalogue of ships" is clear;
But a mere modern must be moderate—
I spare you then the furniture and plate.

The mellow autumn came, and with it came
   The promised party, to enjoy its sweets.
The corn is cut, the manor full of game;
   The pointer ranges, and the sportsman beats
In russet jacket:—lynx-like is his aim;
   Full grows his bag, and wonder*ful* his feats.
Ah, nutbrown partridges! Ah, brilliant pheasants!
And ah, ye poachers!—'Tis no sport for peasants.

An English autumn, though it hath no vines,
   Blushing with Bacchant coronals along
The paths, o'er which the far festoon entwines
   The red grape in the sunny lands of song,
Hath yet a purchased choice of choicest wines;
   The claret light, and the Madeira strong.

If Britain mourn her bleakness, we can tell her,
The very best of vineyards is the cellar.

Then, if she hath not that serene decline
    Which makes the southern autumn's day appear
As if 'twould to a second spring resign
    The season, rather than to winter drear,—
Of in-door comforts still she hath a mine,—
    The sea-coal fires, the "earliest of the year";
Without doors, too, she may compete in mellow,
As what is lost in green is gain'd in yellow.

And for the effeminate *villeggiatura*—
    Rife with more horns than hounds—she hath the
        chase,
So animated that it might allure a
    Saint from his beads to join the jocund race;
Even Nimrod's self might leave the plains of Dura,
    And wear the Melton jacket for a space:
If she hath no wild boars, she hath a tame
Preserve of bores, who ought to be made game.

The noble guests, assembled at the Abbey,
    Consisted of—we give the sex the *pas*—
The Duchess of Fitz-Fulke; the Countess Crabby;
    The Ladies Scilly, Busey;—Miss Eclat,
Miss Bombazeen, Miss Mackstay, Miss O'Tabby,
    And Mrs. Rabbi, the rich banker's squaw;
Also the honourable Mrs. Sleep,
Who look'd a white lamb, yet was a black sheep:

With other Countesses of Blank—but rank;
    At once the "lie" and the "élite" of crowds;
Who pass'd like water filter'd in a tank,
    All purged and pious from their native clouds;
Or paper turn'd to money by the Bank:
    No matter how or why, the passport shrouds

The "passée" and the past; for good society
Is no less famed for tolerance than piety,—

That is, up to a certain point; which point
  Forms the most difficult in punctuation.
Appearances appear to form the joint
  On which it hinges in a higher station;
And so that no explosion cry "Aroint
  Thee, witch!" or each Medea has her Jason;
Or (to the point with Horace and with Pulci)
"*Omne tulit punctum, quæ miscuit utile dulci.*"

I can't exactly trace their rule of right,
  Which hath a little leaning to a lottery.
I've seen a virtuous woman put down quite
  By the mere combination of a coterie;
Also a so-so matron boldly fight
  Her way back to the world by dint of plottery,
And shine the very *Siria* of the spheres,
Escaping with a few slight, scarless sneers.

I have seen more than I'll say:—but we will see
  How our *villeggiatura* will get on.
The party might consist of thirty-three
  Of highest caste—the Brahmins of the ton.
I have named a few, not foremost in degree,
  But ta'en at hazard as the rhyme may run.
By way of sprinkling, scatter'd amongst these
There also were some Irish absentees.

There was Parolles, too, the legal bully,
  Who limits all his battles to the bar
And senate: when invited elsewhere, truly,
  He shows more appetite for words than war.
There was the young bard Rackrhyme, who had newly
  Come out and glimmer'd as a six weeks' star.

There was Lord Pyrrho, too, the great free-thinker;
And Sir John Pottledeep, the mighty drinker.

There was the Duke of Dash, who was a—duke,
  "Ay, every inch a" duke; there were twelve peers
Like Charlemagne's—and all such peers in look
  And intellect, that neither eyes nor ears
For commoners had ever them mistook.
  There were the six Miss Rawbolds—pretty dears!
All song and sentiment; whose hearts were set
Less on a convent than a coronet.

There were four Honourable Misters, whose
  Honour was more before their names than after;
There was the preux Chevalier de la Ruse,
  Whom France and Fortune lately deign'd to waft
    here,
Whose chiefly harmless talent was to amuse;
  But the clubs found it rather serious laughter,
Because—such was his magic power to please—
The dice seem'd charm'd, too, with his repartees.

There was Dick Dubious, the metaphysician,
  Who loved philosophy and a good dinner;
Angle, the soi-disant mathematician;
  Sir Henry Silvercup, the great race-winner.
There was the Reverend Rodomont Precisian,
  Who did not hate so much the sin as sinner;
And Lord Augustus Fitz-Plantagenet,
Good at all things, but better at a bet.

There was Jack Jargon, the gigantic guardsman;
  And General Fireface, famous in the field,
A great tactician, and no less a swordsman,
  Who ate, last war, more Yankees than he kill'd.
There was the waggish Welsh Judge, Jefferies Hards-
    man,

In his grave office so completely skill'd,
That when a culprit came for condemnation,
He had his judge's joke for consolation.

Good company's a chess-board—there are kings,
    Queens, bishops, knights, rooks, pawns; the world's a
      game;
Save that the puppets pull at their own strings,
    Methinks gay Punch hath something of the same.
My Muse, the butterfly hath but her wings,
    Not stings, and flits through ether without aim,
Alighting rarely:—were she but a hornet,
Perhaps there might be vices which would mourn it.

I had forgotten—but must not forget—
    An orator, the latest of the session,
Who had deliver'd well a very set
    Smooth speech, his first and maidenly transgression
Upon debate: the papers echoed yet
    With his début, which made a strong impression,
And rank'd with what is every day display'd—
"The best first speech that ever yet was made."

Proud of his "Hear hims!" proud, too, of his vote
    And lost virginity of oratory,
Proud of his learning (just enough to quote),
    He revell'd in his Ciceronian glory:
With memory excellent to get by rote,
    With wit to hatch a pun or tell a story,
Graced with some merit, and with more effrontery,
"His country's pride," he came down to the country.

There also were two wits by acclamation,
    Longbow from Ireland, Strongbow from the Tweed,
Both lawyers and both men of education;
    But Strongbow's wit was of more polish'd breed;
Longbow was rich in an imagination

As beautiful and bounding as a steed,
But sometimes stumbling over a potato,—
While Strongbow's best things might have come from
    Cato.

Strongbow was like a new-tuned harpsichord;
   But Longbow wild as an Æolian harp,
With which the winds of heaven can claim accord,
   And make a music, whether flat or sharp.
Of Strongbow's talk you would not change a word:
   At Longbow's phrases you might sometimes carp:
Both wits—one born so, and the other bred,
This by his heart—his rival by his head.

If all these seem an heterogeneous mass
   To be assembled at a country seat,
Yet think, a specimen of every class
   Is better than a humdrum tête-à-tête.
The days of Comedy are gone, alas!
   When Congreve's fool could vie with Molière's *bête:*
Society is smooth'd to that excess,
That manners hardly differ more than dress.

Our ridicules are kept in the back ground—
   Ridiculous enough, but also dull;
Professions, too, are no more to be found
   Professional; and there is nought to cull
Of folly's fruit: for though your fools abound,
   They're barren, and not worth the pains to pull.
Society is now one polish'd horde,
Form'd of two mighty tribes, the *Bores* and *Bored.*

But from being farmers, we turn gleaners, gleaning
   The scanty but right-well thresh'd ears of truth;
And, gentle reader! when you gather meaning,
   You may be Boaz, and I—modest Ruth.
Further I'd quote, but Scripture intervening

Forbids. A great impression in my youth
Was made by Mrs. Adams, where she cries
"That Scriptures out of church are blasphemies."

But what we can we glean in this vile age
  Of chaff, although our gleanings be not grist.
I must not quite omit the talking sage,
  Kit-Cat, the famous conversationist,
Who, in his common-place book, had a page
  Prepared each morn for evenings. "List, oh list!"
"Alas, poor ghost!"—What unexpected woes
Await those who have studied their bons-mots!

Firstly, they must allure the conversation
  By many windings to their clever clinch;
And secondly, must let slip no occasion,
  Nor *bate* (abate) their hearers of an *inch*,
But take an ell—and make a great sensation,
  If possible; and thirdly, never flinch
When some smart talker puts them to the test,
But seize the last word, which no doubt's the best.

Lord Henry and his lady were the hosts;
  The party we have touch'd on were the guests.
Their table was a board to tempt even ghosts
  To pass the Styx for more substantial feasts.
I will not dwell upon ragoûts or roasts,
  Albeit all human history attests
That happiness for man—the hungry sinner!—
Since Eve ate apples, much depends on dinner.

Witness the lands which "flow'd with milk and honey,"
  Held out unto the hungry Israelites:
To this we have added since, the love of money,
  The only sort of pleasure which requites.
Youth fades, and leaves our days no longer sunny;
  We tire of mistresses and parasites;

But oh, ambrosial cash! Ah! who would lose thee?
When we no more can use, or even abuse thee!

The gentlemen got up betimes to shoot,
   Or hunt: the young, because they liked the sport—
The first thing boys like after play and fruit;
   The middle-aged, to make the day more short;
For *ennui* is a growth of English root,
   Though nameless in our language:—we retort
The fact for words, and let the French translate
That awful yawn which sleep cannot abate.

The elderly walk'd through the library,
   And tumbled books, or criticised the pictures,
Or saunter'd through the gardens piteously,
   And made upon the hot-house several strictures,
Or rode a nag which trotted not too high,
   Or on the morning papers read their lectures,
Or on the watch their longing eyes would fix.
Longing at sixty for the hour of six.

But none were "gêné": the great hour of union
   Was rung by dinner's knell; till then all were
Masters of their own time—or in communion,
   Or solitary, as they chose to bear
The hours, which how to pass is but to few known.
   Each rose up at his own, and had to spare
What time he chose for dress, and broke his fast
When, where, and how he chose for that repast.

The ladies—some rouged, some a little pale—
   Met the morn as they might. If fine, they rode,
Or walk'd; if foul, they read, or told a tale,
   Sung, or rehearsed the last dance from abroad;
Discuss'd the fashion which might next prevail,
   And settled bonnets by the newest code,

Or cramm'd twelve sheets into one little letter,
To make each correspondent a new debtor.

For some had absent lovers, all had friends.
   The earth has nothing like a she epistle,
And hardly heaven—because it never ends.
   I love the mystery of a female missal,
Which, like a creed, ne'er says all it intends,
   But full of cunning as Ulysses' whistle,
When he allured poor Dolon:—you had better
Take care what you reply to such a letter.

Then there were billiards; cards, too, but *no* dice;—
   Save in the clubs no man of honour plays;—
Boats when 'twas water, skating when 'twas ice,
   And the hard frost destroy'd the scenting days:
And angling, too, that solitary vice,
   Whatever Izaak Walton sings or says:
The quaint, old, cruel coxcomb, in his gullet
Should have a hook, and a small trout to pull it.

With evening came the banquet and the wine;
   The conversazione; the duet,
Attuned by voices more or less divine
   (My heart or head aches with the memory yet).
The four Miss Rawbolds in a glee would shine;
   But the two youngest loved more to be set
Down to the harp—because to music's charms
They added graceful necks, white hands and arms.

Sometimes a dance (though rarely on field days,
   For then the gentlemen were rather tired)
Display'd some sylph-like figures in its maze;
   Then there was small-talk ready when required;
Flirtation—but decorous; the mere praise
   Of charms that should or should not be admired.

The hunters fought their fox-hunt o'er again,
And then retreated soberly—at ten.

The politicians, in a nook apart,
  Discuss'd the world, and settled all the spheres;
The wits watch'd every loophole for their art,
  To introduce a bon-mot head and ears;
Small is the rest of those who would be smart,
  A moment's good thing may have cost them years
Before they find an hour to introduce it;
And then, even *then*, some bore may make them lose it.

But all was gentle and aristocratic
  In this our party; polish'd, smooth, and cold,
As Phidian forms cut out of marble Attic,
  There now are no Squire Westerns as of old;
And our Sophias are not so emphatic,
  But fair as then, or fairer to behold.
We have no accomplish'd blackguards, like Tom Jones,
But gentlemen in stays, as stiff as stones.

They separated at an early hour;
  That is, ere midnight—which is London's noon:
But in the country ladies seek their bower
  A little earlier than the waning moon.
Peace to the slumbers of each folded flower—
  May the rose call back its true colour soon!
Good hours of fair cheeks are the fairest tinters,
And lower the price of rouge—at least some winters.

                                        (Canto xiii, entire)

# Percy Bysshe Shelley

(1792–1822)

## Lines Written Among the Euganean Hills

*October, 1818*

Many a green isle needs must be
In the deep wide sea of Misery,
Or the mariner, worn and wan,
Never thus could voyage on—
Day and night, and night and day
Drifting on his dreary way,
With the solid darkness black
Closing round his vessel's track;
Whilst above the sunless sky,
Big with clouds, hangs heavily,
And behind the tempest fleet
Hurries on with lightning feet,
Riving sail, and cord, and plank,
Till the ship has almost drank
Death from the o'er-brimming deep;
And sinks down, down, like that sleep
When the dreamer seems to be
Weltering through eternity;
And the dim low line before
Of a dark and distant shore
Still recedes, as ever still
Longing with divided will,
But no power to seek or shun,
He is ever drifted on

O'er the unreposing wave
To the haven of the grave.
What, if there no friends will greet;
What, if there no heart will meet
His with love's impatient beat;
Wander wheresoe'er he may,
Can he dream before that day
To find refuge from distress
In friendship's smile, in love's caress?
Then 'twill wreak him little woe
Whether such there be or no:
Senseless is the breast, and cold,
Which relenting love would fold;
Bloodless are the veins and chill,
Which the pulse of pain did fill;
Every little living nerve
That from bitter words did swerve
Round the tortured lips and brow,
Are like sapless leaflets now
Frozen upon December's bough.

On the beach of a northern sea
Which tempests shake eternally,
As once the wretch there lay to sleep,
Lies a solitary heap,
One white skull and seven dry bones,
On the margin of the stones,
Where a few gray rushes stand,
Boundaries of the sea and land:
Nor is heard one voice of wail
But the sea-mews, as they sail
O'er the billows of the gale;
Or the whirlwind up and down
Howling, like a slaughtered town,
When a king in glory rides

Through the pomp of fratricides:
Those unburied bones around
There is many a mournful sound;
There is no lament for him,
Like a sunless vapour, dim,
Who once clothed with life and thought
What now moves nor murmurs not.

Ay, many flowering islands lie
In the waters of wide Agony:
To such a one this morn was led,
My bark by soft winds piloted:
'Mid the mountains Euganean
I stood listening to the paean
With which the legioned rooks did hail
The sun's uprise majestical;
Gathering round with wings all hoar,
Through the dewy mist they soar
Like gray shades, till the eastern heaven
Bursts, and then, as clouds of even,
Flecked with fire and azure, lie
In the unfathomable sky,
So their plumes of purple grain,
Starred with drops of golden rain,
Gleam above the sunlight woods,
As in silent multitudes
On the morning's fitful gale
Through the broken mist they sail,
And the vapours cloven and gleaming
Follow, down the dark steep streaming,
Till all is bright, and clear, and still,
Round the solitary hill.

Beneath is spread like a green sea
The waveless plain of Lombardy,
Bounded by the vaporous air,

Islanded by cities fair;
Underneath Day's azure eyes
Ocean's nursling, Venice lies,
A peopled labyrinth of walls,
Amphitrite's destined halls,
Which her hoary sire now paves
With his blue and beaming waves.
Lo! the sun upsprings behind,
Broad, red, radiant, half-reclined
On the level quivering line
Of the waters crystalline;
And before that chasm of light,
As within a furnace bright,
Column, tower, and dome, and spire,
Shine like obelisks of fire,
Pointing with inconstant motion
From the altar of dark ocean
To the sapphire-tinted skies;
As the flames of sacrifice
From the marble shrines did rise,
As to pierce the dome of gold
Where Apollo spoke of old.

Sun-girt City, thou hast been
Ocean's child, and then his queen;
Now is come a darker day,
And thou soon must be his prey,
If the power that raised thee here
Hallow so thy watery bier.
A less drear ruin then than now,
With thy conquest-branded brow
Stooping to the slave of slaves
From thy throne, among the waves
Wilt thou be, when the sea-mew
Flies, as once before it flew,

O'er thine isles depopulate,
And all is in its ancient state,
Save where many a palace gate
With green sea-flowers overgrown
Like a rock of Ocean's own,
Topples o'er the abandoned sea
As the tides change sullenly.
The fisher on his watery way,
Wandering at the close of day,
Will spread his sail and seize his oar
Till he pass the gloomy shore,
Lest thy dead should, from their sleep
Bursting o'er the starlight deep,
Lead a rapid masque of death
O'er the waters of his path.

Those who alone thy towers behold
Quivering through aëreal gold,
As I now behold them here,
Would imagine not they were
Sepulchres, where human forms,
Like pollution-nourished worms,
To the corpse of greatness cling,
Murdered, and now mouldering:
But if Freedom should awake
In her omnipotence, and shake
From the Celtic Anarch's hold
All the keys of dungeons cold,
Where a hundred cities lie
Chained like thee, ingloriously,
Thou and all thy sister band
Might adorn this sunny land,
Twining memories of old time
With new virtues more sublime;
If not, perish thou and they!—

Clouds which stain truth's rising day
By her sun consumed away—
Earth can spare ye: while like flowers,
In the waste of years and hours,
From your dust new nations spring
With more kindly blossoming.

Perish—let there only be
Floating o'er thy heartless sea
As the garment of thy sky
Clothes the world immortally,
One remembrance, more sublime
Than the tattered pall of time,
Which scarce hides thy visage wan;—
That a tempest-cleaving Swan
Of the songs of Albion,
Driven from his ancestral streams
By the might of evil dreams,
Found a nest in thee; and Ocean
Welcomed him with such emotion
That its joy grew his, and sprung
From his lips like music flung
O'er a mighty thunder-fit,
Chastening terror:—what though yet
Poesy's unfailing River,
Which through Albion winds forever
Lashing with melodious wave
Many a sacred Poet's grave,
Mourn its latest nursling fled?
What though thou with all thy dead
Scarce can for this fame repay
Aught thine own? oh, rather say
Though thy sins and slaveries foul
Overcloud a sunlike soul?
As the ghost of Homer clings

Round Scamander's wasting springs;
As divinest Shakespeare's might
Fills Avon and the world with light
Like omniscient power which he
Imaged 'mid mortality;
As the love from Petrarch's urn,
Yet amid yon hills doth burn,
A quenchless lamp by which the heart
Sees things unearthly;—so thou art,
Mighty spirit—so shall be
The City that did refuge thee.

Lo, the sun floats up the sky
Like thought-wingèd Liberty,
Till the universal light
Seems to level plain and height;
From the sea a mist has spread,
And the beams of morn lie dead
On the towers of Venice now,
Like its glory long ago.
By the skirts of that gray cloud
Many-domèd Padua proud
Stands, a peopled solitude,
'Mid the harvest-shining plain,
Where the peasant heaps his grain
In the garner of his foe,
And the milk-white oxen slow
With the purple vintage strain,
Heaped upon the creaking wain,
That the brutal Celt may swill
Drunken sleep with savage will;
And the sickle to the sword
Lies unchanged, though many a lord,
Like a weed whose shade is poison,
Overgrows this region's foison,

Sheaves of whom are ripe to come
To destruction's harvest-home:
Men must reap the things they sow,
Force from force must ever flow,
Or worse; but 'tis a bitter woe
That love or reason cannot change
The despot's rage, the slave's revenge.

Padua, thou within whose walls
Those mute guests at festivals,
Son and Mother, Death and Sin,
Played at dice for Ezzelin,
Till Death cried, "I win, I win!"
And Sin cursed to lose the wager,
But Death promised, to assuage her,
That he would petition for
Her to be made Vice-Emperor,
When the destined years were o'er,
Over all between the Po
And the eastern Alpine snow,
Under the mighty Austrian.
Sin smiled so as Sin only can,
And since that time, ay, long before,
Both have ruled from shore to shore,—
That incestuous pair, who follow
Tyrants as the sun the swallow,
As Repentance follows Crime,
And as changes follow Time.

In thine halls the lamp of learning,
Padua, now no more is burning;
Like a meteor, whose wild way
Is lost over the grave of day,
It gleams betrayed and to betray:
Once remotest nations came
To adore that sacred flame,

When it lit not many a hearth
On this cold and gloomy earth:
Now new fires from antique light
Spring beneath the wide world's might;
But their spark lies dead in thee,
Trampled out by Tyranny.
As the Norway woodman quells,
In the depth of piny dells,
One light flame among the brakes,
While the boundless forest shakes,
And its mighty trunks are torn
By the fire thus lowly born;—
The spark beneath his feet is dead,
He starts to see the flames it fed
Howling through the darkened sky
With a myriad tongues victoriously,
And sinks down in fear: so thou,
O Tyranny, beholdest now
Light around thee, and thou hearest
The loud flames ascend, and fearest:
Grovel on the earth; ay, hide
In the dust thy purple pride!

Noon descends around me now:
'Tis the noon of autumn's glow,
When a soft and purple mist
Like a vaporous amethyst,
Or an air-dissolvèd star
Mingling light and fragrance, far
From the curved horizon's bound
To the point of Heaven's profound,
Fills the overflowing sky;
And the plains that silent lie
Underneath, the leaves unsodden
Where the infant Frost has trodden

With his morning-wingèd feet,
Whose bright print is gleaming yet;
And the red and golden vines,
Piercing with their trellised lines
The rough, dark-skirted wilderness;
The dun and bladed grass no less,
Pointing from this hoary tower
In the windless air; the flower
Glimmering at my feet; the line
Of the olive-sandalled Apennine
In the south dimly islanded;
And the Alps, whose snows are spread
High between the clouds and sun;
And of living things each one;
And my spirit which so long
Darkened this swift stream of song,—
Interpenetrated lie
By the glory of the sky:
Be it love, light, harmony,
Odour, or the soul of all
Which from Heaven like dew doth fall,
Or the mind which feeds this verse
Peopling the lone universe.

Noon descends, and after noon
Autumn's evening meets me soon,
Leading the infantine moon,
And that one star, which to her
Almost seems to minister
Half the crimson light she brings
From the sunset's radiant springs:
And the soft dreams of the morn
(Which like wingèd winds had borne
To that silent isle, which lies
Mid remembered agonies,

The frail bark of this lone being)
Pass, to other sufferers fleeing,
And its ancient pilot, Pain,
Sits beside the helm again.

Other flowering isles must be
In the sea of Life and Agony:
Other spirits float and flee
O'er that gulf: even now, perhaps,
On some rock the wild wave wraps,
With folded wings they waiting sit
For my bark, to pilot it
To some calm and blooming cove,
Where for me, and those I love,
May a windless bower be built,
Far from passion, pain, and guilt,
In a dell mid lawny hills,
Which the wild sea-murmur fills,
And soft sunshine, and the sound
Of old forests echoing round,
And the light and smell divine
Of all flowers that breathe and shine:
We may live so happy there,
That the Spirits of the Air,
Envying us, may even entice
To our healing Paradise
The polluting multitude;
But their rage would be subdued
By that clime divine and calm,
And the winds whose wings rain balm
On the uplifted soul, and leaves
Under which the bright sea heaves;
While each breathless interval
In their whisperings musical
The inspired soul supplies

With its own deep melodies,
And the love which heals all strife
Circling, like the breath of life,
All things in that sweet abode
With its own mild brotherhood:
They, not it, would change; and soon
Every sprite beneath the moon
Would repent its envy vain,
And the earth grow young again.

### FROM *Charles the First*

#### SONG

A widow bird sate mourning for her love
   Upon a wintry bough;
The frozen wind crept on above,
   The freezing stream below.

There was no leaf upon the forest bare,
   No flower upon the ground,
And little motion in the air
   Except the mill-wheel's sound.

### FROM *Prometheus Unbound*

Life of Life! thy lips enkindle
   With their love the breath between them;
And thy smiles before they dwindle
   Make the cold air fire; then screen them
In those looks, where whoso gazes
Faints, entangled in their mazes.

Child of Light! thy limbs are burning
  Through the vest which seems to hide them;
As the radiant lines of morning
  Through the clouds ere they divide them;
And this atmosphere divinest
Shrouds thee wheresoe'er thou shinest.

Fair are others; none beholds thee,
  But thy voice sounds low and tender
Like the fairest, for it folds thee
  From the sight, that liquid splendour,
And all feel, yet see thee never,
As I feel now, lost for ever!

Lamp of Earth! where'er thou movest
  Its dim shapes are clad with brightness,
And the souls of whom thou lovest
  Walk upon the winds with lightness,
Till they fail, as I am failing,
Dizzy, lost, yet unbewailing!

## Ode to the West Wind

### I

O wild West Wind, thou breath of Autumn's being,
Thou, from whose unseen presence the leaves dead
Are driven, like ghosts from an enchanter fleeing,

Yellow, and black, and pale, and hectic red,
Pestilence-stricken multitudes: O thou,
Who chariotest to their dark wintry bed

The wingèd seeds, where they lie cold and low,
Each like a corpse within its grave, until
Thine azure sister of the Spring shall blow

Her clarion o'er the dreaming earth, and fill
(Driving sweet buds like flocks to feed in air)
With living hues and odours plain and hill:

Wild Spirit, which art moving everywhere;
Destroyer and preserver; hear, oh, hear!

## II

Thou on whose stream, mid the steep sky's commotion,
Loose clouds like earth's decaying leaves are shed,
Shook from the tangled boughs of Heaven and Ocean,

Angels of rain and lightning: there are spread
On the blue surface of thine aëry surge,
Like the bright hair uplifted from the head

Of some fierce Maenad, even from the dim verge
Of the horizon to the zenith's height,
The locks of the approaching storm. Thou dirge

Of the dying year, to which this closing night
Will be the dome of a vast sepulchre,
Vaulted with all thy congregated might

Of vapours, from whose solid atmosphere
Black rain, and fire, and hail will burst: oh, hear!

## III

Thou who didst waken from his summer dreams
The blue Mediterranean, where he lay,
Lulled by the coil of his crystàlline streams,

Beside a pumice isle in Baiae's bay,
And saw in sleep old palaces and towers
Quivering within the wave's intenser day,

All overgrown with azure moss and flowers
So sweet, the sense faints picturing them! Thou
For whose path the Atlantic's level powers

Cleave themselves into chasms, while far below
The sea-blooms and the oozy woods which wear
The sapless foliage of the ocean, know

Thy voice, and suddenly grow gray with fear,
And tremble and despoil themselves: oh, hear!

### IV

If I were a dead leaf thou mightest bear;
If I were a swift cloud to fly with thee;
A wave to pant beneath thy power, and share

The impulse of thy strength, only less free
Than thou, O uncontrollable! If even
I were as in my boyhood, and could be

The comrade of thy wanderings over Heaven,
As then, when to outstrip thy skiey speed
Scarce seemed a vision; I would ne'er have striven

As thus with thee in prayer in my sore need.
Oh, lift me as a wave, a leaf, a cloud!
I fall upon the thorns of life! I bleed!

A heavy weight of hours has chained and bowed
One too like thee: tameless, and swift, and proud.

### V

Make me thy lyre, even as the forest is:
What if my leaves are falling like its own!
The tumult of thy mighty harmonies

Will take from both a deep, autumnal tone,
Sweet though in sadness. Be thou, Spirit fierce,
My spirit! Be thou me, impetuous one!

Drive my dead thoughts over the universe
Like withered leaves to quicken a new birth!
And, by the incantation of this verse,

Scatter, as from an unextinguished hearth
Ashes and sparks, my words among mankind!
Be through my lips to unawakened earth

The trumpet of a prophecy! O, Wind,
If Winter comes, can Spring be far behind?

## The Cloud

I bring fresh showers for the thirsting flowers,
    From the seas and the streams;
I bear light shade for the leaves when laid
    In their noonday dreams.
From my wings are shaken the dews that waken
    The sweet buds every one,
When rocked to rest on their mother's breast,
    As she dances about the sun.
I wield the flail of the lashing hail,
    And whiten the green plains under,
And then again I dissolve it in rain,
    And laugh as I pass in thunder.

I sift the snow on the mountains below,
    And their great pines groan aghast;
And all the night 'tis my pillow white,
    While I sleep in the arms of the blast.

Sublime on the towers of my skiey bowers,
    Lightning my pilot sits;
In a cavern under is fettered the thunder,
    It struggles and howls at fits;
Over earth and ocean, with gentle motion,
    This pilot is guiding me,
Lured by the love of the genii that move
    In the depths of the purple sea;
Over the rills, and the crags, and the hills,
    Over the lakes and the plains,
Wherever he dream, under mountain or stream,
    The Spirit he loves remains;
And I all the while bask in Heaven's blue smile,
    Whilst he is dissolving in rains.

The sanguine Sunrise, with his meteor eyes,
    And his burning plumes outspread,
Leaps on the back of my sailing rack,
    When the morning star shines dead;
As on the jag of a mountain crag,
    Which an earthquake rocks and swings,
An eagle alit one moment may sit
    In the light of its golden wings.
And when Sunset may breathe, from the lit sea beneath,
    Its ardours of rest and of love,
And the crimson pall of eve may fall
    From the depth of Heaven above,
With wings folded I rest, on mine aëry nest,
    As still as a brooding dove.

That orbèd maiden with white fire laden,
    Whom mortals call the Moon,
Glides glimmering o'er my fleece-like floor,
    By the midnight breezes strewn;
And wherever the beat of her unseen feet,
    Which only the angels hear,

May have broken the woof of my tent's thin roof,
    The stars peep behind her and peer;
And I laugh to see them whirl and flee,
    Like a swarm of golden bees,
When I widen the rent in my wind-built tent,
    Till the calm rivers, lakes, and seas,
Like strips of the sky fallen through me on high,
    Are each paved with the moon and these.

I bind the Sun's throne with a burning zone,
    And the Moon's with a girdle of pearl;
The volcanoes are dim, and the stars reel and swim,
    When the whirlwinds my banner unfurl.
From cape to cape, with a bridge-like shape,
    Over a torrent sea,
Sunbeam-proof, I hang like a roof,—
    The mountains its columns be.
The triumphal arch through which I march
    With hurricane, fire, and snow,
When the Powers of the air are chained to my chair,
    Is the million-coloured bow;
The sphere-fire above its soft colours wove,
    While the moist Earth was laughing below.

I am the daughter of Earth and Water,
    And the nursling of the Sky;
I pass through the pores of the ocean and shores;
    I change, but I cannot die.
For after the rain when with never a stain
    The pavilion of Heaven is bare,
And the winds and sunbeams with their convex gleams
    Build up the blue dome of air,
I silently laugh at my own cenotaph,
    And out of the caverns of rain,
Like a child from the womb, like a ghost from the tomb,
    I arise and unbuild it again.

# Hymn of Pan

From the forests and highlands
　　We come, we come;
From the river-girt islands,
　　Where loud waves are dumb
　　　　Listening to my sweet pipings.
The wind in the reeds and the rushes,
　　The bees on the bells of thyme,
The birds on the myrtle bushes,
　　The cicale above in the lime,
And the lizards below in the grass,
Were as silent as ever old Timolus was,
　　　　Listening to my sweet pipings.

Liquid Peneus was flowing,
　　And all dark Tempe lay
In Pelion's shadow, outgrowing
　　The light of the dying day,
　　　　Speeded by my sweet pipings.
The Sileni, and Sylvans, and Fauns,
　　And the Nymphs of the woods and the waves,
To the edge of the moist river-lawns,
　　And the brink of the dewy caves,
And all that did then attend and follow,
Were silent with love, as you now, Apollo,
　　　　With envy of my sweet pipings.

I sang of the dancing stars,
　　I sang of the daedal Earth,
And of Heaven—and the giant wars,
　　And Love, and Death, and Birth,—
　　　　And then I changed my pipings,—

Singing how down the vale of Maenalus
 I pursued a maiden and clasped a reed.
Gods and men, we are all deluded thus!
 It breaks in our bosom and then we bleed:
All wept, as I think both ye now would,
If envy or age had not frozen your blood,
 At the sorrow of my sweet pipings.


## To ——


Music, when soft voices die,
Vibrates in the memory;
Odors, when sweet violets sicken,
Live within the sense they quicken.

Rose leaves, when the rose is dead,
Are heaped for the belovèd's bed;
And so thy thoughts, when thou art gone,
Love itself shall slumber on.


### FROM *Hellas*


#### CHORUS

The world's great age begins anew,
 The golden years return,
The earth doth like a snake renew
 Her winter weeds outworn;
Heaven smiles, and faiths and empires gleam,
Like wrecks of a dissolving dream.

A brighter Hellas rears its mountains
 From waves serener far;
A new Peneus rolls his fountains

Against the morning-star.
Where fairer Tempes bloom, there sleep
Young Cyclads on a sunnier deep.

A loftier Argo cleaves the main,
   Fraught with a later prize;
Another Orpheus sings again,
   And loves, and weeps, and dies.
A new Ulysses leaves once more
Calypso for his native shore.

Oh, write no more the tale of Troy,
   If earth Death's scroll must be!
Nor mix with Laian rage the joy
   Which dawns upon the free;
Although a subtler Sphinx renew
Riddles of death Thebes never knew.

Another Athens shall arise,
   And to remoter time
Bequeath, like sunset to the skies,
   The splendor of its prime;
And leave, if nought so bright may live,
All earth can take or Heaven can give.

Saturn and Love their long repose
   Shall burst, more bright and good
Than all who fell, than One who rose,
   Than many unsubdued;
Not gold, not blood, their altar dowers,
But votive tears and symbol flowers.

Oh, cease! must hate and death return?
   Cease! must men kill and die?
Cease! drain not to its dregs the urn
   Of bitter prophecy.
The world is weary of the past,
Oh, might it die or rest at last!

# Adonais

### AN ELEGY ON THE DEATH OF JOHN KEATS, AUTHOR OF ENDYMION, HYPERION, ETC.

Ἀστὴρ πρὶν μὲν ἔλαμπες ἐνὶ ζωοῖσιν Ἑῷος.
νῦν δὲ θανὼν λάμπεις Ἕσπερος ἐν φθιμένοις.—PLATO

I weep for Adonais—he is dead!
O, weep for Adonais! though our tears
Thaw not the frost which binds so dear a head!
And thou, sad Hour, selected from all years
To mourn our loss, rouse thy obscure compeers,
And teach them thine own sorrow, say: "With me
Died Adonais; till the Future dares
Forget the Past, his fate and fame shall be
An echo and a light unto eternity!"

Where wert thou, mighty Mother, when he lay,
When thy Son lay, pierced by the shaft which flies
In darkness? where was lorn Urania
When Adonais died? With veilèd eyes,
'Mid listening Echoes, in her Paradise
She sate, while one, with soft enamoured breath,
Rekindled all the fading melodies,
With which, like flowers that mock the corse beneath,
He had adorned and hid the coming bulk of Death.

Oh, weep for Adonais—he is dead!
Wake, melancholy Mother, wake and weep!
Yet wherefore? Quench within their burning bed
Thy fiery tears, and let thy loud heart keep
Like his, a mute and uncomplaining sleep;
For he is gone, where all things wise and fair
Descend;—oh, dream not that the amorous Deep

Will yet restore him to the vital air;
Death feeds on his mute voice, and laughs at our despair.

Most musical of mourners, weep again!
Lament anew, Urania!—He died,
Who was the Sire of an immortal strain,
Blind, old, and lonely, when his country's pride,
The priest, the slave, and the liberticide,
Trampled and mocked with many a loathèd rite
Of lust and blood; he went, unterrified,
Into the gulf of death; but his clear Sprite
Yet reigns o'er earth; the third among the sons of light.

Most musical of mourners, weep anew!
Not all to that bright station dared to climb;
And happier they their happiness who knew,
Whose tapers yet burn through that night of time
In which suns perished; others more sublime,
Struck by the envious wrath of man or god,
Have sunk, extinct in their refulgent prime;
And some yet live, treading the thorny road,
Which leads, through toil and hate, to Fame's serene
abode.

But now, thy youngest, dearest one, has perished—
The nursling of thy widowhood, who grew,
Like a pale flower by some sad maiden cherished,
And fed with true-love tears, instead of dew;
Most musical of mourners, weep anew!
Thy extreme hope, the loveliest and the last,
The bloom, whose petals nipped before they blew
Died on the promise of the fruit, is waste;
The broken lily lies—the storm is overpast.

To that high Capital, where kingly Death
Keeps his pale court in beauty and decay,

He came; and bought, with price of purest breath,
A grave among the eternal.—Come away!
Haste, while the vault of blue Italian day
Is yet his fitting charnel-roof! while still
He lies, as if in dewy sleep he lay;
Awake him not! surely he takes his fill
Of deep and liquid rest, forgetful of all ill.

He will awake no more, oh, never more!—
Within the twilight chamber spreads apace
The shadow of white Death, and at the door
Invisible Corruption waits to trace
His extreme way to her dim dwelling-place;
The eternal Hunger sits, but pity and awe
Soothe her pale rage, nor dares she to deface
So fair a prey, till darkness, and the law
Of change, shall o'er his sleep the mortal curtain draw.

Oh, weep for Adonais!—The quick Dreams,
The passion-wingèd Ministers of thought,
Who were his flocks, whom near the living streams
Of his young spirit he fed, and whom he taught
The love which was its music, wander not,—
Wander no more, from kindling brain to brain,
But droop there, whence they sprung; and mourn
    their lot
Round the cold heart, where, after their sweet pain,
They ne'er will gather strength, or find a home again.

And one with trembling hands clasps his cold head,
And fans him with her moonlight wings, and cries;
"Our love, our hope, our sorrow, is not dead;
See, on the silken fringe of his faint eyes,
Like dew upon a sleeping flower, there lies
A tear some Dream has loosened from his brain."
Lost Angel of a ruined Paradise!

She knew not 'twas her own; as with no stain
She faded, like a cloud which had outwept its rain.

One from a lucid urn of starry dew
Washed his light limbs as if embalming them;
Another clipped her profuse locks, and threw
The wreath upon him, like an anadem,
Which frozen tears instead of pearls begem;
Another in her wilful grief would break
Her bow and wingèd reeds, as if to stem
A greater loss with one which was more weak;
And dull the barbèd fire against his frozen cheek.

Another Splendour on his mouth alit,
That mouth, whence it was wont to draw the breath
Which gave it strength to pierce the guarded wit,
And pass into the panting heart beneath
With lightning and with music: the damp death
Quenched its caress upon his icy lips;
And, as a dying meteor stains a wreath
Of moonlight vapour, which the cold night clips,
It flushed through his pale limbs, and passed to its
    eclipse.

And others came . . . Desires and Adorations,
Wingèd Persuasions and veiled Destinies,
Splendours, and Glooms, and glimmering Incarna-
    tions
Of hopes and fears, and twilight Phantasies;
And Sorrow, with her family of Sighs,
And Pleasure, blind with tears, led by the gleam
Of her own dying smile instead of eyes,
Came in slow pomp;—the moving pomp might seem
Like pageantry of mist on an autumnal stream.

All he had loved, and moulded into thought,
From shape, and hue, and odour, and sweet sound,

Lamented Adonais. Morning sought
Her eastern watch-tower, and her hair unbound,
Wet with the tears which should adorn the ground,
Dimmed the aëreal eyes that kindle day;
Afar the melancholy thunder moaned,
Pale Ocean in unquiet slumber lay,
And the wild Winds flew round, sobbing in their dis-
    may.

Lost Echo sits amid the voiceless mountains,
And feeds her grief with his remembered lay,
And will no more reply to winds or fountains,
Or amorous birds perched on the young green spray,
Or herdsman's horn, or bell at closing day;
Since she can mimic not his lips, more dear
Than those for whose disdain she pined away
Into a shadow of all sounds:—a drear
Murmur, between their songs, is all the woodmen hear.

Grief made the young Spring wild, and she threw
    down
Her kindling buds, as if she Autumn were,
Or they dead leaves; since her delight is flown,
For whom should she have waked the sullen year?
To Phoebus was not Hyacinth so dear
Nor to himself Narcissus, as to both
Thou, Adonais: wan they stand and sere
Amid the faint companions of their youth,
With dew all turned to tears; odour, to sighing ruth.

Thy spirit's sister, the lorn nightingale
Mourns not her mate with such melodious pain;
Not so the eagle, who like thee could scale
Heaven, and could nourish in the sun's domain
Her mighty youth with morning, doth complain,
Soaring and screaming round her empty nest,

As Albion wails for thee: the curse of Cain
Light on his head who pierced thy innocent breast,
And scared the angel soul that was its earthly guest!

Ah, woe is me! Winter is come and gone,
But grief returns with the revolving year;
The airs and streams renew their joyous tone;
The ants, the bees, the swallows reappear;
Fresh leaves and flowers deck the dead Seasons' bier;
The amorous birds now pair in every brake,
And build their mossy homes in field and brere;
And the green lizard, and the golden snake,
Like unimprisoned flames, out of their trance awake.

Through wood and stream and field and hill and
        Ocean
A quickening life from the Earth's heart has burst
As it has ever done, with change and motion,
From the great morning of the world when first
God dawned on Chaos; in its stream immersed,
The lamps of Heaven flash with a softer light;
All baser things pant with life's sacred thirst;
Diffuse themselves; and spend in love's delight,
The beauty and the joy of their renewèd might.

The leprous corpse, touched by this spirit tender,
Exhales itself in flowers of gentle breath;
Like incarnations of the stars, when splendour
Is changed to fragrance, they illumine death
And mock the merry worm that wakes beneath;
Nought we know, dies. Shall that alone which knows
Be as a sword consumed before the sheath
By sightless lightning?—the intense atom glows
A moment, then is quenched in a most cold repose.

Alas! that all we loved of him should be,
But for our grief, as if it had not been,

And grief itself be mortal! Woe is me!
Whence are we, and why are we? of what scene
The actors or spectators? Great and mean
Meet massed in death, who lends what life must bor-
    row.
As long as skies are blue, and fields are green,
Evening must usher night, night urge the morrow,
Month follow month with woe, and year wake year to
    sorrow.

*He* will awake no more, oh, never more!
"Wake thou," cried Misery, "childless Mother, rise
Out of thy sleep, and slake, in thy heart's core,
A wound more fierce than his, with tears and sighs."
And all the Dreams that watched Urania's eyes,
And all the Echoes whom their sister's song
Had held in holy silence, cried: "Arise!"
Swift as a Thought by the snake Memory stung,
From her ambrosial rest the fading Splendour sprung.

She rose like an autumnal Night, that springs
Out of the East, and follows wild and drear
The golden Day, which, on eternal wings,
Even as a ghost abandoning a bier,
Had left the Earth a corpse. Sorrow and fear
So struck, so roused, so rapt Urania;
So saddened round her like an atmosphere
Of stormy mist; so swept her on her way
Even to the mournful place where Adonais lay.

Out of her secret Paradise she sped,
Through camps and cities rough with stone, and steel,
And human hearts, which to her aery tread
Yielding not, wounded the invisible
Palms of her tender feet where'er they fell:

And barbèd tongues, and thoughts more sharp than
    they,
Rent the soft Form they never could repel,
Whose sacred blood, like the young tears of May,
Paved with eternal flowers that undeserving way.

In the death-chamber for a moment Death,
Shamed by the presence of that living Might,
Blushed to annihilation, and the breath
Revisited those lips, and Life's pale light
Flashed through those limbs, so late her dear delight.
"Leave me not wild and drear and comfortless,
As silent lightning leaves the starless night!
Leave me not!" cried Urania: her distress
Roused Death: Death rose and smiled, and met her vain
    caress.

"Stay yet awhile! speak to me once again;
Kiss me, so long but as a kiss may live;
And in my heartless breast and burning brain
That word, that kiss, shall all thoughts else survive,
With food of saddest memory kept alive,
Now thou art dead, as if it were a part
Of thee, my Adonais! I would give
All that I am to be as thou now art!
But I am chained to Time, and cannot thence depart!

"O gentle child, beautiful as thou wert,
Why didst thou leave the trodden paths of men
Too soon, and with weak hands though mighty heart
Dare the unpastured dragon in his den?
Defenceless as thou wert, oh, where was then
Wisdom the mirrored shield, or scorn the spear?
Or hadst thou waited the full cycle, when
Thy spirit should have filled its crescent sphere,
The monsters of life's waste had fled from thee like deer.

"The herded wolves, bold only to pursue;
The obscene ravens, clamorous o'er the dead;
The vultures to the conqueror's banner true
Who feed where Desolation first has fed,
And whose wings rain contagion;—how they fled,
When, like Apollo, from his golden bow
The Pythian of the age one arrow sped
And smiled!—The spoilers tempt no second blow,
They fawn on the proud feet that spurn them lying low.

"The sun comes forth, and many reptiles spawn;
He sets, and each ephemeral insect then
Is gathered into death without a dawn,
And the immortal stars awake again;
So is it in the world of living men:
A godlike mind soars forth, in its delight
Making earth bare and veiling heaven, and when
It sinks, the swarms that dimmed or shared its light
Leave to its kindred lamps the spirit's awful night."

Thus ceased she: and the mountain shepherds came,
Their garlands sere, their magic mantles rent;
The Pilgrim of Eternity, whose fame
Over his living head like Heaven is bent,
An early but enduring monument,
Came, veiling all the lightnings of his song
In sorrow; from her wilds Ierne sent
The sweetest lyrist of her saddest wrong,
And Love taught Grief to fall like music from his
    tongue.

Midst others of less note, came one frail Form,
A phantom among men; companionless
As the last cloud of an expiring storm
Whose thunder is its knell; he, as I guess,

Had gazed on Nature's naked loveliness,
Actaeon-like, and now he fled astray
With feeble steps o'er the world's wilderness,
And his own thoughts, along that rugged way,
Pursued, like raging hounds, their father and their prey.

A pardlike Spirit beautiful and swift—
A Love in desolation masked;—a Power
Girt round with weakness;—it can scarce uplift
The weight of the superincumbent hour;
It is a dying lamp, a falling shower,
A breaking billow;—even whilst we speak
Is it not broken? On the withering flower
The killing sun smiles brightly: on a cheek
The life can burn in blood, even while the heart may
    break.

His head was bound with pansies overblown,
And faded violets, white, and pied, and blue;
And a light spear topped with a cypress cone,
Round whose rude shaft dark ivy-tresses grew
Yet dripping with the forest's noonday dew,
Vibrated, as the ever-beating heart
Shook the weak hand that grasped it; of that crew
He came the last, neglected and apart;
A herd-abandoned deer struck by the hunter's dart.

All stood aloof, and at his partial moan
Smiled through their tears; well knew that gentle
    band
Who in another's fate now wept his own,
As in the accents of an unknown land
He sung new sorrow; sad Urania scanned
The Stranger's mien, and murmured: "Who art
    thou?"

He answered not, but with a sudden hand
Made bare his branded and ensanguined brow,
Which was like Cain's or Christ's—oh! that it should
    be so!

What softer voice is hushed over the dead?
Athwart what brow is that dark mantle thrown?
What form leans sadly o'er the white death-bed,
In mockery of monumental stone,
The heavy heart heaving without a moan?
If it be He, who, gentlest of the wise,
Taught, soothed, loved, honoured the departed one,
Let me not vex, with inharmonious sighs,
The silence of that heart's accepted sacrifice.

Our Adonais has drunk poison—oh!
What deaf and viperous murderer could crown
Life's early cup with such a draught of woe?
The nameless worm would now itself disown:
It felt, yet could escape, the magic tone
Whose prelude held all envy, hate, and wrong,
But what was howling in one breast alone,
Silent with expectation of the song,
Whose master's hand is cold, whose silver lyre unstrung.

Live thou, whose infamy is not thy fame!
Live! fear no heavier chastisement from me,
Thou noteless blot on a remembered name!
But be thyself, and know thyself to be!
And ever at thy season be thou free
To spill the venom when thy fangs o'erflow;
Remorse and Self-contempt shall cling to thee;
Hot Shame shall burn upon thy secret brow,
And like a beaten hound tremble thou shalt—as now.

Nor let us weep that our delight is fled
Far from these carrion kites that scream below;

He wakes or sleeps with the enduring dead;
Thou canst not soar where he is sitting now.—
Dust to the dust! but the pure spirit shall flow
Back to the burning fountain whence it came,
A portion of the Eternal, which must glow
Through time and change, unquenchably the same,
Whilst thy cold embers choke the sordid hearth of
 shame.

Peace, peace! he is not dead, he doth not sleep—
He hath awakened from the dream of life—
'Tis we, who lost in stormy visions, keep
With phantoms an unprofitable strife,
And in mad trance, strike with our spirit's knife
Invulnerable nothings.—*We* decay
Like corpses in a charnel; fear and grief
Convulse us and consume us day by day,
And cold hopes swarm like worms within our living
 clay.

He has outsoared the shadow of our night;
Envy and calumny and hate and pain,
And that unrest which men miscall delight,
Can touch him not and torture not again;
From the contagion of the world's slow stain
He is secure, and now can never mourn
A heart grown cold, a head grown gray in vain;
Nor, when the spirit's self has ceased to burn,
With sparkless ashes load an unlamented urn.

He lives, he wakes—'tis Death is dead, not he;
Mourn not for Adonais.—Thou young Dawn,
Turn all thy dew to splendour, for from thee
The spirit thou lamentest is not gone;
Ye caverns and ye forests, cease to moan!
Cease, ye faint flowers and fountains, and thou Air,

Which like a mourning veil thy scarf hadst thrown
O'er the abandoned Earth, now leave it bare
Even to the joyous stars which smile on its despair!

He is made one with Nature: there is heard
His voice in all her music, from the moan
Of thunder, to the song of night's sweet bird;
He is a presence to be felt and known
In darkness and in light, from herb and stone,
Spreading itself where'er that Power may move
Which has withdrawn his being to its own;
Which wields the world with never-wearied love,
Sustains it from beneath, and kindles it above.

He is a portion of the loveliness
Which once he made more lovely: he doth bear
His part, while the one Spirit's plastic stress
Sweeps through the dull dense world, compelling
    there,
All new successions to the forms they wear;
Torturing th' unwilling dross that checks its flight
To its own likeness, as each mass may bear;
And bursting in its beauty and its might
From trees and beasts and men into the Heaven's light.

The splendours of the firmament of time
May be eclipsed, but are extinguished not;
Like stars to their appointed height they climb,
And death is a low mist which cannot blot
The brightness it may veil. When lofty thought
Lifts a young heart above its mortal lair,
And love and life contend in it, for what
Shall be its earthly doom, the dead live there
And move like winds of light on dark and stormy air.

The inheritors of unfulfilled renown
Rose from their thrones, built beyond mortal thought,

Far in the Unapparent. Chatterton
Rose pale,—his solemn agony had not
Yet faded from him; Sidney, as he fought
And as he fell and as he lived and loved
Sublimely mild, a Spirit without spot,
Arose; and Lucan, by his death approved:
Oblivion as they rose shrank like a thing reproved.

And many more, whose names on Earth are dark,
But whose transmitted effluence cannot die
So long as fire outlives the parent spark,
Rose, robed in dazzling immortality.
"Thou art become as one of us," they cry,
"It was for thee yon kingless sphere has long
Swung blind in unascended majesty,
Silent alone amid an Heaven of Song.
Assume thy wingèd throne, thou Vesper of our throng!"

Who mourns for Adonais? Oh, come forth,
Fond wretch! and know thyself and him aright.
Clasp with thy panting soul the pendulous Earth;
As from a centre, dart thy spirit's light
Beyond all worlds, until its spacious might
Satiate the void circumference: then shrink
Even to a point within our day and night;
And keep thy heart light lest it make thee sink
When hope has kindled hope, and lured thee to the
    brink.

Or go to Rome, which is the sepulchre,
Oh, not of him, but of our joy: 'tis nought
That ages, empires, and religions there
Lie buried in the ravage they have wrought;
For such as he can lend,—they borrow not
Glory from those who made the world their prey;
And he is gathered to the kings of thought

Who waged contention with their time's decay,
And of the past are all that cannot pass away.

Go thou to Rome,—at once the Paradise,
The grave, the city, and the wilderness;
And where its wrecks like shattered mountains rise,
And flowering weeds, and fragrant copses dress
The bones of Desolation's nakedness
Pass, till the spirit of the spot shall lead
Thy footsteps to a slope of green access
Where, like an infant's smile, over the dead
A light of laughing flowers along the grass is spread;

And gray walls moulder round, on which dull Time
Feeds, like slow fire upon a hoary brand;
And one keen pyramid with wedge sublime,
Pavilioning the dust of him who planned
This refuge for his memory, doth stand
Like flame transformed to marble; and beneath,
A field is spread, on which a newer band
Have pitched in Heaven's smile their camp of death,
Welcoming him we lose with scarce extinguished
    breath.

Here pause: these graves are all too young as yet
To have outgrown the sorrow which consigned
Its charge to each; and if the seal is set,
Here, on one fountain of a mourning mind,
Break it not thou! too surely shalt thou find
Thine own well full, if thou returnest home,
Of tears and gall. From the world's bitter wind
Seek shelter in the shadow of the tomb.
What Adonais is, why fear we to become?

The One remains, the many change and pass;
Heaven's light forever shines, Earth's shadows fly;
Life, like a dome of many-coloured glass,

Stains the white radiance of Eternity,
Until Death tramples it to fragments.—Die,
If thou wouldst be with that which thou dost seek!
Follow where all is fled!—Rome's azure sky,
Flowers, ruins, statues, music, words, are weak
The glory they transfuse with fitting truth to speak,

Why linger, why turn back, why shrink, my Heart?
Thy hopes are gone before: from all things here
They have departed; thou shouldst now depart!
A light is passed from the revolving year,
And man, and woman; and what still is dear
Attracts to crush, repels to make thee wither.
The soft sky smiles,—the low wind whispers near:
'Tis Adonais calls! oh, hasten thither,
No more let Life divide what Death can join together.

That Light whose smile kindles the Universe,
That Beauty in which all things work and move,
That Benediction which the eclipsing Curse
Of birth can quench not, that sustaining Love
Which through the web of being blindly wove
By man and beast and earth and air and sea,
Burns bright or dim, as each are mirrors of
The fire for which all thirst; now beams on me,
Consuming the last clouds of cold mortality.

The breath whose might I have invoked in song
Descends on me; my spirit's bark is driven,
Far from the shore, far from the trembling throng
Whose sails were never to the tempest given;
The massy earth and spherèd skies are riven!
I am borne darkly, fearfully, afar;
Whilst, burning through the inmost veil of Heaven,
The soul of Adonais, like a star,
Beacons from the abode where the Eternal are.

## Lines

When the lamp is shattered,
The light in the dust lies dead;
  When the cloud is scattered,
The rainbow's glory is shed;
  When the lute is broken,
Sweet tones are remembered not;
  When the lips have spoken,
Loved accents are soon forgot.

  As music and splendor
Survive not the lamp and the lute,
  The heart's echoes render
No song when the spirit is mute:—
  No song but sad dirges,
Like the wind through a ruined cell,
  Or the mournful surges
That ring the dead seaman's knell.

  When hearts have once mingled,
Love first leaves the well-built nest;
  The weak one is singled
To endure what it once possessed.
  O Love! who bewailest
The frailty of all things here,
  Why choose you the frailest
For your cradle, your home, and your bier?

  Its passions will rock thee,
As the storms rock the ravens on high;
  Bright reason will mock thee,
Like the sun from a wintry sky.

From thy nest every rafter
Will rot, and thine eagle home
Leave thee naked to laughter,
When leaves fall and cold winds come.


## The Triumph of Life

Swift as a spirit hastening to his task
Of glory and of good, the Sun sprang forth
Rejoicing in his splendour, and the mask

Of darkness fell from the awakened Earth—
The smokeless altars of the mountain snows
Flamed above crimson clouds, and at the birth

Of light, the Ocean's orison arose,
To which the birds tempered their matin lay.
All flowers in field or forest which unclose

Their trembling eyelids to the kiss of day,
Swinging their censers in the element,
With orient incense lit by the new ray

Burned slow and inconsumably, and sent
Their odorous sighs up to the smiling air;
And, in succession due, did continent,

Isle, ocean, and all things that in them wear
The form and character of mortal mould,
Rise as the Sun their father rose, to bear

Their portion of the toil, which he of old
Took as his own, and then imposed on them:
But I, whom thoughts which must remain untold

Had kept as wakeful as the stars that gem
The cone of night, now they were laid asleep
Stretched my faint limbs beneath the hoary stem

Which an old chestnut flung athwart the steep
Of a green Apennine: before me fled
The night; behind me rose the day; the deep

Was at my feet, and Heaven above my head,—
When a strange trance over my fancy grew
Which was not slumber, for the shade it spread

Was so transparent, that the scene came through
As clear as when a veil of light is drawn
O'er evening hills they glimmer; and I knew

That I had felt the freshness of that dawn
Bathe in the same cold dew my brow and hair,
And sate as thus upon that slope of lawn

Under the self-same bough, and heard as there
The birds, the fountains and the ocean hold
Sweet talk in music through the enamoured air,
And then a vision on my brain was rolled.

———

As in that trance of wondrous thought I lay,
This was the tenour of my waking dream:—
Methought I sate beside a public way

Thick strewn with summer dust, and a great stream
Of people there was hurrying to and fro,
Numerous as gnats upon the evening gleam,

All hastening onward, yet none seemed to know
Whither he went, or whence he came, or why
He made one of the multitude, and so

Was borne amid the crowd, as through the sky
One of the million leaves of summer's bier;
Old age and youth, manhood and infancy,

Mixed in one mighty torrent did appear,
Some flying from the thing they feared, and some
Seeking the object of another's fear;

And others, as with steps towards the tomb,
Pored on the trodden worms that crawled beneath,
And others mournfully within the gloom

Of their own shadow walked, and called it death;
And some fled from it as it were a ghost,
Half fainting in the affliction of vain breath:

But more, with motions which each other crossed,
Pursued or shunned the shadows the clouds threw,
Or birds within the noonday aether lost,

Upon that path where flowers never grew,—
And, weary with vain toil and faint for thirst,
Heard not the fountains, whose melodious dew

Out of their mossy cells forever burst;
Nor felt the breeze which from the forest told
Of grassy paths and wood-lawns interspersed

With overarching elms and caverns cold,
And violet banks where sweet dreams brood, but they
Pursued their serious folly as of old.

And as I gazed, methought that in the way
The throng grew wilder, as the woods of June
When the south wind shakes the extinguished day,

And a cold glare, intenser than the noon,
But icy cold, obscured with blinding light
The sun, as he the stars. Like the young moon—

When on the sunlit limits of the night
Her white shell trembles amid crimson air,
And whilst the sleeping tempest gathers might—

Doth, as the herald of its coming, bear
The ghost of its dead mother, whose dim form
Bends in dark aether from her infant's chair,—

So came a chariot on the silent storm
Of its own rushing splendour, and a Shape
So sate within, as one whom years deform,

Beneath a dusky hood and double cape,
Crouching within the shadow of a tomb;
And o'er what seemed the head a cloud-like crape

Was bent, a dun and faint aethereal gloom
Tempering the light. Upon the chariot-beam
A Janus-visaged Shadow did assume

The guidance of that wonder-wingèd team;
The shapes which drew it in thick lightenings
Were lost:—I heard alone on the air's soft stream

The music of their ever-moving wings.
All the four faces of that Charioteer
Had their eyes banded; little profit brings

Speed in the van and blindness in the rear,
Nor then avail the beams that quench the sun,—
Or that with banded eyes could pierce the sphere

Of all that is, has been or will be done;
So ill was the car guided—but it passed
With solemn speed majestically on.

The crowd gave way, and I arose aghast,
Or seemed to rise, so mighty was the trance,
And saw, like clouds upon the thunder-blast,

The million with fierce song and maniac dance
Raging around—such seemed the jubilee
As when to greet some conqueror's advance

Imperial Rome poured forth her living sea
From senate-house, and forum, and theatre,
When                              upon the free

Had bound a yoke, which soon they stooped to bear.
Nor wanted here the just similitude
Of a triumphal pageant, for where'er

The chariot rolled, a captive multitude
Was driven;—and all those who had grown old in power
Or misery,—all who had their age subdued

By action or by suffering, and whose hour
Was drained to its last sand in weal or woe,
So that the trunk survived both fruit and flower;—

All those whose fame or infamy must grow
Till the great winter lay the form and name
Of this green earth with them for ever low;—

All but the sacred few who could not tame
Their spirits to the conquerors—but as soon
As they had touched the world with living flame,

Fled back like eagles to their native noon,
Or those who put aside the diadem
Of earthly thrones or gems . . .

Were there, of Athens or Jerusalem,
Were neither mid the mighty captives seen,
Nor mid the ribald crowd that followed them,

Nor those who went before fierce and obscene.
The wild dance maddens in the van, and those
Who lead it—fleet as shadows on the green,

Outspeed the chariot, and without repose
Mix with each other in tempestuous measure
To savage music, wilder as it grows,

They, tortured by their agonizing pleasure,
Convulsed and on the rapid whirlwinds spun
Of that fierce Spirit, whose unholy leisure

Was soothed by mischief since the world begun,
Throw back their heads and loose their streaming hair;
And in their dance round her who dims the sun,

Maidens and youths fling their wild arms in air
As their feet twinkle; they recede, and now
Bending within each other's atmosphere,

Kindle invisibly—and as they glow,
Like moths by light attracted and repelled,
Oft to their bright destruction come and go,

Till like two clouds into one vale impelled,
That shake the mountains when their lightnings mingle
And die in rain—the fiery band which held

Their natures, snaps—while the shock still may tingle;
One falls and then another in the path
Senseless—nor is the desolation single,

Yet ere I can say *where*—the chariot hath
Passed over them—nor other trace I find
But as of foam after the ocean's wrath

Is spent upon the desert shore;—behind,
Old men and women foully disarrayed,
Shake their gray hairs in the insulting wind,

And follow in the dance, with limbs decayed,
Seeking to reach the light which leaves them still
Farther behind and deeper in the shade.

But not the less with impotence of will
They wheel, though ghastly shadows interpose
Round them and round each other, and fulfil

Their work, and in the dust from whence they rose
Sink, and corruption veils them as they lie,
And past in these performs what        in those.

Struck to the heart by this sad pageantry,
Half to myself I said—"And what is this?
Whose shape is that within the car? And why—"

I would have added—"is all here amiss?—"
But a voice answered—"Life!"—I turned, and knew
(O Heaven, have mercy on such wretchedness!)

That what I thought was an old root which grew
To strange distortion out of the hill side,
Was indeed one of those deluded crew,

And that the grass, which methought hung so wide
And white, was but his thin discoloured hair,
And that the holes he vainly sought to hide,

Were or had been eyes:—"If thou canst, forbear
To join the dance, which I had well forborne!"
Said the grim Feature (of my thought aware).

"I will unfold that which to this deep scorn
Led me and my companions, and relate
The progress of the pageant since the morn;

"If thirst of knowledge shall not then abate,
Follow it thou even to the night, but I
Am weary."—Then like one who with the weight

Of his own words is staggered, wearily
He paused; and ere he could resume, I cried:
"First, who art thou?"—"Before thy memory,

"I feared, loved, hated, suffered, did and died,
And if the spark with which Heaven lit my spirit
Had been with purer nutriment supplied,

"Corruption would not now this much inherit
Of what was once Rousseau,—nor this disguise
Stain that which ought to have disdained to wear it;

"If I have been extinguished, yet there rise
A thousand beacons from the spark I bore"—
"And who are those chained to the car?"—"The wise,

"The great, the unforgotten,—they who wore
Mitres and helms and crowns, or wreaths of light,
Signs of thought's empire over thought—their lore

"Taught them not this, to know themselves; their might
Could not repress the mystery within,
And for the morn of truth they feigned, deep night

"Caught them ere evening."—"Who is he with chin
Upon his breast, and hands crossed on his chain?"—
"The child of a fierce hour; he sought to win

"The world, and lost all that it did contain
Of greatness, in its hope destroyed; and more
Of fame and peace than virtue's self can gain

"Without the opportunity which bore
Him on its eagle pinions to the peak
From which a thousand climbers have before

"Fallen, as Napoleon fell."—I felt my cheek
Alter, to see the shadow pass away,
Whose grasp had left the giant world so weak

That every pigmy kicked it as it lay;
And much I grieved to think how power and will
In opposition rule our mortal day,

And why God made irreconcilable
Good and the means of good; and for despair
I half disdained mine eyes' desire to fill

With the spent vision of the times that were
And scarce have ceased to be.—"Dost thou behold,"
Said my guide, "those spoilers spoiled, Voltaire,

"Frederick, and Paul, Catherine, and Leopold,
And hoary anarchs, demagogues, and sage—names
  which the world thinks always old,

"For in the battle Life and they did wage,
She remained conqueror. I was overcome
By my own heart alone, which neither age,

"Nor tears, nor infamy, nor now the tomb
Could temper to its object."—"Let them pass,"
I cried, "the world and its mysterious doom

"Is not so much more glorious than it was,
That I desire to worship those who drew
New figures on its false and fragile glass

"As the old faded."—"Figures ever new
Rise on the bubble, paint them as you may;
We have but thrown, as those before us threw,

"Our shadows on it as it passed away.
But mark how chained to the triumphal chair
The mighty phantoms of an elder day;

"All that is mortal of great Plato there
Expiates the joy and woe his master knew not;
The star that ruled his doom was far too fair,

"And life, where long that flower of Heaven grew not,
Conquered that heart by love, which gold, or pain,
Or age, or sloth, or slavery could subdue not.

"And near him walk the           twain,
The tutor and his pupil, whom Dominion
Followed as tame as vulture in a chain.

"The world was darkened beneath either pinion
Of him whom from the flock of conquerors
Fame singled out for her thunder-bearing minion;

"The other long outlived both woes and wars,
Throned in the thoughts of men, and still had kept
The jealous key of Truth's eternal doors,

"If Bacon's eagle spirit had not lept
Like lightning out of darkness—he compelled
The Proteus shape of Nature, as it slept

"To wake, and lead him to the caves that held
The treasure of the secrets of its reign.
See the great bards of elder time, who quelled

"The passions which they sung, as by their strain
May well be known: their living melody
Tempers its own contagion to the vein

"Of those who are infected with it—I
Have suffered what I wrote, or viler pain!
And so my words have seeds of misery—

"Even as the deeds of others, not as theirs."
And then he pointed to a company,

'Midst whom I quickly recognized the heirs
Of Caesar's crime, from him to Constantine;
The anarch chiefs, whose force and murderous snares

Had founded many a sceptre-bearing line,
And spread the plague of gold and blood abroad:
And Gregory and John, and men divine,

Who rose like shadows between man and God;
Till that eclipse, still hanging over heaven,
Was worshipped by the world o'er which they strode,

For the true sun it quenched—"Their power was given
But to destroy," replied the leader:—"I
Am one of those who have created, even

"If it be but a world of agony."—
"Whence camest thou? and whither goest thou?
How did thy course begin?" I said, "and why?

"Mine eyes are sick of this perpetual flow
Of people, and my heart sick of one sad thought—
Speak!"—"Whence I am, I partly seem to know,

"And how and by what paths I have been brought
To this dread pass, methinks even thou mayest guess;—
Why this should be, my mind can compass not;

"Whither the conqueror hurries me, still less;—
But follow thou, and from spectator turn
Actor or victim in this wretchedness,

"And what thou wouldst be taught I then may learn
From thee. Now listen:—In the April prime,
When all the forest-tips began to burn

"With kindling green, touched by the azure clime
Of the young season, I was laid asleep
Under a mountain, which from unknown time

"Had yawned into a cavern, high and deep;
And from it came a gentle rivulet,
Whose water, like clear air, in its calm sweep

"Bent the soft grass, and kept for ever wet
The stems of the sweet flowers, and filled the grove
With sounds, which whoso hears must needs forget

"All pleasure and all pain, all hate and love,
Which they had known before that hour of rest;
A sleeping mother then would dream not of

"Her only child who died upon the breast
At eventide—a king would mourn no more
The crown of which his brows were dispossessed

"When the sun lingered o'er his ocean floor
To gild his rival's new prosperity.
Thou wouldst forget thus vainly to deplore

"Ills, which if ills can find no cure from thee,
The thought of which no other sleep will quell,
Nor other music blot from memory,

"So sweet and deep is the oblivious spell;
And whether life had been before that sleep
The Heaven which I imagine, or a Hell

"Like this harsh world in which I wake to weep,
I know not. I arose, and for a space
The scene of woods and waters seemed to keep,

"Though it was now broad day, a gentle trace
Of light diviner than the common sun
Sheds on the common earth, and all the place

"Was filled with magic sounds woven into one
Oblivious melody, confusing sense
Amid the gliding waves and shadows dun;

"And, as I looked, the bright omnipresence
Of morning through the orient cavern flowed,
And the sun's image radiantly intense

"Burned on the waters of the well that glowed
Like gold, and threaded all the forest's maze
With winding paths of emerald fire; there stood

"Amid the sun, as he amid the blaze
Of his own glory, on the vibrating
Floor of the fountain, paved with flashing rays,

"A Shape all light, which with one hand did fling
Dew on the earth, as if she were the dawn,
And the invisible rain did ever sing

"A silver music on the mossy lawn;
And still before me on the dusky grass,
Iris her many-coloured scarf had drawn:

"In her right hand she bore a crystal glass,
Mantling with bright Nepenthe; the fierce splendour
Fell from her as she moved under the mass

"Of the deep cavern, and with palms so tender,
Their tread broke not the mirror of its billow,
Glided along the river, and did bend her

"Head under the dark boughs, till like a willow
Her fair hair swept the bosom of the stream
That whispered with delight to be its pillow.

"As one enamoured is upborne in dream
O'er lily-paven lakes, mid silver mist,
To wondrous music, so this shape might seem

"Partly to tread the waves with feet which kissed
The dancing foam; partly to glide along
The air which roughened the moist amethyst,

"Or the faint morning beams that fell among
The trees, or the soft shadows of the trees;
And her feet, ever to the ceaseless song

"Of leaves, and winds, and waves, and birds, and bees,
And falling drops, moved in a measure new
Yet sweet, as on the summer evening breeze,

"Up from the lake a shape of golden dew
Between two rocks, athwart the rising moon,
Dances i' the wind, where never eagle flew;

"And still her feet, no less than the sweet tune
To which they moved, seemed as they moved to blot
The thoughts of him who gazed on them; and soon

"All that was, seemed as if it had been not;
And all the gazer's mind was strewn beneath
Her feet like embers; and she, thought by thought,

"Trampled its sparks into the dust of death;
As day upon the threshold of the east
Treads out the lamps of night, until the breath

"Of darkness re-illumine even the least
Of heaven's living eyes—like day she came,
Making the night a dream; and ere she ceased

"To move, as one between desire and shame
Suspended, I said—If, as it doth seem,
Thou comest from the realm without a name

"Into this valley of perpetual dream,
Show whence I came, and where I am, and why—
Pass not away upon the passing stream.

"Arise and quench thy thirst, was her reply.
And as a shut lily stricken by the wand
Of dewy morning's vital alchemy,

"I rose; and, bending at her sweet command,
Touched with faint lips the cup she raised,
And suddenly my brain became as sand

"Where the first wave had more than half erased
The track of deer on desert Labrador;
Whilst the wolf, from which they fled amazed,

"Leaves his stamp visibly upon the shore,
Until the second bursts;—so on my sight
Burst a new vision, never seen before,

"And the fair shape waned in the coming light,
As veil by veil the silent splendour drops
From Lucifer, amid the chrysolite

"Of sunrise, ere it tinge the mountain-tops;
And as the presence of that fairest planet,
Although unseen, is felt by one who hopes

"That his day's path may end as he began it,
In that star's smile, whose light is like the scent
Of a jonquil when evening breezes fan it,

"Or the soft note in which his dear lament
The Brescian shepherd breathes, or the caress
That turned his weary slumber to content;

"So knew I in that light's severe excess
The presence of that Shape which on the stream
Moved, as I moved along the wilderness,

"More dimly than a day-appearing dream,
The ghost of a forgotten form of sleep;
A light of heaven, whose half-extinguished beam

"Through the sick day in which we wake to weep
Glimmers, for ever sought, for ever lost;
So did that shape its obscure tenour keep

"Beside my path, as silent as a ghost;
But the new Vision, and the cold bright car,
With solemn speed and stunning music, crossed

"The forest, and as if from some dread war
Triumphantly returning, the loud million
Fiercely extolled the fortune of her star.

"A moving arch of victory, the vermilion
And green and azure plumes of Iris had
Built high over her wind-wingèd pavilion,

"And underneath aethereal glory clad
The wilderness, and far before her flew
The tempest of the splendour, which forbade

"Shadow to fall from leaf and stone; the crew
Seemed in that light, like atomies to dance
Within a sunbeam;—some upon the new

"Embroidery of flowers, that did enhance
The grassy vesture of the desert, played,
Forgetful of the chariot's swift advance;

"Others stood gazing, till within the shade
Of the great mountain its light left them dim;
Others outspeeded it; and others made

"Circles around it, like the clouds that swim
Round the high moon in a bright sea of air;
And more did follow, with exulting hymn,

"The chariot and the captives fettered there:—
But all like bubbles on an eddying flood
Fell into the same track at last, and were

"Borne onward.—I among the multitude
Was swept—me, sweetest flowers delayed not long;
Me, not the shadow nor the solitude;

"Me, not that falling stream's Lethean song;
Me, not the phantom of that early Form
Which moved upon its motion—but among

"The thickest billows of that living storm
I plunged, and bared my bosom to the clime
Of that cold light, whose airs too soon deform.

"Before the chariot had begun to climb
The opposing steep of that mysterious dell,
Behold a wonder worthy of the rhyme

"Of him who from the lowest depths of hell,
Through every paradise and through all glory,
Love led serene, and who returned to tell

"The words of hate and awe; the wondrous story
How all things are transfigured except Love;
For deaf as is a sea, which wrath makes hoary,

"The world can hear not the sweet notes that move
The sphere whose light is melody to lovers—
A wonder worthy of his rhyme.—The grove

"Grew dense with shadows to its inmost covers,
The earth was gray with phantoms, and the air
Was peopled with dim forms, as when there hovers

"A flock of vampire-bats before the glare
Of the tropic sun, bringing, ere evening,
Strange night upon some Indian isle;—thus were

"Phantoms diffused around; and some did fling
Shadows of shadows, yet unlike themselves,
Behind them; some like eaglets on the wing

"Were lost in the white day; others like elves
Danced in a thousand unimagined shapes
Upon the sunny streams and grassy shelves;

"And others sate chattering like restless apes
On vulgar hands, . . .
Some made a cradle of the ermined capes

"Of kingly mantles; some across the tiar
Of pontiffs sate like vultures; others played
Under the crown which girt with empire

"A baby's or an idiot's brow, and made
Their nests in it. The old anatomies
Sate hatching their bare broods under the shade

"Of daemon wings, and laughed from their dead eyes
To reassume the delegated power,
Arrayed in which those worms did monarchize,

"Who made this earth their charnel. Others more
Humble, like falcons, sate upon the fist
Of common men, and round their heads did soar;

"Or like small gnats and flies, as thick as mist
On evening marshes, thronged about the brow
Of lawyers, statesmen, priest and theorist;—

"And others, like discoloured flakes of snow
On fairest bosoms and the sunniest hair,
Fell, and were melted by the youthful glow

"Which they extinguished; and, like tears, they were
A veil to those from whose faint lids they rained
In drops of sorrow. I became aware

"Of whence those forms proceeded which thus stained
The track in which we moved. After brief space,
From every form the beauty slowly waned;

"From every firmest limb and fairest face
The strength and freshness fell like dust, and left
The action and the shape without the grace

"Of life. The marble brow of youth was cleft
With care; and in those eyes where once hope shone,
Desire, like a lioness bereft

"Of her last cub, glared ere it died; each one
Of that great crowd sent forth incessantly
These shadows, numerous as the dead leaves blown

"In autumn evening from a poplar tree.
Each like himself and like each other were
At first; but some distorted seemed to be

"Obscure clouds, moulded by the casual air;
And of this stuff the car's creative ray
Wrought all the busy phantoms that were there,

"As the sun shapes the clouds; thus on the way
Mask after mask fell from the countenance
And form of all; and long before the day

"Was old, the joy which waked like heaven's glance
The sleepers in the oblivious valley, died;
And some grew weary of the ghastly dance,

"And fell, as I have fallen, by the wayside;—
Those soonest from whose forms most shadows passed,
And least of strength and beauty did abide.

"Then, what is life? I cried."—

# George Darley

(1795–1846)

FROM *Nepenthe*

## THE UNICORN

Lo! in the mute, mid wilderness,
What wondrous Creature?—of no kind!—
His burning lair doth largely press,—
Gaze fixt, and feeding on the wind?
His fell is of the desert dye,
And tissue adust, dun-yellow and dry,
Compact of living sands; his eye
Black luminary, soft and mild,
With its dark lustre cools the wild;
From his stately forehead springs,
Piercing to heaven, a radiant horn,—
Lo! the compeer of lion-kings!
The steed self-armed, the Unicorn!
Ever heard of, never seen,
With a main of sands between
Him and approach; his lonely pride
To course his arid arena wide,
Free as the hurricane, or lie here,
Lord of his couch as his career!—
Wherefore should this foot profane
His sanctuary, still domain?
Let me turn, ere eye so bland
Perchance be fire-shot, like heaven's brand,

To wither my boldness! Northward now,
Behind the white star on his brow
Glittering straight against the sun,
Far athwart his lair I run.


## The Mermaidens' Vesper-Hymn

Troop home to silent grots and caves!
   Troop home! and mimic as you go
The mournful winding of the waves
   Which to their dark abysses flow.

At this sweet hour, all things beside
   In amorous pairs to covert creep;
The swans that brush the evening tide
   Homeward in snowy couples keep.

In his green den the murmuring seal
   Close by his sleek companion lies;
While singly we to bedward steal,
   And close in fruitless sleep our eyes.

In bowers of love men take their rest,
   In loveless bowers we sigh alone,
With bosom-friends are others blest,—
   But we have none! but we have none!


### FROM *Ethelstan*

#### O'ER THE WILD GANNET'S BATH

    O'er the wild gannet's bath
    Come the Norse coursers!
    O'er the whale's heritance

Gloriously steering!
With beaked heads peering,
Deep-plunging, high-rearing,
Tossing their foam abroad,
Shaking white manes aloft,
Creamy-neck'd, pitchy-ribb'd,
Steeds of the Ocean!

O'er the Sun's mirror green
Come the Norse coursers!
Trampling its glassy breadth
Into bright fragments!
Hollow-back'd, huge-bosom'd,
Fraught with mail'd riders,
Clanging with hauberks,
Shield, spear, and battleaxe.
Canvas-wing'd, cable-rein'd,
Steeds of the Ocean!

O'er the Wind's ploughing field
Come the Norse coursers!
By a hundred each ridden,
To the bloody feast bidden,
They rush in their fierceness
And ravine all round them!
Their shoulders enriching
With fleecy-light plunder,
Fire-spreading, foe-spurning,
Steeds of the Ocean!—

# John Keats

(1795–1821)

## On First Looking into Chapman's Homer

Much have I travell'd in the realms of gold,
   And many goodly states and kingdoms seen;
   Round many western isles have I been
Which bards in fealty to Apollo hold.
Oft of one wide expanse had I been told
   That deep-brow'd Homer ruled as his demesne;
   Yet did I never breathe its pure serene
Till I heard Chapman speak out loud and bold:
Then felt I like some watcher of the skies
   When a new planet swims into his ken;
Or like stout Cortez when with eagle eyes
   He star'd at the Pacific—and all his men
Look'd at each other with a wild surmise—
   Silent, upon a peak in Darien.

## Sonnet

Keen, fitful gusts are whisp'ring here and there
   Among the bushes half leafless, and dry;
   The stars look very cold about the sky,
And I have many miles on foot to fare.
Yet feel I little of the cool bleak air,
   Or of the dead leaves rustling drearily,

Or of those silver lamps that burn on high,
  Or of the distance from home's pleasant lair:
For I am brimfull of the friendliness
    That in a little cottage I have found;
Of fair hair'd Milton's eloquent distress,
    And of his love for gentle Lycid drown'd;
Of lovely Laura in her light green dress,
    And faithful Petrarch gloriously crown'd.

# To Sleep

O soft embalmer of the still midnight,
    Shutting, with careful fingers and benign,
Our gloom-pleas'd eyes, embower'd from the light,
    Enshaded in forgetfulness divine:
O soothest Sleep! if so it please thee, close,
    In midst of this thine hymn, my willing eyes,
Or wait the amen, ere thy poppy throws
    Around my bed its lulling charities.
Then save me, or the passéd day will shine
Upon my pillow, breeding many woes;
    Save me from curious conscience, that still lords
Its strength for darkness, burrowing like a mole;
    Turn the key deftly in the oilèd wards,
And seal the hushèd casket of my soul.

## Sonnet

WRITTEN ON A BLANK PAGE IN
SHAKESPEARE'S POEMS, FACING
"A LOVER'S COMPLAINT"

Bright star! would I were steadfast as thou art—
   Not in lone splendor hung aloft the night
And watching, with eternal lids apart,
   Like nature's patient, sleepless Eremite,
The moving waters at their priest-like task
   Of pure ablution round earth's human shores,
Or gazing on the new soft fallen mask
   Of snow upon the mountains and the moors—
No—yet still steadfast, still unchangeable,
   Pillow'd upon my fair love's ripening breast,
To feel for ever its soft fall and swell,
   Awake for ever in a sweet unrest,
Still, still to hear her tender-taken breath,
And so live ever—or else swoon to death.

## A Song About Myself

FROM A LETTER TO FANNY KEATS

There was a naughty Boy,
   A naughty boy was he,
He would not stop at home,
   He could not quiet be—
     He took
     In his Knapsack

A Book
Full of vowels
And a shirt
With some towels—
A slight cap
For night cap—
A hair brush,
Comb ditto,
New Stockings
For old ones
Would split O!
This Knapsack
Tight at's back
He rivetted close
And followed his Nose
To the North,
To the North,
And follow'd his nose to the North.

There was a naughty boy
And a naughty boy was he,
For nothing would he do
But scribble poetry—
He took
An ink stand
In his hand
And a Pen
Big as ten
In the other.
And away
In a Pother
He ran
To the mountains
And fountains
And ghostes

And Postes
And witches
And ditches
And wrote
In his coat
When the weather
Was cool,
Fear of gout,
And without
When the weather
Was warm—
Och the charm
When we choose
To follow one's nose
To the North,
To the North,
To follow one's nose to the North!

There was a naughty boy
And a naughty boy was he,
He kept little fishes
In washing tubs three
In spite
Of the might
Of the Maid
Nor affraid
Of his Granny-good—
He often would
Hurly burly
Get up early
And go
By hook or crook
To the brook
And bring home
Miller's thumb,

                Tittlebat
                Not over fat,
                Minnows small
                As the stall
                Of a glove,
                Not above
                The size
                Of a nice
                Little Baby's
                Little fingers—
                O he made
                'Twas his trade
            Of Fish a pretty Kettle
                A Kettle—a Kettle
            Of Fish a pretty Kettle
                A Kettle!


    There was a naughty Boy,
        And a naughty boy was he,
    He ran away to Scotland
        The people for to see—
                Then he found
                That the ground
                Was as hard,
                That a yard
                Was as long,
                That a song
                Was as merry,
                That a cherry
                Was as red—
                That lead
                Was as weighty,
                That fourscore
                Was as eighty,
                That a door

Was as wooden
As in England—
So he stood in
His shoes and he wonder'd,
He wonder'd,
He stood in
His shoes and he wonder'd.


## Ode to a Nightingale

My heart aches, and a drowsy numbness pains
　My sense, as though of hemlock I had drunk,
Or emptied some some dull opiate to the drains
　One minute past, and Lethe-wards had sunk:
'Tis not through envy of thy happy lot,
　But being too happy in thy happiness,—
　　That thou, light-wingèd Dryad of the trees,
　　　In some melodious plot
　Of beechen green, and shadows numberless,
　　Singest of summer in full-throated ease.

O, for a draught of vintage! that hath been
　Cool'd a long age in the deep-delvèd earth,
Tasting of Flora and the country green,
　Dance, and Provençal song, and sunburnt mirth!
O for a beaker full of the warm South,
　Full of the true, the blushful Hippocrene,
　　With beaded bubbles winking at the brim,
　　　And purple-stainèd mouth;
　That I might drink, and leave the world unseen,
　　And with thee fade away into the forest dim:

Fade far away, dissolve, and quite forget
　What thou among the leaves hast never known,

The weariness, the fever, and the fret
    Here, where men sit and hear each other groan;
Where palsy shakes a few, sad, last grey hairs,
    Where youth grows pale, and spectre-thin, and dies;
        Where but to think is to be full of sorrow
            And leaden-eyed despairs,
    Where Beauty cannot keep her lustrous eyes,
        Or new Love pine at them beyond to-morrow.

Away! away! for I will fly to thee,
    Not charioted by Bacchus and his pards,
But on the viewless wings of Poesy,
    Though the dull brain perplexes and retards:
Already with thee! tender is the night,
    And haply the Queen-Moon is on her throne,
        Cluster'd around by all her starry Fays;
            But here there is no light,
    Save what from heaven is with the breezes blown
        Through verdurous glooms and winding mossy
            ways.

I cannot see what flowers are at my feet,
    Nor what soft incense hangs upon the boughs,
But, in embalmèd darkness, guess each sweet
    Wherewith the seasonable month endows
The grass, the thicket, and the fruit-tree wild;
    White hawthorn, and the pastoral eglantine; (sweet briar)
        Fast fading violets cover'd up in leaves;
            And mid-May's eldest child,
    The coming musk-rose, full of dewy wine,
        The murmurous haunt of flies on summer eves.

Darkling I listen; and, for many a time
    I have been half in love with easeful Death,
Call'd him soft names in many a musèd rhyme,
    To take into the air my quiet breath;

Now more than ever seems it rich to die,
　　To cease upon the midnight with no pain,
　　While thou art pouring forth thy soul abroad
　　　　In such an ecstasy!
　　Still wouldst thou sing, and I have ears in vain—
　　　　To thy high requiem become a sod.

*[one who overdoses on a drug]*

Thou wast not born for death, immortal Bird!
　　No hungry generations tread thee down;
The voice I hear this passing night was heard
　　In ancient days by emperor and clown:
Perhaps the self-same song that found a path
　　Through the sad heart of Ruth, when, sick for home, *[Bably lower caption]*
　　　　She stood in tears amid the alien corn;
　　　　The same that oft-times hath
　　Charm'd magic casements, opening on the foam
　　Of perilous seas, in faery lands forlorn.

Forlorn! the very word is like a bell
　　To toll me back from thee to my sole self!
Adieu! the fancy cannot cheat so well
　　As she is fam'd to do, deceiving elf.
Adieu! adieu! thy plaintive anthem fades
　　Past the near meadows, over the still stream,
　　Up the hillside; and now 'tis buried deep
　　　　In the next valley-glades:
　　Was it a vision, or a waking dream?
　　Fled is that music:—Do I wake or sleep?

*motionless remaining yet*

## Ode on a Grecian Urn   [1819]

　　Thou still unravish'd bride of quietness,
　　　　Thou foster-child of silence and slow time,
　　Sylvan historian, who canst thus express

*urn tells a story*　　*It interrogates an unanswering urn.*

A flowery tale more sweetly than our rhyme:
What leaf-fring'd legend haunts about thy shape
   Of deities or mortals, or of both,
     In Tempe or the dales of Arcady?
   What men or gods are these? What maidens loth?
What mad pursuit? What struggle to escape?
   What pipes and timbrels? What wild ecstasy?

Heard melodies are sweet, but those unheard
   Are sweeter; therefore, ye soft pipes, play on;
Not to the sensual ear, but, more endear'd,
   Pipe to the spirit ditties of no tone:
Fair youth, beneath the trees, thou canst not leave
   Thy song, nor ever can those trees be bare;
    Bold Lover, never, never canst thou kiss,
Though winning near the goal—yet, do not grieve;
   She cannot fade, though thou hast not thy bliss,
    For ever wilt thou love, and she be fair!

Ah, happy, happy boughs! that cannot shed
   Your leaves, nor ever bid the Spring adieu;
And, happy melodist, unwearièd,
   For ever piping songs for ever new;
More happy love! more happy, happy love!
   For ever warm and still to be enjoy'd,
    For ever panting, and for ever young;
All breathing human passion far above,
   That leaves a heart high-sorrowful and cloy'd,
    A burning forehead, and a parching tongue.

Who are these coming to the sacrifice?
   To what green altar, O mysterious priest,
Lead'st thou that heifer lowing at the skies,
   And all her silken flanks with garlands drest?
What little town by river or sea shore,
   Or mountain-built with peaceful citadel,

Is emptied of this folk, this pious morn?
And, little town, thy streets for evermore
　　Will silent be; and not a soul to tell
　　Why thou art desolate, can e'er return.

O Attic shape! Fair attitude! with brede *embroidery*
　　Of marble men and maidens overwrought,
With forest branches and the trodden weed;
　　Thou, silent form, dost tease us out of thought
As doth eternity: Cold Pastoral!
　　When old age shall this generation waste,
　　　Thou shalt remain, in midst of other woe
Than ours, a friend to man, to whom thou say'st,
　　"Beauty is truth, truth beauty,"—that is all
　　　Ye know on earth, and all ye need to know.

*① Temptation to / miscerund*
*② Recognition of mortality*

*to Reader or Urn?*

*accusation*

*The urn does not know life, woes*

## Ode to Psyche

O Goddess! hear these tuneless numbers, wrung
　　By sweet enforcement and remembrance dear,
And pardon that thy secrets should be sung
　　Even into thine own soft-conchèd ear:
Surely I dreamt today, or did I see
　　The wingèd Psyche with awaken'd eyes?
I wander'd in a forest thoughtlessly,
　　And, on the sudden, fainting with surprise,
Saw two fair creatures, couchèd side by side
　　In deepest grass, beneath the whisp'ring roof
　　Of leaves and trembled blossoms, where there ran
　　　A brooklet, scarce espied:

'Mid hush'd, cool-rooted flowers, fragrant-eyed,
　　Blue, silver-white, and budded Tyrian,
They lay calm-breathing, on the bedded grass;

Their arms embracèd, and their pinions too;
Their lips touched not, but had not bade adieu,
As if disjoinèd by soft-handed slumber,
And ready still past kisses to outnumber
  At tender eye-dawn of aurorean love:
    The wingèd boy I knew;
  But who wast thou, O happy, happy dove?
    His Psyche true!

O latest born and loveliest vision far
  Of all Olympus' faded hierarchy!
Fairer than Phœbe's sapphire-region'd star,
  Or Vesper, amorous glow-worm of the sky;
Fairer than these, though temple thou hast none,
    Nor altar heap'd with flowers;
Nor virgin-choir to make delicious moan
    Upon the midnight hours;
No voice, no lute, no pipe, no incense sweet
  From chain-swung censer teeming;
No shrine, no grove, no oracle, no heat
  Of pale-mouth'd prophet dreaming.

O brightest! though too late for antique vows,
  Too, too late for the fond believing lyre,
When holy were the haunted forest boughs,
  Holy the air, the water, and the fire;
Yet even in these days so far retir'd
  From happy pieties, thy lucent fans,
  Fluttering among the faint Olympians,
I see, and sing, by my own eyes inspired.
So let me be thy choir, and make a moan
    Upon the midnight hours;
Thy voice, thy lute, thy pipe, thy incense sweet
  From swingèd censer teeming;
Thy shrine, thy grove, thy oracle, thy heat
  Of pale-mouth'd prophet dreaming.

Yes, I will be thy priest, and build a fane
  In some untrodden region of my mind,
Where branchèd thoughts, new grown with pleasant
        pain
  Instead of pines shall murmur in the wind:
Far, far around shall those dark-clustered trees
  Fledge the wild-ridgèd mountains steep by steep;
And there by zephyrs, streams, and birds, and bees,
  The moss-lain Dryads shall be lulled to sleep;
And in the midst of this wide quietness
A rosy sanctuary will I dress
With the wreath'd trellis of a working brain,
  With buds, and bells, and stars without a name,
With all the gardener Fancy e'er could feign,
  Who breeding flowers, will never breed the same:
And there shall be for thee all soft delight
  That shadowy thought can win,
A bright torch, and a casement ope at night,
  To let the warm Love in!


# To Autumn


Season of mists and mellow fruitfulness,
  Close bosom-friend of the maturing sun;
Conspiring with him how to load and bless
  With fruit the vines that round the thatch-eaves run;
To bend with apples the moss'd cottage trees,
  And fill all fruit with ripeness to the core;
    To swell the gourd, and plump the hazel shells
  With a sweet kernel; to set budding more,
And still more, later flowers for the bees,
Until they think warm days will never cease,
    For Summer has o'er-brimmed their clammy cells.

Who hath not seen thee oft amid thy store?
    Sometimes whoever seeks abroad may find
Thee sitting careless on a granary floor,
    Thy hair soft-lifted by the winnowing wind;
Or on a half-reap'd furrow sound asleep,
    Drows'd with the fume of poppies, while thy hook
        Spares the next swath and all its twinèd flowers:
And sometimes like a gleaner thou dost keep
    Steady thy laden head across a brook;
    Or by a cider-press, with patient look,
        Thou watchest the last oozings hours by hours.

Where are the songs of Spring? Aye, where are they?
    Think not of them, thou hast thy music too,—
While barrèd clouds bloom the soft-dying day,
    And touch the stubble-plains with rosy hue;
Then in a wailful choir the small gnats mourn
    Among the river sallows, borne aloft
        Or sinking as the light wind lives or dies;
And full-grown lambs loud bleat from hilly bourn;
    Hedge-crickets sing; and now with treble soft
The red-breast whistles from a garden-croft;
    And gathering swallows twitter in the skies.


## Ode on Melancholy

No, no, go not to Lethe, neither twist
    Wolfs-bane, tight-rooted, for its poisonous wine;
Nor suffer thy pale forehead to be kiss'd
    By nightshade, ruby grape of Proserpine;
Make not your rosary of yew-berries,
    Nor let the beetle, nor the death-moth be
        Your mournful Psyche, nor the downy owl

A partner in your sorrow's mysteries;
  For shade to shade will come too drowsily,
    And drown the wakeful anguish of the soul.

But when the melancholy fit shall fall
  Sudden from heaven like a weeping cloud,
That fosters the droop-headed flowers all,
  And hides the green hill in an April shroud;
Then glut thy sorrow on a morning rose,
  Or on the rainbow of the salt sand-wave,
    Or on the wealth of globèd peonies;
Or if thy mistress some rich anger shows,
  Emprison her soft hand, and let her rave,
    And feed deep, deep upon her peerless eyes.

She dwells with Beauty—Beauty that must die;
  And Joy, whose hand is ever at his lips
Bidding adieu; and aching Pleasure nigh,
  Turning to poison while the bee-mouth sips:
Ay, in the very temple of Delight
  Veil'd Melancholy has her sovran shrine,
    Though seen of none save him whose strenuous
      tongue
  Can burst Joy's grape against his palate fine;
His soul shall taste the sadness of her might,
    And be among her cloudy trophies hung.

## Fragment of an Ode to Maia

### Written on May Day, 1818

Mother of Hermes! and still youthful Maia!
    May I sing to thee
As thou wast hymned on the shores of Baiæ?
    Or may I woo thee

In earlier Sicilian? or thy smiles
Seek as they once were sought, in Grecian isles,
By bards who died content on pleasant sward,
   Leaving great verse unto a little clan?
O, give me their old vigour, and unheard
   Save of the quiet Primrose, and the span
        Of heaven and few ears,
Rounded by thee, my song should die away
        Content as theirs,
Rich in the simple worship of a day.


## FROM *Endymion*

### [*Hymn to Pan*]

"O thou, whose mighty palace roof doth hang
From jagged trunks, and overshadoweth
Eternal whispers, glooms, the birth, life, death
Of unseen flowers in heavy peacefulness;
Who lov'st to see the hamadryads dress
Their ruffled locks where meeting hazels darken;
And through whole solemn hours dost sit, and hearken
The dreary melody of bedded reeds—
In desolate places, where dank moisture breeds
The pipy hemlock to strange overgrowth;
Bethinking thee, how melancholy loth
Thou wast to lose fair Syrinx—do thou now,
By thy love's milky brow!
By all the trembling mazes that she ran,
Hear us, great Pan!

"O thou, for whose soul-soothing quiet, turtles
Passion their voices cooingly 'mong myrtles,
What time thou wanderest at eventide

Through sunny meadows, that outskirt the side
Of thine enmossed realms; O thou, to whom
Broad leaved fig trees even now foredoom
Their ripened fruitage; yellow girted bees
Their golden honeycombs; our village leas
Their fairest blossom'd beans and poppied corn;
The chuckling linnet its five young unborn,
To sing for thee; low creeping strawberries
Their summer coolness; pent up butterflies
Their freckled wings; yea, the fresh budding year
All its completions—be quickly near,
By every wind that nods the mountain pine,
O forester divine!

  "Thou, to whom every faun and satyr flies
For willing service; whether to surprise
The squatted hare while in half sleeping fit;
Or upward ragged precipices flit
To save poor lambkins from the eagle's maw;
Or by mysterious enticement draw
Bewildered shepherds to their path again;
Or to tread breathless round the frothy main,
And gather up all fancifullest shells
For thee to tumble into Naiad's cells,
And, being hidden, laugh at their out-peeping;
Or to delight thee with fantastic leaping,
The while they pelt each other on the crown
With silvery oak apples, and fir cones brown—
By all the echoes that about thee ring,
Hear us, O satyr king!

  "O Hearkener to the loud clapping shears,
While ever and anon to his shorn peers
A ram goes bleating: Winder of the horn,
When snouted wild-boars routing tender corn
Anger our huntsmen: Breather round our farms,

To keep off mildews, and all weather harms:
Strange ministrant of undescribed sounds,
That comes a swooning over hollow grounds,
And wither drearily on barren moors:
Dread opener of the mysterious doors
Leading to universal knowledge—see,
Great son of Dryope,
The many that are come to pay their vows
With leaves about their brows!

   "Be still the unimaginable lodge
For solitary thinkings; such as dodge
Conception to the very bourne of heaven,
Then leave the naked brain: be still the leaven,
That spreading in this dull and clodded earth
Gives it a touch ethereal—a new birth:
Be still a symbol of immensity;
A firmament reflected in a sea;
An element filling the space between,
An unknown—but no more; we humbly screen
With uplift hands our foreheads, lowly bending,
And giving out a shout most heaven rending,
Conjure thee to receive our humble Pæan,
Upon thy Mount Lycean!"

(Book I, 232–306)

## La Belle Dame sans Merci

O what can ail thee, knight-at-arms,
   Alone and palely loitering?
The sedge has wither'd from the lake,
   And no birds sing.

O what can ail thee, knight-at-arms,
   So haggard and so woe-begone?

The squirrel's granary is full,
 And the harvest's done.

I see a lilly on thy brow
 With anguish moist and fever dew
And on thy cheeks a fading rose
 Fast withereth too.

I met a lady in the meads,
 Full beautiful—a faery's child,
Her hair was long, her foot was light,
 And her eyes were wild.

I made a garland for her head,
 And bracelets too, and fragrant zone;
She look'd at me as she did love,
 And made sweet moan.

I set her on my pacing steed,
 And nothing else saw all day long,
For sidelong would she bend, and sing
 A faery's song.

She found me roots of relish sweet,
 And honey wild, and manna dew,
And sure in language strange she said,
 "I love thee true."

She took me to her elfin grot,
 And there she wept, and sigh'd full sore,
And there I shut her wild wild eyes
 With kisses four.

And there she lullèd me asleep
 And there I dream'd—Ah! woe betide!
The latest dream I ever dream'd
 On the cold hill side.

I saw pale kings, and princes too,
    Pale warriors, death-pale were they all;
They cried—"La belle Dame sans Merci
    Hath thee in thrall!"

I saw their starved lips in the gloam
    With horrid warning gapèd wide,
And I awoke and found me here
    On the cold hill's side.

And this is why I sojourn here
    Alone and palely loitering,
Though the sedge is wither'd from the lake,
    And no birds sing.

## The Eve of St. Agnes

St. Agnes' Eve—Ah, bitter chill it was!
The owl, for all his feathers, was a-cold;
The hare limped trembling through the frozen grass,
And silent was the flock in woolly fold:
Numb were the Beadsman's fingers, while he told
His rosary, and while his frosted breath,
Like pious incense from a censer old,
Seem'd taking flight for heaven, without a death,
Past the sweet Virgin's picture, while his prayer he
    saith.

His prayer he saith, this patient, holy man;
Then takes his lamp, and riseth from his knees,
And back returneth, meagre, barefoot, wan,
Along the chapel aisle by slow degrees:
The sculptur'd dead, on each side, seem to freeze,
Emprison'd in black, purgatorial rails:

Knights, ladies, praying in dumb orat'ries,
He passeth by; and his weak spirit fails
To think how they may ache in icy hoods and mails.

Northward he turneth through a little door,
And scarce three steps, ere Music's golden tongue
Flatter'd to tears this agèd man and poor;
But no—already had his deathbell rung;
The joys of all his life were said and sung:
His was harsh penance on St. Agnes' Eve:
Another way he went, and soon among
Rough ashes sat he for his soul's reprieve,
And all night kept awake, for sinners' sake to grieve.

That ancient Beadsman heard the prelude soft;
And so it chanc'd, for many a door was wide,
From hurry to and fro. Soon, up aloft,
The silver, snarling trumpets 'gan to chide:
The level chambers, ready with their pride,
Were glowing to receive a thousand guests:
The carvèd angels, ever eager-eyed,
Star'd, where upon their heads the cornice rests,
With hair blown back, and wings put cross-wise on their
       breasts.

At length burst in the argent revelry,
With plume, tiara, and all rich array,
Numerous as shadows, haunting fairily
The brain, new stuff'd, in youth, with triumphs gay
Of old romance. These let us wish away,
And turn, sole-thoughted, to one Lady there,
Whose heart had brooded, all that wintry day,
On love, and wing'd St. Agnes' saintly care,
As she had heard old dames full many times declare.

They told her how, upon St. Agnes' Eve,
Young virgins might have visions of delight,

And soft adorings from their loves receive
Upon the honey'd middle of the night,
If ceremonies due they did aright;
As, supperless to bed they must retire,
And couch supine their beauties, lily white;
Nor look behind, nor sideways, but require
Of Heaven with upward eyes for all that they desire.

Full of this whim was thoughtful Madeline:
The music, yearning like a God in pain,
She scarcely heard: her maiden eyes divine,
Fix'd on the floor, saw many a sweeping train
Pass by—she heeded not at all: in vain
Came many a tiptoe, amorous cavalier,
And back retir'd: not cool'd by high disdain,
But she saw not: her heart was otherwhere:
She sigh'd for Agnes' dreams, the sweetest of the year.

She danc'd along with vague, regardless eyes,
Anxious her lips, her breathing quick and short:
The hallow'd hour was near at hand: she sighs
Amid the timbrels, and the throng'd resort
Of whisperers in anger, or in sport;
'Mid looks of love, defiance, hate, and scorn,
Hoodwink'd with faery fancy; all amort,
Save to St. Agnes and her lambs unshorn,
And all the bliss to be before to-morrow morn.

So, purposing each moment to retire,
She linger'd still. Meantime, across the moors,
Had come young Porphyro, with heart on fire
For Madeline. Beside the portal doors,
Buttress'd from moonlight, stands he, and implores
All saints to give him sight of Madeline,
But for one moment in the tedious hours,
That he might gaze and worship all unseen;

Perchance speak, kneel, touch, kiss—in sooth such
    things have been.

He ventures in: let no buzz'd whisper tell:
All eyes be muffled, or a hundred swords
Will storm his heart, Love's fev'rous citadel:
For him, those chambers held barbarian hordes,
Hyena foemen, and hot-blooded lords,
Whose very dogs would execrations howl
Against his lineage: not one breast affords
Him any mercy, in that mansion foul,
Save one old beldame, weak in body and in soul.

Ah, happy chance! the agèd creature came,
Shuffling along with ivory-headed wand,
To where he stood, hid from the torch's flame,
Being a broad hall-pillar, far beyond
The sound of merriment and chorus bland:
He startled her; but soon she knew his face,
And grasped his fingers in her palsied hand,
Saying, "Mercy, Porphyro! hie thee from this place;
They are all here to-night, the whole blood-thirsty race!

"Get hence! get hence! there's dwarfish Hildebrand;
He had a fever late, and in the fit
He cursèd thee and thine, both house and land:
Then there's that old Lord Maurice, not a whit
More tame for his grey hairs—Alas me! flit!
Flit like a ghost away."—"Ah, Gossip dear,
We're safe enough; here in this arm-chair sit,
And tell me how"—"Good Saints! not here, not here;
Follow me, child, or else these stones will be thy bier."

He followed through a lowly archèd way,
Brushing the cobwebs with his lofty plume,
And as she muttered "Well-a—well-a-day!"
He found him in a little moonlight room,

Pale, lattic'd, chill, and silent as a tomb.
"Now tell me where is Madeline," said he,
"O tell me, Angela, by the holy loom
Which none but secret sisterhood may see,
When they St. Agnes' wool are weaving piously."

"St. Agnes! Ah! it is St. Agnes' Eve—
Yet men will murder upon holy days:
Thou must hold water in a witch's sieve,
And be liege-lord of all the Elves and Fays,
To venture so: it fills me with amaze
To see thee, Porphyro!—St. Agnes' Eve!
God's help! my lady fair the conjuror plays
This very night: good angels her deceive!
But let me laugh awhile, I've mickle time to grieve."

Feebly she laugheth in the languid moon,
While Porphyro upon her face doth look,
Like puzzled urchin on an agèd crone
Who keepeth clos'd a wond'rous riddle-book,
As spectacled she sits in chimney nook.
But soon his eyes grew brilliant, when she told
His lady's purpose; and he scarce could brook
Tears, at the thought of those enchantments cold,
And Madeline asleep in lap of legends old.

Sudden a thought came like a full-blown rose,
Flushing his brow, and in his painèd heart
Made purple riot: then doth he propose
A stratagem, that makes the beldame start:
"A cruel man and impious thou art:
Sweet lady, let her pray, and sleep, and dream
Alone with her good angels, far apart
From wicked men like thee. Go, go!—I deem
Thou canst not surely be the same that thou didst
    seem."

"I will not harm her, by all saints I swear,"
Quoth Porphyro: "O may I ne'er find grace
When my weak voice shall whisper its last prayer,
If one of her soft ringlets I displace,
Or look with ruffian passion in her face:
Good Angela, believe me by these tears;
Or I will, even in a moment's space,
Awake, with horrid shout, my foemen's ears,
And beard them, though they be more fang'd than
    wolves and bears."

"Ah! why wilt thou affright a feeble soul?
A poor, weak, palsy-stricken, churchyard thing,
Whose passing-bell may ere the midnight toll;
Whose prayers for thee, each morn and evening,
Were never miss'd."—Thus plaining, doth she bring
A gentler speech from burning Porphyro;
So woful, and of such deep sorrowing,
That Angela gives promise she will do
Whatever he shall wish, betide her weal or woe.

Which was, to lead him, in close secrecy,
Even to Madeline's chamber, and there hide
Him in a closet, of such privacy
That he might see her beauty unespied,
And win perhaps that night a peerless bride,
While legion'd fairies paced the coverlet,
And pale enchantment held her sleepy-eyed.
Never on such a night have lovers met,
Since Merlin paid his Demon all the monstrous debt.

"It shall be as thou wishest," said the Dame:
"All cates and dainties shall be storèd there
Quickly on this feast-night: by the tambour frame
Her own lute thou wilt see: no time to spare,
For I am slow and feeble, and scarce dare

On such a catering trust my dizzy head.
Wait here, my child, with patience; kneel in prayer
The while: Ah! thou must needs the lady wed,
Or may I never leave my grave among the dead."

So saying, she hobbled off with busy fear.
The lover's endless minutes slowly pass'd;
The Dame return'd, and whisper'd in his ear
To follow her; with agèd eyes aghast
From fright of dim espial. Safe at last,
Through many a dusky gallery, they gain
The maiden's chamber, silken, hush'd, and chaste;
Where Porphyro took covert, pleas'd amain.
His poor guide hurried back with agues in her brain.

Her falt'ring hand upon the balustrade,
Old Angela was feeling for the stair,
When Madeline, St. Agnes' charmèd maid,
Rose, like a mission'd spirit, unaware:
With silver taper's light, and pious care,
She turned, and down the agèd gossip led
To a safe level matting. Now prepare,
Young Porphyro, for gazing on that bed;
She comes, she comes again, like ring-dove fray'd and
    fled.

Out went the taper as she hurried in;
Its little smoke, in pallid moonshine, died:
She clos'd the door, she panted, all akin
To spirits of the air, and visions wide:
No uttered syllable, or, woe betide!
But to her heart, her heart was voluble,
Paining with eloquence her balmy side;
As though a tongueless nightingale should swell
Her throat in vain, and die, heart-stifled, in her dell.

A casement high and triple-arched there was,
All garlanded with carven imag'ries
Of fruits, and flowers, and bunches of knot-grass,
And diamonded with panes of quaint device,
Innumerable of stains and splendid dyes,
As are the tiger-moth's deep-damask'd wings;
And in the midst, 'mong thousand heraldries,
And twilight saints, and dim emblazonings,
A shielded scutcheon blush'd with blood of queens and
    kings.

Full on this casement shone the wintry moon,
And threw warm gules on Madeline's fair breast,
As down she knelt for heaven's grace and boon;
Rose-bloom fell on her hands, together prest,
And on her silver cross soft amethyst,
And on her hair a glory, like a saint:
She seem'd a splendid angel, newly dressed,
Save wings, for heaven:—Porphyro grew faint:
She knelt, so pure a thing, so free from mortal taint.

Anon his heart revives: her vespers done,
Of all its wreathèd pearls her hair she frees;
Unclasps her warmèd jewels one by one;
Loosens her fragrant boddice; by degrees
Her rich attire creeps rustling to her knees:
Half-hidden, like a mermaid in sea-weed,
Pensive awhile she dreams awake, and sees,
In fancy, fair St. Agnes in her bed,
But dares not look behind, or all the charm is fled.

Soon, trembling in her soft and chilly nest,
In sort of wakeful swoon, perplex'd she lay,
Until the poppied warmth of sleep oppress'd
Her soothèd limbs, and soul fatigued away;

Flown, like a thought, until the morrow-day;
Blissfully haven'd both from joy and pain;
Clasp'd like a missal where swart Paynims pray;
Blinded alike from sunshine and from rain,
As though a rose should shut, and be a bud again.

Stol'n to this paradise, and so entranced,
Porphyro gazed upon her empty dress,
And listen'd to her breathing, if it chanced
To wake into a slumberous tenderness:
Which when he heard, that minute did he bless,
And breath'd himself: then from the closet crept,
Noiseless as fear in a wide wilderness,
And over the hush'd carpet, silent, stept,
And 'tween the curtains peep'd, where, lo!—how fast
    she slept.

Then by the bed-side, where the faded moon
Made a dim, silver twilight, soft he set
A table and, half anguish'd, threw thereon
A cloth of woven crimson, gold, and jet:—
O for some drowsy Morphean amulet!
The boisterous, midnight, festive clarion,
The kettledrum, and far-heard clarinet,
Affray his ears, though but in dying tone:—
The hall door shuts again, and all the noise is gone.

And still she slept an azure-lidded sleep,
In blanchèd linen, smooth, and lavender'd,
While he from forth the closet brought a heap
Of candied apple, quince, and plum, and gourd;
With jellies soother than the creamy curd,
And lucent syrops, tinct with cinnamon;
Manna and dates, in argosy transferr'd
From Fez; and spicèd dainties, every one,
From silken Samarcand to cedar'd Lebanon.

These delicates he heap'd with glowing hand
On golden dishes and in baskets bright
Of wreathèd silver: sumptuous they stand
In the retirèd quiet of the night,
Filling the chilly room with perfume light.—
"And now, my love, my seraph fair, awake!
Thou art my heaven, and I thine eremite:
Open thine eyes, for meek St. Agnes' sake,
Or I shall drowse beside thee, so my soul doth ache."

Thus whispering, his warm, unnervèd arm
Sank in her pillow. Shaded was her dream
By the dusk curtains:—'twas a midnight charm
Impossible to melt as icèd stream:
The lustrous salvers in the moonlight gleam;
Broad golden fringe upon the carpet lies:
It seem'd he never, never could redeem
From such a steadfast spell his lady's eyes;
So mus'd awhile, entoil'd in woofèd phantasies.

Awakening up, he took her hollow lute,—
Tumultuous,—and, in chords that tenderest be,
He play'd an ancient ditty, long since mute,
In Provence call'd, "La belle dame sans merci":
Close to her ear touching the melody;—
Wherewith disturb'd, she utter'd a soft moan:
He ceased—she panted quick—and suddenly
Her blue affrayèd eyes wide open shone:
Upon his knees he sank, pale as smooth-sculptured
    stone.

Her eyes were open, but she still beheld,
Now wide awake, the vision of her sleep:
There was a painful change, that nigh expell'd
The blisses of her dream so pure and deep,
At which fair Madeline began to weep,

And moan forth witless words with many a sigh;
While still her gaze on Porphyro would keep;
Who knelt, with joinèd hands and piteous eye,
Fearing to move or speak, she look'd so dreamingly.

"Ah, Porphyro!" said she, "but even now
Thy voice was at sweet tremble in mine ear,
Made tuneable with every sweetest vow;
And those sad eyes were spiritual and clear:
How chang'd thou art! how pallid, chill, and drear!
Give me that voice again, my Porphyro,
Those looks immortal, those complainings dear!
Oh leave me not in this eternal woe,
For if thou diest, my Love, I know not where to go."

Beyond a mortal man impassion'd far
At these voluptuous accents, he arose,
Ethereal, flush'd, and like a throbbing star
Seen mid the sapphire heaven's deep repose;
Into her dream he melted, as the rose
Blendeth its odor with the violet,—
Solution sweet: meantime the frost-wind blows
Like Love's alarum pattering the sharp sleet
Against the window-panes; St. Agnes' moon hath set.

'Tis dark: quick pattereth the flaw-blown sleet.
"This is no dream, my bride, my Madeline!"
'Tis dark: the icèd gusts still rave and beat:
"No dream, alas! alas! and woe is mine!
Porphyro will leave me here to fade and pine.—
Cruel! what traitor could thee hither bring?
I curse not, for my heart is lost in thine,
Though thou forsakest a deceivèd thing;—
A dove forlorn and lost with sick unprunèd wing."

"My Madeline! sweet dreamer! lovely bride!
Say, may I be for aye thy vassal blest?

Thy beauty's shield, heart-shap'd and vermeil dyed?
Ah, silver shrine, here will I take my rest
After so many hours of toil and quest,
A famish'd pilgrim,—saved by miracle.
Though I have found, I will not rob thy nest
Saving of thy sweet self; if thou think'st well
To trust, fair Madeline, to no rude infidel.

"Hark! 'tis an elfin-storm from faery land
Of haggard seeming, but a boon indeed:
Arise—arise! the morning is at hand;—
The bloated wassailers will never heed:—
Let us away, my love, with happy speed;
There are no ears to hear, or eyes to see,—
Drown'd all in Rhenish and the sleepy mead:
Awake! arise! my love, and fearless be,
For o'er the southern moors I have a home for thee."

She hurried at his words, beset with fears,
For there were sleeping dragons all around,
At glaring watch, perhaps, with ready spears—
Down the wide stairs a darkling way they found.—
In all the house was heard no human sound.
A chain-droop'd lamp was flickering by each door;
The arras, rich with horseman, hawk, and hound,
Flutter'd in the besieging wind's uproar;
And the long carpets rose along the gusty floor.

They glide, like phantoms, into the wide hall;
Like phantoms, to the iron porch, they glide;
Where lay the Porter, in uneasy sprawl,
With a huge empty flaggon by his side:
The wakeful bloodhound rose, and shook his hide,
But his sagacious eye an inmate owns:
By one, and one, the bolts full easy slide:—
The chains lie silent on the footworn stones;—
The key turns, and the door upon its hinges groans.

And they are gone: ay, ages long ago
These lovers fled away into the storm.
That night the Baron dreamt of many a woe,
And all his warrior-guests, with shade and form
Of witch, and demon, and large coffin-worm,
Were long be-nightmar'd. Angela the old
Died palsy-twitch'd, with meagre face deform;
The Beadsman, after a thousand aves told,
For aye unsought-for slept among his ashes cold.

## FROM *Hyperion*

### A FRAGMENT

Deep in the shady sadness of a vale
Far sunken from the healthy breath of morn,
Far from the fiery noon, and eve's one star,
Sat gray-hair'd Saturn, quiet as a stone,
Still as the silence round about his lair;
Forest on forest hung about his head
Like cloud on cloud. No stir of air was there,
Not so much life as on a summer's day
Robs not one light seed from the feather'd grass,
But where the dead leaf fell, there did it rest.
A stream went voiceless by, still deadened more
By reason of his fallen divinity
Spreading a shade: the Naiad 'mid her reeds
Press'd her cold finger closer to her lips.

Along the margin-sand large foot-marks went,
No further than to where his feet had stray'd,
And slept there since. Upon the sodden ground
His old right hand lay nerveless, listless, dead,
Unsceptred; and his realmless eyes were closed;

While his bow'd head seem'd list'ning to the Earth,
His ancient mother, for some comfort yet.

   It seem'd no force could wake him from his place;
But there came one, who with a kindred hand
Touch'd his wide shoulders, after bending low
With reverence, though to one who knew it not.
She was a Goddess of the infant world;
By her in stature the tall Amazon
Had stood a pigmy's height: she would have ta'en
Achilles by the hair and bent his neck;
Or with a finger stay'd Ixion's wheel.
Her face was large as that of Memphian sphinx,
Pedestal'd haply in a palace court,
When sages look'd to Egypt for their lore.
But oh! how unlike marble was that face:
How beautiful, if sorrow had not made
Sorrow more beautiful than Beauty's self.
There was a listening fear in her regard,
As if calamity had but begun;
As if the vanward clouds of evil days
Had spent their malice, and the sullen rear
Was with its stored thunder labouring up.
One hand she press'd upon that aching spot
Where beats the human heart, as if just there,
Though an immortal, she felt cruel pain:
The other upon Saturn's bended neck
She laid, and to the level of his ear
Leaning with parted lips, some words she spake
In solemn tenour and deep organ tone:
Some mourning words, which in our feeble tongue
Would come in these like accents; O how frail
To that large utterance of the early Gods!
"Saturn, look up!—though wherefore, poor old King?
I have no comfort for thee, no not one:

I cannot say, 'O wherefore sleepest thou?'
For heaven is parted from thee, and the earth
Knows thee not, thus afflicted, for a God;
And ocean too, with all its solemn noise,
Has from thy sceptre pass'd; and all the air
Is emptied of thine hoary majesty.
Thy thunder, conscious of the new command,
Rumbles reluctant o'er our fallen house;
And thy sharp lightning in unpractised hands
Scorches and burns our once serene domain.
O aching time! O moments big as years!
All as ye pass swell out the monstrous truth,
And press it so upon our weary griefs
That unbelief has not a space to breathe.
Saturn, sleep on:—O thoughtless, why did I
Thus violate thy slumbrous solitude?
Why should I ope thy melancholy eyes?
Saturn, sleep on! while at thy feet I weep."

As when, upon a tranced summer-night,
Those green-rob'd senators of mighty woods,
Tall oaks, branch-charmed by the earnest stars,
Dream, and so dream all night without a stir,
Save from one gradual solitary gust
Which comes upon the silence, and dies off,
As if the ebbing air had but one wave;
So came these words and went; the while in tears
She touch'd her fair large forehead to the ground,
Just where her falling hair might be outspread
A soft and silken mat for Saturn's feet.
One moon, with alteration slow, had shed
Her silver seasons four upon the night,
And still these two were postured motionless,
Like natural sculpture in cathedral cavern;
The frozen God still couchant on the earth,

And the sad Goddess weeping at his feet:
Until at length old Saturn lifted up
His faded eyes, and saw his kingdom gone,
And all the gloom and sorrow of the place,
And that fair kneeling Goddess; and then spake,
As with a palsied tongue, and while his beard
Shook horrid with such aspen-malady:
"O tender spouse of gold Hyperion,
Thea, I feel thee ere I see thy face;
Look up, and let me see our doom in it;
Look up, and tell me if this feeble shape
Is Saturn's; tell me, if thou hear'st the voice
Of Saturn; tell me, if this wrinkling brow,
Naked and bare of its great diadem,
Peers like the front of Saturn. Who had power
To make me desolate? whence came the strength?
How was it nurtur'd to such bursting forth,
While Fate seem'd strangled in my nervous grasp?
But it is so; and I am smother'd up,
And buried from all godlike exercise
Of influence benign on planets pale,
Of admonitions to the winds and seas,
Of peaceful sway above man's harvesting,
And all those acts which Deity supreme
Doth ease its heart of love in.—I am gone
Away from my own bosom: I have left
My strong identity, my real self,
Somewhere between the throne, and where I sit
Here on this spot of earth. Search, Thea, search!
Open thine eyes eterne, and sphere them round
Upon all space: space starr'd, and lorn of light;
Space region'd with life-air; and barren void;
Spaces of fire, and all the yawn of hell.—
Search, Thea, search! and tell me, if thou seest
A certain shape or shadow, making way

With wings or chariot fierce to repossess
A heaven he lost erewhile: it must—it must
Be of ripe progress—Saturn must be King.
Yes, there must be a golden victory;
There must be Gods thrown down, and trumpets blown
Of triumph calm, and hymns of festival
Upon the gold clouds metropolitan,
Voices of soft proclaim, and silver stir
Of strings in hollow shells; and there shall be
Beautiful things made new, for the surprise
Of the sky-children; I will give command:
Thea! Thea! Thea! where is Saturn?"

This passion lifted him upon his feet,
And made his hands to struggle in the air,
His Druid locks to shake and ooze with sweat,
His eyes to fever out, his voice to cease.
He stood, and heard not Thea's sobbing deep;
A little time, and then again he snatch'd
Utterance thus.—"But cannot I create?
Cannot I form? Cannot I fashion forth
Another world, another universe,
To overbear and crumble this to naught?
Where is another chaos? Where?"—That word
Found way unto Olympus, and made quake
The rebel three.—Thea was startled up,
And in her bearing was a sort of hope,
As thus she quick-voic'd spake, yet full of awe.

"This cheers our fallen house: come to our friends,
O Saturn! come away, and give them heart;
I know the covert, for thence came I hither."
Thus brief; then with beseeching eyes she went
With backward footing through the shade a space:
He follow'd, and she turn'd to lead the way

Through aged boughs, that yielded like the mist
Which eagles cleave upmounting from their nest.

Meanwhile in other realms big tears were shed,
More sorrow like to this, and such like woe,
Too huge for mortal tongue or pen of scribe:
The Titans fierce, self-hid, or prison-bound,
Groan'd for the old allegiance once more,
And listen'd in sharp pain for Saturn's voice.
But one of the whole mammoth-brood still kept
His sov'reignty, and rule, and majesty;—
Blazing Hyperion on his orbed fire
Still sat, still snuff'd the incense, teeming up
From Man to the sun's God; yet unsecure:
For as among us mortals omens drear
Fright and perplex, so also shuddered he—
Not at dog's howl, or gloom-bird's hated screech,
Or the familiar visiting of one
Upon the first toll of his passing-bell,
Or prophesyings of the midnight lamp;
But horrors, portion'd to a giant nerve,
Oft made Hyperion ache. His palace bright
Bastion'd with pyramids of glowing gold,
And touch'd with shade of bronzed obelisks,
Glar'd a blood-red through all its thousand courts,
Arches, and domes, and fiery galleries;
And all its curtains of Aurorian clouds
Flush'd angerly: while sometimes eagles' wings,
Unseen before by Gods or wondering men,
Darken'd the place; and neighing steeds were heard,
Not heard before by Gods or wondering men.
Also, when he would taste the spicy wreaths
Of incense, breath'd aloft from sacred hills,
Instead of sweets, his ample palate took

Savour of poisonous brass and metal sick:
And so, when harbour'd in the sleepy west,
After the full completion of fair day,—
For rest divine upon exalted couch
And slumber in the arms of melody,
He pac'd away the pleasant hours of ease
With stride colossal, on from hall to hall;
While far within each aisle and deep recess,
His winged minions in close clusters stood,
Amaz'd and full of fear; like anxious men
Who on wide plains gather in panting troops,
When earthquakes jar their battlements and towers.
Even now, while Saturn, rous'd from icy trance,
Went step for step with Thea through the woods,
Hyperion, leaving twilight in the rear,
Came slope upon the threshold of the west;
Then, as was wont, his palace-door flew ope
In smoothest silence, save what solemn tubes,
Blown by the serious Zephyrs, gave of sweet
And wandering sounds, slow-breathed melodies;
And like a rose in vermeil tint and shape,
In fragrance soft, and coolness to the eye,
That inlet to severe magnificence
Stood full blown, for the God to enter in.

He enter'd, but he enter'd full of wrath;
His flaming robes stream'd out beyond his heels,
And gave a roar, as if of earthly fire,
That scar'd away the meek ethereal Hours
And made their dove-wings tremble. On he flared,
From stately nave to nave, from vault to vault,
Through bowers of fragrant and enwreathed light,
And diamond-paved lustrous long arcades,
Until he reach'd the great main cupola;
There standing fierce beneath he stampt his foot,

And from the basements deep to the high towers
Jarr'd his own golden region; and before
The quavering thunder thereupon had ceas'd,
His voice leapt out, despite of godlike curb,
To this result: "O dreams of day and night!
O monstrous forms! O effigies of pain!
O spectres busy in a cold, cold gloom!
O lank-ear'd Phantoms of black-weeded pools!
Why do I know ye? why have I seen ye? why
Is my eternal essence thus distraught
To see and to behold these horrors new?
Saturn is fallen, am I too to fall?
Am I to leave this haven of my rest,
This cradle of my glory, this soft clime,
This calm luxuriance of blissful light,
These crystalline pavilions, and pure fanes,
Of all my lucent empire? It is left
Deserted, void, nor any haunt of mine.
The blaze, the splendour, and the symmetry,
I cannot see—but darkness, death and darkness.
Even here, into my centre of repose,
The shady visions come to domineer,
Insult, and blind, and stifle up my pomp.—
Fall!—No, by Tellus and her briny robes!
Over the fiery frontier of my realms
I will advance a terrible right arm
Shall scare that infant thunderer, rebel Jove,
And bid old Saturn take his throne again."—
He spake, and ceas'd, the while a heavier threat
Held struggle with his throat but came not forth:
For as in theatres of crowded men
Hubbub increases more they call out "Hush!"
So at Hyperion's words the Phantoms pale
Bestirr'd themselves, thrice horrible and cold;
And from the mirror'd level where he stood

A mist arose, as from a scummy marsh.
At this, through all his bulk an agony
Crept gradual, from the feet unto the crown,
Like a lithe serpent vast and muscular
Making slow way, with head and neck convuls'd
From over-strained might. Releas'd, he fled
To the eastern gates, and full six dewy hours
Before the dawn in season due should blush,
He breath'd fierce breath against the sleepy portals,
Clear'd them of heavy vapours, burst them wide
Suddenly on the ocean's chilly streams.
The planet orb of fire, whereon he rode
Each day from east to west the heavens through,
Spun round in sable curtaining of clouds;
Not therefore veiled quite, blindfold, and hid,
But ever and anon the glancing spheres,
Circles, and arcs, and broad-belting colure,
Glow'd through, and wrought upon the muffling dark
Sweet-shaped lightnings from the nadir deep
Up to the zenith,—hieroglyphics old
Which sages and keen-eyed astrologers
Then living on the earth, with labouring thought
Won from the gaze of many centuries:
Now lost, save what we find on remnants huge
Of stone, or marble swart; their import gone,
Their wisdom long since fled.—Two wings this orb
Possess'd for glory, two fair argent wings,
Ever exalted at the God's approach:
And now, from forth the gloom their plumes immense
Rose, one by one, till all outspreaded were;
While still the dazzling globe maintain'd eclipse,
Awaiting for Hyperion's command.
Fain would he have commanded, fain took throne
And bid the day begin, if but for change.
He might not:—No, though a primeval God:

The sacred seasons might not be disturb'd.
Therefore the operations of the dawn
Stay'd in their birth, even as here 'tis told.
Those silver wings expanded sisterly,
Eager to sail their orb; the porches wide
Open'd upon the dusk demesnes of night;
And the bright Titan, phrenzied with new woes,
Unus'd to bend, by hard compulsion bent
His spirit to the sorrow of the time;
And all along a dismal rack of clouds,
Upon the boundaries of day and night,
He stretch'd himself in grief and radiance faint.
There as he lay, the Heaven with its stars
Look'd down on him with pity, and the voice
Of Cœlus, from the universal space,
Thus whisper'd low and solemn in his ear.
"O brightest of my children dear, earth-born
And sky-engendered, Son of Mysteries
All unrevealed even to the powers
Which met at thy creating; at whose joys
And palpitations sweet, and pleasures soft,
I, Cœlus, wonder, how they came and whence;
And at the fruits thereof what shapes they be,
Distinct, and visible; symbols divine,
Manifestations of that beauteous life
Diffus'd unseen throughout eternal space:
Of these new-form'd art thou, oh brightest child!
Of these, thy brethren and the Goddesses!
There is sad feud among ye, and rebellion
Of son against his sire. I saw him fall,
I saw my first-born tumbled from his throne!
To me his arms were spread, to me his voice
Found way from forth the thunders round his head!
Pale wox I, and in vapours hid my face.
Art thou, too, near such doom? vague fear there is:

For I have seen my sons most unlike Gods.
Divine ye were created, and divine
In sad demeanour, solemn, undisturb'd,
Unruffled, like high Gods, ye liv'd and ruled:
Now I behold in you fear, hope, and wrath;
Actions of rage and passion; even as
I see them, on the mortal world beneath,
In men who die.—This is the grief, O Son!
Sad sign of ruin, sudden dismay, and fall!
Yet do thou strive; as thou art capable,
As thou canst move about, an evident God;
And canst oppose to each malignant hour
Ethereal presence:—I am but a voice;
My life is but the life of winds and tides,
No more than winds and tides can I avail:—
But thou canst.—Be thou therefore in the van
Of Circumstance; yea, seize the arrow's barb
Before the tense string murmur.—To the earth!
For there thou wilt find Saturn, and his woes.
Meantime I will keep watch on thy bright sun,
And of thy seasons be a careful nurse."—
Ere half this region-whisper had come down,
Hyperion arose, and on the stars
Lifted his curved lids, and kept them wide
Until it ceas'd; and still he kept them wide:
And still they were the same bright, patient stars.
Then with a slow incline of his broad breast,
Like to a diver in the pearly seas,
Forward he stoop'd over the airy shore,
And plung'd all noiseless into the deep night.

(Book I, entire)

# Leigh Hunt

(1784–1859)

## The Fish, the Man, and the Spirit

### TO A FISH

You strange, astonished-looking, angle-faced,
  Dreary-mouthed, gaping wretches of the sea,
  Gulping salt-water everlastingly,
Cold-blooded, though with red your blood be graced,
And mute, though dwellers in the roaring waste;
  And you, all shapes beside, that fishy be,—
  Some round, some flat, some long, all devilry,
Legless, unloving, infamously chaste:—

O scaly, slippery, wet, swift, staring wights,
  What is't ye do? What life lead? eh, dull goggles?
How do ye vary your vile days and nights?
  How pass your Sundays? Are ye still but joggles
In ceaseless wash? Still nought but gapes and bites,
  And drinks, and stares, diversified with boggles?

### A FISH ANSWERS

Amazing monster! that, for aught I know,
  With the first sight of thee didst make our race
  For ever stare! O flat and shocking face,
Grimly divided from the breast below!
Thou that on dry land horribly dost go
  With a split body and most ridiculous pace,

Prong after prong, disgracer of all grace,
Long-useless-finned, haired, upright, unwet, slow!

O breather of unbreathable, sword-sharp air,
　How canst exist? How bear thyself, thou dry
And dreary sloth? What particle canst share
　Of the only blessed life, the watery?
I sometimes see of ye an actual *pair*
　Go by! linked fin by fin! most odiously.


## THE FISH TURNS INTO A MAN, AND THEN
## INTO A SPIRIT, AND AGAIN SPEAKS

Indulge thy smiling scorn, if smiling still,
　O man! and loathe, but with a sort of love;
　For difference must its use by difference prove,
And, in sweet clang, the spheres with music fill.
One of the spirits am I, that at his will
　Live in whate'er has life—fish, eagle, dove—
　No hate, no pride, beneath nought, nor above,
A visitor of the rounds of God's sweet skill.

Man's life is warm, glad, sad, 'twixt loves and graves,
　Boundless in hope, honoured with pangs austere,
Heaven-gazing; and his angel-wings he craves:—
　The fish is swift, small-needing, vague yet clear,
A cold, sweet, silver life, wrapped in round waves,
　Quickened with touches of transporting fear.

# Thomas Hood

(1799–1845)

## Sonnet to Vauxhall

*"The English Garden."*—MASON

The cold transparent ham is on my fork—
   It hardly rains—and hark the bell!—ding-dingle—
Away! Three thousand feet at gravel work,
   Mocking a Vauxhall shower!—Married and Single
Crush—rush;—Soak'd Silks with wet white Satin
   mingle.
   Hengler! Madame! round whom all bright sparks
   lurk,
Calls audibly on Mr. and Mrs. Pringle
   To study the Sublime, &c.—(vide Burke)
All Noses are upturn'd!—Whish-ish!—On high
   The rocket rushes—trails—just steals in sight—
Then droops and melts in bubbles of blue light—
   And Darkness reigns—Then balls flare up and die—
Wheels whiz—smack crackers—serpents twist—and
   then
   Back to the cold transparent ham again!

## Our Village

### BY A VILLAGER

Sweet Auburn, loveliest village of the plain.—GOLDSMITH

Our village, that's to say not Miss Mitford's village, but
our village of Bullock Smithy,
Is come into by an avenue of trees, three oak pollards,
two elders, and a withy;
And in the middle, there's a green of about not exceed-
ing an acre and a half;
It's common to all, and fed off by nineteen cows, six
ponies, three horses, five asses, two foals, seven pigs,
and a calf!
Besides a pond in the middle, as is held by a similar sort
of common law lease,
And contains twenty ducks, six drakes, three ganders,
two dead dogs, four drown'd kittens, and twelve
geese.
Of course the green's cropt very close, and does famous
for bowling when the little village boys play at
cricket;
Only some horse, or pig, or cow, or great jackass, is sure
to come and stand right before the wicket.
There's fifty-five private houses, let alone barns and
workshops, and pigstyes, and poultry huts, and such-
like sheds;
With plenty of public-houses—two Foxes, one Green
Man, three Bunch of Grapes, one Crown, and six
King's Heads.
The Green Man is reckon'd the best, as the only one
that for love or money can raise

A postilion, a blue jacket, two deplorable lame white
  horses, and a ramshackled "neat postchaise."
There's one parish church for all the people, whatsoever
  may be their ranks in life or their degrees,
Except one very damp, small, dark, freezing-cold, little
  Methodist chapel of Ease;
And close by the church-yard there's a stone-mason's
  yard, that when the time is seasonable
Will furnish with afflictions sore and marble urns and
  cherubims very low and reasonable.
There's a cage, comfortable enough; I've been in it with
  old Jack Jeffrey and Tom Pike;
For the Green Man next door will send you in ale, gin,
  or any thing else you like.
I can't speak of the stocks, as nothing remains of them
  but the upright post;
But the pound is kept in repairs for the sake of Cob's
  horse, as is always there almost.
There's a smithy of course, where that queer sort of a
  chap in his way, Old Joe Bradley,
Perpetually hammers and stammers, for he stutters and
  shoes horses very badly.
There's a shop of all sorts, that sells every thing, kept
  by the widow of Mr. Task;
But when you go there it's ten to one she's out of every
  thing you ask.
You'll know her house by the swarm of boys, like flies,
  about the old sugary cask:
There are six empty houses, and not so well paper'd in-
  side as out,
For bill-stickers won't beware, but sticks notices of sales
  and election placards all about.
That's the Doctor's with a green door, where the garden
  pots in the windows is seen;
A weakly monthly rose that don't blow, and a dead

geranium, and a tea-plant with five black leaves and one green.

As for hollyoaks at the cottage doors, and honeysuckles and jasmines, you may go and whistle;

But the Tailor's front garden grows two cabbages, a dock, a ha'porth of pennyroyal, two dandelions, and a thistle.

There are three small orchards—Mr. Busby's the school-master's is the chief—

With two pear-trees that don't bear; one plum and an apple, that every year is stripped by a thief.

There's another small day-school too, kept by the re-spectable Mrs. Gaby.

A select establishment, for six little boys and one big, and four little girls and a baby;

There's a rectory, with pointed gables and strange odd chimneys that never smokes,

For the rector don't live on his living like other Chris-tian sort of folks;

There's a barber's, once a week well filled with rough black-bearded, shock-headed churls,

And a window with two feminine men's heads, and two masculine ladies in false curls;

There's a butcher's, and a carpenter's, and a plumber's, and a small green-grocer's, and a baker,

But he won't bake on a Sunday, and there's a sexton that's a coal-merchant besides, and an undertaker;

And a toy-shop, but not a whole one, for a village can't compare with the London shops;

One window sells drums, dolls, kites, carts, bats, Clout's balls, and the other sells malt and hops.

And Mrs. Brown, in domestic economy not to be a bit behind her betters,

Lets her house to a milliner, a watchmaker, a rat-

catcher, a cobler, lives in it herself, and it's the post-
office for letters.
Now I've gone through all the village—ay, from end
to end, save and except one more house,
But I haven't come to that—and I hope I never shall—
and that's the Village Poor House!

## A Friendly Address

### TO MRS. FRY IN NEWGATE

Sermons in stones.—*As You Like It*.
Out! out! damned spot.—*Macbeth*.

I like you, Mrs. Fry! I like your name!
    It speaks the very warmth you feel in pressing
In daily act round Charity's great flame—
    I like the crisp Browne way you have of dressing,
Good Mrs. Fry! I like the placid claim
    You make to Christianity,—professing
Love, and good *works*—of course you buy of Barton,
Beside the young *fry's* bookseller, Friend Darton!

I like, good Mrs. Fry, your brethren mute—
    Those serious, solemn gentlemen that sport—
I should have said, that *wear*, the sober suit
    Shap'd like a court dress—but for heaven's court.
I like your sisters too,—sweet Rachel's fruit—
    Protestant nuns! I like their stiff support
Of virtue—and I like to see them clad
With such a difference—just like good from bad!

I like the sober colours—not the wet;
    Those gaudy manufactures of the rainbow—

Green, orange, crimson, purple, violet—
　　In which the fair, the flirting, and the vain, go—
The others are a chaste, severer set,
　　In which the good, the pious, and the plain, go—
They're moral *standards,* to know Christians by—
In short, they are your *colours,* Mrs. Fry!

As for the naughty tinges of the prism—
　　Crimson's the cruel uniform of war—
Blue—hue of brimstone! minds no catechism;
　　And green is young and gay—not noted for
Goodness, or gravity, or quietism,
　　Till it is sadden'd down to tea-green, or
Olive—and purple's giv'n to wine, I guess;
And yellow is a convict by its dress!

They're all the devil's liveries, that men
　　And women wear in servitude to sin—
But how will they come off, poor motleys, when
　　Sin's wages are paid down, and they stand in
The Evil presence? You and I know, then,
　　How all the party colours will begin
To part—the *Pitt*ite hues will sadden there,
Whereas the *Fox*ite shades will all show fair!

Witness their goodly labours one by one!
　　*Russet* makes garments for the needy poor—
*Dove-colour* preaches love to all—and *dun*
　　Calls every day at Charity's street-door—
*Brown* studies scripture, and bids woman shun
　　All gaudy furnishings—*olive* doth pour
Oil into wounds: and *drab* and *slate* supply
Scholar and book in Newgate, Mrs. Fry!

Well! Heaven forbid that I should discommend
　　The gratis, charitable, jail-endeavour!
When all persuasions in your praises blend—

The Methodist's creed and cry are, *Fry for ever!*
No—I will be your friend—and, like a friend,
   Point out your very worst defect—Nay, never
Start at that word!—But I *must* ask you why
You keep your school *in* Newgate, Mrs. Fry?

Too well I know the price our mother Eve
   Paid for *her* schooling: but must all her daughters
Commit a petty larceny, and thieve—
   Pay down a crime for *"entrance"* to your *"quarters"?*
Your classes may increase, but I must grieve
   Over your pupils at their bread and waters!
Oh, tho' it cost you rent—(and rooms run high!)
Keep your school *out* of Newgate, Mrs. Fry!

O save the vulgar soul before it's spoil'd!
   Set up your mounted sign *without* the gate—
And there inform the mind before 'tis soil'd!
   'Tis sorry writing on a greasy slate!
Nay, if you would not have your labours foil'd,
   Take it *inclining* tow'rds a virtuous state,
Not prostrate and laid flat—else, woman meek!
The *upright* pencil will but hop and shriek!

Ah, who can tell how hard it is to drain
   The evil spirit from the heart it preys in,—
To bring sobriety to life again,
   Chok'd with the vile Anacreontic raisin,—
To wash Black Betty when her black's ingrain,—
   To stick a moral lacquer on Moll Brazen,
Of Suky Tawdry's habits to deprive her;
To tame the wild-fowl-ways of Jenny Diver!

Ah, who can tell how hard it is to teach
   Miss Nancy Dawson on her bed of straw—
To make Long Sal sew up the endless breach
   She made in manners—to write heaven's own law

On hearts of granite.—Nay, how hard to preach,
    In cells, that are not memory's—to draw
The moral thread, thro' the immoral eye
Of blunt Whitechapel natures, Mrs. Fry!

In vain you teach them baby-work within:
    'Tis but a clumsy botchery of crime;
'Tis but a tedious darning of old sin—
    Come out yourself, and stitch up souls in time—
It is too late for scouring to begin
    When virtue's ravell'd out, when all the prime
Is worn away, and nothing sound remains;
You'll fret the fabric out before the stains!

I like your chocolate, good Mistress Fry!
    I like your cookery in every way;
I like your shrove-tide service and supply;
    I like to hear your sweet *Pandeans* play;
I like the pity in your full-brimm'd eye;
    I like your carriage and your silken grey,
Your dove-like habits, and your silent preaching;
But I don't like your Newgatory teaching.

Come out of Newgate, Mrs. Fry! Repair
    Abroad, and find your pupils in the streets.
O, come abroad into the wholesome air,
    And take your moral place, before Sin seats
Her wicked self in the Professor's chair.
    Suppose some morals raw! the true receipt's
To dress them in the pan, but do not try
To cook them in the fire, good Mrs. Fry!

Put on your decent bonnet, and come out!
    Good lack! the ancients did not set up schools
In jail—but at the *Porch!* hinting, no doubt,
    That Vice should have a lesson in the rules

Before 'twas whipt by law.—O come about,
  Good Mrs. Fry! and set up forms and stools
All down the Old Bailey, and thro' Newgate-street,
But not in Mr. Wontner's proper seat!

Teach Lady Barrymore, if, teaching, you
  That peerless Peeress can absolve from dolour;
Teach her it is not virtue to pursue
  Ruin of blue, or any other colour;
Teach her it is not Virtue's crown to rue,
  Month after month, the unpaid drunken dollar;
Teach her that "flooring Charleys" is a game
Unworthy one that bears a Christian name.

O come and teach our children—that ar'n't *ours*—
  That heaven's straight pathway is a narrow way,
Not Broad St. Giles's, where fierce Sin devours
  Children, like Time—or rather they both prey
On youth together—meanwhile Newgate low'rs
  Ev'n like a black cloud at the close of day,
To shut them out from any more blue sky:
Think of these hopeless wretches, Mrs. Fry!

You are not nice—go into their retreats,
  And make them Quakers, if you will.—'Twere best
They wore straight collars, and their shirts sans *pleats;*
  That they had hats *with* brims,—that they were drest
In garbs without *lappels*—than shame the streets
  With so much raggedness.—You may invest
Much cash this way—but it will cost its price,
To give a good, round, real *cheque* to Vice!

In brief,—oh teach the child its moral rote,
  Not *in* the way from which it won't depart,—
But *out*—out—out! Oh, bid it walk remote!
  And if the skies are clos'd against the smart,

Ev'n let him wear the single-breasted coat,
  For that ensureth singleness of heart.—
Do what you will, his every want supply,
*Keep* him—but *out* of Newgate, Mrs. Fry!

## Silence

There is a silence where hath been no sound,
  There is a silence where no sound may be,
  In the cold grave—under the deep deep sea,
Or in wide desert where no life is found,
Which hath been mute, and still must sleep profound;
  No voice is hush'd—no life treads silently,
  But clouds and cloudy shadows wander free,
That never spoke, over the idle ground:
But in green ruins, in the desolate walls
  Of antique palaces, where Man hath been,
Though the dun fox, or wild hyena, calls,
  And owls, that flit continually between,
Shriek to the echo, and the low winds moan,
There the true Silence is, self-conscious and alone.

## I remember, I remember

I remember, I remember,
The house where I was born,
The little window where the sun
Came peeping in at morn;
He never came a wink too soon,
Nor brought too long a day,

But now, I often wish the night
Had borne my breath away!

I remember, I remember,
The roses, red and white,
The vi'lets, and the lily-cups,
Those flowers made of light!
The lilacs where the robin built,
And where my brother set
The laburnum on his birthday,—
The tree is living yet!

I remember, I remember,
Where I was used to swing,
And thought the air must rush as fresh
To swallows on the wing;
My spirit flew in feathers then,
That is so heavy now,
And summer pools could hardly cool
The fever on my brow!

I remember, I remember,
The fir trees dark and high;
I used to think their slender tops
Were close against the sky:
It was a childish ignorance,
But now 'tis little joy
To know I'm farther off from heav'n
Than when I was a boy.

# The Sea of Death

## A FRAGMENT

—Methought I saw
Life swiftly treading over endless space;
And, at her foot-print, but a bygone pace,
The ocean-past, which, with increasing wave,
Swallow'd her steps like a pursuing grave.
Sad were my thoughts that anchor'd silently
On the dead waters of that passionless sea,
Unstirr'd by any touch of living breath:
Silence hung over it, and drowsy Death,
Like a gorged sea-bird, slept with folded wings
On crowded carcases—sad passive things
That wore the thin grey surface, like a veil
Over the calmness of their features pale.

And there were spring-faced cherubs that did sleep
Like water-lilies on that motionless deep,
How beautiful! with bright unruffled hair
On sleek unfretted brows, and eyes that were
Buried in marble tombs, a pale eclipse!
And smile-bedimpled cheeks, and pleasant lips,
Meekly apart, as if the soul intense
Spake out in dreams of its own innocence:
And so they lay in loveliness, and kept
The birth-night of their peace, that Life e'en wept
With very envy of their happy fronts;
For there were neighbour brows scarr'd by the brunts
Of strife and sorrowing—where Care had set
His crooked autograph, and marr'd the jet
Of glossy locks with hollow eyes forlorn,

And lips that curl'd in bitterness and scorn—
Wretched,—as they had breathed of this world's pain,
And so bequeath'd it to the world again
Through the beholder's heart in heavy sighs.

So lay they garmented in torpid light,
Under the pall of a transparent night,
Like solemn apparitions lull'd sublime
To everlasting rest,—and with them Time
Slept, as he sleeps upon the silent face
Of a dark dial in a sunless place.

## Ode: Autumn

I saw old Autumn in the misty morn
Stand shadowless like Silence, listening
To silence, for no lonely bird would sing
Into his hollow ear from woods forlorn,
Nor lowly hedge nor solitary thorn;—
Shaking his languid locks all dewy bright
With tangled gossamer that fell by night,
   Pearling his coronet of golden corn.

Where are the songs of Summer?—With the sun,
Oping the dusky eyelids of the south,
Till shade and silence waken up as one,
And Morning sings with a warm odorous mouth.
Where are the merry birds?—Away, away,
On panting wings through the inclement skies,
   Lest owls should prey
   Undazzled at noon-day,
And tear with horny beak their lustrous eyes.

Where are the blooms of Summer?—In the west,
Blushing their last to the last sunny hours,

When the mild Eve by sudden Night is prest
Like tearful Proserpine, snatch'd from her flow'rs
　　To a most gloomy breast.
Where is the pride of Summer,—the green prime,—
The many, many leaves all twinkling?—Three
　　On the moss'd elm; three on the naked lime
Trembling,—and one upon the old oak tree!
　　Where is the Dryads' immortality?—
Gone into mournful cypress and dark yew,
Or wearing the long gloomy Winter through
　　In the smooth holly's green eternity.

The squirrel gloats on his accomplish'd hoard,
The ants have brimm'd their garners with ripe grain,
　　And honey bees have stor'd
The sweets of Summer in their luscious cells;
The swallows all have wing'd across the main;
But here the Autumn melancholy dwells,
　　And sighs her tearful spells
Amongst the sunless shadows of the plain.
　　　　Alone, alone,
　　　　Upon a mossy stone,
She sits and reckons up the dead and gone
With the last leaves for a love-rosary,
Whilst all the wither'd world looks drearily,
Like a dim picture of the drowned past
In the hush'd mind's mysterious far away,
Doubtful what ghostly thing will steal the last
Into that distance, grey upon the grey.

O go and sit with her, and be o'ershaded
Under the languid downfall of her hair:
She wears a coronal of flowers faded
Upon her forehead, and a face of care;—
There is enough of wither'd every where
To make her bower,—and enough of gloom;

There is enough of sadness to invite,
If only for the rose that died,—whose doom
Is Beauty's,—she that with the living bloom
Of conscious cheeks most beautifies the light;—
There is enough of sorrowing, and quite
Enough of bitter fruits the earth doth bear,—
Enough of chilly droppings for her bowl;
Enough of fear and shadowy despair,
To frame her cloudy prison for the soul!

# Winthrop Mackworth Praed

(1802–1839)

## FROM Every Day Characters

### THE VICAR

Some years ago, ere time and taste
   Had turned our parish topsy-turvy,
When Darnel Park was Darnel Waste,
   And roads as little known as scurvy,
The man who lost his way, between
   St. Mary's Hill and Sandy Thicket,
Was always shown across the green,
   And guided to the Parson's wicket.

Back flew the bolt of lissom lath;
   Fair Margaret, in her tidy kirtle,
Led the lorn traveller up the path,
   Through clean-clipt rows of box and myrtle;
And Don and Sancho, Tramp and Tray,
   Upon the parlour steps collected,
Wagged all their tails, and seemed to say—
   "Our master knows you—you're expected."

Uprose the Reverend Dr. Brown,
   Uprose the Doctor's winsome marrow;
The lady laid her knitting down,
   Her husband clasped his ponderous Barrow;
Whate'er the stranger's caste or creed,
   Pundit or Papist, saint or sinner,

436

He found a stable for his steed,
   And welcome for himself, and dinner.

If, when he reached his journey's end,
   And warmed himself in Court or College,
He had not gained an honest friend
   And twenty curious scraps of knowledge,—
If he departed as he came,
   With no new light on love or liquor,—
Good sooth, the traveller was to blame,
   And not the Vicarage, nor the Vicar.

His talk was like a stream, which runs
   With rapid change from rocks to roses:
It slipped from politics to puns,
   It passed from Mahomet to Moses;
Beginning with the laws which keep
   The planets in their radiant courses,
And ending with some precept deep
   For dressing eels, or shoeing horses.

He was a shrewd and sound Divine,
   Of loud Dissent the mortal terror;
And when, by dint of page and line,
   He 'stablished Truth, or started Error,
The Baptist found him far too deep;
   The Deist sighed with saving sorrow;
And the lean Levite went to sleep,
   And dreamed of tasting pork to-morrow.

His sermon never said or showed
   That Earth is foul, that Heaven is gracious,
Without refreshment on the road
   From Jerome, or from Athanasius:
And sure a righteous zeal inspired
   The hand and head that penned and planned them,

For all who understood admired,
    And some who did not understand them.

He wrote, too, in a quiet way,
    Small treatises, and smaller verses,
And sage remarks on chalk and clay,
    And hints to noble Lords—and nurses;
True histories of last year's ghost,
    Lines to a ringlet, or a turban,
And trifles for the Morning Post,
    And nothings for Sylvanus Urban.

He did not think all mischief fair,
    Although he had a knack of joking;
He did not make himself a bear,
    Although he had a taste for smoking;
And when religious sects ran mad,
    He held, in spite of all his learning,
That if a man's belief is bad,
    It will not be improved by burning.

And he was kind, and loved to sit
    In the low hut or garnished cottage,
And praise the farmer's homely wit,
    And share the widow's homelier pottage:
At his approach complaint grew mild;
    And when his hand unbarred the shutter,
The clammy lips of fever smiled
    The welcome which they could not utter.

He always had a tale for me
    Of Julius Caesar, or of Venus;
From him I learnt the rule of three,
    Cat's cradle, leap-frog, and *Quae genus:*
I used to singe his powdered wig,
    To steal the staff he put such trust in,

And make the puppy dance a jig,
   When he began to quote Augustine.

Alack the change! in vain I look
   For haunts in which my boyhood trifled,—
The level lawn, the trickling brook,
   The trees I climbed, the beds I rifled;
The church is larger than before;
   You reach it by a carriage entry;
It holds three hundred people more,
   And pews are fitted up for gentry.

Sit in the Vicar's seat: you'll hear
   The doctrine of a gentle Johnian,
Whose hand is white, whose tone is clear,
   Whose phrase is very Ciceronian.
Where is the old man laid?—look down,
   And construe on the slab before you,
"*Hic jacet GULIELMUS BROWN,*
   *Vir nullâ non donandus laura.*"

## PORTRAIT OF A LADY
### IN THE EXHIBITION OF THE ROYAL ACADEMY

What are you, Lady?—naught is here
   To tell us of your name or story;
To claim the gazer's smile or tear,
   To dub you Whig, or damn you Tory.
It is beyond a poet's skill
   To form the slightest notion, whether
We e'er shall walk through one quadrille,
   Or look upon one moon together.

You're very pretty!—all the world
   Are talking of your bright brow's splendor,

And of your locks, so softly curled,
   And of your hands, so white and slender:
Some think you're blooming in Bengal;
   Some say you're blowing in the city;
Some know you're nobody at all;
   I only feel, you're very pretty.

But bless my heart! it's very wrong:
   You're making all our belles ferocious;
Anne "never saw a chin so long";
   And Laura thinks your dress "atrocious";
And Lady Jane, who now and then
   Is taken for the village steeple,
Is sure you can't be four feet ten,
   And "wonders at the taste of people."

Soon pass the praises of a face;
   Swift fades the very best vermilion;
Fame rides a most prodigious pace;
   Oblivion follows on the pillion;
And all, who, in these sultry rooms,
   To-day have stared, and pushed, and fainted,
Will soon forget your pearls and plumes,
   As if they never had been painted.

You'll be forgotten—as old debts
   By persons who are used to borrow;
Forgotten—as the sun that sets,
   When shines a new one on the morrow;
Forgotten—like the luscious peach,
   That blessed the school-boy last September;
Forgotten—like a maiden speech,
   Which all men praise, but none remember.

Yet, ere you sink into the stream,
   That whelms alike sage, saint, and martyr,
And soldier's sword, and minstrel's theme,

And Canning's wit, and Gratton's charter,
Here of the fortunes of your youth
    My fancy weaves her dim conjectures,
Which have, perhaps, as much of truth
    As Passion's vows, or Cobbett's lectures.

Was't in the north or in the south,
    That summer-breezes rocked your cradle?
And had you in your baby mouth
    A wooden or a silver ladle?
And was your first, unconscious sleep,
    By Brownie banned, or blessed by fairy?
And did you wake to laugh or weep?
    And were you christened Maud or Mary?

And was your father called "your grace?"
    And did he bet at Ascot races?
And did he chat at common-place?
    And did he fill a score of places?
And did your lady-mother's charms
    Consist in picklings, broilings, bastings?
Or did she prate about the arms
    Her brave forefathers wore at Hastings?

Where were you "finished?" tell me where!
    Was it at Chelsea, or at Chiswick?
Had you the ordinary share
    Of books and backboard, harp and physic?
And did they bid you banish pride,
    And mind your oriental tinting?
And did you learn how Dido died,
    And who found out the art of printing?

And are you fond of lanes and brooks,
    A votary of the sylvan muses?
Or do you con the little books
    Which Baron Brougham and Vaux diffuses?

Or do you love to knit and sew,
   The fashionable world's Arachne?
Or do you canter down the Row,
   Upon a very long-tailed hackney?

And do you love your brother James?
   And do you pet his mares and setters?
And have your friends romantic names?
   And do you write them long, long letters?
And are you—since the world began
   All women are—a little spiteful?
And don't you dote on Malibran?
   And don't you think Tom Moore delightful?

I see they've brought you flowers to-day,
   Delicious food for eyes and noses;
But carelessly you turn away
   From all the pinks, and all the roses;
Say, is that fond look sent in search
   Of one whose look as fondly answers?
And is he, fairest, in the Church,
   Or is he—ain't he—in the Lancers?

And is your love a motley page
   Of black and white, half joy, half sorrow?
Are you to wait till you're of age?
   Or are you to be his to-morrow?
Or do they bid you, in their scorn,
   Your pure and sinless flame to smother?
Is he so very meanly born?
   Or are you married to another?

Whate'er you are, at last, adieu!
   I think it is your bounden duty
To let the rhymes I coin for you,
   Be prized by all who prize your beauty.

From you I seek nor gold nor fame;
  From you I fear no cruel strictures;
I wish some girls that I could name
  Were half as silent as their pictures!


## Good-Night to the Season

So runs the world away.—*Hamlet*

Good-night to the Season! 'tis over!
  Gay dwellings no longer are gay;
The courtier, the gambler, the lover,
  Are scattered like swallows away;
There's nobody left to invite one,
  Except my good uncle and spouse;
My mistress is bathing at Brighton,
  My patron is sailing at Cowes;
For want of a better employment,
  Till Ponto and Don can get out,
I'll cultivate rural enjoyment,
  And angle immensely for trout.

Good-night to the Season! the lobbies,
  Their changes, and rumours of change,
Which startled the rustic Sir Bobbies,
  And made all the Bishops look strange;
The breaches, and battles, and blunders,
  Performed by the Commons and Peers;
The Marquis's eloquent thunders,
  The Baronet's eloquent ears;
Denouncings of Papists and treasons,
  Of foreign dominion, and oats;
Misrepresentations of reasons,
  And misunderstandings of notes.

Good-night to the Season! the building's
   Enough to make Inigo sick;
The paintings, and plasterings, and gildings
   Of stucco, and marble, and brick;
The orders deliciously blended,
   From love of effect, into one;
The club-houses only intended,
   The palaces only begun;
The hell, where the fiend in his glory
   Sits staring at putty and stones,
And scrambles from story to story,
   To rattle at midnight his bones.

Good-night to the Season! the dances,
   The fillings of hot little rooms,
The glancings of rapturous glances,
   The fancyings of fancy costumes;
The pleasures which fashion makes duties,
   The praisings of fiddles and flutes,
The luxury of looking at beauties,
   The tedium of talking to mutes;
The female diplomatists, planners
   Of matches for Laura and Jane,
The ice of her Ladyship's manners,
   The ice of his Lordship's champagne.

Good-night to the Season! the rages
   Led off by the chiefs of the throng,
The Lady Matilda's new pages,
   The Lady Eliza's new song,
Miss Fennel's macaw, which at Boodle's
   Was held to have something to say;
Mrs. Splenetic's musical poodles,
   Which bark "Batti—Batti!" all day;
The pony Sir Araby sported,
   As hot and as black as a coal,

And the lion his mother imported,
   In bearskins and grease, from the Pole.

Good-night to the Season! the Toso,
   So very majestic and tall;
Miss Ayton, whose singing was so-so,
   And Pasta, divinest of all;
The labour in vain of the ballet,
   So sadly deficient in stars;
The foreigners thronging the Alley,
   Exhaling the breath of cigars;
The *loge*, where some heiress, how killing,
   Environed with exquisites, sits,
The lovely one out of her drilling,
   The silly ones out of their wits.

Good-night to the Season! the splendor
   That beamed in the Spanish bazaar,
Where I purchased—my heart was so tender—
   A card-case,—a pasteboard guitar,—
A bottle of perfume,—a girdle,—
   A lithographed Riego, full-grown,
Whom bigotry drew on a hurdle,
   That artists might draw him on stone,—
A small panorama of Seville,—
   A trap for demolishing flies,—
A caricature of the Devil,—
   And a look from Miss Sheridan's eyes.

Good-night to the Season! the flowers
   Of the grand horticultural fête,
When boudoirs were quitted for bowers,
   And the fashion was, not to be late;
When all who had money and leisure
   Grew rural o'er ices and wines,
All pleasantly toiling for pleasure,

All hungrily pining for pines,
And making of beautiful speeches,
    And marring of beautiful shows,
And feeding on delicate peaches,
    And treading on delicate toes.

Good-night to the Season! another
    Will come with its trifles and toys,
And hurry away, like its brother,
    In sunshine, and odour, and noise.
Will it come with a rose, or a brier?
    Will it come with a blessing, or curse?
Will its bonnets be lower, or higher?
    Will its morals be better, or worse?
Will it find me grown thinner, or fatter,
    Or fonder of wrong or of right,
Or married, or buried?—no matter,—
    Good-night to the Season!—Good-night!

# John Clare

(1793–1864)

## I Am

I am: yet what I am none cares or knows
  My friends forsake me like a memory lost,
I am the self-consumer of my woes—
  They rise and vanish in oblivious host,
Like shadows in love's frenzied stifled throes:—
And yet I am, and live—like vapours tost

Into the nothingness of scorn and noise,
  Into the living sea of waking dreams,
Where there is neither sense of life or joys,
  But the vast shipwreck of my life's esteems;
Even the dearest, that I love the best,
Are strange—nay, rather stranger than the rest.

I long for scenes, where man hath never trod,
  A place where woman never smiled or wept—
There to abide with my Creator, God,
  And sleep as I in childhood sweetly slept,
Untroubling, and untroubled where I lie,
The grass below—above the vaulted sky.

## The Ploughboy

Soon the night in mantle dark
Disperses at the singing lark,
When the morning breaks the cloud,
And the yard dog, barking loud,
Calls the men and maidens up;
And the fowl, a noisy crowd,
From the hen-roost cackle loud,
When the farm-boy blundering up
Drives the old hens 'neath the coop,
And from the stack, at maid's desire,
Throws the faggot for the fire,
Then in the hovel milks the cow
And from the stackyard drives the sow;
And when the chimney smokes, goes in
Till breakfast's ready to begin,
And in the corner grunts to stoop
And does his unlaced hightops up;
Then off behind the plough afield
He goes, the whalebone whip to yield.

## Birds' Lament

Oh, says the linnet, if I sing,
My love forsook me in the spring,
And nevermore will I be seen
Without my satin gown of green.

Oh, says the pretty-feathered jay,
Now my love is fled away

For the memory of my dear
A feather of each sort I'll wear.

Oh, says the sparrow, my love is gone,
She so much that I doted on,
And e'er since for that selfsame thing
I've made a vow I ne'er will sing.

Oh, says the water-wag-my-tail,
I courted a fair one but could not prevail,
I could not with my love prevail,
So that is the reason I wag my tail.

Oh, says the pretty speckled thrush,
That changes its note from bush to bush,
My love has left me here alone
And I fear she never will return.

Oh, says the rook, and eke the crow,
The reason why in black we go—
Because our love has us forsook,
So pity us, poor crow and rook.

Oh, says the owl, my love is gone,
It was her I doted on;
Since she has gone I know not where to follow,
But after her I'll whoop and hollo.

## Emmonsail's Heath in Winter

I love to see the old heath's withered brake
Mingle its crimpled leaves with furze and ling,
While the old heron from the lonely lake
Starts slow and flaps his melancholy wing,
And oddling crow in idle motions swing

On the half-rotten ash-tree's topmost twig,
Beside whose trunk the gipsy makes his bed.
Up flies the bouncing woodcock from the brig
Where a black quagmire quakes beneath the tread;
The fieldfares chatter in the whistling thorn
And for the haw round fields and closen rove,
And coy bumbarrels, twenty in a drove,
Flit down the hedgerows in the frozen plain
And hang on little twigs and start again.

## Schoolboys in Winter

The schoolboys still their morning rambles take
To neighbouring village school with playing speed,
Loitering with pastime's leisure till they quake,
Oft looking up the wild-geese droves to heed,
Watching the letters which their journeys make;
Or plucking haws on which the fieldfares feed,
And hips, and sloes! and on each shallow lake
Making glib slides, where they like shadows go
Till some fresh pastimes in their minds awake.
Then off they start anew and hasty blow
Their numbed and clumpsing fingers till they glow;
Then races with their shadows wildly run
That stride huge giants o'er the shining snow
In the pale splendour of the winter sun.

## Badger

When midnight comes a host of dogs and men
Go out and track the badger to his den,
And put a sack within the hole, and lie

Till the old grunting badger passes by.
He comes and hears—they let the strongest loose.
The old fox hears the noise and drops the goose.
The poacher shoots and hurries from the cry,
And the old hare half wounded buzzes by.
They get a forkèd stick to bear him down
And clap the dogs and take him to the town,
And bait him all the day with many dogs,
And laugh and shout and fright the scampering hogs.
He runs along and bites at all he meets:
They shout and hollo down the noisy streets.

He turns about to face the loud uproar
And drives the rebels to their very door.
The frequent stone is hurled where'er they go;
When badgers fight, then every one's a foe.
The dogs are clapt and urged to join the fray;
The badger turns and drives them all away.
Though scarcely half as big, demure and small,
He fights with dogs for hours and beats them all.
The heavy mastiff, savage in the fray,
Lies down and licks his feet and turns away.
The bulldog knows his match and waxes cold,
The badger grins and never leaves his hold.
He drives the crowd and follows at their heels
And bites them through—the drunkard swears and
   reels.

The frightened women take the boys away,
The blackguard laughs and hurries on the fray.
He tries to reach the woods, an awkward race,
But sticks and cudgels quickly stop the chase.
He turns agen and drives the noisy crowd
And beats the dogs in noises loud.
He drives away and beats them every one,
And then they loose them all and set them on.

He falls as dead and kicked by boys and men,
Then starts and grins and drives the crowd agen;
Till kicked and torn and beaten out he lies
And leaves his hold and cackles, groans, and dies.

## The Frightened Ploughman

I went to the fields with the leisure I got;
The stranger might smile but I heeded him not;
The hovel was ready to screen from a shower,
And the book in my pocket was read in an hour.

The bird came for shelter, but soon flew away;
The horse came to look, and seemed happy to stay;
He stood up in quiet, and hung down his head,
And seemed to be hearing the poem I read.

The ploughman would turn from his plough in the day
And wonder what being had come in his way,
To lie on a mole-hill and read the day long
And laugh out aloud when he'd finished his song.

The pewit turned over and stoop'd o'er my head
Where the raven croaked loud like the ploughman ill-
    bred,
But the lark high above charmed me all the day long,
So I sat down and joined in the chorus of song.

The foolhardy ploughman I well could endure;
His praise was worth nothing, his censure was poor;
Fame bade me go on, and I toiled the day long,
Till the fields where he lived should be known in my
    song.

## Gipsies

The snow falls deep; the forest lies alone;
The boy goes hasty for his load of brakes,
Then thinks upon the fire and hurries back;
The gipsy knocks his hands and tucks them up,
And seeks his squalid camp, half hid in snow,
Beneath the oak which breaks away the wind,
And bushes close in snow like hovel warm;
There tainted mutton wastes upon the coals,
And the half-wasted dog squats close and rubs,
Then feels the heat too strong, and goes aloof;
He watches well, but none a bit can spare,
And vainly waits the morsel thrown away.
'Tis thus they live—a picture to the place,
A quiet, pilfering, unprotected race.

## Autumn

The thistledown's flying
Though the winds are all still,
On the green grass now lying,
Now mounting the hill,
The spring from the fountain
Now boils like a pot,
Through stones past the counting,
It bubbles red hot.

The ground parched and cracked is
Like overbaked bread,
The greensward all wracked is,

Bents dried up and dead.
The fallow fields glitter
Like water indeed,
And gossamers twitter,
Flung from weed unto weed.

Hill-tops like hot iron
Glitter hot i' the sun.
And the rivers we're eyeing
Burn to gold as they run.
Burning hot is the ground,
Liquid gold is the air;
Whoever looks round
Sees Eternity there.

## Clock-a-clay
### (The Ladybird)

In the cowslip pips I lie
Hidden from the buzzing fly,
While green grass beneath me lies
Pearled wi' dew like fishes' eyes.
Here I lie, a clock-a-clay,
Waiting for the time o' day.

While grassy forests quake surprise,
And the wild wind sobs and sighs,
My gold home rocks as like to fall
On its pillar green and tall;
When the parting rain drives by
Clock-a-clay keeps warm and dry.

Day by day and night by night
All the week I hide from sight.

In the cowslip pips I lie,
In rain and dew still warm and dry.
Day and night, and night and day,
Red, black-spotted clock-a-clay.

My home it shakes in wind and showers,
Pale green pillar topped wi' flowers,
Bending at the wild wind's breath
Till I touch the grass beneath.
Here I live, lone clock-a-clay,
Watching for the time of day.

## Secret Love

I hid my love when young till I
Couldn't bear the buzzing of a fly;
I hid my life to my despite
Till I could not bear to look at light:
I dare not gaze upon her face
But left her memory in each place;
Where'er I saw a wild flower lie
I kissed and bade my love good-bye.

I met her in the greenest dells,
Where dewdrops pearl the wood bluebells;
The lost breeze kissed her bright blue eye,
The bee kissed and went singing by,
A sunbeam found a passage there,
A gold chain round her neck so fair;
As secret as the wild bee's song
She lay there all the summer long.

I hid my love in field and town
Till e'en the breeze would knock me down;

The bees seemed singing ballads o'er,
The fly's bass turned a lion's roar;
And even silence found a tongue,
To haunt me all the summer long;
The riddle nature could not prove
Was nothing else but secret love.

## Invitation to Eternity

Say, wilt thou go with me, sweet maid,
Say, maiden, wilt thou go with me
Through the valley-depths of shade,
Of night and dark obscurity;
Where the path has lost its way,
Where the sun forgets the day,
Where there's nor light nor life to see,
Sweet maiden, wilt thou go with me?

Where stones will turn to flooding streams,
Where plains will rise like ocean's waves,
Where life will fade like visioned dreams
And mountains darken into caves,
Say, maiden, wilt thou go with me
Through this sad non-identity,
Where parents live and are forgot,
And sisters live and know us not?

Say, maiden, wilt thou go with me
In this strange death-in-life to be,
To live in death and be the same,
Without this life or home or name,
At once to be and not to be—
That was and is not—yet to see

Things pass like shadows, and the sky
Above, below, around us lie?

The land of shadows wilt thou trace,
Nor look nor know each other's face;
The present marred with reason gone,
And past and present all as one?
Say, maiden, can thy life be led
To join the living and the dead?
Then trace thy footsteps on with me;
We are wed to one eternity.

## Fragment

Language has not the power to speak what love indites:
The soul lies buried in the ink that writes.

# Ralph Waldo Emerson

(1803–1882)

## Hamatreya

Bulkeley, Hunt, Willard, Hosmer, Meriam, Flint,
Possessed the land which rendered to their toil
Hay, corn, roots, hemp, flax, apples, wool, and wood.
Each of these landlords walked amidst his farm,
Saying, " 'Tis mine, my children's and my name's.
How sweet the west wind sounds in my own trees!
How graceful climb those shadows on my hill!
I fancy these pure waters and the flags
Know me, as does my dog: we sympathize;
And, I affirm, my actions smack of the soil."


Where are these men? Asleep beneath their grounds:
And strangers, fond as they, their furrows plough.
Earth laughs in flowers, to see her boastful boys
Earth-proud, proud of the earth which is not theirs;
Who steer the plough, but cannot steer their feet
Clear of the grave.
They added ridge to valley, brook to pond,
And sighed for all that bounded their domain;
"This suits me for a pasture; that's my park;
We must have clay, lime, gravel, granite-ledge,
And misty lowland, where to go for peat.
The land is well,—lies fairly to the south.
'Tis good, when you have crossed the sea and back,
To find the sitfast acres where you left them."

Ah! the hot owner sees not Death, who adds
Him to his land, a lump of mould the more.
Hear what the Earth says:—

### EARTH-SONG

"Mine and yours;
Mine, not yours.
Earth endures;
Stars abide—
Shine down in the old sea;
Old are the shores;
But where are old men?
I who have seen much,
Such have I never seen.

"The lawyer's deed
Ran sure,
In tail,
To them and to their heirs
Who shall succeed,
Without fail,
Forevermore.

"Here is the land,
Shaggy with wood,
With its old valley,
Mound and flood.
But the heritors?—
Fled like the flood's foam.
The lawyer, and the laws,
And the kingdom,
Clean swept herefrom.

"They called me theirs,
Who so controlled me;
Yet every one

Wished to stay, and is gone,
How am I theirs,
If they cannot hold me,
But I hold them?"

When I heard the Earth-song
I was no longer brave;
My avarice cooled
Like lust in the chill of the grave.


## Water

The water understands
Civilization well;
It wets my foot, but prettily,
It chills my life, but wittily,
It is not disconcerted,
It is not broken-hearted:
Well used, it decketh joy,
Adorneth, doubleth joy:
Ill used, it will destroy,
In perfect time and measure
With a face of golden pleasure
Elegantly destroy.


## The Snow-Storm

Announced by all the trumpets of the sky,
Arrives the snow, and, driving o'er the fields,
Seems nowhere to alight: the whited air
Hides hills and woods, the river, and the heaven,

And veils the farm-house at the garden's end.
The sled and traveller stopped, the courier's feet
Delayed, all friends shut out, the housemates sit
Around the radiant fireplace, enclosed
In a tumultuous privacy of storm.

Come see the north wind's masonry.
Out of an unseen quarry evermore
Furnished with tile, the fierce artificer
Curves his white bastions with projected roof
Round every windward stake, or tree, or door.
Speeding, the myriad-handed, his wild work
So fanciful, so savage, nought cares he
For number or proportion. Mockingly,
On coop or kennel he hangs Parian wreaths;
A swan-like form invests the hidden thorn;
Fills up the farmer's lane from wall to wall,
Maugre the farmer's sighs; and at the gate
A tapering turret overtops the work.
And when his hours are numbered, and the world
Is all his own, retiring, as he were not,
Leaves, when the sun appears, astonished Art
To mimic in slow structures, stone by stone,
Built in an age, the mad wind's night-work,
The frolic architecture of the snow.

## Parks and ponds

Parks and ponds are good by day;
I do not delight
In black acres of the night,
Nor my unseasoned step disturbs
The sleeps of trees or dreams of herbs.

## Give all to love

Give all to love;
Obey thy heart;
Friends, kindred, days,
Estate, good-fame,
Plans, credit and the Muse,—
Nothing refuse.

'Tis a brave master;
Let it have scope:
Follow it utterly,
Hope beyond hope:
High and more high
It dives into noon,
With wing unspent,
Untold intent;
But it is a god,
Knows its own path
And the outlets of the sky.

It was never for the mean;
It requireth courage stout.
Souls above doubt,
Valor unbending,
It will reward,—
They shall return
More than they were,
And ever ascending.

Leave all for love;
Yet, hear me, yet,
One word more thy heart behoved,
One pulse more of firm endeavor,—

Keep thee to-day,
To-morrow, forever,
Free as an Arab
Of thy beloved.

Cling with life to the maid;
But when the surprise,
First vague shadow of surmise
Flits across her bosom young,
Of a joy apart from thee,
Free be she, fancy-free;
Nor thou detain her vesture's hem,
Nor the palest rose she flung
From her summer diadem.

Though thou loved her as thyself,
As a self of purer clay,
Though her parting dims the day,
Stealing grace from all alive;
Heartily know,
When half-gods go,
The gods arrive.

## Bacchus

Bring me wine, but wine which never grew
In the belly of the grape,
Or grew on vine whose tap-roots, reaching through
Under the Andes to the Cape,
Suffered no savor of the earth to scape.

Let its grapes the morn salute
From a nocturnal root,
Which feels the acrid juice

Of Styx and Erebus;
And turns the woe of Night,
By its own craft, to a more rich delight.

We buy ashes for bread;
We buy diluted wine;
Give me of the true,—
Whose ample leaves and tendrils curled
Among the silver hills of heaven
Draw everlasting dew;
Wine of wine,
Blood of the world,
Form of forms, and mould of statures,
That I intoxicated,
And by the draught assimilated,
May float at pleasure through all natures;
The bird-language rightly spell,
And that which roses say so well.

Wine that is shed
Like the torrents of the sun
Up the horizon walls,
Or like the Atlantic streams, which run
When the South Sea calls.

Water and bread,
Food which needs no transmuting,
Rainbow-flowering, wisdom-fruiting,
Wine which is already man,
Food which teach and reason can.

Wine which Music is,—
Music and wine are one,—
That I, drinking this,
Shall hear far Chaos talk with me;
Kings unborn shall walk with me;
And the poor grass shall plot and plan

What it will do when it is man.
Quickened so, will I unlock
Every crypt of every rock.

I thank the joyful juice
For all I know;—
Winds of remembering
Of the ancient being blow,
And seeming-solid walls of use
Open and flow.

Pour, Bacchus! the remembering wine;
Retrieve the loss of me and mine!
Vine for vine be antidote,
And the grape requite the lote!
Haste to cure the old despair,—
Reason in Nature's lotus drenched,
The memory of ages quenched;
Give them again to shine;
Let wine repair what this undid;
And where the infection slid,
A dazzling memory revive;
Refresh the faded tints,
Recut the aged prints,
And write my old adventures with the pen
Which on the first day drew,
Upon the tablets blue,
The dancing Pleiads and eternal men.

## Days

Daughters of Time, the hypocritic Days,
Muffled and dumb like barefoot dervishes,
And marching single in an endless file,

Bring diadems and fagots in their hands.
To each they offer gifts after his will,
Bread, kingdoms, stars, and sky that holds them all.
I, in my pleached garden, watched the pomp,
Forgot my morning wishes, hastily
Took a few herbs and apples, and the Day
Turned and departed silent. I, too late,
Under her solemn fillet saw the scorn.

## Merlin: II

The rhyme of the poet
Modulates the king's affairs;
Balance-loving Nature
Made all things in pairs.
To every foot its antipode;
Each color with its counter glowed;
To every tone beat answering tones,
Higher or graver;
Flavor gladly blends with flavor;
Leaf answers leaf upon the bough;
And match the paired cotyledons.
Hands to hands, and feet to feet,
In one body grooms and brides;
Eldest rite, two married sides
In every mortal meet.
Light's far furnace shines,
Smelting balls and bars,
Forging double stars,
Glittering twins and trines.
The animals are sick with love,
Lovesick with rhyme;
Each with all propitious Time

Into chorus wove.
Like the dancers' ordered band,
Thoughts come also hand in hand,
In equal couples mated,
Or else alternated;
Adding by their mutual gage,
One to other, health and age.
Solitary fancies go
Short-lived wandering to and fro,
Most like to bachelors,
Or an ungiven maid,
Not ancestors,
With no posterity to make the lie afraid,
Or keep truth undecayed.
Perfect-paired as eagle's wings,
Justice is the rhyme of things;
Trade and counting use
The self-same tuneful muse;
And Nemesis,
Who with even matches odd,
Who athwart space redresses
The partial wrong,
Fills the just period,
And finishes the song.

Subtle rhymes, with ruin rife,
Murmur in the house of life,
Sung by the Sisters as they spin;
In perfect time and measure they
Build and unbuild our echoing clay.
As the two twilights of the day
Fold us music-drunken in.

## Ode to Beauty

Who gave thee, O Beauty,
The keys of this breast,—
Too credulous lover
Of blest and unblest?
Say, when in lapsed ages
Thee knew I of old?
Or what was the service
For which I was sold?
When first my eyes saw thee,
I found me thy thrall,
By magical drawings,
Sweet tyrant of all!
I drank at thy fountain
False waters of thirst;
Thou intimate stranger,
Thou latest and first!
Thy dangerous glances
Make women of men;
New-born, we are melting
Into nature again.

Lavish, lavish promiser,
Nigh persuading gods to err!
Guest of million painted forms,
Which in turn thy glory warms!
The frailest leaf, the mossy bark,
The acorn's cup, the raindrop's arc,
The swinging spider's silver line,
The ruby of the drop of wine,
The shining pebble of the pond,

Thou inscribest with a bond,
In thy momentary play,
Would bankrupt nature to ·epay.

Ah, what avails it
To hide or to shun
Whom the Infinite One
Hath granted his throne?
The heaven high over
Is the deep's lover;
The sun and sea,
Informed by thee,
Before me run
And draw me on,
Yet fly me still,
As Fate refuses
To me the heart Fate for me chooses.
Is it that my opulent soul
Was mingled from the generous whole;
Sea-valleys and the deep of skies
Furnished several supplies;
And the sands whereof I'm made
Draw me to them, self-betrayed?
I turn the proud portfolio
Which holds the grand designs
Of Salvator, of Guercino,
And Piranesi's lines.
I hear the lofty paeans
Of the masters of the shell,
Who heard the starry music
And recount the numbers well;
Olympian bards who sung
Divine Ideas below,
Which always find us young
And always keep us so.

Oft, in streets or humblest places,
I detect far-wandered graces,
Which, from Eden wide astray,
In lowly homes have lost their way.

Thee gliding through the sea of form,
Like the lightning through the storm,
Somewhat not to be possessed,
Somewhat not to be caressed,
No feet so fleet could ever find,
No perfect form could ever bind.
Thou eternal fugitive,
Hovering over all that live,
Quick and skilful to inspire
Sweet, extravagant desire,
Starry space and lily-bell
Filling with thy roseate smell,
Wilt not give the lips to taste
Of the nectar which thou hast.

All that's good and great with thee
Works in close conspiracy;
Thou hast bribed the dark and lonely
To report thy features only,
And the cold and purple morning
Itself with thoughts of thee adorning;
The leafy dell, the city mart,
Equal trophies of thine art;
E'en the flowing azure air
Thou hast touched for my despair;
And, if I languish into dreams,
Again I meet the ardent beams.

Queen of things! I dare not die
In Being's deeps past ear and eye;
Lest there I find the same deceiver.

And be the sport of Fate forever.
Dread Power, but dear! if God thou be,
Unmake me quite, or give thyself to me!


# Limits

Who knows this or that?
Hark in the wall to the rat:
Since the world was, he has gnawed;
Of his wisdom, of his fraud
What dost thou know?
In the wretched little beast
Is life and heart,
Child and parent,
Not without relation
To fruitful field and sun and moon.
What art thou? His wicked eye
Is cruel to thy cruelty.


# Experience

The lords of life, the lords of life,—
I saw them pass
In their own guise,
Like and unlike,
Portly and grim,—
Use and Surprise,
Surface and Dream,
Succession swift, and spectral Wrong,
Temperament without a tongue,

And the inventor of the game
Omnipresent without name;—
Some to see, some to be guessed,
They marched from east to west:
Little man, least of all,
Among the legs of his guardians tall,
Walked about with puzzled look.
Him by the hand dear Nature took,
Dearest Nature, strong and kind,
Whispered, "Darling, never mind!
To-morrow they will wear another face,
The founder thou; these are thy race!"


## The Past

The debt is paid,
The verdict said,
The Furies laid,
The plague is stayed,
All fortunes made;
Turn the key and bolt the door,
Sweet is death forevermore.
Nor haughty hope, nor swart chagrin,
Nor murdering hate, can enter in.
All is now secure and fast;
Not the gods can shake the Past;
Flies-to the adamantine door
Bolted down forevermore.
None can re-enter there,—
No thief so politic,
No Satan with a royal trick
Steal in by window, chink, or hole,
To bind or unbind, add what lacked,

Insert a leaf, or forge a name,
New-face or finish what is packed,
Alter or mend eternal Fact.


## Terminus

It is time to be old,
To take in sail:—
The god of bounds,
Who sets to seas a shore,
Came to me in his fatal rounds,
And said: "No more!
No farther shoot
Thy broad ambitious branches, and thy root.
Fancy departs: no more invent;
Contract thy firmament
To compass of a tent.
There's not enough for this and that,
Make thy option which of two;
Economize the failing river,
Not the less revere the Giver,
Leave the many and hold the few.
Timely wise accept the terms,
Soften the fall with wary foot;
A little while
Still plan and smile,
And,—fault of novel germs,—
Mature the unfallen fruit.
Curse, if thou wilt, thy sires,
Bad husbands of their fires,
Who, when they gave thee breath,
Failed to bequeath
The needful sinew stark as once,

The Baresark marrow to thy bones,
But left a legacy of ebbing veins,
Inconstant heat and nerveless reins,—
Amid the Muses, left thee deaf and dumb,
Amid the gladiators, halt and numb."

As the bird trims her to the gale,
I trim myself to the storm of time,
I man the rudder, reef the sail,
Obey the voice at eve obeyed at prime:
"Lowly faithful, banish fear,
Right onward drive unharmed;
The port, well worth the cruise, is near,
And every wave is charmed."

# Henry David Thoreau

(1817–1862)

## The Old Marlborough Road

Where they once dug for money,
But never found any;
Where sometimes Martial Miles
Singly files,
And Elijah Wood,
I fear for no good:
No other man,
Save Elisha Dugan—
O man of wild habits,
Partridges and rabbits,
Who hast no cares
Only to set snares,
Who liv'st alone,
Close to the bone,
And where life is sweetest
Constantly eatest.
When the spring stirs my blood
With the instinct to travel,
I can get enough gravel
On the Old Marlborough Road.
Nobody repairs it,
For nobody wears it;
It is a living way,
As the Christians say.
Not many there be

Who enter therein,
Only the guests of the
    Irishman Quin.
What is it, what is it,
    But a direction out there,
And the bare possibility
    Of going somewhere?
        Great guide-boards of stone,
        But travellers none;
        Cenotaphs of the towns
        Named on their crowns.
        It is worth going to see
        Where you *might* be.
        What king
        Did the thing,
        I am still wondering;
        Set up how or when,
        By what selectmen,
        Gourgas or Lee,
        Clark or Darby?
        They're a great endeavor
        To be something forever;
        Blank tablets of stone,
        Where a traveller might groan,
        And in one sentence
        Grave all that is known;
        Which another might read,
        In his extreme need.
        I know one or two
        Lines that would do.
        Literature that might stand
        All over the land,
        Which a man could remember
        Till next December,
        And read again in the spring,

After the thawing.
If with fancy unfurled
   You leave your abode,
You may go round the world
   By the Old Marlborough Road.


## What's the railroad to me?

What's the railroad to me?
I never go to see
Where it ends.
It fills a few hollows,
And makes banks for the swallows,
It sets the sand a-blowing,
And the blackberries a-growing.


## I am a parcel of vain strivings tied

I am a parcel of vain strivings tied
   By a chance bond together,
   Dangling this way and that, their links
     Were made so loose and wide,
       Methinks,
     For milder weather.

A bunch of violets without their roots,
   And sorrel intermixed,
   Encircled by a wisp of straw
     Once coiled about their shoots,
       The law
     By which I'm fixed.

A nosegay which Time clutched from out
   Those fair Elysian fields,
With weeds and broken stems, in haste,
   Doth make the rabble rout
      That waste
   The day he yields.

And here I bloom for a short hour unseen,
   Drinking my juices up,
With no root in the land
   To keep my branches green,
      But stand
   In a bare cup.

Some tender buds were left upon my stem
   In mimicry of life,
But ah! the children will not know,
   Till time has withered them,
      The woe
   With which they're rife.

But now I see I was not plucked for naught,
   And after in life's vase
Of glass set while I might survive,
   But by a kind hand brought
      Alive
   To a strange place.

That stock thus thinned will soon redeem its hours,
   And by another year,
Such as God knows, with freer air,
   More fruits and fairer flowers
      Will bear,
   While I droop here.

## Who sleeps by day and walks by night

> Who sleeps by day and walks by night,
> Will meet no spirit but some sprite.

## I was born upon thy bank, river

> I was born upon thy bank, river,
>     My blood flows in thy stream,
> And thou meanderest forever
>     At the bottom of my dream.

## On the Sun Coming Out in the Afternoon

Methinks all things have travelled since you shined,
But only Time, and clouds, Time's team, have moved;
Again foul weather shall not change my mind,
But in the shade I will believe what in the sun I loved.

## The moon now rises to her absolute rule

> The moon now rises to her absolute rule,
> And the husbandman and hunter
> Acknowledge her for their mistress.
> Asters and golden reign in the fields

And the life everlasting withers not.
The fields are reaped and shorn of their pride
But an inward verdure still crowns them;
The thistle scatters its down on the pool
And yellow leaves clothe the river—
And nought disturbs the serious life of men.
But behind the sheaves and under the sod
There lurks a ripe fruit which the reapers have not
  gathered,
The true harvest of the year—the boreal fruit
Which it bears forever,
With fondness annually watering and maturing it.
But man never severs the stalk
Which bears this palatable fruit.


## To a Marsh Hawk in Spring

There is health in thy gray wing,
Health of nature's furnishing.
Say, thou modern-winged antique,
Was thy mistress ever sick?
In each heaving of thy wing
Thou dost health and leisure bring,
Thou dost waive disease and pain
And resume new life again.


## Great Friend

I walk in nature still alone
    And know no one,
Discern no lineament nor feature
    Of any creature.

Though all the firmament
  Is o'er me bent,
Yet still I miss the grace
  Of an intelligent and kindred face.

I still must seek the friend
Who does with nature blend,
Who is the person in her mask,
He is the man I ask.

Who is the expression of her meaning,
Who is the uprightness of her leaning,
Who is the grown child of her weaning.

The center of this world,
The face of nature,
The site of human life,
Some sure foundation
And nucleus of a nation—
At least a private station.

We twain would walk together
Through every weather,
And see this aged nature
Go with a bending stature.


## At midnight's hour I raised my head

At midnight's hour I raised my head,
The owls were seeking for their bread;
The foxes barked impatient still,
At their wan fate they bear so ill.—
I thought me of eternities delayed
And of commands but half obeyed.—
The night wind rustled through the glade

As if a force of men there staid;
The word was whispered through the ranks
And every hero seized his lance;
The word was whispered through the ranks,
    Advance.


# Among the worst of men that ever lived

Among the worst of men that ever lived,
However we did seriously attend,
A little space we let our thoughts ascend,
Experienced our religion and confessed
'Twas good for us to be there—be anywhere:
Then to a heap of apples we addressed
And cleared the topmost rider *sine* care,
But our Icarian thoughts returned to ground
And we went on to heaven the long way round.


## Tall Ambrosia

Among the signs of autumn I perceive
The Roman wormwood (called by learned men
*Ambrosia elatior*, food for gods,—
For to impartial science the humblest weed
Is as immortal once as the proudest flower—)
Sprinkles its yellow dust over my shoes
As I cross the now neglected garden.
—We trample under foot the food of gods
And spill their nectar in each drop of dew—
My honest shoes, fast friends that never stray

Far from my couch, thus powdered, countryfied,
Bearing many a mile the marks of their adventure,
At the post-house disgrace the Gallic gloss
Of those well dressed ones who no morning dew
Nor Roman wormwood ever have been through,
Who never walk but are *transported* rather—
For what old crime of theirs I do not gather.

## Forever in my dream
## and in my morning thought

Forever in my dream and in my morning thought
    Eastward a mount ascends—
But when in the sunbeam its hard outline is sought—
    It all dissolves and ends.
The woods that way are gates—the pastures too slope
      up
    To an unearthly ground—
But when I ask my mates, to take the staff and cup,
    It can no more be found—
Perchance I have no shoes fit for the lofty soil
    Where my thoughts graze—
No properly spun clues—nor well strained mid-day oil
    Or—must I mend my ways?
It is a promised land which I have not yet earned,
    I have not made beginning
With consecrated hand—I have not even learned
    To lay the underpinning.
The mountain sinks by day—as do my lofty thoughts,
    Because I'm not highminded.
If I could think alway above these hills and warts
    I should see it, though blinded.

It is a spiral path within the pilgrim's soul
    Leads to this mountain's brow,
Commencing at his hearth he reaches to this goal:
    He knows not when nor how.


## For though the caves were rabbited

For though the caves were rabbited,
    And the well sweeps were slanted,
Each house seemed not inhabited
    But haunted.

The pensive traveller held his way,
    Silent and melancholy,
For every man an idiot was,
    And every house a folly.


## I was made erect and lone

I was made erect and lone,
And within me is the bone;
Still my vision will be clear,
Still my life will not be drear,
To the center all is near.
Where I sit there is my throne.
If age choose to sit apart,
If age choose, give me the start,
Take the sap and leave the heart.

## To the Mountains

And when the sun puts out his lamp
We'll sleep serene within the camp,
Trusting to his invet'rate skill
Who leads the stars o'er yonder hill,
Whose discipline doth never cease
To watch the slumberings of peace,
And from the virtuous hold afar
The melancholy din of war.—
For ye our sentries still outlie,
The earth your pallet and your screen the sky.

From steadfastness I will not swerve,
Remembering my sweet reserve.

With all your kindness shown from year to year
Ye do but civil demons still appear;
Still to my mind
Ye are inhuman and unkind,
And bear an untamed aspect to my sight
After the "civil-suited" night,
As if ye had lain out
Like to the Indian scout
Who lingers in the purlieus of the towns
With unexplored grace and savage frowns.

## Between the traveller and the setting sun

Between the traveller and the setting sun,
Upon some drifting sand heap of the shore,
A hound stands o'er the carcass of a man.

# I'm thankful that my life doth not deceive

I'm thankful that my life doth not deceive
Itself with a low loftiness, half height,
And think it soars when still it dip its way
Beneath the clouds on noiseless pinion
Like the crow or owl, but it doth know
The full extent of all its trivialness,
Compared with the splendid heights above.

See how it waits to watch the mail come in
While 'hind its back the sun goes out perchance.
And yet their lumbering cart brings me no word,
Not one scrawled leaf such as my neighbors get
To cheer them with the slight events forsooth,
Faint ups and downs of their far distant friends—
And now 'tis passed. What next? See the long train
Of teams wreathed in dust, their atmosphere;
Shall I attend until the last is passed?
Else why these ears that hear the leader's bells
Or eyes that link me in procession?
But hark! the drowsy day has done its task,
Far in yon hazy field where stands a barn,
Unanxious hens improve the sultry hour
And with contented voice now brag their deed—
A new laid egg—Now let the day decline—
They'll lay another by tomorrow's sun.

# William Barnes

(1801–1886)

## Zun-zet

Where the western zun, unclouded,
   Up above the grey hill-tops,
Did sheen drough ashes, lofty sh'ouded,
   On the turf bezide the copse,
     In zummer weather,
     We together,
     Sorrow-slightèn, work-vorgettèn,
     Gambol'd wi' the zun a-zettèn.

There, by flow'ry bows o' bramble,
   Under hedge, in ash-tree sheädes,
The dun-heäir'd ho'se did slowly ramble
   On the grasses' dewy bleädes,
     Zet free o' lwoads,
     An' stwony rwoads,
     Vorgetvul o' the lashes frettèn,
     Grazèn wi' the zun a-zettèn.

There wer rooks a-beätèn by us
   Drough the aïr, in a vlock,
An' there the lively blackbird, nigh us,
   On the meäple bough did rock,
     Wi' ringèn droat,
     Where zunlight smote
     The yollow boughs o' zunny hedges
     Over western hills' blue edges.

Waters, drough the meäds a-purlèn,
  Glissen'd in the evenèn's light,
An' smoke, above the town a-curlèn,
    Melted slowly out o' zight;
    An' there, in glooms
    Ov unzunn'd rooms,
    To zome, wi' idle sorrows frettèn,
    Zuns did set avore their zettèn.

We were out in geämes and reäces,
  Loud a-laughèn, wild in me'th,
Wi' windblown heäir, an' zunbrowned feäces,
    Leäpèn on the high-sky'd e'th,
    Avore the lights
    Wer tin'd o' nights,
    An' while the gossamer's light nettèn
    Sparkled to the zun a-zettèn.


## The Clote (Water-Lily)

O zummer clote! when the brook's a-glidèn
  So slow an' smooth down his zedgy bed,
Upon thy broad leaves so seäfe a-ridèn
    The water's top wi' thy yollow head,
    By alder sheädes, O,
    An' bulrush beds, O,
Thou then dost float, goolden zummer clote!

The grey-bough'd withy's a-leänèn lowly
  Above the water thy leaves do hide;
The bènden bulrush, a-swaÿèn slowly,
    Do skirt in zummer thy river's zide;
    An' perch in shoals, O,

Do vill the holes, O,
Where thou dost float, goolden zummer clote!

Oh! when thy brook-drinkèn flow'r's a-blowèn,
  The burnèn zummer's a-zettèn in;
The time o' greenness, the time o' mowèn,
  When in the haÿ-vield, wi' zunburnt skin,
        The vo'k do drink, O,
        Upon the brink, O,
Where thou dost float, goolden zummer clote!

Wi' eärms a-spreadèn, an' cheäks a-blowèn,
  How proud wer I when I vu'st could zwim
Athirt the deep pleäce where thou bist growèn,
  Wi' thy long more vrom the bottom dim;
        While cows, knee-high, O,
        In brook, wer nigh, O,
Where thou dost float, goolden zummer clote!

Ov all the brooks drough the meäds a-windèn,
  Ov all the meäds by a river's brim,
There's nwone so feäir o' my own heart's vindèn
  As where the maïdens do zee thee zwim,
        An' stan' to teäke, O,
        Wi' long-stemm'd reäke, O,
Thy flow'r afloat, goolden zummer clote!


## The Wind at the Door

As day did darken on the dewless grass,
There, still, wi' nwone a-come by me
To stay a-while at hwome by me
Within the house, all dumb by me,
I zot me sad as the eventide did pass.

An' there a win'blast shook the rattlèn door,
An' seemed, as win' did mwoan without,
As if my Jeäne, alwone without,
A-stannèn on the stwone without,
Wer there a-come wi' happiness oonce mwore.

I went to door; an' out vrom trees above
My head, upon the blast by me,
Sweet blossoms wer a-cast by me,
As if my Love, a-past by me,
Did fling em down—a token ov her love.

"Sweet blossoms o' the tree where I do murn,"
I thought, "if you did blow vor her,
Vor apples that should grow vor her,
A-vallèn down below vor her,
O then how happy I should zee you kern!"

But no. Too soon I voun my charm a-broke.
Noo comely soul in white like her—
Noo soul a-steppèn light like her—
An' nwone o' comely height like her
Went by; but all my grief ageän awoke.

## The Lost Little Sister

O' zummer night, as day did gleam,
   Wi' weänèn light, vrom red to wan,
An' we did play above the stream
   Avore our house a-windèn on,
Our little sister, light o' tooe,
   Did skip about in all her pride
O' snow-white frock an' sash o' blue,
   A sheäpe that night wer slow to hide,

Bezide the brook a-tricklèn thin
Among the poppies, out an' in.

If periwinkles' buds o' blue
  By lilies' hollow cups do wind,
What then can their two colours do
  But call our sister back to mind?
She wore noo black—she wore her white;
  She wore noo black—she wore her blue;
She never murn'd another's flight,
  Vor she's avore us all to goo
Vrom where our litty veet did tread
Vrom stwone to stwone the water's bed.


## My Love's Guardian Angel

As in the cool-aïr'd road I come by,
              —in the night,
Under the moon-clim'd height o' the sky,
              —in the night,
There by the lime's broad lim's I did staÿ,
While in the aïr dark sheädes wer at plaÿ
Up on the window-glass, that did keep
Lew vrom the wind my true love asleep,
              —in the night.

While in the grey-wall'd height o' the tow'r,
              —in the night,
Sounded the midnight bell wi' the hour,
              —in the night,
There come a bright-heäir'd angel that shed
Light vrom her white robe's zilvery thread,
Wi' her vore-vinger hild up to meäke
Silence around lest sleepers mid weäke,
              —in the night.

"Oh! then," I whisper'd, "do I behold
————in the night,
Linda, my true-love, here in the cwold,
————in the night?"
"No," she meäde answer, "you do misteäke:
She is asleep, but I that do weäke
Here be on watch, an angel a-blest,
Over her slumber while she do rest,
————in the night."

"Zee how the winds, while brisk by the bough,
————in the night,
They do pass on, don't smite on her brow,
————in the night;
Zee how the cloud-sheädes naïseless do zweep
Over the house-top where she's asleep.
You, too, goo by, though times mid be near,
When you, wi' me, mid speäk to her ear
————in the night."


## To Me

At night, as drough the meäd I took my waÿ,
In aïr a-sweeten'd by the new-meäde haÿ,
A stream a-vallèn down a rock did sound,
Though out o' zight wer foam an' stwone to me.

Behind the knap, above the gloomy copse,
The wind did russle in the trees' high tops,
Though evenèn darkness, an' the risèn hill,
Kept all the quiv'rèn leaves unshown to me.

Within the copse, below the zunless sky,
I heärd a nightèngeäle, a-warblèn high

Her lwoansome zong, a-hidden vrom my zight,
An' showèn nothèn but her mwoan to me.

An' by a house, where rwoses hung avore
The thatch-brow'd window, an' the open door,
I heärd the merry words, an' hearty laugh,
O' zome feäir maïd, as eet unknown to me.

High over head the white-rimm'd clouds went on,
Wi' woone a-comèn up, vor woone a-gone;
An feäir they floated in their sky-back'd flight,
But still they never meäde a sound to me.

An' there the miller, down the stream did float
Wi' all his childern, in his white-saïl'd bwoat,
Vur off, beyond the stragglèn cows in meäd,
But zent noo vaïce athirt the ground to me.

An' then a buttervlee, in zultry light,
A-wheelèn on about me, vier-bright,
Did show the gaÿest colors to my eye,
But still did bring noo vaïce around to me.

I met the merry laugher on the down,
Beside her mother, on the path to town,
An' oh! her sheäpe wer comely to the zight,
But wordless thèn wer she a-vound to me.

Zoo, sweet ov unzeen things mid be the sound,
An' feäir to zight mid soundless things be vound,
But I've the laugh to hear, an' feäce to zee,
Vor they be now my own, a-bound to me.

## Tokens

Green mwold on zummer bars do show
   That they've a-dripp'd in winter wet;
The hoof-worn ring o' groun' below
   The tree, do tell o' storms or het;
The trees in rank along a ledge
Do show where woonce did bloom a hedge;
An' where the vurrow-marks do stripe
The down, the wheat woonce rustled ripe.
Each mark ov things a-gone vrom view—
To eyezight's woone, to soulzight two.

The grass ageän the mwoldrèn door
   'S a tóken sad o' vo'k a-gone,
An' where the house, bwoth wall an' vloor,
   'S a-lost, the well mid linger on.
What tokens, then, could Meäry gi'e
That she'd a-liv'd, an' liv'd vor me,
But things a-done vor thought an' view?
Good things that nwone ageän can do,
An' every work her love ha' wrought
To eyezight's woone, but two to thought.

## The Fall

   The length o' days ageän do shrink
    An' flowers be thin in meäd, among
    The eegrass a-sheenèn bright, along
   Brook upon brook, an' brink by brink.

Noo starlèns do rise in vlock on wing—
Noo goocoo in nest-green leaves do sound—
Noo swallows be now a-wheelèn round—
Dip after dip, an' swing by swing.

The wheat that did leätely rustle thick
Is now up in mows that still be new,
An' yollow bevore the sky o' blue—
Tip after tip, an' rick by rick.

While now I can walk a dusty mile
I'll teäke me a day, while days be clear,
To vind a vew friends that still be dear,
Feäce after feäce, an' smile by smile.

# John Greenleaf Whittier

(1807–1892)

## Ichabod

So fallen! so lost! the light withdrawn
    Which once he wore!
The glory from his gray hairs gone
    Forevermore!

Revile him not, the Tempter hath
    A snare for all;
And pitying tears, not scorn and wrath,
    Befit his fall!

Oh, dumb be passion's stormy rage,
    When he who might
Have lighted up and led his age,
    Falls back in night.

Scorn! would the angels laugh, to mark
    A bright soul driven,
Fiend-goaded, down the endless dark,
    From hope and heaven!

Let not the land once proud of him
    Insult him now,
Nor brand with deeper shame his dim,
    Dishonored brow.

But let its humbled sons, instead,
    From sea to lake,

A long lament, as for the dead,
  In sadness make.

Of all we loved and honored, naught
  Save power remains;
A fallen angel's pride of thought,
  Still strong in chains.

All else is gone; from those great eyes
  The soul has fled:
When faith is lost, when honor dies,
  The man is dead!

Then, pay the reverence of old days
  To his dead fame;
Walk backward, with averted gaze,
  And hide the shame!

## For Righteousness' Sake

### INSCRIBED TO FRIENDS UNDER ARREST FOR TREASON AGAINST THE SLAVE POWER

The age is dull and mean. Men creep,
  Not walk; with blood too pale and tame
  To pay the debt they owe to shame;
Buy cheap, sell dear; eat, drink, and sleep
  Down-pillowed, deaf to moaning want;
Pay tithes for soul-insurance; keep
  Six days to Mammon, one to Cant.

In such a time, give thanks to God,
  That somewhat of the holy rage
  With which the prophets in their age
On all its decent seemings trod,

Has set your feet upon the lie,
That man and ox and soul and clod
  Are market stock to sell and buy!

The hot words from your lips, my own,
  To caution trained, might not repeat;
  But if some tares among the wheat
Of generous thought and deed were sown,
  No common wrong provoked your zeal;
The silken gauntlet that is thrown
  In such a quarrel rings like steel.

The brave old strife the fathers saw
  For Freedom calls for men again
  Like those who battled not in vain
For England's Charter, Alfred's law;
  And right of speech and trial just
Wage in your name their ancient war
  With venal courts and perjured trust.

God's ways seem dark, but, soon or late,
  They touch the shining hills of day;
  The evil cannot brook delay,
The good can well afford to wait.
  Give ermined knaves their hour of crime;
Ye have the future grand and great,
  The safe appeal of Truth to Time!


FROM *Among the Hills*

### PRELUDE

Along the roadside, like the flowers of gold
That tawny Incas for their gardens wrought,
Heavy with sunshine droops the golden-rod,

And the red pennons of the cardinal-flowers
Hang motionless upon their upright staves.
The sky is hot and hazy, and the wind,
Wing-weary with its long flight from the south,
Unfelt; yet, closely scanned, yon maple leaf
With faintest motion, as one stirs in dreams,
Confesses it. The locust by the wall
Stabs the noon-silence with his sharp alarm.
A single hay-cart down the dusty road
Creaks slowly, with its driver fast asleep
On the load's top. Against the neighboring hill,
Huddled along the stone wall's shady side,
The sheep show white, as if a snowdrift still
Defied the dog-star. Through the open door
A drowsy smell of flowers—gray heliotrope,
And white sweet clover, and shy mignonette—
Comes faintly in, and silent chorus lends
To the pervading symphony of peace.
No time is this for hands long over-worn
To task their strength: and (unto Him be praise
Who giveth quietness!) the stress and strain
Of years that did the work of centuries
Have ceased, and we can draw our breath once more
Freely and full. So, as yon harvesters
Make glad their nooning underneath the elms
With tale and riddle and old snatch of song,
I lay aside grave themes and idly turn
The leaves of memory's sketch-book, dreaming o'er
Old summer pictures of the quiet hills,
And human life, as quiet, at their feet.

And yet not idly all. A farmer's son,
Proud of field-lore and harvest craft, and feeling
All their fine possibilities, how rich
And restful even poverty and toil

Become when beauty, harmony, and love
Sit at their humble hearth as angels sat
At evening in the patriarch's tent, when man
Makes labor noble, and his farmer's frock
The symbol of a Christian chivalry
Tender and just and generous to her
Who clothes with grace all duty; still, I know
Too well the picture has another side,—
How wearily the grind of toil goes on
Where love is wanting, how the eye and ear
And heart are starved amidst the plenitude
Of nature, and how hard and colorless
Is life without an atmosphere. I look
Across the lapse of half a century,
And call to mind old homesteads, where no flower
Told that the spring had come, but evil weeds,
Nightshade and rough-leaved burdock in the place
Of the sweet doorway greeting of the rose
And honeysuckle, where the house walls seemed
Blistering in sun, without a tree or vine
To cast the tremulous shadow of its leaves
Across the curtainless windows, from whose panes
Fluttered the signal rags of shiftlessness.
Within, the cluttered kitchen-floor, unwashed
(Broom-clean I think they called it); the best room
Stifling with cellar damp, shut from the air
In hot midsummer, bookless, pictureless
Save the inevitable sampler hung
Over the fireplace, or a mourning piece,
A green-haired woman, peony-cheeked, beneath
Impossible willows; the wide-throated hearth
Bristling with faded pine-boughs half concealing
The piled-up rubbish at the chimney's back;
And, in sad keeping with all things about them,
Shrill, querulous women, sour and sullen men,

Untidy, loveless, old before their time,
With scarce a human interest save their own
Monotonous round of small economies,
Or the poor scandal of the neighborhood;
Blind to the beauty everywhere revealed,
Treading the May-flowers with regardless feet;
For them the song-sparrow and the bobolink
Sang not, nor winds made music in the leaves;
For them in vain October's holocaust
Burned, gold and crimson, over all the hills,
The sacred mystery of the woods.
Church-goers, fearful of the unseen Powers,
But grumbling over pulpit-tax and pew-rent,
Saving, as shrewd economists, their souls
And winter pork with the least possible outlay
Of salt and sanctity; in daily life
Showing as little actual comprehension
Of Christian charity and love and duty,
As if the Sermon on the Mount had been
Outdated like a last year's almanac:
Rich in broad woodlands and in half-tilled fields,
And yet so pinched and bare and comfortless,
The veriest straggler limping on his rounds,
The sun and air his sole inheritance,
Laughed at a poverty that paid its taxes,
And hugged his rags in self-complacency!

Not such should be the homesteads of a land
Where whoso wisely wills and acts may dwell
As king and lawgiver, in broad-acred state,
With beauty, art, taste, culture, books, to make
His hour of leisure richer than a life
Of fourscore to the barons of old time,
Our yeoman should be equal to his home
Set in the fair, green valleys, purple walled,

A man to match his mountains, not to creep
Dwarfed and abased below them. I would fain
In this light way (of which I needs must own
With the knife-grinder of whom Canning sings,
"Story, God bless you! I have none to tell you!")
Invite the eye to see and heart to feel
The beauty and the joy within their reach,—
Home, and home loves, and the beatitudes
Of nature free to all. Happly in years
That wait to take the places of our own,
Heard where some breezy balcony looks down
On happy homes, or where the lake in the moon
Sleeps dreaming of the mountains, fair as Ruth,
In the old Hebrew pastoral, at the feet
Of Boaz, even this simple lay of mine
May seem the burden of a prophecy,
Finding its late fulfilment in a change
Slow as the oak's growth, lifting manhood up
Through broader culture, finer manners, love,
And reverence, to the level of the hills.

O Golden Age, whose light is of the dawn,
And not of sunset, forward, not behind,
Flood the new heavens and earth, and with thee bring
All the old virtues, whatsoever things
Are pure and honest and of good repute,
But add thereto whatever bard has sung
Or seer has told of when in trance and dream
They saw the Happy Isles of prophecy!
Let Justice hold her scale, and Truth divide
Between the right and wrong; but give the heart
The freedom of its fair inheritance;
Let the poor prisoner, cramped and starved so long,
At Nature's table feast his ear and eye
With joy and wonder; let all harmonies

Of sound, form, color, motion, wait upon
The princely guest, whether in soft attire
Of leisure clad, or the coarse frock of toil,
And, lending life to the dead form of faith,
Give human nature reverence for the sake
Of One who bore it, making it divine
With the ineffable tenderness of God;
Let common need, the brotherhood of prayer,
The heirship of an unknown destiny,
The unsolved mystery round about us, make
A man more precious than the gold of Ophir
Sacred, inviolate, unto whom all things
Should minister, as outward types and signs
Of the eternal beauty which fulfils
The one great purpose of creation, Love,
The sole necessity of Earth and Heaven!


## The Dead Feast of the Kol-Folk

We have opened the door,
   Once, twice, thrice!
We have opened the door,
   We have boiled the rice.
Come hither, come hither!
Come from the far lands,
Come from the star lands,
   Come as before!
We have lived long together,
We loved one another;
   Come back to our life.
Come father, come mother,
Come sister and brother,
   Child, husband, and wife,

For you we are sighing.
Come take your old places,
Come look in our faces,
The dead on the dying,
 Come home!

We have opened the door,
 Once, twice, thrice!
We have kindled the coals,
 And we boil the rice
For the feast of the souls.
 Come hither, come hither!
Think not we fear you,
Whose hearts are so near you.
Come tenderly thought on,
Come all unforgotten,
Come from the shadow-lands,
From the dim meadow-lands
Where the pale grasses bend
 Low to our sighing.
Come father, come mother,
Come sister and brother,
Come husband and friend,
The dead to the dying,
 Come home!

We have opened the door
 You entered so oft;
For the feast of the souls
We have kindled the coals,
 And we boil the rice soft.
Come you who are dearest
To us who are nearest,
Come hither, come hither,
From out the wild weather;
The storm clouds are flying,

The peepul is sighing;
  Come in from the rain.
Come father, come mother,
Come sister and brother,
Come husband and lover,
Beneath our roof-cover.
  Look on us again,
The dead on the dying,
  Come home!

We have opened the door!
For the feast of the souls
We have kindled the coals
  We may kindle no more.
Snake, fever, and famine,
The curse of the Brahmin,
  The sun and the dew,
They burn us, they bite us,
They waste us and smite us;
  Our days are but few!
In strange lands far yonder
To wonder and wander
  We hasten to you.
List then to our sighing,
  While yet we are here:
Nor seeing nor hearing,
We wait without fearing,
  To feel you draw near.
O dead, to the dying
  Come home!

## The Brewing of Soma

These libations mixed with milk have been prepared for
Indra: offer Soma to the drinker of Soma.
—*Vashista*, translated by Max Müller

The fagots blazed, the caldron's smoke
  Up through the green wood curled;
"Bring honey from the hollow oak,
Bring milky sap," the brewers spoke,
  In the childhood of the world.

And brewed they well or brewed they ill,
  The priests thrust in their rods,
First tasted, and then drank their fill,
And shouted, with one voice and will,
  "Behold the drink of gods!"

They drank, and lo! in heart and brain
  A new, glad life began;
The gray of hair grew young again,
The sick man laughed away his pain,
  The cripple leaped and ran.

"Drink, mortals, what the gods have sent,
  Forget your long annoy."
So sang the priests. From tent to tent
The Soma's sacred madness went,
  A storm of drunken joy.

Then knew each rapt inebriate
  A winged and glorious birth,
Soared upward, with strange joy elate,
Beat, with dazed head, Varuna's gate,
  And, sobered, sank to earth.

The land with Soma's praises rang;
  On Gihon's banks of shade
Its hymns the dusky maidens sang;
In joy of life or mortal pang
  All men to Soma prayed.

The morning twilight of the race
  Sends down these matin psalms;
And still with wondering eyes we trace
That simple prayers to Soma's grace,
  That Vedic verse embalms.

As in that child-world's early year,
  Each after age has striven
By music, incense, vigils drear,
And trance, to bring the skies more near,
  Or lift men up to heaven!

Some fever of the blood and brain,
  Some self-exalting spell,
The scourger's keen delight of pain,
The Dervish dance, the Orphic strain,
  The wild-haired Bacchant's yell,—

The desert's hair-grown hermit sunk
  The saner brute below;
The naked Santon, hashish-drunk,
The cloister madness of the monk,
  The fakir's torture-show!

And yet the past comes round again,
  And new doth old fulfil;
In sensual transports wild as vain
We brew in many a Christian lane
  The heathen Soma still!

Dear Lord and Father of mankind,
  Forgive our foolish ways!

Reclothe us in our rightful mind,
In purer lives Thy service find,
  In deeper reverence, praise.

In simple trust like theirs who heard
  Beside the Syrian sea
The gracious calling of the Lord,
Let us, like them, without a word,
  Rise up and follow Thee.

O Sabbath rest by Galilee!
  O calm of hills above,
Where Jesus knelt to share with Thee
The silence of eternity
  Interpreted by love!

With that deep hush subduing all
  Our words and works that drown
The tender whisper of Thy call,
As noiseless let Thy blessing fall
  As fell Thy manna down.

Drop Thy still dews of quietness,
  Till all our strivings cease;
Take from our souls the strain and stress,
And let our ordered lives confess
  The beauty of Thy peace.

Breathe through the heats of our desire
  Thy coolness and Thy balm;
Let sense be dumb, let flesh retire;
Speak through the earthquake, wind, and fire,
  O still, small voice of calm!

# Jones Very

## (1813–1880)

## Yourself

'Tis to yourself I speak; you cannot know
Him whom I call in speaking such an one,
For thou beneath the earth lie buried low,
Which he alone as living walks upon;
Thou mayst at times have heard him speak to you,
And often wished perchance that you were he;
And I must ever wish that it were true,
For then thou couldst hold fellowship with me;
But now thou hear'st us talk as strangers, met
Above the room wherein thou liest abed;
A word perhaps loud spoken thou mayst get,
Or hear our feet when heavily they tread;
But he who speaks, or him who's spoken to,
Must both remain as strangers still to you.

## The hand and foot

The hand and foot that stir not, they shall find
Sooner than all the rightful place to go;
Now in their motion free as roving wind,
Though first no snail more limited and slow;
I mark them full of labor all the day,
Each active motion made in perfect rest;

They cannot from their path mistaken stray,
Though 'tis not theirs, yet in it they are blest;
The bird has not their hidden track found out,
Nor cunning fox, though full of art he be;
It is the way unseen, the certain route,
Where ever bound, yet thou art ever free;
The path of Him, whose perfect law of love
Bids spheres and atoms in just order move.


## Thy Brother's Blood

I have no Brother,—they who meet me now
Offer a hand with their own wills defiled,
And, while they wear a smooth unwrinkled brow,
Know not that Truth can never be beguiled;
Go wash the hand that still betrays thy guilt;
Before the spirit's gaze what stain can hide?
Abel's red blood upon the earth is spilt,
And by thy tongue it cannot be denied;
I hear not with my ear,—the heart doth tell
Its secret deeds to me untold before;
Go, all its hidden plunder quickly sell,
Then shalt thou cleanse thee from thy brother's gore,
Then will I take thy gift; that bloody stain
Shall not be seen upon thy hand again.

# Thomas Lovell Beddoes

(1803–1849)

## FROM Death's Jest-Book

### DIRGE

If thou wilt ease thine heart
Of love and all its smart,
   Then sleep, dear, sleep;
And not a sorrow
  Hang any tear on your eyelashes;
   Lie still and deep,
  Sad soul, until the sea-wave washes
The rim o' the sun to-morrow,
   In eastern sky.

But wilt thou cure thine heart
Of love and all its smart,
   Then die, dear, die;
'Tis deeper, sweeter,
  Than on a rose bank to lie dreaming
   With folded eye;
  And then alone, amid the beaming
Of love's stars, thou'lt meet her
   In eastern sky.

### SONG

Old Adam, the carrion crow,
   The old crow of Cairo;
He sat in the shower, and let it flow

511

Under his tail and over his crest;
   And through every feather
   Leaked the wet weather;
And the bough swung under his nest;
For his beak it was heavy with marrow.
   Is that the wind dying? O no;
   It's only two devils, that blow
   Through a murderer's bones, to and fro,
     In the ghosts' moonshine.

Ho! Eve, my grey carrion wife,
   When we have supped on kings' marrow,
Where shall we drink and make merry our life?
   Our nest it is queen Cleopatra's skull,
     'Tis cloven and cracked,
     And battered and hacked,
   But with tears of blue eyes it is full:
Let us drink then, my raven of Cairo.
   Is that the wind dying? O no;
   It's only two devils, that blow
   Through a murderer's bones, to and fro,
     In the ghosts' moonshine.


## EPITHALAMIA

**BY FEMALE VOICES:**

We have bathed, where none have seen us,
   In the lake and in the fountain,
     Underneath the charmed statue
Of the timid, bending Venus,
   When the water-nymphs were counting
In the waves the stars of night,
     And those maidens started at you,
Your limbs shone through so soft and bright.
   But no secrets dare we tell,

For thy slaves unlace thee,
And he, who shall embrace thee,
Waits to try thy beauty's spell.

BY MALE VOICES:

We have crowned thee queen of women,
Since love's love, the rose, hath kept her
Court within thy lips and blushes,
And thine eye, in beauty swimming,
Kissing, we rendered up the sceptre,
At whose touch the startled soul
Like an ocean bounds and gushes,
And spirits bend at thy controul.
But no secrets dare we tell,
For thy slaves unlace thee,
And he, who shall embrace thee,
Is at hand, and so farewell.


DIRGE

A VOICE FROM THE WATERS:

The swallow leaves her nest,
The soul my weary breast;
But therefore let the rain
On my grave
Fall pure; for why complain?
Since both will come again
O'er the wave.
The wind dead leaves and snow
Doth scurry to and fro;
And, once a day shall break
O'er the wave,
When a storm of ghosts shall shake
The dead, until they wake
In the grave.

### FROM *Torrismond*

#### SONG

How many times do I love thee, dear?
  Tell me how many thoughts there be
     In the atmosphere
     Of a new-fall'n year,
Whose white and sable hours appear
  The latest flake of Eternity:—
So many times do I love thee, dear.

How many times do I love again?
  Tell me how many beads there are
     In a silver chain
     Of evening rain,
Unravelled from the tumbling main,
  And threading the eye of a yellow star:—
So many times do I love again.

## *Dream-Pedlary*

If there were dreams to sell,
  What would you buy?
Some cost a passing bell;
  Some a light sigh,
That shakes from Life's fresh crown
Only a rose-leaf down.
If there were dreams to sell,
Merry and sad to tell,

And the crier rung the bell,
  What would you buy?

A cottage lone and still,
  With bowers nigh,
Shadowy, my woes to still,
  Until I die.
Such pearl from Life's fresh crown
Fain would I shake me down.
Were dreams to have at will,
This would best heal my ill,
  This would I buy.

But there were dreams to sell
  Ill didst thou buy;
Life is a dream, they tell,
  Waking, to die.
Dreaming a dream to prize,
In wishing ghosts to rise;
And, if I had the spell
To call the buried well,
      Which one would I?

If there are ghosts to raise,
  What shall I call,
Out of hell's murky haze,
  Heaven's blue pall?
Raise my loved long-lost boy
To lead me to his joy.—
There are no ghosts to raise;
Out of death lead no ways;
      Vain is the call.

Know'st thou not ghosts to sue?
  No love thou hast.
Else lie, as I will do,
  And breathe thy last.

So out of Life's fresh crown
Fall like a rose-leaf down.
Thus are the ghosts to woo;
Thus are all dreams made true,
      Ever to last!

# Edgar Allan Poe

(1809–1849)

## The City in the Sea

Lo! Death has reared himself a throne
In a strange city lying alone
Far down within the dim West,
Where the good and the bad and the worst and the best
Have gone to their eternal rest.
There shrines and palaces and towers
(Time-eaten towers that tremble not!)
Resemble nothing that is ours.
Around, by lifting winds forgot,
Resignedly beneath the sky
The melancholy waters lie.

No rays from the holy heaven come down
On the long night-time of that town;
But light from out the lurid sea
Streams up the turrets silently—
Gleams up the pinnacles far and free—
Up domes—up spires—up kingly halls—
Up fanes—up Babylon-like walls—
Up shadowy long-forgotten bowers
Of sculptured ivy and stone flowers—
Up many and many a marvellous shrine
Whose wreathèd friezes intertwine
The viol, the violet, and the vine.

Resignedly beneath the sky
The melancholy waters lie.
So blend the turrets and shadows there
That all seem pendulous in air,
While from a proud tower in the town
Death looks gigantically down.

There open fanes and gaping graves
Yawn level with the luminous waves;
But not the riches there that lie
In each idol's diamond eye—
Not the gayly-jewelled dead
Tempt the waters from their bed;
For no ripples curl, alas!
Along that wilderness of glass—
No swellings tell that winds may be
Upon some far-off happier sea—
No heavings hint that winds have been
On seas less hideously serene.

But lo, a stir is in the air!
The wave—there is a movement there!
As if the towers had thrust aside,
In slightly sinking, the dull tide—
As if their tops had feebly given
A void within the filmy Heaven.
The waves have now a redder glow—
The hours are breathing faint and low—
And when, amid no earthly moans,
Down, down that town shall settle hence,
Hell, rising from a thousand thrones,
Shall do it reverence.

## The Sleeper

At midnight, in the month of June,
I stand beneath the mystic moon.
An opiate vapor, dewy, dim,
Exhales from out her golden rim,
And, softly dripping, drop by drop,
Upon the quiet mountain top,
Steals drowsily and musically
Into the universal valley.
The rosemary nods upon the grave;
The lily lolls upon the wave;
Wrapping the fog about its breast,
The ruin moulders into rest;
Looking like Lethe, see! the lake
A conscious slumber seems to take,
And would not, for the world, awake.
All Beauty sleeps!—and lo! where lies
Irene, with her Destinies!

Oh, lady bright! can it be right—
This window open to the night?
The wanton airs, from the tree-top,
Laughingly through the lattice drop—
The bodiless airs, a wizard rout,
Flit through thy chamber in and out,
And wave the curtain canopy
So fitfully—so fearfully—
Above the closed and fringèd lid
'Neath which thy slumb'ring soul lies hid,
That, o'er the floor and down the wall,
Like ghosts the shadows rise and fall!

Oh, lady dear, hast thou no fear?
Why and what art thou dreaming here?
Sure thou art come o'er far-off seas,
A wonder to these garden trees!
Strange is thy pallor! strange thy dress!
Strange, above all, thy length of tress,
And this all solemn silentness!

The lady sleeps! Oh, may her sleep,
Which is enduring, so be deep!
Heaven have her in its sacred keep!
This chamber changed for one more holy,
This bed for one more melancholy,
I pray to God that she may lie
Forever with unopened eye,
While the pale sheeted ghosts go by!

My love, she sleeps! Oh, may her sleep,
As it is lasting, so be deep!
Soft may the worms about her creep!
Far in the forest, dim and old,
For her may some tall vault unfold—
Some vault that oft hath flung its black
And wingèd pannels fluttering back,
Triumphant, o'er the crested palls
Of her grand family funerals—

Some sepulchre, remote, alone,
Against whose portal she hath thrown,
In childhood, many an idle stone—
Some tomb from out whose sounding door
She ne'er shall force an echo more,
Thrilling to think, poor child of sin!
It was the dead who groaned within.

## The Valley of Unrest

Once it smiled a silent dell
Where the people did not dwell;
They had gone unto the wars,
Trusting to the mild-eyed stars,
Nightly, from their azure towers,
To keep watch above the flowers,
In the midst of which all day
The red sun-light lazily lay.
*Now* each visitor shall confess
The sad valley's restlessness.
Nothing there is motionless—
Nothing save the airs that brood
Over the magic solitude.
Ah, by no wind are stirred those trees
That palpitate like the chill seas
Around the misty Hebrides!
Ah, by no wind those clouds are driven
That rustle through the unquiet Heaven
Uneasily, from morn till even,
Over the violets there that lie
In myriad types of the human eye—
Over the lilies there that wave
And weep above a nameless grave!
They wave:—from out their fragrant tops
Eternal dews come down in drops.
They weep:—from off their delicate stems
Perennial tears descend in gems.

# The Haunted Palace

In the greenest of our valleys
   By good angels tenanted,
Once a fair and stately palace—
   Radiant palace—reared its head.
In the monarch Thought's dominion,
   It stood there!
Never seraph spread a pinion
   Over fabric half so fair!

Banners yellow, glorious, golden,
   On its roof did float and flow
(This—all this—was in the olden
   Time long ago)
And every gentle air that dallied,
   In that sweet day,
Along the ramparts plumed and pallid,
   A wingèd odor went away.

Wanderers in that happy valley,
   Through two luminous windows, saw
Spirits moving musically
   To a lute's well-tunèd law,
Round about a throne where, sitting,
   Porphyrogene!
In state his glory well befitting,
   The ruler of the realm was seen.

And all with pearl and ruby glowing
   Was the fair palace door,
Through which came flowing, flowing, flowing
   And sparkling evermore,

A troop of Echoes, whose sweet duty
  Was but to sing,
In voices of surpassing beauty,
  The wit and wisdom of their king.

But evil things, in robes of sorrow,
  Assailed the monarch's high estate;
(Ah, let us mourn!—for never morrow
  Shall dawn upon him, desolate!)
And round about his home the glory
  That blushed and bloomed
Is but a dim-remembered story
  Of the old time entombed.

And travellers, now, within that valley,
  Through the red-litten windows see
Vast forms that move fantastically
  To a discordant melody;
While, like a ghastly rapid river,
  Through the pale door
A hideous throng rush out forever,
  And laugh—but smile no more.

## To Helen

Helen, thy beauty is to me
  Like those Nicéan barks of yore,
That gently, o'er a perfumed sea,
  The weary, way-worn wanderer bore
  To his own native shore.

On desperate seas long wont to roam,
  Thy hyacinth hair, thy classic face,

Thy Naiad airs have brought me home
  To the glory that was Greece,
And the grandeur that was Rome.

Lo! in yon brilliant window-niche
  How statue-like I see thee stand,
  The agate lamp within thy hand!
Ah, Psyche, from the regions which
  Are Holy Land!

## Israfel

And the angel Israfel, whose heart-strings are a lute, and
who has the sweetest voice of all God's creatures.—KORAN

In Heaven a spirit doth dwell
  "Whose heart-strings are a lute";
None sing so wildly well
As the angel Israfel,
And the giddy stars (so legends tell),
Ceasing their hymns, attend the spell
  Of his voice, all mute.

Tottering above
  In her highest noon,
  The enamored moon
Blushes with love,
  While, to listen, the red levin
  (With the rapid Pleiads, even,
  Which were seven,)
  Pauses in Heaven.

And they say (the starry choir
  And the other listening things)
That Israfeli's fire

Is owing to that lyre
  By which he sits and sings—
The trembling living wire
  Of those unusual strings.

But the skies that angel trod,
  Where deep thoughts are a duty,
Where Love's a grown-up God,
  Where the Houri glances are
Imbued with all the beauty
  Which we worship in a star.

Therefore, thou art not wrong,
  Israfeli, who despisest
An unimpassioned song;
To thee the laurels belong,
  Best bard, because the wisest!
Merrily live, and long!

The ecstasies above
  With thy burning measures suit—
Thy grief, thy joy, thy hate, thy love,
  With the fervor of thy lute—
  Well may the stars be mute!

Yes, Heaven is thine; but this
  Is a world of sweets and sours;
  Our flowers are merely—flowers,
And the shadow of thy perfect bliss
  Is the sunshine of ours.

If I could dwell
Where Israfel
  Hath dwelt, and he where I,
He might not sing so wildly well
  A mortal melody,
While a bolder note than this might swell
  From my lyre within the sky.

## From childhood's hour

From childhood's hour I have not been
As others were; I have not seen
As others saw; I could not bring
My passions from a common spring.
From the same source I have not taken
My sorrow; I could not awaken
My heart to joy at the same tone;
And all I loved, I loved alone.
Then—in my childhood, in the dawn
Of a most stormy life—was drawn
From every depth of good and ill
The mystery which binds me still:
From the torrent or the fountain,
From the red cliff of the mountain,
From the sun that round me rolled
In its autumn tint of gold,
From the lightning in the sky
As it passed me flying by,
From the thunder and the storm,
And the cloud that took the form
(When the rest of Heaven was blue)
Of a demon in my view.

# Index of Titles and First Lines

# Biographical Notes

BARNES, WILLIAM (1801–1886), born in Dorset, was educated by tutors and himself, becoming remarkably proficient in linguistics. He was registered as rector at St. John's College, Cambridge (1838–50), graduating as B.D. He was ordained in 1847, finally settling as rector at Came in 1862. In addition to his work as archaeologist and linguist, he published verse, based on "purity of the language," of which *Poems of Rural Life: in the Dorset Dialect* (1844) was the first. W. E. Henley, ed., *Collected Poems* (1901); Thomas Hardy, ed., *Selected Poems* (1908); G. Grigson, ed., *Selected Poems* (1950). L. Baxter, *The Life of William Barnes* (1887).

BEDDOES, THOMAS LOVELL (1803–1849), born at Rodney Place, Clifton, was educated at the Charterhouse and Pembroke College, Oxford (1825), after which he went abroad (1825) to study medicine, remaining on the continent as writer and physiologist. His first verses appeared in 1817, and *The Bride's Tragedy* (1822) was written in 1819. *Death's Jest-Book* (1850) was begun about 1825. H. W. Donner, ed., *The Works* (1935). H. W. Donner, *Thomas Lovell Beddoes* (1935).

BLAKE, WILLIAM (1757–1827), born in London, the son of a Swedenborgian hosier, attended drawing school and was apprenticed (1771–78) to an engraver. Afterwards he studied briefly at the Royal Academy. He began writing verse at 12. Always poor, he tried to earn his living as engraver, art teacher, and dealer in prints. Unable to find a publisher, he himself engraved and published *Songs of Innocence* (1789), *The Book of Thel* (1789), and others. From 1793–1804 he wrote and published his prophetic books, but thereafter was chiefly an artist. G. Keynes, ed., *The Writings* (1925), 3 vols. S. F. Damon, *William Blake, His Philosophy and Symbols* (1924); M. Wilson, *The Life of William Blake* (rev. ed., 1948). A. Kazin, ed., *The Portable Blake.*

BRYANT, WILLIAM CULLEN (1794–1878), born at Cummington, Mass., the son of a physician, was educated at Williams College. *The Embargo* (1808), a political satire, and "Thanatopsis," written in 1811 and printed in revised form in 1817, were forerunners of his quasi-Wordsworthian *Poems* (1821). He was admitted to the bar in 1815, but his literary successes pulled him toward journalism. From 1829 he was editor-in-chief and part owner of the *New York Evening Post.* Parke Godwin, ed., *The Poetical Works* (1883), 2 vols. Parke Godwin, *A Biography of William Cullen Bryant* (1883), 2 vols.

BURNS, ROBERT (1759–1796), born at Alloway, Scotland, worked as a farm laborer and, 1784–88, farmed with his brother. *Poems, Chiefly in the Scottish Dialect* (1786), published at Kilmarnock, brought him some fame, and *Poems* (1787) enough money to settle on a farm of his own, and belatedly marry. In 1791 the farm failed and he moved to Dumfries where he ob-

tained a position in the excise. C. S. Dougall, *Robert Burns: The Poems* (1927). F. B. Snyder, *Life of Robert Burns* (1932); J. De L. Ferguson, *Pride and Passion* (1939).

BYRON, GEORGE GORDON, LORD (1788–1824), born at London, succeeding to the title at 10, was educated at Harrow and Trinity College, Cambridge (1808). The poor reception of his *Hours of Idleness* (1807) gave the cue for the satiric *English Bards and Scotch Reviewers* (1809). In 1809–11 he traveled in the Mediterranean area, publishing the first two cantos of *Childe Harold's Pilgrimage* in 1812. He spent the years 1816–23 in Italy, writing *Manfred* (1817), *Beppo* (1818), and *Don Juan* (1819–24). He joined the Greek insurgents against Turkey in 1823, and died of fever on that expedition. E. H. Coleridge, ed., *Poetry*; and R. E. Prothero, ed., *Letters and Journals* (together, rev. ed., 1905–1924), 13 vols. J. Murray, ed., *Correspondence* (1922), 2 vols. E. Mayne, *Byron* (1912), 2 vols.; John Drinkwater, *The Pilgrim of Eternity* (1925).

CLARE, JOHN (1793–1864), born at Helpston, Northamptonshire, was a plowboy, tavern servant, etc. Largely self-educated, he fell under the spell of Thomson's *Seasons*, and began writing verses, eventually publishing *Poems Descriptive of Rural Life and Scenery* (1820), which had a striking success. *The Village Minstrel* (1821), *The Shepherd's Calendar* (1827), and *The Rural Muse* (1835) met a less enthusiastic reception. His life of constant poverty was complicated by mental illness. J. W. Tibble, ed., *The Poems* (1935), 2 vols.; G. Grigson, *Poems of John Clare's Madness* (1949). J. W.

and Anne Tibble, *John Clare* (1932).

**COLERIDGE, HARTLEY** (1796–1849), born at Clevedon, Somersetshire, the son of Samuel Taylor Coleridge (q.v.), was reared in Southey's family after his parents' separation, and was educated at Ambleside and Merton College, Oxford. He was for a time probation fellow of Oriel College, Oxford, tried schoolmastering, and then lived chiefly, and aimlessly, as a writer at Grasmere. *Poems* (1833) was the only volume of verse published in his lifetime. R. Colles, ed., *The Complete Poetical Works* (1908), 2 vols.; E. L. Griggs, ed., *New Poems* (1942). E. L. Griggs, *Hartley Coleridge* (1929); H. Hartman, *Hartley Coleridge* (1931).

**COLERIDGE, SAMUEL TAYLOR** (1772–1834), born at Ottery St. Mary, Devon, was educated at Christ's Hospital and Jesus College, Cambridge. After a period of planning a "pantisocratic" community, with Southey, on the banks of the Susquehanna, and spasmodic Unitarian preaching, he began a precarious livelihood as writer, existing mostly by the support of patrons. The years when he was intimate with Wordsworth were the period of most of his poems, marked by their joint *Lyrical Ballads* (1798) and *Christabel, Kubla Khan, The Pains of Sleep* (1816). *Biographia Literaria* (1817) and *Aids to Reflection* (1825) have brought him stature as critic and philosopher. E. H. Coleridge, ed., *Complete Poetical Works* (1912), 2 vols. J. L. Lowes, *The Road to Xanadu* (1927); E. K. Chambers, *Samuel Taylor Coleridge* (1938). I. A. Richards, ed., *The Portable Coleridge*.

**CRABBE, GEORGE** (1754–1832), was born at Aldeburgh.

Apprenticed to a doctor, he later practiced medicine in his home village, and, still later, having been ordained, was curate there. The harsh local scenes became the themes of such poems as *The Village* (1783), *Poems* (1807), and *The Borough* (1810). A. W. Ward, ed., *Poems* (1905–07), 3 vols. George Crabbe, Jr., *The Life of the Rev. George Crabbe* (1834, reprinted 1947); J. H. Evans, *The Poems of George Crabbe: a Literary and Historical Study* (1933).

**DARLEY, GEORGE** (1795–1846), born at Dublin, was educated at Trinity College, Dublin (1820). He quarreled with his parents because of his desire for a literary career, and left for London where he published *The Errors of Ecstacie* (1822), and lived as critic and poet. He wrote mathematical texts (1826–28). *Sylvia, or the May Queen* (1827), a poetic drama; *Nepenthe* (1835); *Ethelstan; or the Battle of Brunaburgh* (1841) were revivals of past ways of poetry. R. Colles, ed., *The Complete Works* (1908). C. C. Abbott, *The Life and Letters of George Darley* (1928).

**EMERSON, RALPH WALDO** (1803–1882), born in Boston, was the son of a clergyman who died in 1811. He was educated at Harvard (1821). He entered the Unitarian ministry, but retired in 1832, and traveled in Europe and in England, where he met Wordsworth, Coleridge, and, most important, Carlyle. From 1834 he resided in Concord, Mass., making a living by his writing and lecture tours. *Nature* (1836)—a Transcendentalist manifesto—and *Essays* (1841) brought him renown. *Poems* (1847) and *May-Day and Other Pieces* (1867) employed his characteristic themes. E. W. Emerson, ed., *The Com-*

*plete Writings* (1903–04), 12 vols. R. L. Rusk, *The Life of Ralph Waldo Emerson* (1949). M. Van Doren, ed., *The Portable Emerson.*

FRENEAU, PHILIP (1752–1832), born in New York City of Huguenot stock, was educated by tutor and at Princeton (1771). He taught school for a while, wrote political verse, and served as secretary to a planter in the West Indies. Returning to the States, he wrote and traveled, frequently as a mariner. *The Poems* (1786) was followed by numerous other publications. F. L. Pattee, ed., *Poems* (1902–07), 3 vols.; Lewis Leary, ed., *The Last Poems* (1946) Lewis Leary, *The Rascal Freneau* (1941).

HALLECK, FITZ-GREENE (1790–1867), was born at Guilford, Conn. In 1811, after six years as clerk, he went to New York where he later became confidential clerk to John Jacob Astor (1832–49). He was self-educated with some *éclat*. *Alnwick Castle* (1827) was followed by his collected works (1847). On the basis of a small annuity at Astor's death, he retired (1849) to Guilford. J. G. Wilson, ed., *The Poetical Writings* (1869). N. F. Adkins, *Fitz-Greene Halleck* (1930).

HOOD, THOMAS (1799–1845), was born in London, educated at private schools, and entered a counting house at 13. His health failed and he turned to writing, after a period as apprentice to engravers. As sub-editor of *The London Magazine* (1821–23), he became a friend of Lamb, Hazlitt, and De Quincey, and as editor of *The Comic Annual* (1830–42) gained a reputation as a wit. W. Jerrold, ed., *Poetical Works* (1906). W. Jerrold, *Thomas Hood* (1907).

HUNT, LEIGH (1784–1859), born at Southgate, Middlesex, was the son of a preacher who was born in Barbados and came to England from Philadelphia after persecution as a loyalist. He was educated at Christ's Hospital. After a period as an editor, he was jailed (1813–15) for editorial remarks on the Prince Regent. *Juvenilia* (1801) was followed by *The Descent of Liberty* (1814), and *The Story of Rimini* (1816). H. S. Milford, ed., *The Poetical Works* (1923). Edmund Blunden, *Leigh Hunt* (1930).

KEATS, JOHN (1795–1821), born in London, the son of a livery-stable keeper, orphaned as a boy, was educated at school in Enfield (1803–11). He was apprenticed to an apothecary-surgeon at Edmonton, and in 1815 became a medical student and dresser at Guy's Hospital, London. He relinquished medicine for poetry, and *Poems* (1817) was published with the help of Shelley. *Endymion* (1818) met with harsh reviews, but he continued with the composition of *Hyperion* (written 1818–19) and his odes. *Lamia, The Eve of St. Agnes, and Other Poems* (1820) appeared just as, ill with tuberculosis, he set sail for Italy where he died. M. Buxton, ed., *Poetical Works and Other Writings* (1938), 8 vols. Amy Lowell, *John Keats* (1925), 2 vols. H. W. Garrod, *Keats* (1926).

LANDOR, WALTER SAVAGE (1775–1864), born in Warwickshire, was educated at Rugby and Trinity College, Oxford. He lived in Italy 1815–35, at Bath 1835–58, and then in Florence. His distinction is based on *Imaginary Conversations* (1824–53), a series in prose, and volumes of lyrics published from

1795 on. T. E. Whelby and S. Wheeler, eds., *The Complete Works* (1927–36), 16 vols. M. Elwin, *Savage Landor* (1941).

MOORE, THOMAS (1779–1852), born at Dublin, the son of a grocer, was educated at Trinity College, Dublin, and entered the law. In 1803–04 he was admiralty registrar in Bermuda, leaving to travel in the United States and Canada. His early poems were satiric, but his true vein was struck in *Irish Melodies* (1820). *Lalla Rookh* (1817) brought him wider reputation A. D Godley, ed., *The Poetical Works* (1910). H. M. Jones, *The Harp that Once—* (1937). L A. G. Strong, *The Minstrel Boy* (1937).

POE, EDGAR ALLAN (1809–1849), born in Boston, Mass., the son of traveling actors, was taken under the protection of John Allan, a Scottish tobacco merchant of Richmond, Va., when his mother died (1812). He lived in England with his foster parents 1815–20, attending school there. He later studied in Richmond and briefly (1826–27) attended the University of Virginia. Having quarreled with Allan, he ran away, published *Tamerlane* (1827), and enlisted in the army. Reconciled, he attended West Point (1830–31). He was thereafter on his own, earning a chaotic living as editor, critic, and writer *Al Aaraaf* (1829), *Poems* (1829), *The Raven and Other Poems* (1845) were his volumes of verse. K. Campbell, ed., *The Poems* (1917). A. H. Quinn, *Edgar Allan Poe* (1941). P. V. D. Stern, ed., *The Portable Poe*.

PRAED, WINTHROP MACK-WORTH (1802–1839), born in London, the son of a sergeant-at-law and chairman of the audit board, was educated at Eton and Trinity College, Cambridge. After practicing as a lawyer, he entered Parliament, and was made secretary to the Board of Control (1834). He published classical verses, but is best known for his *vers de société*. D. Coleridge, ed., *Poems* (1864), 2 vols. D. Hudson, *A Poet in Parliament* (1939).

SCOTT, SIR WALTER (1771–1832), born at Edinburgh, was educated at Edinburgh University. After apprenticeship to his father, he practiced law but increasingly devoted himself to writing. He edited, with Leyden, *Minstrelsy of the Scottish Border* (1802–03), a collection of ballads, many of which he rewrote. *The Lay of the Last Minstrel* (1805) brought him fame, and *Marmion* (1808), *The Lady of the Lake* (1810), and other similar poems followed. From *Waverly* (1814) on, he turned his attention to historical novels. J. L. Robertson, ed., *The Poetical Works* (1904). J. G. Lockhart, *Memoirs of the Life of Sir Walter Scott* (1837–38), 7 vols.; H. J. C. Grierson, *Sir Walter Scott, Bart.* (1938).

SHELLEY, PERCY BYSSHE (1792–1822), born at Field Place, Sussex, was educated at Eton and University College, Oxford, from which he was expelled for his pamphlet *The Necessity of Atheism* (1811). He then married Harriet Westbrook, aged 16, from whom he separated after three years. *Queen Mab* was published in 1813, and in 1814 he eloped to Italy with Mary Godwin, who became his second wife. *The Cenci* (1820), a poetic drama; *Prometheus Unbound* (1820); *Adonais* (1821); and *Hellas* (1822) were his chief later works. He was drowned while sailing near Spezzia. R. Ingpen and W. E. Peck, eds., *Complete*

*Works* (1926–30), 10 vols. N. I. White, *Shelley* (1940), 2 vols.

THOREAU, HENRY DAVID (1817–1862), born at Concord, Mass., was educated at Concord Academy and at Harvard (1837). He kept a school with his brother 1838–41, later going to live with Emerson whose protégé he had become. *A Week on the Concord and Merrimac Rivers* (1849) contained, with poems, an account of a trip with his brother; *Walden* (1854) is a philosophical treatment of his sojourn as recluse (1845–47). Little of his poetry was published during his life. C. Bode, ed., *Collected Poems* (1943). H. S. Canby, *Thoreau* (1939). C. Bode, ed., *The Portable Thoreau.*

VERY, JONES (1813–1880), was born at Salem, Mass. In 1827 he interrupted his schooling to serve as errand boy to an auctioneer, but after being tutored became assistant in a Latin school and was graduated from Harvard (1836). An ardent Unitarian, he studied divinity and was moved to the "inspired" writing of sacred sonnets. He was briefly (1838) the inmate of a mental institution. *Essays and Poems* (1839) had a great vogue among Transcendentalists. J. F. Clarke, ed., *The Works* (1886). W. I. Bartlett, *Jones Very* (1942); Yvor Winters, *In Defense of Reason* (1947), pp. 344–57.

WHITTIER, JOHN GREENLEAF (1807–1892), born at Haverhill, Mass., the son of a Quaker farmer, was educated briefly at the Haverhill Academy. Already a prolific poet in the press, he later held various editorial positions and in 1831 published *Legends of New England in Prose and Verse.* By 1833 he had become an ardent abolitionist. His fame as political and rural poet increased with many volumes, and *Snow-Bound* (1866), brought him a comfortable living. His hymns are the finest written by an American. H. E. Scudder, ed., *The Complete Poetical Works* (1894). J. Pollard, *John Greenleaf Whittier* (1949).

WORDSWORTH, WILLIAM (1770–1850), born at Cockermouth, Cumberland, was educated at St. John's College, Cambridge (1791), and in his holidays traveled in the Lake Country, France, and Switzerland. He returned to France, but his revolutionary enthusiasm was dimmed. After a period of despair, he went to live with his sister Dorothy (1795). With Coleridge, he published *Lyrical Ballads* (1798). In 1799 he settled at Grasmere. In 1805 he wrote his first version of *The Prelude*, later revised, and published in 1850. Other works were *Descriptive Sketches in Verse* (1793), *Poems* (1807), and *The Excursion* (1814). In 1843 he was made Poet Laureate. E. de Selincourt, ed., *The Poems* (1940–49), 5 vols. H. W. Garrod, *Wordsworth* (1927); R. D. Havens, *The Mind of a Poet* (1941).